AF541807

New Facets of Tourism Management

New Facets of Tourism Management

Varinder Rana

RANDOM PUBLICATIONS
NEW DELHI (INDIA)

New Facets of Tourism Management

ISBN 978-93-5111-942-5

Published in 2016 in India by

RANDOM PUBLICATIONS

4376-A/4B, Gali Murari Lal, Ansari Road
New Delhi-110 002
Phone : +9111-43580356, 011-23289044, 011-43142548
e-mail: sales@randompublications.com,
info@randompublications.com, randomexports@gmail.com

Type Setting by : Friends Media, Delhi-110089
Digitally Printed at : Replika Press Pvt. Ltd.

Preface

Tourism impacts are multi-faceted and therefore are difficult to plan for and manage. This title looks at all the key players involved - be they tourists, host communities or industry members - and considers a number of approaches and techniques for managing tourism impacts successfully.

Although many of us have been "tourists" at some point in our lives, defining what tourism actually is can be difficult. Tourism is the activities of people traveling to and staying in places outside their usual environment for leisure, business or other purposes for not more than one consecutive year.

Tourism can be domestic or international, and international tourism has both incoming and outgoing implications on a country's balance of payments. Today, tourism is a major source of income for many countries, and affects the economy of both the source and host countries, in some cases being of vital importance.

In a tourism context, the economics of tourism has been defined by one writer as being. The concerned with the use of scare resource, labour, capital, land, and environmental resources, to produce the product, tourism, and with the distribution of this product between different.

Tourism is a collection of activities, services and industries which deliver a travel experience comprising transportation, accommodation, eating and drinking establishments, retail shops, entertainment businesses and othe hospitality services provided for individuals or groups traveling away from home.

This book attempts to provide a fresh perspective on the existing and emerging areas of travel and tourism industry by focusing on contemporary problems and prospects.

– Author

Contents

1

Forms of Tourism

ADVENTURE TOURISM

Adventure tourism is a type of tourism involving exploration or travel to remote areas, where the traveller should expect the unexpected. Adventure tourism is rapidly growing in popularity as tourists seek unusual holidays, different from the typical beach vacation. Adventure tourism typically involves travelling into remote, inaccessible and possibly hostile areas. It may include the performance of acts that require significant effort and grit and may also involve some degree of risk. Adventure Tourism becoming more and more Famous specially among youth. India is not a country but a world in itself.

Here one can find World's biggest river for rafting and endless mountains for trekking. It is a country who has something for every kind of Adventure lover. For Mountainerring and Trekking one can go to Sikkim, the home of mighty Kunchnjanga and situated within eastern himalayas. Jummu and Kashmir the heaven on earth. The place for Ski lovers and wonderful for backpackers. Himachal one of the best sites for Pargaliding in World and famous for beautiful gentle hills and Where glaciers are not far from mainland.

Uttranchal a place where every single person wants to go, famous for valley of flowers and for Shiva Dhams and Last but not least Leh and Ladakh the cold deasert of India a place where one cannot find Trees and find really cold and different culture much closer to Tibtian culture and a starting point for Extreme tourism lovers who want to travel beyond the main land towards zanskar and nubra valleys. For Rafting India is heaven the rivers like Ganga, Teesta, and Brahamaputra provide rafters a real thrill and challenge. Rafting is becoming very popular among the corporates combined with Stay in riverside resorts and team building exercises.

MOUNTAINEERING

Mountaineering is the sport, hobby or profession of walking, hiking and climbing up mountains. It is also sometimes known as alpinism, particularly in Europe. It may be said to consist of two main aspects, rock-craft and snow-craft, depending on whether the route chosen is over rock or over snow and ice. Both require great gymnastic and technical ability, but experience is also a very important part of the latter. Training in these areas for several months enhances a person's abilities and increases their chances for survival while climbing.

AGRITOURISM

Agritourism is a style of vacation in which hospitality is offered on farms. This may include the opportunity to assist with farming tasks during the visit. Agritourism is often practiced in wine growing regions, as in Italy, France and Spain. In America, Agritourism is wide-spread and includes any farm open to the public at least part of the year. Tourists can pick fruits and vegetables, ride horses, taste honey, learn about wine, shop in gift shops and farm stands for local and regional produce or hand-crafted gifts, and much more. Each farm generally offers a unique and memorable experience suitable for the entire family.

Agritourism is being developed as a valuable component of a business model to support many agricultural entities when the farm products they produce are no longer economically competitive otherwise. To help promote the single agritourism operations, farms get together and form festivals or tours, such as Agri-tours, a two-weekend festival in September celebrating the lower Ottawa Valley's unique farms. This festival includes over a dozen non-traditional farms that specialize in everything from deer and pheasant, to apples and wine. People are more interested in how their food is produced and want to meet the producers and talk with them about what goes into food production.

Children who visit the farms often have not seen a live duck, or goat, and have not picked an apple right off the tree. This form of expanded agri-tourism has given birth to what are often called "entertainment farms." These farms cater to the pick-your-own crowd, offering not only regular farm products, but also food, mazes, open-pen animals, train rides, picnic facilities and pick-your-own produce. Dude ranches offer tourists the chance to work on cattle ranches and sometimes include cattle drives.

CULTURAL TOURISM

Cultural tourism and ecotourism, the number of living cultural areas is continually droping off. For an indigenous culture that has stayed largely separated from the surrounding majority culture, tourism can present both advantages and problems on to it. On the positive side are the unique cultural practices and arts that attract the curiosity of tourists and provide opportunities for tourism and economic development. On the negative side is the issue of how to control tourism so that those same cultural amenities are not destroyed and the people do not feel violated.

DESTINATION PLANNING RESOURCES

It is important that the destination planner takes into account the diverse definition of culture as the term is subjective. Satisfying tourists' interests such as landscapes, seascapes, art, nature, traditions, ways of life and other products associated to them -which may be categorized cultural in the broadest sense of the word, is a prime consideration as it marks the initial phase of the development of a cultural destination.

The quality of service and destination, which doesn't solely depend on the cultural heritage but more importantly to the cultural environment, can further be developed by setting controls and policies which shall govern the community and its stakeholders.

It is therefore safe to say that the planner should be on the ball with the varying meaning of culture itself as this fuels the formulation of development policies that shall entail efficient planning and monitored growth. While satisfying tourists' interests and demands may be a top priority, it is also imperative to ruminate the subsystems of the destinatons. Development pressures should be anticipated and set to their minimum level so as to conserve the area's resources and prevent a saturation of the destination as to not abuse the product and the residents correspondingly.

The plan should incorporate the locals to its gain by training and employing them and in the process encourage them to participate to the travel business. Keep in mind that the plan should make travellers not only aware about the destination but also concern on how to help it sustain its character while broadening their travelling experience.

CULTURAL VALUES

To grasp tourist motivation at sites of dark tourism, it is essential to understand the memorialization process of such sites, the how and why they were initially erected. Not all sites of death, disaster, and destruction are memorialized, nor do all sites evolve into tourist destinations. Much of this commemoration is shaped by cultural values. As Foote reported, "...attitudes towards violence and tragedy are closely aligned with cultural values".

In his aptly named book, Shadowed Ground: America's Landscapes of Violence and Tragedy, Foote discusses at length the impacts cultural values have on forging both a nation's memory and its commemorative landscape. The memorializing sites seen today have all been shaped by political, social and/or economic factors, sometimes over a number of decades.

According to Foote, when a site experiences a tragic or violent event, one of four outcomes results: sanctification, designation, rectification, or obliteration. Most relevant to this study are the former two, and they are discussed in detail below.

SANCTIFICATION

The most common motives for sanctification are to honour martyrs, fallen heroes, great leaders and community loss. The process involves the creation of a sacred place, often identified by a durable marker such as a statue, building, monument or memorial garden. It also involves some form of formal consecration, a ceremony explaining the site's history and significance. However, this is not always an objective process as illustrated by the sanctification of Abraham Lincoln. Bodnar explains, "...the shaping of a past worthy of public commemoration in the present is contested and involves a struggle for supremacy between advocates of various political ideas and sentiments".

Although today Lincoln is regarded by many as one of the greatest American presidents, his memorial in Washington D.C. was not completed until 1922, fifty-seven years after his death. Foote states that, "...the heart of the problem of building a larger memorial was that Americans did not agree on how Lincoln should be remembered". At the time of his death in 1865, Lincoln was considered a polarizing leader who was responsible for dividing the nation. His name was synonymous with the American Civil War and any efforts to commemorate him were overshadowed by the after-effects of the war. However, these aftereffects began to fade with time.

- Gradually, over several decades, the Civil War came to assume new meaning for Americans in both the North and the South. Whereas early assessments stressed only the issue of victory and defeat, by the late nineteenth century the war was being cast in heroic terms by both sides...both North and South could maintain that they had fought the good fight for causes each side held dear...Only a step separated this view from seeing the war as a struggle that tested-and strengthened-the nation.

As American cultural values began to alter the status of the Civil War at the turn of the 19th century, they also began to transform Lincoln's reputation. No longer vilified as the president who divided the nation, the Lincoln Memorial was dedicated in Washington, D.C., in 1922 to the *defender* of the nation.

DESIGNATION

Designated sites, "...arise from events that are viewed as important but somehow lacking the heroic or sacrificial qualities associated with sanctification". Due to a number of reasons, they omit the rituals of ceremony and consecration. For example, the designation of a site may be a transitional phase. The site could, over time, either be consecrated or eventually obliterated from memory. The commemoration process of Martin Luther King Jr. illustrates this idea. After King's assassination at the Lorraine Motel, Walter Bailey, building's owner, marked the site to venerate the Black hero. However, the wider American population did not immediately accept King' as a heroic symbol, and therefore sanctification was not forthcoming. This is due in part because, "...commemoration is primarily enacted by former victims, survivors or relatives...Rarely does any state commemorate its own crimes...".

Young supports this idea. "Only rarely does a nation call upon itself to remember the victims of crimes it has perpetrated. Where are the national monuments to the genocide of American Indians, to the millions of Africans enslaved...? They barely exist". For a group that has suffered such negative images and stereotypes, or who simply has not molded into American ideals, preservation has been limited. It took twenty years before the Black struggle was integrated into American cultural values and therefore King to reach national recognition. As Foote noted, the changing political climate finally allowed such black minority sites to be commemorated. Changes included, "...downsizing controversial divisive issues and instead stressing values and virtues held in common by parties on both sides... and canonizing heroes, and creating shared monuments...". Foote is not the sole academic to recognize the influence of cultural values on the commemoration of dark places.

Preservation is a selective process for Barthel and that which is selected often reflects the interests of those in power. Similarly, Tunbridge and Ashworth found motives behind some interpretation, which, "...may include the manipulation of...essentially sensitive heritage so that it contributes to a variety of contemporary goals even though these may historically have had little relevance to the original atrocity events". For Goodey, cultural influence does not lie solely in the hands of politicians: "There has always been those rich enough to create taste in landscape". Tunbridge and Ashworth reminded us that media is also highly selective in its choice of victims thereby influencing cultural values.

For instance, the British Broadcasting Company (BBC) was not in Rwanda and, "...world interest in East Timor was stirred only after the broadcast of a 1990's videotape, some 15 years after the violence had begun". A number of additional academic works have looked at cultural values and commemoration. Also using the Black example, Crew noted that interest in Black History did not begin until the two decades after World War II. While initial commemoration took place with local, grass roots movements, it was not until the early 1970's that mainstream America began to pay heed to Black History.

Much of this change came with the political activism of the 1960's. However, despite recent commemorations of Black History, certain parts of history remain vague, especially antebellum plantations and slavery: perhaps because this subservient part of history continues to diverge from overriding American values. Compare this to modern slavery commemoration Britain. Until the last century, Unite Kingdom perceptions of Britain's role in slavery were that of social reform. With an absence of physical evidence, a smaller Black population, and no watershed mark to signify slavery as being important, Britons until recently have been removed from their role in the slavery triangle.

It was easier to focus on the positive aspects of slavery that the historic sites postulated. For example, there is the abolition campaign led by William Wilberforce. The change came when a leading white, British philanthropist traveled to Barbados and discovered Britain's ignorance about slavery. He funded a permanent exhibit at the Maritime Museum in Liverpool, England, and today, all aspects of slavery in Britain are interpreted. Another illustrative example is to compare the sinking of the *Titanic* to that of the *S.S. Atlantic*, which sank in 1898, killing 562 persons.

Until 1912, the *Atlantic's* sinking had the distinction of being the worst single-vessel maritime disaster. Unlike the *Titanic* that carried a number of rich, influential individuals, the Atlantic was carrying mostly European immigrants to the United States. As a result, there is little commemoration to the victims except within the tiny Canadian fishing villages that played rescuers' roles in the tragedy. Another manifestation of conflicting cultural values is what Tunbridge and Ashworth define as heritage dissonance. As the authors noted, "All heritage is someone's heritage and therefore logically not someone else's". Hence, when individuals attempt to lay claim to a part of someone else's heritage, conflict can arise. Furthermore, conflict is exacerbated when one party is comprised of tourists and tourism providers. Lennon and Foley note,

- Viewing the past – as opposed to history – as a set of discourses aimed at a particular group highlights the suggestion that history is for someone and that the contemporary dominant power élites are most likely to play a significant part in shaping that reality when the target group is ordinary citizens in the guise of tourists. Thus those with the responsibilities for tourism promotion and development may have a previously unrecognized ethical dilemma – that of adjudicating in debates over 'whose history' prevails in interpretation.

This is well illustrated in a question posed by Tunbridge and Ashworth. Is a British bomber pilot or German U-boat captain a hero, villain, or both simultaneously? For the allies during World War II, the British bomber pilot was a hero; however, the citizens of Dresden did not likely feel the same way after their city was bombed in 1945 by allied air raids. The question becomes even more profound looking at contemporary interpretation of the events in Dresden.

Although Britain and the United States devastated the city in 1945, the issue today is often skirted in the retelling of the war for, "...fear of offending the English-speaking tourism market". Consequently, tourism creates dissonance as people cater to the tourism dollar rather than adhering to authenticity. The literature cites a number of additional relationships between tourism and heritage dissonance.

Foote discusses the 1889 Johnstown flood that killed almost 1,800 of the town's residents. Although a marker was erected in commemoration, little else was done. "Many residents felt that it was now time...to put the flood behind them and move forward with reconstruction, that further memorialization would only prolong painful memories". However, journalists and tourists continued to inundate the region in attempt to keep the story alive. Over one hundred years later, cultural values have changed, and now the town is the site of a flood museum and a national memorial. Rather than wanting to turn away tourists, tourism is, "...seen as a way to turn a past catastrophe into a present-day asset". Lennon and Foley discuss heritage dissonance regarding the Sixth Floor Depository in Dallas, Texas. Although a popular tourist site today, the Depository was not always seen in a positive light. "After the assassination, the building was clearly a difficult real estate proposition and state employees were understandably less than enthusiastic working on the sixth floor".

A former mayor of Dallas was quoted as saying, "For my part, I don't want anything to remind me that a President was killed on the streets of Dallas. I want to forget". However, tourists and other well-wishers flocked to the assassination site, leaving behind a collection of remembrances: flowers, madonnas, wreaths. Today a number of memorials commemorate the life of John F. Kennedy, including the Sixth Floor Book Depository, which is Dallas' number one tourist attraction. Dann and Potter noted that plantation and slavery tourism in Barbados often created dissonance by putting dollars first and people last. The island was,

- ...quick to realize that it cannot portray its history as it really happened, since the presentation of centuries of overt racism...is hardly a recipe for touristic success. There has consequently been a selective rendition of the past...[resulting]...in a loss of identification for the provider, and indigenous culture becomes reduced....

This premise is supported by Tunbridge and Ashworth who quote, "This shaping of past oppression, perhaps as a reaction to the perceived contemporary problems of these groups, creates obvious dissonance possibilities in the interpretation of this historical period...". While tourists and tourism-providers may not want to confront the island's history of suffering, for many islanders who endured slavery, telling their story may be vital. The Jersey Islands off the coast of England also illustrate a history at odds with tourism.

Today, "The 'ill wind' of the war years has been turned to the good. The relics and remains of Hitler's British stronghold have now taken their place...Jersey's German occupation is now big business, with more war museums per square mile than anywhere else in Europe". However, any reminders tarnishing the island's image during the war are sanitized or hidden: the collaborations, fraternization and compromises. Moreover, the whole issue of collaboration is dealt with in only one museum on Jersey in a minor display area. This is because collaboration brings into question the belief that Britain stood alone against Hitler during the dark days of World War II, thereby hurting national identity and the tourism dollar. Light found dissonance to be alive and well in post-communist Romania. Like other Eastern and Central European nations, Romania has little desire to commemorate and interpret their communist past for, "...the physical legacy of Ceausescu's rule is an unwelcome reminder of a period of history which Romania is attempting to forget". As proof, after the 1998 revolution, statues of all communist leaders were torn down and streets were renamed.

However, there is considerable interest from tourists. In 1990, a year after the overthrow of communism in Romania, the country saw a 67 per cent increase in tourism. "Independent travelers took the opportunity to see for themselves the site and sights of Eastern Europe's most violent revolution, while travel companies hastily arranged packages for visitors wanting to see the locations associated with the collapse of communism". In Romania then, the desire to forget the past conflicts with the desire to maximize the economic benefits of tourism. Such heritage dissonance between survivors and tourism has possible ramifications aside from direct, human conflict. Firstly, as Henderson points out, "There is potential conflict between the functions of education and entertainment...".

If hosts ignore the interpretation that is being offered to guests, the line between education and spectacle may easily be crossed. Secondly, host sites may be missing opportunities to tell their stories. Using Light's Romanian example, tourists are left uninformed about the meaning of communism to the country and why they are so unwilling to share their stories. Conversely, tourism may be rushing the country to confront a past they are not yet ready to face. Cultural values dominate history, heritage, and the memorialization process. Frequently, those in power manipulate which stories are told for political, economic, and nationalistic purposes. This alone can create conflict between the prevailing forces and victims and survivors as they battle for the ownership of the past.

Survivors and victims themselves do not always agree on the shaping of memory. However, the situation is intensified when tourists and tourism dollars enter into the equation. The literature was clear in outlining the conflict between hosts' wants and guests' demands. Unfortunately, the tourism dollar often triumphs over victims' wishes and historical fact. There are severe repercussions to this situation. As illustrated in Dresden, Germany and Jersey, England, some historical facts were disregarded in order to satisfy tourists. In Dallas, Texas, there was a division in the community. In Romania, educational opportunities were lost due to the impatience of the tourism industry. Some sites may even be threatened with spectacle as tourism operators' rush to capitalize on tragic events. Dark tourism sites are particularly susceptible to heritage dissonance given the gravity and sensitivity of their origins. For those who have undergone such traumatic events, forgetting may be an instinctual reaction. Yet given the pervasiveness of the media, touristic interest is often immediate. It follows that these sites must be managed with heritage dissonance in mind in order to reduce conflict.

CULTURAL VALUES AND THE HOLOCAUST

The commemoration of the Holocaust is no different from the previous examples in that it, too, is impacted by prevailing cultural values. As Gourevitch notes, "In America...we recast the story of the Holocaust to teach fundamental American values...pluralism, democracy, restraint on government, the inalienable right of individuals, the inability of government to enter into freedom of religion". The USHMM in Washington, D.C. provides a highly illustrative example of this. In the years following World War II, the world tried to come to grips with a number of conflicting emotions, especially regarding the Holocaust. Veterans who liberated concentration camps endured, "...an almost unbearable mixture of empathy, disgust, guilt, anger and alienation". Bystanders experienced guilt for not having taken a more active part, while perpetrators attempted to forget their actions.

The implications of the events were simply too threatening for public examination. In America, reactions to the Holocaust were similar, and the reactions of survivors who had come to the country were equally as mixed. Some simply wanted to forget, while others did not want to identify with the victims. Others starting a new life, "...were more concerned about acting as Americans than as Jews". The political climate of the decades following World War II proved conducive to sustaining these conflicting emotions. Post-war America had allied itself with Germany against Cold War communism. Holocaust perpetrators had suddenly become the allies, while some liberators such as the Soviet Union were now considered the enemy. "Active memory of the Nazi past was considered a needless complication in the struggle to win the Cold War".

A number of international and national events began to change American opinions towards the Holocaust in the 1960's. May of 1967 saw the Six-Day War in Israel, with the ultimate Egyptian goal of annihilating Israel. For Jews in both the United States and abroad, this awakened dormant memories of the Holocaust and brought about a 'collapse of complacency'. The Jewish struggle for 'Never Again' was born. On another foreign shore, America was fighting a losing battle against North Vietnam. As the conflict began to erode the American belief in the, "...righteousness of the American fighting man..." the Holocaust provided a foundation for good versus evil after the, "...disorientation of Vietnam...". Americans were forced to reconsider their values. On the home shores, the late 1960's saw a rise in ethnic particularism as an accepted form of cultural expression. It became acceptable to be different and to express those differences; therefore, many Jews became less reserved about demonstrating their Jewish identity in public. In the late 1970's, a number of additional events transpired. There were proposed anti-Semitic marches in Skokie, Illinois by American Nazis.

The American Office of Special Investigations began prosecuting war criminals. The NBC aired a miniseries on the Holocaust, and in 1978 then-president Jimmy Carter commissioned a presidential report on the Holocaust. Finally, and pointedly, the changing political climate was in Washington, D.C. directly influenced the commemoration of the Holocaust in the capital. As Linenthal relates, "The motivation to build a Holocaust memorial was linked with a clear message of the administration's support for the State of Israel". This was desperately needed as Carter wanted to appease the Jewish constituency after the sale of F-15 fighter jets to Saudi Arabia.

President Carter was using the, "...power of the government to do something many would perceive as good, and at the same time, reach out to an increasingly alienated ethnic constituency". In 1980, the Carter administration created a Campaign to Remember, a mail-out fundraising campaign targeting the American Jewish population. Throughout the 1960's and 70's, the above factors combined with others to bring about the genesis of a Holocaust museum in Washington D.C. However, this museum would not only commemorate the Holocaust, it would be a, "...repository of American identity". The story, instead of focusing solely on the Jewish experience, would have to be told in a way that would be significant to an American audience: it needed to move beyond the limits of ethnic memory. To do so, the museum would reinforce, "...American identity by graphically revealing what America is not", "...through stark presentation of their antitheses in Nazi Germany".

Krauthammer reinforces this idea. Located in the Washington Mall, "...home of the monumental expressions of core national narratives", the museum provides excellent views of the Washington Monument and Jefferson Memorial. Here, "...juxtaposition is not just redemptive. It is reassuring. The angels of democracy stand watch on this temple of evil. It is as if only in the heart of the world's most tolerant and powerful democracy can such terrible testimony be safely contained". Outwardly, the commemoration process appears to be an easy practice. Americans flock in droves to the Sixth Floor Museum, the Lincoln Monument, and Gettysburg to venerate their heroes. However, these heroes and events, which we take for, granted were likely once victims of debate and conflict over what accurately represented a national identity. The enshrinement of disaster and tragedy is not accidental: it is shaped by prevailing cultural values that forge and maintain a national identity. 'Remember the Alamo', the 'Maine' and 'Pearl Harbour' have all served as rallying cries to rouse patriotic fervour in the pursuit of justice. These words conjure up visions of freedom, bravery and liberty. Rarely does one hear reminders of unpopular events such as 'Remember Kent State' or 'Remember Saigon'. This is because shame and loss are not values governments want to instill in their constituency.

Therefore, the commemoration of dark tourism sites must be looked at under this light. Violence and tragedy are widespread in society; however, not all sites and events are memorialized. Social and political forces have moulded much of what is seen. Similarly, interpretation at sites of death and disaster must be viewed with skepticism. The truth may not be the ultimate ideal because it is more important to shape displays and exhibits into a marketable commodity.

UNDERSTANDING THE HOLOCAUST

For many, the scope of the Holocaust is beyond belief: that one state sponsored regime could systematically annihilate mass populations is unfathomable. Beginning in 1933 with Hitler's investiture as German chancellor, the Third Reich eventually exterminated approximately eleven million individuals before the 1945 Nazi surrender. Those targeted included, but were not limited to, communists and other political prisoners, Gypsies, homosexuals, and the mentally disabled. Of those eleven million, however, over half were of Jewish origin. In Poland alone, 90 per cent of the Judaic population was wiped out. Pre-1933, there were 3.5 million Jews living in the country: approximately 300,000 survived. In Czechoslovakia, the ancient fortress city of Terezin was converted into a transit camp where 138,000 Jews died. Jewry in Austria, France, Holland, Belgium, Denmark, Norway, Luxembourg, Ukraine, Hungry and Lithuania suffered similar fates.

All totaled, 6 million Jews lost their lives during the Holocaust, including 1.5 million children. Whether termed Shoah or Holocaust, the remembrance and commemoration of such events are also overwhelming and are as varied as the individual experiences themselves. Much of the literature on memorializing the period emphasizes a deep divergence in commemoration, particularly between countries; for it is there cultural values dictate public memory. Furthermore, the stakes of remembrance are high for those involved. Holocaust commemoration not only involves veneration, but also perceived ownership of the events and subsequently the sculpting of a nation's identity. To illustrate, two countries are examined: Israel, and most importantly for this study, the United States.

ISRAEL AND SHOAH

Today, Israel is a nation indelibly tied to Shoah. For some, the events of 1933- 1945 were precursors to the establishment of a Jewish state. The Israeli army's Informational Guidelines to the Commander on Yom Hashoah goes as far as quoting, "By standing under these conditions and refusing to surrender to despair the Jews made it possible the continuation of the Jewish people even in the inferno of the Holocaust and thereby helped created the State of Israel". This form of recognition however, was not always the case, for Israel, like all nations, remembers according to national myths and political will. In the years immediately following the war, Israel had an ambiguous relationship with the destruction of the Shoah, particularly after statehood in 1948. Native-born Israeli's could not understand the mass extermination and did not care to commemorate the powerlessness of their people.

Similarly, many of the 350,000 survivors that settled there after the war found the past too painful to confront. There was little desire to commemorate what was perceived to be victimization and as a result, remembrance was greeted with silence. This silence was shattered with the 1961 trial of Adolph Eichmann. Hundreds of survivors stood to give testimony and emotion to their Holocaust experiences, and this soon opened dialogue between varying Israeli factions.

"The trial created a climate of opinion in which the Holocaust...became the central topic of conversation... [it]...ceased to be a taboo, and instead assumed an increasingly central – if contestedposition in Israeli society and politics". The trial brought together the dueling reactions to the Holocaust, thus reconciling Israelis with their past. Furthermore, it brought about the genesis of modern remembrance in Israel: that of rebirth. Today in Israel, memory is devoted to heroism and yesterday's victims have become modern martyrs. Where European museums focus on the annihilation of the Jews, at museums such as Yad Vashem in Jerusalem, the Holocaust links a, "...millennium of Jewish life in Europe before the war...to Jewish National Rebirth afterwards".

THE UNITED STATES OF AMERICA

Like Israel, both native-born Americans and immigrant survivors sought to put the past behind them immediately after the war. For Americans, Germany had become an ally in the Cold War; for survivors, the memories were too painful. Attitudes have changed dramatically in the past 60 years, and today the United States embraces the events. Now, what is, "...beyond dispute is that in the 1990's the 'Holocaust' is being made in America".

Holocaust history has become American history, justified by the country's roles as bystander, liberator, and haven for survivors. As a result, the Holocaust has become Americanized and the numerous Holocaust museums and memorials dotting the country exemplify this. From Dallas and Boston to Miami and Tucson, America remembers. Yet, America remembers through American ideals. Perhaps no other museum illustrates this better than the United States Holocaust Memorial Museum in Washington, D.C. Where European sites focus on victims and Israelis on rebirth, in the American focus in on what it means to be American. As the USHMM's Memorial Council stated during the museum's inception,

- This museum belongs at the center of American life because as a democratic civilization America is the enemy of racism and its ultimate expression, genocide. An event of universal significance, the Holocaust has special importance for Americans: in act and word the Nazis denied the deepest tenets of the American people.
- A number of other sources endorse this doctrine. Max Kampelman, Ronald Reagan's chief arms negotiator felt that,
- ...Europeans probably should have built such museums in their capitals, but they haven't and most probably won't...But our building will demonstrate the tolerance of our culture, its ability to empathize with the suffering of all its people. Or decision to build such a museum says something about our commitment to human rights and to the kind of nation we want to be.

Michael Berenbaum, director of the museum, commented that, "When people leave the U.S. Holocaust Memorial Museum, the monuments to democracy that surround it – to Lincoln and Jefferson and Washington – will taken on new meaning". For Cole, this indicates the museum's ability to affect all Americans. For him, "...the museum just off the Mall...gives an 'Americanised' telling of the 'Holocaust' to a target audience of non-Jewish mom, dad and kids from Iowa...[it]...talks of 'victims'/'survivors' and 'liberators'". Ownership of the Holocaust, then, must be understood in the context of this research.

The paper's focus is an American Holocaust museum and its American visitors, hence, an Americanization of the events. Should someone initiate a similar study in Israel, Poland or Germany, the results will likely differ, for each country comprehends the Holocaust differently. The events will be interpreted according to each country's own unique cultural value systems. For visitors to the Holocaust Museum Houston, according to the literature, their experience will revolve around key

American tenets. As bystander to many of the events, America will reach out through such museums to promise Nie Wider – Never Again. Exhibits will stand, "...as an explicit judgement on past inaction, and an implicit call to America (as self-styled 'policeman of the world') not to stand idly by in the future". Via Holocaust museums such as in Houston, America may also overlay this inaction through her roles of liberator and haven for survivors. Once again, national cultural values such as pluralism, democracy, liberty and heroism are interwoven with other stories from the Holocaust. While Jewish death and destruction is commemorated, it is done so in an American context. Therefore, visitors to the Holocaust Museum Houston are not just experiencing the Holocaust, they are experiencing an American version of the events.

DEPENDENCE ON TOURISM

Permitting tourism to become the subsistence industry is not desirable for a number of reasons. First, tourism is by its very nature subject to considerable seasonality. While seasonal fluctuations in demand can sometimes be reduced, they cannot be eliminated. Thus, when tourism is the primary industry in an area, the off-season periods inevitably result in serious unemployment problems. Such areas find that the seasonal character of tourism leaves severe economic and social effects on the host region.

Another very important reason relates to the source of demand for tourism. The demand for tourism depends largely on the income and the tastes of tourists, both of which are beyond the control of the host region. When the American economy goes through a slump, demand for travel to a foreign destination by Americans will fall off. A destination area can do precious little, in this case, to increase the level of demand. If the tastes of the people in the tourist-generating area change—that is, they decide to travel to a new destination—tourism in the old area will decline, causing economic and social problems.

Again, the destination can do little or nothing to avoid this. In fact, as Plog points out, there is reason to believe that such a decline in an area's popularity may be largely inevitable. Quite clearly, then, tourism should not be allowed to grow to an extent that the destination area becomes totally dependent on it. In other words, total dependence on a single industrial sector is undesirable. If it cannot be avoided, then dependence on domestic agriculture is in many ways preferable to dependence on tourism. The country has presumably adapted itself economically and socially to dependence on agriculture over several centuries. The demand for agricultural output is also unlikely to suffer from a secular decline, because people must eat. Also, it is the residents, not foreigners as in tourism, who directly benefit from agricultural production.

ECOTOURISM

Ecotourism means ecological tourism, where ecological has both environmental and social connotations. It is defined both as a concept-tourism movement and as a tourism section. Born in its current form in the late 1980's, Ecotourism came of age in 2002, when the United Nations celebrated the "International Year of Ecotourism". The meeting was a watershed event, but it was not created with those who had pioneered the niche. There are various definitions as this is a vibrant movement and ecotourism may be defined by its lack of definition.

Generally speaking, ecotourism focuses on local cultures, wilderness adventures, volunteering, personal growth and learning new ways to live on the planet. It is typically defined as travel to destinations where the flora, fauna, and cultural heritage are the primary attractions. Responsible ecotourism includes Programmes that minimize the adverse effects of traditional tourism on the natural environment, and enhance the cultural integrity of local people. Therefore, in addition to evaluating environmental and cultural factors, initiatives by hospitality providers to promote recycling, energy efficiency, water reuse, and the creation of economic opportunities for local communities are an integral part of ecotourism. Many global environmental organizations and aid agencies favour ecotourism as a vehicle to sustainable development.

Ideally, true ecotourism should satisfy several criteria, such as:

- Conservation of biological diversity and cultural diversity, through ecosystems protection
- Promotion of sustainable use of biodiversity, by providing jobs to local populations
- Sharing of socio-economic benefits with local communities and indigenous people by having their informed consent and participation in the management of ecotourism enterprises.
- Increase of environmental and cultural knowledge
- Minimisation of tourism's own environmental impact
- Affordability and lack of waste in the form of luxury
- Local culture, flora and fauna being the main attractions

For many countries, ecotourism is not so much seen as a marginal activity intended to finance protection of the environment than as a major sector of national economy and as a means of attracting tourists. For example, in countries such as Costa Rica, Ecuador, Nepal, Kenya, Madagascar and Antarctica, ecotourism represents a significant portion of the gross domestic product. The concept of ecotourism is widely misunderstood and, in practice, is often simply used as a marketing tool to promote tourism that is related to nature. Critics claim that ecotourism as practiced and abused often consists of placing a hotel in a splendid landscape, to the detriment of the ecosystem. According to them, ecotourism must above all sensitize people with the beauty and the fragility of nature.

They condemn some operators as "green-washing" their operations — that is, using the label of "ecotourism" and "green-friendly", while behaving in environmentally irresponsible ways. Although academics argue about who can be classified as an ecotourist, and there is precious little statistical data, some estimate that more than five million ecotourists — the majority of the worldwide population — come from the United States, with other ecotourists coming from Europe, Canada and Australia. Currently there are various moves to create national and international ecotourism certification Programmes, although the process is causing controversy.

One example of ecoturism certificates has been put into place at Costa Rica, though the Programmes has been dismissed as green-washing by others. One criticism against ecotourism is that the air travel to often remote places is not included in the "environmental impact calculation". A journey to a place 10,000 kilometers away and home consumes about 700 litres of fuel per person. Another problem is that some of the destinations visited by ecotourists are extremely sensitive to environmental impact from human use and can be damaged even by careful travellers. A new form of tourism is called Clean Tourism.

ECOLOGICAL MASS TOURISM

When people think about the word 'Ecological Mass Tourism' they normally link it with negative thoughts of mass tourism that is associated with environmental degradation. The truth is we believe that Ecological Mass Tourism is beneficial for everyone, but in essence we must first understand what Ecological Mass Tourism actually encompasses: Mass Tourism: "refers to the steady stream of large numbers of tourists to holiday destinations."

Ecotourism "nature based tourism involving the education and interpretation of the natural environment and is managed to be ecologically sustainable. This definition also recognises that 'natural environment' includes cultural components and that 'ecologically sustainable' involves an appropriate return to the local community and long term conservation of the resource" Ecotourists: are tourists who participate in different sorts of nature based tourism. Furthermore "most ecotourists are often found to be residents of the developed world with above average incomes and educations." By integrating all 3 words into 1 we have constructed our definition of Ecological Mass Tourism or for short. Ecological Mass Tourism or: are large numbers of educated tourists and ecotourists participating within the realms of diversified forms of managed ecotourism.

EMT also attracts tourists who not only participate in ecotourism, but also recognise its cultural components and its involvement with giving a fitting return to the local community and long term conservation of the resource. In properly defining EMT we believe that it is beneficial to all parties involved, and more importantly it can also be perceived to be sustainable. In addition to this EMT also has the ability to be managed properly and has definite infrastructure, cultural and social benefits linked Ecological Mass Tourism does not go against the principle of mass tourism on the basis that it contains financial, cultural and social benefits associated with its concept.

HERITAGE TOURISM

Cultural heritage tourism is a branch of tourism oriented towards the cultural heritage. Culture has always been a major object of travel, as the development of the Grand Tour from the 16th century onwards attests. In the 20th century, some people have claimed, culture ceased to be the objective of tourism: tourism is now culture. Cultural attractions play an important role in tourism at all levels, from the global highlights of world culture to attractions that underpin local identities. According to the Weiler and Hall, culture, heritage and the arts have long contributed to appeal of tourist destination. However, in recent years 'culture' has been rediscovered as an important marketing tool to attract those travellers with special interests in heritage and arts. According to the Hollinshead, cultural heritage tourism defines as cultural heritage tourism is the fastest growing segment of the tourism industry because there is a trend towards an increase specialization among tourist.

This trend is evident in the rise in the volume of tourists who seek adventure, culture, history, archaeology and interaction with local people. Cultural heritage tourism is important for various reasons; it has a positive economic and social impact, it establishes and reinforces identity, it helps preserve the cultural heritage, with culture as an instrument it facilitates harmony and understanding among people, it supports culture and helps renew tourism. Cultural heritage tourism has a number of objectives that must be met within the context of sustainable development such as; the conservation of cultural resources, accurate interpretation of resources, authentic visitors experience, and the stimulation of the earned revenues of cultural resources.

We can see therefore, that cultural heritage tourism is not only concerned with identification, management and protection of the heritage values but it must also be involved in understanding the impact of tourism on communities and regions, achieving economic and social benefits, providing financial resources for protection, as well as marketing and promotion. Heritage tourism involves visiting historical or industrial sites that may include old canals, railways, battlegrounds, etc. The overall purpose is to gain an appreciation of the past. It also refers to the marketing of a location to members of a diaspora who have distant family roots there. Heritage tourism is distinct from visiting a family member in a faraway place because the connection to the original homeland is removed; a recent Irish immigrant to the US, for example, may return home to see relatives but would probably not be considered a heritage tourist.

On the other hand, an Irish-American whose family emigrated in the 19th century, also going to Ireland but rather to see the country generally, would be partaking in heritage tourism. This is particularly relevant to European areas where large numbers of people emigrated to North America in the 19th century and early 20th century. People from Quebec have been moving back and forth to France for centuries in fairly significant numbers, as have their counterparts with ties to the British Isles and other countries for more recent immigrants. Other examples include Black/African Americans who visit Africa and Hispanics who visit Spain. The purpose can be education, fun, marriage, employment, etc. Permanent emigration tied to heritage tourism is less common but increasing. Diagonalization and immigration form the major background of much contemporary heritage tourism. Falling travel costs have also made heritage tourism possible for more people. Another possible form involves religious travel or pilgrimages.

Many Catholics from around the world come to the Vatican and other sites such as Lourdes or Fatima. Large numbers of Jews have both visited Israel and emigrated there. Many have also gone to Holocaust sites and memorials. Islam commands its followers to take the hajj to Mecca, thus differentiating it somewhat from tourism in the usual sense, though the trip can also be a culturally important event for the pilgrim. Heritage Tourism can also be attributed to historical events that have been dramatised to make them more entertaining. For example a historical tour of a town or city using a theme such as ghosts or vikings.

INVESTMENT PRIORITIES

Sometimes, governments of developing countries take an overly optimistic view of tourism. They undertake aggressive investment Programmes to develop tourism, assigning it top priority in their development plans. In extreme cases, such an approach can lead to the neglect of more fundamental investment needs of the country. For example, funds can be channeled into tourism development at the cost of education, health, and other social services—aspects of the social well-being of the population that should be of primary concern for a developing country.

Not only is undue glamorization of tourism unwise because it usurps this position, but such a strategy only speeds up the process of dependence on tourism, which, as discussed earlier, is itself undesirable. Moreover, investment in tourism at the cost of health and education Programmes also slows down the rate at which the local population is assimilated into the modern market economy of the country. Under certain circumstances, it may actually retard development rather than enhance it.

The conclusion is that although tourism has tremendous potential as a tool in economic development, it is no panacea. Governments should attempt to optimize the benefits that tourism provides, being ever mindful of the costs that it can impose. It should be noted also that the probability and the intensity of the economic costs of tourism are greater for developing nations than for wealthy ones. Wealthy nations, by definition, possess robust economies that can more easily absorb the cost of tourism. Typically, such economies are well diversified, and government investment Programme are not so central to development efforts. The social benefits and costs of tourism should be viewed similarly. While the host community seeks to maximize the benefits, it must weigh these against the social costs. The social costs are likewise higher in both probability and magnitude when tourism is being considered for development in an area that still possesses a traditional social structure.

INCOME ELASTICITY OF DEMAND

As income rises, more travel is demanded at any given price. Thus, the relationship between income and demand is positive. The responsiveness of demand to changes in income is called income elasticity of demand. It is defined as the percentage. Tourism makes a major economic contribution to the world economy. Despite this economic significance, tourism managers have for some time been met with complaints such as "All the type about tourism's contribution to economic growth and job creation is a gross exaggeration." As well, members of the industry itself want to be sure that the economic impact figures are indeed accurate so that they can better plan their investments and improve their productivity and performance.

In an attempt to ensure the accuracy and reliability of the measures of tourism's economic impact, the World Tourism Organization in collaboration with the World Travel and Tourism Council and with the support of the Canadian Tourism Commission have undertaken to develop a tourism accounting system that is not only rigorous, but consistent with the national accounts of every country. This system has been named Tourism Satellite Account.

MEDICAL TOURISM

Medical tourism is the act of travelling to other countries to obtain medical, dental, and surgical care. The term was initially coined by travel agencies and the media as a catchall phrase to describe a rapidly growing industry where people travel to other countries to obtain medical care while at the same time touring, vacationing and enjoying the attractions of the countries which they are visiting.

A combination of many factors has led to the recent increase in popularity of medical tourism: the high cost of health care in industrialized nations, the ease and affordability of international travel, and the improvement of technology and standards of care in many countries of the world. A large draw to medical tourism is the convenience in comparison to that of other countries. Some countries that operate from a public health-care system are so taxed that it can take a considerable amount of time, sometimes even years, to get needed medical care. The time spent waiting for a procedure, such as a hip replacement, can be a year or more in Britain and Canada; however, in Bangkok or Bangalore, a patient could feasibly have an operation the day after their arrival. The real lure to medical tourism is saving money on costly procedures. According to research found in an article by UDaily: the cost of surgery in India, Thailand or South Africa can be one-tenth of what it is in the United States or Western Europe, and sometimes even less. A heart-valve replacement that would cost US$200,000 or more in the U.S., for example, goes for $10,000 in India—and that includes round-trip airfare and a brief vacation package. Similarly, a metal-free dental bridge worth $5,500 in the U.S. costs $500 in India, a knee replacement in Thailand with six days of physical therapy costs about one-fifth of what it would in the States, and Lasik eye surgery worth $3,700 in the U.S. is available in many other countries for only $730. Cosmetic surgery savings are even greater: A full facelift that would cost $20,000 in the U.S. runs about $1,250 in South Africa."

Medical tourists are generally residents of the industrialized nations of the world. The countries to which they travel are typically less developed and have a lower cost of medical care. This is, in some cases, due to Favourable currency exchange ratios. Currently, many of the procedures accessed are considered "elective procedures," such as cosmetic surgery. Because elective procedures are rarely covered through health insurance plans, there may be greater incentive to find such care at lower costs. The list of countries currently promoting medical tourism include: Bolivia, Brazil, Cuba, Costa Rica, Hungary, India, Israel, Jordan, Lithuania, Malaysia, The Philippines, and Thailand with the Joint Commission International accredited Bumrungrad Hospital. Belgium, Poland and Singapore are also breaking into the business. South Africa is taking the term "medical tourism" very literally by promoting their "medical safaris": Come to see African wildlife and get a facelift in the same trip. However, feelings towards medical tourism are not always positive. In places like the US, where most have insurance and access to quality health care, medical tourism is viewed as risky.

While the tourism component might be a big draw for Southeast Asia countries that focus on simple procedures, India is positioning itself the primary medical destination for the most complex medical procedures in the world. India's commitment to this is demonstrated with an ever growing number of hospitals that are attaining the US Joint Commission International accreditation. Singapore has made international news for providing complex neurosurgical procedures. Currently Singapore boasts the largest number of US Joint Commission accredited hospitals in the region. There are companies emerging to offer global health care options that will allow North American patients to take full advantage of dramatic reductions in air travel and access world class health care at a fraction of the cost.

Companies that focus on 'Medical Value Travel' typically will have experienced nurse case managers to assist patients with pre- and post-travel medical issues. They will also help provide resources for follow-up care upon the patient's return. While these services will initially be of interest to the self-insured patient, several studies indicate that the rapid growth of Health Savings Accounts will also drive interest to health care in other countries.

POP-CULTURE TOURISM

Pop-culture tourism is the act of travelling to locations featured in literature, film, music, or any other form of popular entertainment. Popular destinations have included the Iowa cornfields featured in Field of Dreams, New Zealand after The Lord of the Rings was filmed there, and The Louvre in which the book and movie The Da Vinci Code takes place. Prince Edward Island, in which the Canadian novel Anne of Green Gables takes place, is a popular attraction for tourists, notably from Japan. Pop-culture tourism is in some respects akin to pilgrimage, with its modern equivalents of places of pilgrimage, such as Elvis Presley's Graceland and the grave of Jim Morrison in Père Lachaise Cemetery.

PILGRIMAGE TOURISM

A pilgrimage is a term primarily used in religion and spirituality of a long journey or search of great moral significance. Sometimes, it is a journey to a sacred place or shrine of importance to a person's beliefs and faith. Members of every religion participate in pilgrimages. A person who makes such a journey is called a pilgrim. Secular and civic pilgrimages are also practiced, without regard for religion but rather of importance to a particular society. For example, many people throughout the world travel to the City of Washington in the United States for a pilgrimage to see the Declaration of Independence and the Constitution of the United States. British people often make pilgrimages to London for public appearances of the monarch of the United Kingdom. Pop culture has also sought to redefine pilgrimages, defining a demoscene party as a pilgrimage.

QUANTITY DEMANDED AND PRICE ELASTICITY

For some products, even a large change in price over a certain range of the demand curve results in only a small change in quantity demanded. In this case, demand is not very responsive to price. For other products, or for the same product over a different range of prices, a relatively small change in price elicits a much larger relative change in quantity demanded. Demand can be classified as inelastic or elastic on the basis of the relative responsiveness of quantity demanded to changes in price. Specifically, price elasticity of demand may be defined as the percentage change in demand resulting from a given percentage change in price. Most tourism products are price elastic. During 1992, when U.S. airlines began offering half fares, the number of air travellers increased to record-high levels.

TOURISM SATELLITE ACCOUNT

A Tourism Satellite Account is a system developed by the United Nations to measure the size of economic sectors that are not defined as industries in national accounts. Tourism, for example, is an amalgam of industries such as transportation, accommodation, food and beverage services, recreation, and entertainment and travel agencies.

Tourism is a unique phenomenon as it is defined by the consumption of the visitor. Visitors buy goods and services associated with both tourism and non-tourism alike. The key from a measurement standpoint is to associate their purchases to the total supply of these goods and services within a country. The TSA is a new statistical instrument designed to measure these goods and services according to international standards of concepts, classifications, and definitions that will allow for valid comparisons with other industries and eventually from country to country and between groups of countries. Such measures will also be comparable with other internationally recognized economic statistics.

In addition, a TSA possesses the following characteristics:

- Provides credible data on the impact of tourism and the associated employment
- Is a standard framework for organizing statistical data on tourism
- Is a new international standard endorsed by the U.N. Statistical Commission
- Is a powerful instrument for designing economic policies related to tourism development
- Provides data on tourism's impact on a nation's balance of payments
- Provides information on tourism human resource characteristics

While it may be obvious, it is useful to stress why a TSA is needed. In brief, there is an acute shortage of information on the increasing role of tourism in national economies worldwide, hence the need for reliable data relative to the importance and magnitude of tourism, using the same concepts, definitions, and measurement approaches as other industries. With the TSA, governments, entrepreneurs, and citizens will be better equipped for designing public policies and business strategies for tourism and for evaluating their effectiveness and efficiency.

Development of a TSA framework has been fueled by the recognition that its implementation will serve to increase and improve knowledge of tourism's importance relative to overall economic activity in a given country. It will also provide an instrument for designing more efficient policies relating to tourism and its employment aspects; and it will create awareness among the various players directly and indirectly involved with tourism of the economic importance of this activity, and by extension its role in all the industries involved in the production of goods and services demanded by visitors.

THE NATURE OF A TSA

A TSA is characterized by the manner in which it seeks to balance measures of tourism demand versus supply. Tourism measurements, in order to be credible and comparable with other industries in a country's economy, must follow concepts and definitions consistent with internationally accepted macroeconomic guidelines, such as the System of National Accounts. The fundamental structure of the TSA therefore relies on the balance existing within an economy between, on one hand, the demand for goods and services generated by visitors and by other consumers and, on the other hand, the overall supply of these goods and services. The idea is to analyse in detail all aspects of demand for goods and services that are associated with tourism within the economy, and to measure the relationship with the supply of such goods and services within the same economy.

*More specifically, a TSA measure*s:

- Tourism's contribution to gross domestic product
- Tourism's ranking compared to other economic sectors
- The number of jobs created by tourism in an economy
- The amount of tourism investment
- Tax revenues generated by tourism industries
- Tourism consumption
- Tourism's impact on a nation's balance of payments
- Characteristics of tourism human resources

Because of its comprehensive nature, a TSA provides decision makers with a valuable tool for planning and policy making. In particular, it provides them with reliable data of tourism's impact on the economy and employment. As well, it permits the measurement of both domestic and non-resident tourism—and the employment associated with each. A TSA, however, can do much more. Following are some examples. A TSA can provide information on how much tourism is worth to the national economy, and how it compares to other industries and other countries. By demonstrating and using the size of tourism, tourism officials and private-sector businesses will have more influence on policy makers at all levels of government. As well, it can make clear which industries benefit from tourism and by how much— in particular, industries not traditionally associated with tourism.

For instance, business enterprises can identify the role tourism plays in their success and develop business strategies accordingly. A TSA is able to provide information regarding how much tax revenue is generated by tourism. This information is useful in convincing municipal, provincial, or federal levels of government to invest further in tourism. In addition, it provides data on visitor demand and how this demand is met by domestic supply. A TSA enables the establishment of a tourism economic impact model, which can be used to estimate the effect on the economy and on employment of various tourism expenditure shocks. Such an impact model provides a better understanding of tourism employment and where each industry ranks compared to other tourism industries. It should be emphasized that the ongoing development of TSAs as national promotion tools has been a process dating back to at least 1993.

The most recent focus of this development was a major international TSA conference held in Vancouver, Canada, in 2001. This and other conferences have brought together the following organizations: World Tourism Organization, World Travel and Tourism Council, Organization for Economic Cooperation and Development, United Nations, Eurostat, and a number of government statistical agencies, national tourism administrators, and central banks. The collaboration demonstrates the general principle that in order to develop a national TSA, it is essential to involve a number of key actors within a country.

The most significant of these are:

- National statistical offices, national tourism administrations, central banks, and associations of national tourism enterprises.
- Information-producing units such as tourism enterprises and establishments, and other public departments.
- Users of the tourism information that is generated, the NTAs themselves, the units responsible for preparing the national accounts and the balance of payments, and others.
- The participation and collaboration of tourism enterprises and, more specifically, their corresponding national associations.

SOURCES OF DATA USED IN A TSA

Canada, as an Example

The data used in the calculation of a TSA in Canada come from a diverse number of surveys produced by Statistics Canada. The preparation of tourism demand estimates involve several surveys that record information on tourism consumption of Canadians traveling in and outside Canada and non-residents traveling to Canada.

These include:

- Canadian Travel Survey
- International Travel Survey of Canadian Residents
- Canadian Resident Questionnaire for same-day automobile travel between the

  United States and Canada:
- United States Resident Questionnaire for same-day automobile travel between the United States and Canada
- Government Travel Survey of U.S. visitors to Canada
- Government Travel Survey of visitors to Canada

Much of the information for the supply-side estimates are drawn from the worksheets used in the making of the input-output tables by industry, commodity, and employment of the System of National Accounts. Data from reference publications, and relevant business surveys and administrative data, are used to obtain as much detail as possible on revenues generated from the sale of tourism commodities. In conclusion, a TSA recognizes that tourism is not an industry in the traditional sense—that is, identified in the System of National Accounts—because industries are classified according to the goods and services they produce, while tourism is a consumption-based concept that depends on the status of the customer. Furthermore, tourists buy many of the same products as other consumers, including items not normally associated with tourism—clothes, groceries— while Canadians at home buy tourism goods and services for non-tourism reasons—restaurant meals, postcards, recreational services.

The TSA brings together these diverse aspects of tourism by providing a tourism dimension to the framework of the System of National Accounts. It makes it possible to separate and examine the demand and supply sides of tourism within an integrated system that describes the production and demand aspects of the whole economy. The recognition of these factors has led to the situation where more than ten countries have a TSA and more than thirty are in the process of developing a TSA. These include Austria, Canada, Chile, the Dominican Republic, France, Mexico, New Zealand, Norway, Singapore, Sweden, the United States, Spain, and Italy. Domestic and international tourism are major economic strengths to many of the world's countries, states, cities, and rural areas. Thus, those who live there are affected by the economic results of tourist spending. This stage explained why these resulting effects vary greatly and what brings about a large measure of benefits or possible detriments to a community.

The main economic phenomena described are various multipliers, balance of payments, investments, tax consideration, employment, economic impact generators, travel expenditures, dependence on tourism, price and income elasticity as related to buying travel experiences, and optimization. The stage also discussed a new method of measuring tourism economic impact, satellite accounting. Many people do not understand or appreciate the economics of tourism.

The following list summarizes the principal economic effects:

1. Expenditures by foreign visitors in one's country become exports. The economic effects are the same as those derived from exporting tangible goods. If there is a Favourable exchange rate, the country that has the devalued currency will experience a higher demand for visitor services than before devaluation.
2. If citizens of one country spend money in foreign countries, these expenditures become imports for the tourists' originating country.
3. Sums of the values of national exports and imports are used when calculating a nation's balance of payments. A positive balance results when exports exceed imports, thus increasing a nation's gross national product.

4. Tourism developments typically require large investments of capital. Thus, local economies where the developments take place are stimulated by such investments.
5. Tourists pay various kinds of taxes directly and indirectly while visiting an area. Thus, tax revenues are increased for all levels of government.
6. Because tourists usually spend more per day at a destination than they do while at home, these extra expenditures may cause inflationary pressures and rising prices for consumer goods in the destination area.
7. Tourism expenditures injected into the economy produce an income multiplier for local people. This is because of the diversity of expenditures made by those receiving tourist payments. Tourist receipts are used to buy a wide variety of goods and services over a year's time. The money turnover creates additional local income.
8. The amount of income multiplication, however, will depend on how much leakage takes place. Leakages are a combination of imported goods and services purchased by tourism suppliers, and savings made of tourist receipts not loaned to another spender within one year of receipt. Thus, the more tourist goods that are supplied locally, the higher will be the multiplier.
9. Income multiplication caused by tourist expenditures necessitates hiring more people. Thus, they also affect an employment multiplier.
10. As increased spending produces more financial transactions, they create a transactions multiplier. These are of particular interest to governments that have a sales or value-added tax on such transactions.
11. As a tourist area grows, more capital is invested in new facilities. This results in a capital multiplier.
12. It is an unwise policy for a society to place too much dependency on tourism as a subsistence industry.
13. Although tourism often has an excellent potential in economic development, it is not a panacea for economic ills. Its economic benefits should be optimized rather than maximized.
14. We believe that tourism products are mainly price elastic, meaning that as prices rise, the quantity demanded tends to drop.
15. In general, we believe that tourism is income elastic. This means that as family income rises, or a particular market's income rises, and tourism prices do not rise proportionally, the demand for travel to that particular area will increase.

2

Tourism Policy of India

The Government of India announced the first Tourism Policy in November 1982. It took ten long years for the Government to feel the need to come up with a possible improvement over this. Thus the National Action Plan for Tourism was announced in May 1992. Between these two policy statements, various legislative and executive measures were brought about. In particular, the report of the National Committee on Tourism, submitted in 1988 needs special mention. In addition, two five-year plans - the Seventh and the Eighth - provided the basic perspective framework for operational initiatives. The Seventh Plan advocated a two-pronged thrust in the area of development of tourism, *viz.,* to vigorously promote domestic tourism and to diversify overseas tourism in India.

While laying stress on creation of beach resorts, conducting of conventions, conferences, winter sports and trekking, the overall intention was to diversify options available for foreign tourists. The Tourism Policy, 1982 was more an aggressive statement in marketing than a perspective plan for development. Its main thrust was aimed at presenting India to the foreigners as the ultimate holiday resort. With a view to reach this destination, the following measures were suggested by the Policy:

1. To take full advantage of the national heritage in arriving at a popular campaign for attracting tourists;
2. To promote tourist resorts and make India a destination of holiday resorts;
3. To grant the status of an export industry to tourism;
4. To adopt a selective approach to develop few tourist circuits; and,
5. To invite private sector participation into the sector.

TOURISM POLICY OF INDIA: AN EXPLORATORY STUDY

The objective here is to assess the impact of Tourism Policy on the tourism sector and make a preliminary study of the possible impact such policy imperatives might have on the socio-economic fabric of the country. The study, commissioned by Equations, Bangalore, utilised a methodology involving a historical preview of the evolution of Tourism Policy since 1982, and an exploratory assessment of the impact. The study material included documentation available at Equations and relevant publications of the Union Government.

The impact assessment of the sectoral policies on the specified sector suffers from a serious methodological problem. Briefly, it may be argued that the development of a sector is not solely dependent on the factors within the sector: it is influenced by the general socio-economic environment, the political system and the overall policy framework. Thus the study integrates within itself the dynamic aspects of historical changes that are taking place at the macro-economic level. Similarly, Tourism Policy would not have evolved on its own without being influenced by the general tenor of macro-economic policy. Tourism policy thus has a socio-political grounding as much as it has a macro-economic colouring.

The 1980s witnessed the era of liberalisation initiated by the Congress Government at the Centre. The process of liberating the Indian economy from the shibboleths of 'license-permit Raj' culminated in the initiation of the structural adjustment programme in 1992. "Objectives, Thrusts and Macro-economic Dimensions of the Eighth Plan" endorsed by the National Development Council, clearly outlines the context within which the structural reforms were initiated: "The need to restructure our systems of economic management has become an imperative if India is to emerge as a vibrant and internationally competitive economy in the 90's. Systems of control and regulation, developed for good reasons in the past have outlived their utility and some positively (sic) stand in the way of further progress.

Such dysfunctional systems have to be overhauled in the light of emerging realities." The process of structural adjustments has brought about far reaching changes in the Indian economy at a breath-taking pace. The impact of these changes over the tourism sector need to be studied in a dynamic context. Nevertheless, the above should not be taken as ignoring the fact that sectoral policy does have a direct and unambiguous impact over the concerned sector. Tourism Policy, as a statement of intent by the Government, would form the reference point for action and criticism. Any initiative by Government in Tourism by way of legislation or direct investment is envisaged within the framework of Tourism Policy.

The debates in Parliament had taken recourse to the received policy of the Union Government while making references to particular cases. The backdrop of a policy always serves as a guideline for further executive and legislative initiatives. It would be cynical to regard these policy statements as mere exercises in eloquence and additions to the already existing volumes of wishful thinking.

Furthermore, Policy statements by Government should be viewed in their evolutionary stance. It would be a negation of the democratic content of our political system to view a Policy statement as a static and rigid formulation, at a point in time, applicable for years to come.

Thus, since 1982, various initiatives undertaken by the Government need to be perceived as additions or modifications to the received Policy. While it may be argued that these changes in the policy are only marginal and superficial from the viewpoint of equity and social justice, it would be an oversimplification to view the latest policy statement as nothing but a certain version of the Policy formulated in 1982. Recognising the all-pervading inertia that looms large in matters governmental, one is often tempted to deny the scope for lobbying which makes possible the desired modifications in the policy corpus. In short, policy, as a body incorporating proactive intentions, is amenable to periodic reviews and possible modifications.

The issues stressed in the preceding paragraphs provide the framework within which Tourism Policy needs to be considered. In brief, there is more to policy in tourism than is found in the Tourism Policy. Perhaps, the links within a macro-economic framework need no special mention.

MAJOR POLICY INITIATIVES

The first ever Tourism Policy was announced by the Government of India in November 1982. It took ten long years for the Government to feel the need to come up with a possible improvement over this. Thus the National Action Plan for Tourism was announced in May 1992. Between these two policy statements, various legislative and executive measures were brought about. In particular, the report of the National Committee on Tourism, submitted in 1988 needs special mention. In addition, two five-year plans-the Seventh and the Eighth-provided the basic perspective framework for operational initiatives.

The Seventh Plan advocated a two-pronged thrust in the area of development of tourism, *viz.,* to vigourously promote domestic tourism and to diversify overseas tourism in India. While laying stress on creation of beach resorts, conducting of conventions, conferences, winter sports and trekking, the overall intention was to diversify options available for foreign tourists. The Tourism Policy, 1982 was more an aggressive statement in marketing than a perspective plan for development. Its main thrust was aimed at presenting India to the foreigners as the ultimate holiday resort.

With a view to reach this destination, the following measures were suggested by the Policy:

- To take full advantage of the national heritage in arriving at a popular campaign for attracting tourists;
- To promote tourist resorts and make India a destination of holiday resorts;

- To grant the status of an export industry to tourism;
- To adopt a selective approach to develop few tourist circuits; and,
- To invite private sector participation into the sector.

The Planning Commission recognised tourism as an industry by June 1982. However, it took ten years to make most of the States to fall in line and accord the same status within their legislative framework. At the beginning of the Eighth Plan (1992-97), 15 States and 3 Union Territories had declared tourism as an industry. Four States had declared hotels as an industry. The National Committee on Tourism was set up in July 1986 by the Planning Commission to prepare a perspective plan for the sector. Within the broad framework of the Seventh Plan, the Committee had to evolve a perspective plan for the coming years.

The Committee, headed by Mr. Mohammed Yunus, submitted its recommendations in November 1987. The list of Members was as impressive Mr. S.K. Mishra (Secretary, Department of Tourism), Mrs. Kapila Vatsayan, Mr. K.L. Thapar, Mr. Rajan Jaitley, Mr. A.B. Kerker, Mr. R.K. Puri and Mr Pran Seth. The Committee in its Report recommended that the existing Department of Tourism be replaced by a National Tourism Board. It suggested that there be a separate cadre of Indian Tourism Service to look after the functioning of the Board. It also submitted proposals for partial privatisation of the two airlines owned by the Union Government.

By September, 1987, the Central Government declared more concessions for the sector: these included tax exemption on foreign exchange earnings from tourism (a 50per cent reduction on rupee earnings and a 100per cent reduction on earnings in dollars), a drastic reduction in tariff on import of capital goods, and concessional finance at the rate of 1 to 5per cent per annum. The Tourism Development Finance Corporation was set up in 1987 with a corpus fund of ₹100 crores. Until then, the sector was financed on commercial lines by the Industrial Development Bank of India, Industrial Credit and Investment Corporation of India and other commercial banks. The National Action Plan for Tourism, published in May 1992, and tabled in the Lok Sabha on 5 May 1992, charts 7 objectives as central concerns of the Ministry:

- Socio-economic development of areas;
- Increasing employment opportunities;
- Developing domestic tourism for the budget category;
- Preserving national heritage and environment;
- Development of international tourism;
- Diversification of the tourism product.,
- Increase in India's share in world tourism (from the present 0.4per cent to 1per cent during next 5 years)

As per the Action Plan, foreign exchange earnings are estimated to increase from ₹10,000 crores in 1992 to ₹24,000 crores by 2000 AD. Simultaneously, the Plan aims at increasing employment in tourism to 28 million from the present 14 million. Hotel accommodation is to be increased from 44,400 rooms to 1,20,000 by 3 years. Other provisions in the Action Plan include a discontinuance of subsidies to star hotels, encouraging foreign investment in tourism and the setting up of a convention city for developing convention tourism. The Action Plan envisages the development of Special Tourism Areas on lines of export processing zones. Special Central assistance is to be provided for the States to improve the infrastructural facilities at pilgrimage places. It proposes to set up a National Culinary Institute, and projects a liberalised framework for recognition of travel agents and tour operators.

The Eighth Plan document makes a special mention that the future expansion of tourism should be achieved mainly by private sector participation. The thrust areas as enumerated in the Plan include development of selected tourist places, diversification from cultural related tourism to holiday and leisure tourism, development of trekking, winter sports, wildlife and beach resort tourism, exploring new source markets, restoration of national heritage projects, launching of national image building, providing inexpensive accommodation in different tourist centres, improving service efficiency in public sector corporations and streamlining of facilitation procedures at airports.

The Eighth Plan aims at luring the high spending tourists from Europe and USA. It also envisages a 'master plan' to integrate area plans with development of tourism. This is envisaged to ensure employment opportunities for the local population. In April 1993, the Government announced further measures aimed at export promotion. The existing Export Promotion of Capital Goods Scheme (EPCG) was extended to tourism and related services. Against the existing 35per cent, the tourism sector would now pay an excise duty of 15per cent only on capital goods import, subject to an export obligation of 4 times the cargo, insurance and freight (CIF) value of imports. With an obligation period of five years, this came as a boon to the hotel industry. The cost of construction had also come down by 20per cent.

In addition to the above policy pronouncements by the Union Government, our planners had envisaged the possibilities of developing specific regions on a zonal plank. Special area programmes like the Hill Area Development Programme and the Western Ghats Development Programme form part of the overall national plan.

The Eighth Plan document stipulates that the strategy in such designated special areas is to devise suitable location-specific solutions, so as to reverse the process of degradation of natural resources and ensure sustainable development. This approach perhaps needs to be integrated into the project of special tourism areas, now being made popular by the Government. Administrative Control and Developmental Compromises The federal principles enshrined in the Indian Constitution require that the tourism sector be treated as a State subject. As such, the Department of Tourism (under the Ministry of Civil Aviation and Tourism at the Centre) undertakes certain promotional and developmental activities with a view to enhance the sectoral potential. The Department has certain regulatory functions to perform involving the hotel industry, travel agencies and tourist operators. Over the years, there has been considerable erosion of powers so far as State Governments are concerned. The sustained campaign for privatisation in all the policy documents has left limited space of operation for the States. The public sector is increasingly being perceived as an agent of inertia than of change and hence the pressure for a hands-off policy.

On the other hand, the Union Government has been usurping the powers of the State with some pretext or the other. Promotion schemes, designed at the Centre, are transferred for implementation at the State level. The special Central Assistance, for example, granted for the development of infrastructure at the pilgrim centres, carries with it a pre-defined scheme and mode of execution. Furthermore, there are occasions when the Centre forces the State Governments to extend certain subsidies and concessions to the sector. The terms of such concessions would have been fixed by the Centre and the States would have no choice but to fall in line. For example, during the State tourism minister's conference in December 1991, the States were urged to freeze water and electricity rates for 10 years.

They were also asked to exempt certain hotels from local and state taxes for 10 years. Seventeen circuits and destinations were identified under the National Action Plan for development through Central assistance and investment by the States and the private sector. The centres were identified by the Centre and the States were asked to do the needful. There were also times when the federal division of power resulted in operational contradictions. For instance, by 1989, many foreign hotel chains like Hilton, Hyatt, Penta and Kempinski had applied for licenses for investing in India.

However, the revenue departments of the respective States failed to locate and allocate land for the construction of hotels. The scheme, thus, fell flat. Curiously, the Union Government was not hesitant to make use of Constitutional provisions when it suited its interests. As has been stated earlier, the Yunus Committee had suggested the creation of the Tourism Board on lines of the existing Railway Board. (Perhaps, it was the brainchild of Mr. K.L. Thapar, then adviser to the Planning Commission, in charge of Transport and Tourism Sector.

Being from the Railway Service, it is not surprising that Thapar thought about a 'Tourism Board'). To begin with, the empowered committee of secretaries challenged the idea of creation of a Board. It was said that the Railway Board as an independent entity was created for historical reasons. It would be difficult for tourism to be looked after by a Board, because legally the sector would come under the Industrial (Development) Act. It was also found that such a Board would not be viable financially. In 1991, the think-tank on tourism created by Minister Madhavarao Scindia rejected the idea of a Board in toto.

It was emphasised that the Board cannot be in charge of a sector that is basically under the jurisdiction of the States! Scope for Federal Interventions The previous section highlights the dubious ways by which the Centre attempts to hijack initiatives at the State-level. This is achieved essentially by threatening to curtail Central assistance or by cajoling through promises of more financial aid. It is common knowledge that the resource-base of the States is very narrow, making them vulnerable at the negotiating table.

However, States have the freedom to resist the Centre's strong- arm tactics, provided State assemblies stand-by the interests of the States. For instance, State legislatures may refuse to freeze water and electricity rates on grounds of revenue generation. In that event, the concerned Chief Minister or the Minister of Tourism may convey the intensity of resistance that he is confronted with, and thus refuse to comply with the Centre's diktats. It is heartening to realise that the States have often exercised their power of self-determination and consequently refused to toe the line drawn by the Centre. This offers enough scope for possible interventions at the federal strata of our political system in matters of policy formulation.

Privatisation and its Implications According to the Approach Paper to the Seventh Plan, " there is a vast potential for development of tourism in the country. Tourism should be accorded the status of an industry. Private sector investment will have to be encouraged in developing tourism and public sector investments should be focused only on development of support infrastructure". Thus the seeds of private initiatives were sown during the Seventh Plan. The Government took the matter of privatising the tourism sector seriously by 1988.

It was during the tenure of Mr. S.K. Mishra as Tourism Secretary that the talk of inviting private investment into the sector began. The Government permitted foreign equity participation up to 5 1 per centin tourism projects. Foreign charters were allowed to operate in the country for the first time. Foreign companies were allowed to repatriate their profits to the extent of 3per cent. The structural adjustment programme, initiated in June, 1992, paved the way for privatisation in almost all sectors of the economy. The Annual Plan (1992-93) document emphatically enunciated the Government's position vis-a-vis tourism: "(T)he future growth of tourism will have to be achieved mainly through private initiative.

The State will contribute to tourism by planning broad strategy of development, provision of monetary and fiscal incentives to catalyse private sector investment." The process of privatisation brought in its wake big investments and private involvement at various levels. As an offshoot, environmental considerations were thrown to the winds and there were instances of large scale human rights violation. The self- correcting nature of policy made provisions for stricter controls in this regard. More seriously, privatisation meant alienation of the majority of our population and their deprivation. Employment generated in tourism is generally seasonal and ill paid. The private sector- induced pockets of tourism had the potential of turning into centres of pollution, drug trafficking and prostitution.

Industry Status Granted to Tourism The Seventh Plan proposed that tourism be declared an industry. However, it took time for the States to implement this, even though they agreed in principle. The smokeless industry had the advantage of generating maximum value-added, because of low-cost inputs. The Tourism Policy Statement carried certain provisions in favour of the hotel industry. It stated that there should be provision for depreciation in the balance sheets of hotels. Being an export industry, hotels were to be given excise concessions. The provisions of the Monopolies and Restrictive Trade Practices (MRTP) Act were relaxed for hotels, because any hotel with 300 or more rooms would have incurred an investment of ₹25 crores.

The document also hinted at lower tariffs for power and water and regulations for easy import of equipment. As a follow-up, hotel and shipping were added to the list of 27 industries exempted from Section 22 A of the MRTP Act. The consequences of declaring tourism as an industry need to be studied in detail. It is not possible to capture its implications in an exploratory work like this. However, it is obvious that the private sector has primarily benefited to a great extent by this measure. Importing Modifications to Policies We have earlier stated that the arena of policy formulation should be self-evaluating and self-correcting. In the case of Tourism Policy, this has proved to be the plus point. As an illustration, the Policy statement of 1982 made no mention of infrastructure development. The successive governments at the Centre failed to create proper tourism infrastructure, thus resulting in loss of traffic.

This lacuna was corrected in the National Action Plan. However, much of this change was due to intensive lobbying by such agencies like the Indian Association of Tour Operators (IATO), the Travel agents Association of India (TAAI) and the Indian Hotels and Restaurants Association (IHRA). It is for the voluntary agencies and pro-people forces to exploit the avenue of lobbying at various levels.

The environmental implications of tourism development did not form part of the 1982 Policy. The consequences are too obvious to be written about. However, the NAP, 1992 did carry specific provisions for environmental protection and harnessing. From Policy to Cartooning Policy statements may also lead to justifiable flights of fantasy. Two examples would illustrate how policies were used to justify stands taken by the politicians: a. Shri Devi Lal, the then Deputy Prime Minister wanted a 50per cent discount for farmers at

Five Star Hotels run by India Tourism Development Corporation. The scheme had teething problems since it was not easy to distinguish a farmer from amongst the clients who visit such hotels. However, on his insistence, the so-called CHAUPALs recreated a village ambience to the amazement of foreign tourists, who took a liking for them. b. Pursuing the objective of the Seventh Plan to diversify overseas tourism to its logical conclusion was what prompted A and. Jagdish Tytler to float the idea of casinos.

It was an attempt to provide some entertainment for foreigners during the evenings. It was said that Indian classical music would not provide much needed entertainment for foreign guests because the artistes spend a lot of time tuning their instruments! Folk dances get over in an hour. So much for our much touted cultural diversity. It is embarrassing to believe that the consultative committee attached to the Ministry of Civil Aviation and Tourism had endorsed the idea. Conclusion Broadly, our successive policy pronouncements in the realm of tourism falls within the "liberalising" framework of the macro- economic policy environment.

The Finance Bill, 1988, had assured 50per cent tax exemption on foreign exchange earnings in the sector, and a further 50per cent exemption if re-invested. In effect, it amounts to 100per cent tax concession. Luxury hotels enjoy exemptions of all kinds with a view to encourage tourism earnings. These tax exemptions coupled with provision of soft loans to the sector led to a boom in the tourism related private investment. The Economic Survey 1991-92 aptly summarises the ultimate aim of such incentives for private sector participation: " The Government has tried to expand the economic space in which the people can exercise their initiative and ingenuity. It hopes to do more to expand their opportunities, to enhance their potential.

But what shape the economy takes ultimately depends on what the people make of it. In that sense, the future is in their hands." We should not forget that tourism is an industry which emerges in the context of unresolved socio-economic structural issues, such as land distribution patterns or the take over of traditional occupations by modem mechanised capital. Tourism happens to be a source of livelihood for millions in India and aggressive privatisation does not ensure social and economic safety nets. In the face of the unhindered entry of international capital and successive alienation, perhaps, it is difficult to agree that "the future is in our hands"

INVESTMENT IN INDIAN TOURISM

India requires considerable investment into infrastructure which could only be met with foreign direct investment. The shortage of rooms in Delhi is adversely affecting the flow of tourists to the capital as well as to other destinations. The accommodation constraints in Delhi will have serious implications on the arrangements for the 2010 Commonwealth Games. It is estimated there will be a requirement of about 40,000-50,000 rooms in the budget category for the tourists visiting Delhi and surrounding areas during the Games.

The issue of giving tax benefit, under section 80 IA of Income Tax Act by declaring them as infrastructure projects for three and four star hotels, which are constructed prior to 2010, has been taken up with ministry of finance. Tourism industry is approximately a $200-billion industry and India doesn't even touch eight per cent of this. We are looking to get a larger chunk of it.

The government of India was considering offering tax incentives for attracting attract investment into building convention centres and halls. Pointing out the country was facing severe shortage of hotel accommodation in the wake of its preparation for 2010 Commonwealth games, The government has outlined plans to facilitate land procurement by hoteliers in order increase number of budget hotels, bed and breakfasts (BandBs) and self-service apartments.

Steps to Promote Tourism

Recently, Indian government adopted a multi-pronged approach for promotion of tourism, which includes new mechanism for speedy implementation of tourism projects, development of integrated tourism circuits and rural destinations, special capacity building in the unorganized hospitality sector and new marketing strategy. A nation wide campaign, for creating awareness about the effects of tourism and preservation of our rich heritage and culture, cleanliness and warm hospitality through a process of training and orientation was launched during 2004-05. The aim was to rebuild that sense of responsibility towards tourists among Indians and re-enforces the confidence of foreign tourist towards India as a preferred holiday destination. More than 6500 taxi drivers, restaurant owners and guides trained under the Programmes. Government also took several other initiatives to promote Indian tourism industry and increased the plan allocation for tourism *i.e.,* from ₹ 325 crore in 2003-04 to ₹ 500 crore in 2004-05. Road shows in key source markets of Europe, Incredible India campaign on prominent TV channels and in magazines across the world were among the few steps taken to advertise Indian tourism. In addition a task force was set up to promote India as prominent health tourism destination.

However, in order to attract more visitors, India still needs to upgrade its airports, roads and other infrastructure to global standards. Even with the recent surge, tourist arrivals are just a mere per centage of those in such popular Asian destinations like Bangkok and Thailand. It is boom time for India's Tourism and Hospitality sector. Driven by a surge in business traveller arrivals and a soaring interest in India as a tourist destination, the year 2005 has been the best year till date, with foreign visitor arrivals reaching a record 3.92 million, resulting in international tourism receipts of US$ 5.7 billion.

BOOM TIME INDIA

According to global hotel and hospitality consulting firm, HVS International, the strong performance in tourist arrivals in 2005 can be attributed to a strong sense of business and investment confidence in India inspired by:

- India's strong GDP performance
- Strengthening of ties with the developed world, and
- Opening of sectors of the economy to private sector/ foreign investment.
- The efforts made by the Ministry of Tourism and Culture in the last few years have had a salutary effect on India's tourism industry.
- Foreign tourist arrivals are expected to witness a growth of 78 per cent in 2006 over 2001 (last 5 years)
- Growth in foreign exchange earnings is expected to be of the order of 122 per cent during this period.
- As per estimates (Ministry of Tourism), on an average, about 3.1 million additional jobs per year have been created directly and indirectly in the tourism sector in the last four years.

India is fast emerging as one of the most enticing destinations for the global leisure traveller. The Readers Travel Awards 2006, conducted by Condé Nast Traveller has recently placed India at number four among the world's must-see countries, up from number nine in 2003. The Incredible India campaign has also been a huge success.

An Economic Growth Engine

As an engine for economic growth, the tourism and hospitality sector cuts across the rural-urban divide, and bridges economic boundaries. According to The World Travel and Tourism Council's 2006 Travel and Tourism Economic Research, the travel and tourism sector in India is expected to generate a total demand of US$ 53,544.5 million of economic activity in 2006, accounting for nearly 5.3 per cent of GDP and 5.4 per cent of total employment.

According to the report, the sector is expected to grow at a rate of 8.4 per cent in 2006 and by 8 per cent per annum, in real terms, between 2007 and 2016.

GDP

Employment

Visitor Exports

Personal TandT

Capital Investment

Government Expenditure

Outlook for 2006 (Real Growth)

7.8 per cent

1.4 per cent
10.9 per cent
6.9 per cent
8.3 per cent
7.7 per cent
(Outlook for the next 10 years 2007-2016)
6.6 per cent
1.0 per cent
7.8 per cent
6.7 per cent
7.8 per cent
6.1 per cent

A Room-Full of Opportunity

As travellers surge into India, the demand for rooms, across segments, has skyrocketed. Hotels in the luxury and business traveller segment are recording nearly 100 per cent occupancy, spiralling tariffs, and a strain on capacity and manpower. Anticipating this demand, around 10,856 hotel rooms in Delhi, 9,318 rooms in Mumbai, 7,794 rooms in Bangalore and 7,408 rooms in Hyderabad are expected to be added by 2011, according to estimates by HVS International.

A Policy Thrust

The objective of the existing Tourism Policy of the Government of India is to position tourism as a major engine of economic growth and to harness its direct and multiplier effects for employment and poverty eradication in an environmentally sustainable manner.

The present government's major policy initiatives include:

- Liberalization in aviation sector
- Pricing policy for aviation turbine fuel which influences internal air fares
- Rationalization in tax rates in the hospitality sector
- Tourist friendly visa regime
- Immigration services
- Procedural changes in making available land for construction of hotels
- Allowing setting up of Guest Houses

The Indian Ministry of Tourism has identified 31 villages across the country to be developed as tourism hubs. The states in which these villages have been identified include Himachal Pradesh, Gujarat, Maharashtra, Bihar, Karnataka, Madhya Pradesh, Andhra Pradesh, Kerala, Tamil Nadu, Orissa, Assam, Sikkim, Rajasthan and West Bengal.

Open Skies, Open Arms

The government's Open Skies policy, permission for domestic airlines to commence international flights, start-up of various low-cost carriers, and fleet expansion by domestic players has created a huge incentive for domestic travellers to explore far-off destinations within and outside India. The booming aviation business is bringing an ever-increasing number of passengers to India, and pulling Indians out of their homes and into hotels.

The numbers, according to the Ministry of Tourism, speak for themselves:

- The number of domestic and international passengers has increased fifteen-fold to 73.34 million in 2005/06 since 1970.
- Domestic air passenger traffic grew by 16.8 per cent in 2005/06 compared to 2004/05.
- International passenger traffic observed a growth of 16.9 per cent in the same period.
- Private airlines accounted for 77.0 per cent of the total domestic traffic.

HEALTH TOURISM

India is gradually gathering popularity as a health tourist destination. A study by McKinsey and Confederation of Indian Industry (CII) says that at its current pace of growth, health care tourism alone can rake over US$ 1.7 billion additional revenues by 2012. Medical tourism is now a US$ 299 million industry, as about 100,000 patients come each year. The country needs to exploit the cost advantage it can offer to a health tourist, the study said.

The biggest driver for health care tourism is the disparity in costs:

- A heart surgery in the US costs US$ 30,000 as compared to US$ 6,000 in India.
- A bone marrow transplant in the US costs US$ 250,000 and US$ 26,000 in India.

"With yoga, meditation, ayurveda, allopathy, and other systems of medicine, India offers a unique basket of services to an individual that is difficult to match by other countries," the CII study said. Clinical outcomes in India are at par with the world's best centres since India has internationally qualified and experienced specialists.

ECO-TOURISM POLICY

The Draft Tourism Policy 1997 states that "in the context of economic liberalisation and globalisation being pursued by the country, the development policies of no sector can remain static. "The policy further states that" the emergence of tourism as an important instrument for sustainable human development including poverty alleviation, employment generation, environmental regeneration and advancement of women and other disadvantaged groups in the country" requires support to realise these goals. India's tourism resources have always been considered immense, in a tourism audit. The geographical features are diverse, colourful and varied. The coastline offers opportunities for developing the best beaches in the world. There are a wealth of eco-systems including bio-sphere reserves, mangroves, coral re-efs, deserts, mountains and forests as well as an equally wide range of flora and fauna.

The Policy further states that "international tourists visiting interiors of the country for reasons of purity of the environment and nature contributes to the development of these areas particularly backward regions". Thus Tourism "should also become a reason for better preservation and protection of our natural resources, environment and ecology".

The policy recognises that sustained growth of tourism can give rise to conflicts.

To ensure that the growth of tourism takes place along desired lines, certain guidelines have been framed:

1. To remove the constraint of the information gap.
2. To create a tourist product that is desirable and supported by an integrated infrastructure.
3. To involve all agencies, public, private and government, in tourism development.
4. To create synergy between departments and agencies that have to deliver the composite tourist product.
5. To use both the circuit and scheme approach so that peoples participation through panchayats, local bodies, NGO's, and youth organisations will create a greater awareness of tourism. The Central Government can thus concentrate on larger investment oriented projects.
6. To create direct access for destinations off the beaten track.
7. To diversify the product with new options like beach tourism, forests, wild life, landscapes and adventure tourism, farm and health tourism.
8. To ensure that the development does not exceed sustainable levels.
9. To develop the seven north-eastern states, the Himalayan region and Islands for tourism.
10. To maintain a balance between the negative and positive impacts of tourism through planning restrictions and through education of the people for conservation and development.

Development Plan

The strategy for development should take into consideration the carrying capacity, local aspirations and benefits likely to accrue to the community. In particular specific policies and guidelines for eco-tourism development and adventure tourism are to be formulated, primarily through a regulatory framework. The Draft Guidelines have been approved at a State Ministers Conference and have been circulated to various trade and industry bodies. The guidelines draw a distinction between mass or resort tourism and nature or Eco-tourism, as the kind of tourism that has a lower impact on the environment and requires less infrastructural development. The Ministry hopes that the environment conscious international tourist will be made aware that India is taking steps to protect its ecology and environment.

Apart from the do's and don'ts, the guidelines are governed by a tourism management plan, the key elements of which are the protection of natural resources and a positive involvement of local communities, along with an optimum number of environmentally conscious visitors. The principles of management are scientific planning, effective control and continuous monitoring, development of physical infrastructure, zoning and a Management plan for public use of natural sites.

The management plan should establish standards for resort development, style and location of structures, waste disposal, treatment of sewage, control of litter, use of public spaces and fragile areas. The operational guidelines rely on sensitisation of all the role players and this Programmes is based on a self-regulated environmental code.

Area specific rather than universal development plans keeping in mind the unique character of the location and its economic and social environment are important. This would help the State Government to coordinate with the industry in managing visitors and their activities. NGO's working on socio-economic Programmes in forest and remote areas could have a closer coordination with tourism service operators to transfer economic benefits, particularly the handicraft production and marketing sector. The guidelines are only a beginning, and it is hoped that with increasing awareness of the visitor the industry will regulate its practices.

Tourism Advisory Committee

There is an emphasis on the needs and perceptions of the international tourist running through the discussion on the guide lines although the data from the National Parks makes it evident that the domestic tourists outnumber international visitors, although they do not pay the same amount as the foreign visitor either in entry fees or for board and lodging and transport facilities. They do however demand a much higher per capita use of resources like water, fuel for heating and cooking and transport. They also make the same intensive use of time and try to maximize their stay by the number of animals and birds they can view in the 24-hour period.

It is interesting to note that no democratic participation has been called for in the policy formulation process, and all the amendments to the policy have come from trade associations and government think tanks. The tourism Advisory Committee also consists of eminent persons and community representation has been ignored.

The policy clearly recognises the debate on the tourism issue which has surfaced wherever tourism development, particularly in the case of tourism projects relating to the "gifts of nature" like beaches, rivers, mountains and forests, have already been developed. However, mere recognition of the hostility of people to tourism development is not enough to change the nature of tourism development or the resistance to tourism or what many have termed a poor tourism culture. Perhaps to understand this in a better perspective, we should look at the issue of sustainable development in a critical way. Perhaps we can question the impact of sustainable development on the environment and sift through the jargon of development planners, international agencies, and environmental activists to see how sustainable development can be achieved without all the contradictions that are apparent as in the case of the tourism sector.

DEVELOPMENT IN TOURISM

The concept of sustainability originated in the context of renewable resources like forests and fisheries and was subsequently adopted by the environmental movement. In most cases it is understood to mean "the existence of the ecological conditions necessary to support human life at a specific level of well being through future generations." However, in addition to ecological conditions there are social conditions that influence ecological sustainability in a nature-people interaction.

The social connotations have been described by Barbier (1987) who has defined social sustainability as "the ability to maintain desired social values, traditions, institutions, cultures or other social characteristics." The term sustainability came into usage in 1980 when the IUCN presented the World Conservation Strategy where sustainable development was linked to conservation of living resources. However, the fundamental goals have often been lost sight of because of operational goals (*e.g.,* food, water, shelter, health are fundamental goals to be realised through self reliance, cost effectiveness, appropriate technology, people centred-ness etc.)

Consequently, the WCED made its definition brief: Social Development is development that meets the needs of the present without compromising the ability of future generations to meet their own needs. They did not make any assumptions on the direction in which changes in demand would take place. (*e.g.,* equity, social justice, self-determination, or cultural diversity).

India's tourism policy follows the mainstream SD (Sustainable Development) thinking by adopting all the critical objectives: revive growth change the quality of growth meet essential needs for jobs, food, energy, water and sanitation ensure sustainable levels of population conserve and enhance the resource base reorient technology and management risk merge environment and economics in decision making reorient international economic relations make development more participatory.

These objectives are responsible for building a very broad consensus on the issue of sustainable development, yet the debate at the operational level continues. Most participants in the debate now accept that many human activities are reducing the long-term ability of the natural environment to provide goods and services, which will eventually affect human health and well being.

Enviromental Degradation

Many also accept that poverty is devastating the lives of millions in the Third World since there is no consensus between what is environmentally necessary and what is economically and developmentally feasible. The level of inter-dependence between the two insights is yet to be incorporated in the concept of Social Development. Some problem areas are: Environmental degradation, already affecting millions in the Third World, is likely to reduce human well being across the globe.

Who is responsible for this rapid degeneration? Is it the poor or the rich? The poor have no option but to exploit resources for short-term survival.

If we take the example of forests and their resources, which have been traditionally outside the market system and in the sphere of tribal or indigenous peoples rights, they are today seen as exploiters of the forests as against tourists, with all their demand for infrastructure and superstructure, who are seen to be conservationists. The inter-linked nature of the problem of sustainability is such that the impact of degradation will be quicker on the poor than on the rich.

Can Sustainable Development be the metafix it claims to be in reconciling increasing industrial, agricultural and resource use productivity with environmental needs. The weakness of the Social Development argument lies in the techno-economic approach to solutions with regard to common property resource management, through know how transfers, resource pricing, subsidy policies and building management capabilities. (World Bank, 1987) Deeper processes such as land reforms, industrial demands on raw materials, over consumption, changing legal and political structures are either ignored or looked at in a cursory manner.

For instance how can we claim a consensus between those who are concerned for the survival of future generations with those who are concerned with the survival of wild life, or human health and subsistence? Unless we can identify the trade-offs necessary for each specific objective of sustainability, we will not have clarity in the discussion.

We will also fail to understand why, even when there is a broad consensus, projects on the ground result in conflicts. Suggested refinements could be:

1. A distinction between ecological and social sustainability and in the process an identification of the inter-linkages a distinction between renewable and non-renewable resources, between environmental processes crucial to human life and crucial to other forms of life dependent on the resources. a distinction between the techno-economic aspects of social sustainability (infrastructure, services, government) with political and cultural sustainability.
2. A distinction between equitable development and local participation, and decentralisation, what many have called NGOisation of sustainable development. This is because no rigorous testing of local participation leading to social equity or to sustainable resource use have been reported.

ENVIRONMENTAL IMPACT

Case studies reflect personal, organisational or political preferences. Tourism is one of the activities which have caused concern because of the effects of increasing human traffic on fragile environments. Countries which are looking towards Tourism as a means of economic growth, like India, have limited resources and cultural restraints and they have the greatest need to pay heed to the possible negative impacts of tourism. The environmental impact of tourism is a basic issue, whether we are looking at a developed or an underdeveloped area, region or country.

The costs of tourism for a country like India include extensive investment in fixed assets with a low rate of return for infrastructure, transportation, accommodation, cultural institutions, exhibition centres, and park facilities.

To this maybe added the social and cultural costs like additional demands on infrastructure like land, water, health services; the creation of new jobs for displaced people; the cost of positive community relationships; the disparity between the lifestyle of visitors and those who serve them; the possible friction between local residents and new users of valued local resources; the perception of local residents of the spending of scarce capital resources on what they consider low priority areas like tourism; cultural cost of alterations in local ceremonial or traditional values; loss of privacy for local communities as tourists come to gape at their living conditions and rituals.

Tourism also causes increasing congestion and pollution as thousands of visitors flock to parks and sanctuaries in motorised vehicles; there are changes in accessibility, landscape and the ecological balance between man and nature; there is the cost, both monetary and human, of creating conservation zones (core/buffer) with unforeseen or undesirable side effects; which have been observed in the Eco-tourism movement.

The benefit of revenue from tourism does not always redress these problems but goes towards the cost of administering the project. The tourism industry is generally self-centred and not given to educational, cultural or exchange Programmes on a philanthropic basis. The natural environment, with the best will in the world, cannot escape damage with the volume of visitors. As more and more tourists, both domestic and international seek the exotic and remote destinations around the world, the likelihood of the environment suffering as a result become greater.

Forests can suffer from trampling, fires, tree felling for facilities and waste. Wildlife, despite the protection in national parks, has suffered a loss of habitat, hunting and poaching, viewing and photographing, leading to an interruption of feeding and breeding patterns or hunting for food undisturbed. These are the prized moments for the viewer. The trade in wild life trophies or tourist souvenirs is the more deliberately destructive aspect of such tourism.

Sanctuaries

The building of tourist lodges in materials that are not integrated with the environment and the pressure they put on the land and water bodies is also wilfully destructive. Management techniques that include being less user friendly or control of numbers by closing access or by multiplying the number of attractions and areas or charging higher admission fees are generally not popular with the tourist or the tour operator and are also difficult to implement because of high administrative costs.

Equations, through its involvement in the field have had a variety of experiences relating to the debate on Eco-tourism and sustainable development. The major issues that have emerged after the policy of notification of wild life sanctuaries and their management by the Forest Departments are quite disturbing. Wherever notification has led to displacement of people the experience of rehabilitation has not been successful and the conservation aims have not been met. Several sanctuaries have witnessed militant action by displaced communities against the developers of tourism. In many cases the tourism aims have also not been met in making the sanctuary accessible to viewers, naturalists, wild life photographers. Tourism has not been able to counteract poaching and the most extensive and the oldest conservation project, Project Tiger has not been able to save the tiger population.

The commercialisation of the experience, like the privileging of one species, for example the tiger, has led to congestion and noise pollution and this has put a pressure on the management of the sanctuary to organise tiger shows which are putting a pressure on the feeding and mating habits of the tiger. These are very invasive techniques of experiencing the wild. On the plus side, the concept of beneficiary led development has helped indigenous people to organise against their displacement and exploitation as well as to fight for the retention of their traditional rights and life styles. Environmentalists have not only been involved in such organisations and movements but have done valuable documentation. This has influenced many urban visitors to be more sensitive to the wild and to follow the rules when participating in eco-tourism. This has also led to the development of a code of conduct for the tourist, the industry and the administrator. These attempts are in a very nascent stage. The kind of co-ordination that is required between the environmentalist and economist is just beginning to emerge and have still to counter the myths of neo-classical economists in the field of tourism. But a beginning has been made.

COASTAL ISSUES

The Coastal Regulation Zone (CRZ) came into existence on February 19, 1991, with the gazetting of the notification by the Union Ministry of Environment and Forests (MoEF) under Sec. 3(1) and Sec. 3(2)(v) of the Environment Protection Act, 1986, and Rule 5(3)(d) of the Environment Protection Rules, 1986.

Through the Notification the Central Government declared the coastal stretches of seas, bays, estuaries, creeks, rivers and backwaters, which are influenced by tidal action (in the land ward side), up to 500m. from the high tide line (HTL) and the land between the low tide line (LTL) and HTL as CRZ. In the case of rivers, creeks and backwaters, the Notification stated that the CRZ could be modified on a case by case basis, on the basis of reasons to be recorded during the preparation of the coastal zone management plan (CZMP). However, the width of the CRZ from each bank could not be less than 100 m., or the width of the water body, whichever was less.

Activities Prohibited in the CRZ:

1. Setting up of new industries and expansion of existing ones, except those directly related to waterfront or requiring foreshore facilities.
2. Manufacture, handling, storage or disposal of hazardous substances.
3. Setting up and expansion of fish processing units including warehousing (excluding hatchery and natural fish drying in permitted areas).
4. · Discharge of untreated wastes and effluents from industries, cities, towns or other human settlements. The existing practices would have to be phased out by the concerned authorities within three years.
5. Dumping of ash or any waste from thermal power plants.
6. Land reclamation, bunding or disturbing the natural course of sea water with similar obstructions. Exceptions are made for activities required for the control of coastal erosion, the maintenance of water ways to ports; clearing sand bars; and for the construction of regulators, storm water drains and structures for the prevention of salinity ingress.

7. Mining of sand, rocks and other substrata materials, except those raw minerals not available outside the CRZ areas.
8. Drawing or harvesting of groundwater and construction of mechanism within 200 m. of the HTL. Between 200 and 500 m. it will be permissible only if done manually through ordinary wells for drinking, horticulture, agriculture and fisheries.
9. Construction activity in ecologically sensitive areas.
10. Any construction activity between LTL and HTL except facilities for carrying treated effluents and waste water discharge into the sea, facilities for carrying sea water for cooling purposes, oil, gas and similar pipelines and facilities essential for facilities permitted under the notification.
11. Dressing or altering of sand dunes, hill, natural features including landscape changes for beautification, recreation and other such purposes, except as permitted under the notification.

Regulated activities (requiring environmental clearance from MoEF):

1. Construction activities related to Defence requirements for which foreshore facilities are essential. Residential office, hospital, workshops will not normally be permitted in the CRZ, except in very special cases.
2. Operational construction for ports and harbours and light house.
3. Foreshore facilities of thermal power plants for transport of raw materials, in-take of cooling water and out fall for discharge of treated wastewater or cooling water.
4. All other activities with investment exceeding. 5 crores.

Coastal Zone Management Plan (CZMP)

All the coastal states have to prepare, within one year, CZMPs identifying and classifying CRZ areas as per the Notification guidelines. These plans have to be approved by MoEF All further development activities should be within the framework of these plans.

In the interim period, before the approval of the plans, development activities should not violate the provisions of the Notification.

Violations are punishable under the provisions of the Environment Protection Act of 1986. For regulating developmental activities, the coastal stretches within 500m of the HTL are classified into CRZ-1, CRZ-11 and CRZ-III.

CRZ-I — Areas that are ecologically sensitive and important (national parks, coral re-efs, mangroves, areas close to the breeding and spawning grounds of fishes, areas of high natural beauty, historical heritage, high genetic diversity, and those likely to be inundated by global warming, 'etc.); and areas within the LTL and HTL.

Regulations in CRZ-I

1. No new construction shall be permitted within 500 m of the HTL.
2. No construction activity except for facility for carrying treated effluents and waste water into the sea or carrying sea water for cooling, oil, gas or similar pipelines will be permitted between the LTL and the HTL.

CRZ-II

Areas that have already been developed up to or close to the shoreline. 'Developed areas' that come within municipal limits or other legally designated urban areas which have been substantially built up and which have been provided with infrastructural facilities like drainage, approach road, water supply and sewage mains.

Regulations in CRZ-III

1. Buildings will not be permitted in the seaward side of existing roads (or those proposed in the CZMP) nor on the seaward side of the existing authorised structures.
2. Reconstruction of authorised buildings to be permitted subject to the existing floor space and without change in existing use CRZ III Areas that are relatively undisturbed and do not belong to either CRZ-I or CRZ-II. This will include coastal zones in the rural areas and also areas within municipal limits or urban areas that are not substantially built up.
3. Areas up to 200 m. from the HTL earmarked as no development zone (NDZ). No construction will be permitted within this zone except for repairs of existing authorised structures not exceeding the existing plinth area and covered apace. Raising of horticultural crops, gardens, pastures, parks, play fields, forestry and salt manufacture from sea water permitted in this zone.
4. Development of vacant plots between 200 m. 500 m. from the HTL, in designated areas with prior approval of MoEF, permitted for hotels and beach resorts.
5. Construction or reconstruction of dwellind units between the 200m and 500m of the HTL permitted so long as it is within the ambit of traditional rights and customary uses such as existing fishing villages and gouthans.

   Building conditions would be based on the conditions that the total number of dwelling units does not increase more than double of the existing units; the total covered area is not more than 33 per cent of the plot area; the overall height is not more than two floors and 9 m. Guidelines for development of beach resorts in the designated areas of CRZ-III · No construction within 200 m. from the HTL and in the area between LTL and HTL.

6. The total plot size should not be less than 0.4 hectare and the covered area should not be more than 33 per cent. · The total height of the construction should not be more than 9 m. and the building should not be more than two floors.
   Groundwater cannot be tapped within 200m of the HTL. Between 200 and 500 m. it can be tapped with the concurrence of the State or Central Groundwater Board.
7. Extraction of sand, leveling or digging of sandy stretches, except for the structural foundation will not be permitted within 500 M. of the HTL.
8. The quality of treated effluents, solid wastes, emissions and noise levels etc. must be within the standards laid down by the central or state pollution control boards. Untreated effluents and solid wastes should not be discharged into the water or beach.
9. To allow public access there should be a gap of 20m. width between two hotels. Two consecutive gaps should not be more than 500 m. apart.

THE WORLD SCENARIO OF TOURISM

In recent years tourism has emerged as a major economic activity that is employment oriented and earns foreign exchange. Its share in the worlds GDP in 1994-95 was 10 per cent which is more than the world military budgets put together. In global terms, the investment in tourism industry and travel trade accounts for 7 per cent of the total capital investment. Today 21.2 crore people around the globe are employed in travel trade and tourism. In future, this industry is likely to see unprecedented growth. According to the World Tourism Council at Brussels, the revenues from travel and tourism in Asia Pacific region will grow at the rate of 7.8 per cent annually over the next decade. Amongst the economic sectors, the tourism sector is highly labour intensive. A survey by the Government of India notes that the rate of employment generation (direct and indirect) in tourism is 52 persons employed per ₹.10 lakh investment (based on 1992-93 Consumer Price Index). This is much higher than the rates of employment generation in most other economic sectors.

Indian tourism industry has also recorded phenomenal growth. The rate of international arrivals in India in recent years has been to the tune of about 19 lakh arrivals per year. The unprecedented growth in tourism in India has made it the third largest foreign exchange earner after gem and jewellery and ready-made garments. This is not surprising since India possesses a whole range of attractive normally sought by tourists and which includes natural attractions like landscapes, scenic beauty, mountains, wildlife, beaches, major rivers and manmade attractions such as monuments, forts, palaces and havelis. However, in global terms, in spite of such attractions, tourist arrivals in India are a mere 0.30 per cent of the world arrivals. Receipts are similarly low, just a 0.50 per cent of the world receipts. We are still quite far from the target of 50 lakh tourist arrivals per year. Travel and Tourism is the world's largest industry and creator of jobs across national and regional economies. WTTC/WEFA research show that in 2000, Travel and Tourism will generate, directly and indirectly, 11.7 per cent of GDP and nearly 200 million jobs in the world-wide economy. Jobs generated by Travel and Tourism are spread across the economy - in retail, construction, manufacturing and telecommunications, as well as directly in Travel and Tourism companies. These jobs employ a large proportion of women, minorities and young people; are predominantly in small and medium sized companies; and offer good training and transferability. Tourism can also be one of the most effective drivers for the development of regional economies. These patterns apply to both developed and emerging economies.

Contributing to Sustainable Development

The 1992 United Nations Conference on Environment and Development (UNCED), the Rio Earth Summit, identified Travel and Tourism as one of the key sectors of the economy which could make a positive contribution to achieving sustainable development. The Earth Summit lead to the adoption of Agenda 21, a comprehensive Programmes of action adopted by 182 governments to provide a global blueprint for achieving sustainable development. Travel and Tourism is the first industry sector to have launched an industry-specific action plan based on Agenda 21.

Travel and Tourism is able to contribute to development which is economically, ecologically and socially sustainable, because it:

1. Has less impact on natural resources and the environment than most other industries;
2. Is based on enjoyment and appreciation of local culture, built heritage, and natural environment, as such that the industry has a direct and powerful motivation to protect these assets;
3. Can play a positive part in increasing consumer commitment to sustainable development principles through its unparalleled consumer distribution channels; and
4. Provides an economic incentive to conserve natural environments and habitats which might otherwise be allocated to more environmentally damaging land uses, thereby, helping to maintain bio-diversity.

There are numerous good examples of where Travel and Tourism is acting as a catalyst for conservation and improvement of the environment and maintenance of local diversity and culture. (Some of these are set out in Section B of this chapter and a fuller illustration of the range of industry action can be found on the World Travel and Tourism Council's Of course, there are also examples where development has not been sustainable.

Providing Infrastructure

To a greater degree than most activities, Travel and Tourism depends on a wide range of infrastructure services - airports, air navigation, roads, railheads and ports, as well as basic infrastructure services required by hotels, restaurants, shops, and recreation facilities (*e.g.,* telecommunications and utilities). It is the combination of tourism and good infrastructure that underpins the economic, environmental and social benefits. It is important to balance any decision to develop an area for tourism against the need to preserve fragile or threatened environments and cultures. However, once a decision has been taken where an area is appropriate for new tourism development, or that an existing tourist site should be developed further, then good infrastructure will be essential to sustain the quality, economic viability and growth of Travel and Tourism. Good infrastructure will also be a key factor in the industry's ability to manage visitor flows in ways that do not affect the natural or built heritage, nor counteract against local interests.

Challenge for the Future

Travel and Tourism creates jobs and wealth and has tremendous potential to contribute to economically, environmentally and socially sustainable development in both developed countries and emerging nations. It has a comparative advantage in that its start up and running costs can be low compared to many other forms of industry development. It is also often one of the few realistic options for development in many areas. Therefore, there is a strong likelihood that the Travel and Tourism industry will continue to grow globally over the short to medium term. Of course, if Travel and Tourism is managed badly, it can have a detrimental effect - it can damage fragile environments and destroy local cultures. The challenge is to manage the future growth of the industry so as to minimise its negative impacts on the environment and host communities whilst maximising the benefits it brings in terms of jobs, wealth and support for local culture and industry, and protection of the built and natural environment.

Objectives

The main objective of the States Tourism Policy will be to undertake intensive development of tourism in the State and thereby increase employment opportunities.

The following related objectives are dovetailed with main objectives:

1. Identify and develop tourist destinations and related activities.
2. Diversifications of tourism products in order to attract more tourists through a varied consumer choice.
3. Comprehensive development of pilgrimage centres as tourist destinations.

4. Create adequate facilities for budget tourists.
5. Strengthen the existing infrastructure and develop new ones where necessary.
6. Creation of tourism infrastructure so as to preserve handicrafts, folk arts and culture of the state and thereby attract more tourists.

Approach and Strategy

In addition to the facilitation role assigned to itself by the Government in the development of tourism, the Government will adopt the following strategy towards the private sector with the objective of securing its active involvement in leading the development of tourism in the State.

1. The tourism will be given the status of industry in order that the facilities and benefits available to the industry are also made available to tourism projects.
2. A special incentives package will be made available for encouraging new tourism projects as well as expansion of existing tourism units.
3. Infrastructural facilities will be strengthened and developed within the State, particularly in Special Tourism Areas which will be notified latter and which will be developed by adopting an integrated-area.
4. Effective mechanisms will be set up to build meaningful co-ordination with the Central Government and the State Governments agencies, the local self-government bodies and the NGOs.
5. Government will encourage building effective linkages with the relevant economic agents and agencies such as the national and international tour operators and travel agents of repute, hotel chains and global institutions connected with tourism such as WTO.

So far, the lending from the State Financial Institutions has been largely confined to hotels only. In reality, the range of activities for tourism projects is far larger than just hotels as can be seen from the following illustrative list

Ten Commandments

1. Respect the frailty of the earth. Realize that unless all are willing to help in its preservation, unique and beautiful destinations may not be here for future generations to enjoy.
2. Leave only footprints. Take only photographs. No graffiti! No litter! Do not take away souvenirs from historical sites and natural areas.
3. To make your travels more meaningful, educate yourself about the geography, customs, manners and cultures of the region you visit. Take time to listen to the people. Encourage local conservation efforts.
4. Respect the privacy and dignity of others. Enquire before photographing people.
5. Do not buy products made from endangered plants or animals, such

as ivory, tortoise shell, animal skins, and feathers. Read Know Before You Go, the U. S. Customs list of products which cannot be imported.

6. Always follow designated trails. Do not disturb animals, plants or their natural habitats.
7. Learn about and support conservation-oriented Programmes and organizations working to preserve the environment.
8. Whenever possible, walk or use environmentally-sound methods of transportation. Encourage drivers of public vehicles to stop engines when parked.
9. Patronize those (hotels, airlines, resorts, cruise lines, tour operators and suppliers) who advance energy and environmental conservation; water and air quality; recycling; safe management of waste and toxic materials; noise abatement, community involvement; and which provide experienced, well-trained staff dedicated to strong principles of conservation.
10. Encourage organizations to subscribe to environmental guidelines. ASTA urges organizations to adopt their own environmental codes to cover special sties and ecosystems.

GROWTH OF TOURISM SECTOR IN INDIA

Tourism is the largest service industry in India, with a contribution of 6.23 per cent to the national GDP and 8.78 per cent of the total employment in India. India witnesses more than 5 million annual foreign tourist arrivals and 562 million domestic tourism visits. The tourism industry in India generated about US$100 billion in 2008 and that is expected to increase to US$275.5 billion by 2018 at a 9.4 per cent annual growth rate.

The Ministry of Tourism is the nodal agency for the development and promotion of tourism in India and maintains the "Incredible India" campaign. World Travel and Tourism Council, India will be a tourism hotspot from 2009-2018, having the highest 10-year growth potential. The Travel and Tourism Competitiveness Report 2007 ranked tourism in India 6th in terms of price competitiveness and 39th in terms of safety and security. Despite short- and medium-term setbacks, such as shortage of hotel rooms, tourism revenues are expected to surge by 42 per cent from 2007 to 2017. India has a growing medical tourism sector. The 2010 Commonwealth Games in Delhi are expected to significantly boost tourism in India.

ANDHRA PRADESH

Andhra Pradesh has a rich cultural heritage and a variety of tourist attractions. The state of Andhra Pradesh comprises scenic hills, forests, beaches and temples. Also known as The City of Nizams and The City of Pearls, Hyderabad is today one of the most developed cities in the country and a modern hub of information technology, ITES, and biotechnology. Hyderabad is known for its rich history, culture and architecture representing its unique character as a meeting point for North and South India, and also its multilingual culture. Andhra Pradesh is the home of many religious pilgrim centres. Tirupati, the abode of Lord Venkateswara, is the richest and most visited religious centre in the world. Srisailam, the abode of Sri Mallikarjuna, is one of twelve Jyothirlingalu in India, Amaravati's Siva temple is one of the Pancharamams, and Yadagirigutta, the abode of an avatara of Vishnu, Sri Lakshmi Narasimha. The Ramappa temple and Thousand Pillars temple in Warangal are famous for some fine temple carvings. The state has numerous Buddhist centres at Amaravati, Nagarjuna Konda, Bhattiprolu, Ghantasala, Nelakondapalli, Dhulikatta, Bavikonda, Thotlakonda, Shalihundam, Pavuralakonda, Sankaram, Phanigiri and Kolanpaka.

The golden beaches at Visakhapatnam, the one-million-year old limestone caves at Borra, picturesque Araku Valley, hill resorts of Horsley Hills, river Godavari racing through a narrow gorge at Papi Kondalu, waterfalls at Ettipotala, Kuntala and rich bio-diversity at Talakona, are some of the natural attractions of the state. Visakhapatnam is home to many tourist attactions such as the INS Karasura Submarine museum, Yarada Beach, Araku Valley, VUDA Park, Indira Gandhi Zoological Gardens. The weather in Andhra Pradesh is mostly tropical and the best time to visit is in November through to January. The monsoon season commences in June and ends in September, so travel would not be advisable during this period. Also worth visiting, the only Indian Buddhism Based Theme Park and Resorts on the Vijayawada-Guntur Highway-Agrigold Haailand.

ARUNACHAL PRADESH

Arunachal Pradesh attracts tourists from many parts of the world. Tourist attractions include Tawang, a beautiful town famous for its Buddhist monastery, Ziro, famous for cultural festivals, the Namdapha tiger project in Changlang district and Sela lake near Bomdila with its bamboo bridges overhanging the river. Religious places of interest include Malinithan in Lekhabali, Rukhmininagar near Roing and Parshuram Kund in Lohit district. Rafting and trekking are common activities. A visitor's permit from the tourism department is required. Places like Tuting have wonderful, undiscovered scenic beauty.

ASSAM

Assam is the central state in the North-East Region of India and serves as the gateway to the rest of the Seven Sister States. Assam boasts of famous wildlife preserves - the Kaziranga National Park, which is home to the Great Indian One-Horned Rhinoceros and the Manas National Park, the largest river island Majuli, historic Sivasagar, famous for the ancient monuments of Ahom Kingdom, the city of eternal romance, Tezpur and tea-estates dating back to time of British Raj. The weather is mostly sub-tropical. Assam experiences the Indian monsoon and has one of the highest forest densities in India. The winter months are the best time to visit. Assam has a rich cultural heritage going back to the Ahom Kingdom, which governed the region for many centuries before the British occupation. Other notable features include the Brahmaputra River, the mystery of the bird suicides in Jatinga, numerous temples including Kamakhya of Tantric sect.

'Gurdwara Sri Guru Tegh Bahadur also known as Damdama Sahib at Dhubri '. This famous Gurudwara is situated in the heart of the Dhubri Town on the bank of the mighty Brahmaputra river in far north-east India. Guru Nanak the first Sikh Guru visited this place in 1505 and met Srimanta Sankardeva as the Guru travelled from Dhaka to Assam, ruins of palaces, etc. Guwahati, the capital city of Assam, boasts many bazaars, temples, and wildlife sanctuaries.

BIHAR

Bihar is one of the oldest continuously inhabited places in the world with history of 3000 years. The rich culture and heritage of Bihar is evident from the innumerable ancient monuments that are dotted all over this state in eastern India. This is the Place of Aryabhata, Great Ashoka, Chanakya and many more. Bihar is one of the most sacred places of various religions such as Hinduism, Buddhism, Jainism, Sikhism and Islam. Famous Attraction includes Mahabodhi Temple, a Buddhist shrine and UNESCO World Heritage Site is also situated in Bihar, Barabar Caves the oldest rockcut caves in India, Khuda Bakhsh Oriental Library the Oldest Library of India.

DELHI

Delhi is the capital city of India. A fine blend of old and new, ancient and modern, Delhi is a melting pot of cultures, religions. Delhi has been the capital of numerous empires that ruled India, making it rich in history. The rulers left behind their trademark architectural styles. Delhi currently has many renowned historic monuments and landmarks such as the Tughlaqabad fort, Qutub Minar, Purana Quila, Lodhi Gardens, Jama Masjid, Humayun's tomb, Red Fort, and Safdarjung's Tomb. Modern monuments include Jantar Mantar, India Gate, Rashtrapati Bhavan, Laxminarayan Temple, Lotus temple and Akshardham Temple. New Delhi is famous for its British colonial architecture, wide roads, and tree-lined boulevards. Delhi is home to numerous political landmarks, national museums, Islamic shrines, Hindu temples, green parks, and trendy malls.

GOA

Goa is one of the most famous tourist destinations in India. A former colony of Portugal, Goa is famous for its excellent beaches, Portuguese churches, Hindu temples, and wildlife sanctuaries. The Basilica of Bom Jesus, Mangueshi Temple, Dudhsagar Falls, and Shantadurga are famous attractions in Goa. Recently a Wax Museum has also opened in Old Goa housing a number of wax personalities of Indian history, culture and heritage. The Goa Carnival is a world famous event, with colourful masks and floats, drums and reverberating music, and dance performances. The celebrations run three days culminating in a carnival parade on fat Tuesday.

HIMACHAL PRADESH

Himachal Pradesh is famous for its Himalayan landscapes and popular hill-stations. Many outdoor activities such as rock climbing, mountain biking, paragliding, ice-skating, and heli-skiing are popular tourist attractions in Himachal Pradesh. Shimla, the state capital, is very popular among tourists. The Kalka-Shimla Railway is a Mountain railway which is a UNESCO World Heritage Site. Shimla is also a famous skiing attraction in India. Other popular hill stations include Manali and Kasauli. Dharamshala, home of the Dalai Lama, is known for its Tibetan monasteries and Buddhist temples. Many trekking expeditions also begin here.

JAMMU AND KASHMIR

Jammu and Kashmir is the northernmost state of India. Jammu is noted for its scenic landscape, ancient temples, Hindu shrines, castles, gardens and forts. The Hindu holy shrines of Amarnath in kashmir attracts about. 4 million Hindu devotees every year. Vaishno Devi alsoattract tens of thousands of Hindu devotees every year. Jammu's historic monuments feature a unique blend of Islamic and Hindu architecture styles. Tourism forms an integral part of the Kashmiri economy. Often dubbed "Paradise on Earth", Kashmir's mountainous landscape has attracted tourists for centuries. Notable places are Dal Lake, Srinagar Phalagam, Gulmarg, Yeusmarg and Mughal Gardens etc. Kashmir's natural landscape has made it one of the popular destinations for adventure tourism in South Asia. Marked by four distinct seasons, Ski enthusiasts can enjoy the exotic himalayan powder during winters. 7000000 tourists arrived in kashmir in the months of April,May and June alone In recent years, Ladakh has emerged as a major hub for adventure tourism. This part of Greater Himalaya called "moon on earth" comprising of naked peaks and deep gorges was once known for the silk route to High Asia from the subcontinent. Leh is also a growing tourist spot.

KARNATAKA

Karnataka has been ranked as fourth most popular destination for tourism among states of India. It has the second highest number of protected monuments in India, at 507. Kannada dynasties like Kadambas, Western Gangas, Chalukyas, Rashtrakutas, Hoysalas and Vijayanagaras, ruled Karnataka particularly North

Karnataka. They built great monuments to Buddhism, Jainism, Shaivism. The monuments are still present at Badami, Aihole, Pattadakal, Hampi, Lakshmeshwar, Sudi, Hooli, Mahadeva Temple, Dambal, Lakkundi, Gadag, Hangal, Halasi, Galaganatha, Chaudayyadanapura, Banavasi, Belur, Halebidu, Shravanabelagola, Sannati and many more. Notable Islamic monuments are present at Bijapur, Bidar, Gulbarga, Raichur and other part of the state. Gol Gumbaz at Bijapur, has the second largest pre-modern dome in the world after the Byzantine Hagia Sophia. Karnataka has two World heritage sites, at Hampi and Pattadakal, both are in North Karnataka. Karnataka is famous for its waterfalls.

Jog falls of Shimoga District is one of the highest waterfalls in Asia. This state has 21 wildlife sanctuaries and five National parks and is home to more than 500 species of birds. Karnataka has many beaches at Karwar, Gokarna, Murdeshwara, Surathkal. Karnataka is a rock climbers paradise. Yana in Uttara Kannada, Fort in Chitradurga, Ramnagara near Bangalore district, Shivagange in Tumkur district and tekal in Kolar district are a rock climbers heaven.

KERALA

Kerala is a state on the tropical Malabar Coast of southwestern India. Nicknamed as one of the "10 paradises of the world" by National Geographic, Kerala is famous especially for its ecotourism initiatives. Its unique culture and traditions, coupled with its varied demography, has made it one of the most popular tourist destinations in India. Growing at a rate of 13.31 per cent, the tourism industry significantly contributes to the state's economy. Kerala is known for its tropical backwaters and pristine beaches such as Kovalam.

MADHYA PRADESH

Madhya Pradesh is called the "Heart of India" because of its location in the centre of the country. It has been home to the cultural heritage of Hinduism, Islam, Buddhism, Sikhism, Jainism. Innumerable monuments, exquisitely carved temples, stupas, forts and palaces are dotted all over the State. The temples of Khajuraho are world-famous for their erotic sculptures, and are a UNESCO World Heritage Site. Gwalior is famous for its forts, the Tomb of Rani Lakshmibai, and the Palace of Tansen. Madhya Pradesh is also known as Tiger State because of the tiger population. Famous national parks like Kanha, Bandhavgadh, Shivpuri, Sanjay, Pench are located in MP. Spectacular mountain ranges, meandering rivers and miles and miles of dense forests offering a unique and exciting panorama of wildlife in sylvan surroundings.

MAHARASHTRA

Maharashtra is the second most visited state in India by foreign tourists, with more than 2 million foreign tourists arrivals annually. Maharashtra boasts of a large number of popular and revered religious venues that are heavily frequented by locals as well as out-of-state visitors. Ajanta Caves, Ellora Caves and Chhatrapati Shivaji Terminus are the three UNESCO World Heritage sites in Maharashtra and are highly responsible for the development of Tourism in the state. Mumbai is the most cosmopolitan city in India, and a great place to experience modern India.

Mumbai famous for Bollywood, the world's largest film industry. In addition, Mumbai is famous for its clubs, shopping, and upscale gastronomy. The city is known for its architecture, from the ancient Elephanta Caves, to the Islamic Haji Ali Mosque, to the colonial architecture of Bombay High Court and Chhatrapati Shivaji Terminus.

Maharashtra also has numerous adventure tourism destinations, including paragliding, rock climbing, canoeing, kayaking, snorkeling, and scuba diving in places like Kolad, Tarkarli, Koyna, Manor. Maharashtra also has several pristine national parks and reserves, some of the best ones are Tadoba with excellent accommodation and safari experiences besides little known by amazing wildlife destinations like Koyna, Nagzira, Melghat, Dajipur, Radhanagari and of course the only national park within metropolic city limits in the world-Sanjay Gandhi National Park. The Bibi Ka Maqbara at Aurangabad the Mahalakshmi temple at Kolhapur, the cities of Nashik, Trimbak famous for religious importance and the city of Pune the seat of the Maratha Empire and the fantastic Ganesh Chaturthi celebrations together contribute for the Tourism sector of Mahrashtra.

MANIPUR

Manipur as the name suggest is a land of jewels. Its rich culture excels in every aspects as in martial arts, dance, theater and sculpture. The charm of the place is the greenery with the moderate climate making it a tourists' heaven. The beautiful and seasonal Shirui Lily at Ukhrul, Sangai and the floating islands at Loktak Lake are few of the rare things found in Manipur. Polo, which can be called a royal game, also originated from Manipur.

MEGHALAYA

Meghalaya has some of the thickest surviving forests in the country and therefore constitutes one of the most important ecotourism circuits in the country today. The Meghalayan subtropical forests support a vast variety of flora and fauna. Meghalaya has 2 National Parks and 3 Wildlife Sanctuaries. Meghalaya also offers many adventure tourism opportunities in the form of mountaineering, rock climbing, trekking and hiking, water sports etc.

The state offers several trekking routes some of which also afford and opportunity to encounter some rare animals such as the slow loris, assorted deer and bear. The Umiam Lake has a water sports complex with facilities such as rowboats, paddleboats, sailing boats, cruise-boats, water-scooters and speedboats. Cherrapunjee is one of the most popular tourist spots in North East of India. It lies to the south of the capital Shillong. The town is very well known and needs little publicity. A rather scenic, 50 kilometer long road, connects Cherrapunjee with Shillong. The popular waterfalls in the state are the Elephant Falls, Shadthum Falls, Weinia falls, Bishop Falls, Nohkalikai Falls, Langshiang Falls and Sweet Falls. The hot springs at Jakrem near Mawsynram are believed to have curative and medicinal properties.

ORISSA

Orissa has been a preferred destination from ancient days for people who have an interest in spirituality, religion, culture, art and natural beauty. Ancient and medieval architecture, pristine sea beaches, the classical and ethnic dance forms and a variety of festivals. Orissa has kept the religion of Buddhism alive. Rock-edicts that have challenged time stand huge and over-powering by the banks of the river Daya. The torch of Buddhism is still ablaze in the sublime triangle at Udayagiri, Lalitagiri and Ratnagiri, on the banks of river Birupa. Precious fragments of a glorious past come alive in the shape of stupas, rock-cut caves, rock-edicts, excavated monasteries, viharas, chaityas and sacred relics in caskets and the Rock-edicts of Ashoka. Orissa is also famous for its well-preserved Hindu Temples, especially the Konark Sun Temple and The Leaning Temple of Huma.

Orissa is the home for various tribal communities who have contributed uniquely to the multicultural and multilingual character of the state. Their handicrafts, different dance forms, jungle products and their unique life style blended with their healing practices have got world wide attention. The Sitalsasthi Carnival is a must see for everyone who wants to see a glimpse of the art and culture of Odisha at one place.

PUDUCHERRY

The Union Territory of Puducherry comprises four coastal regions *viz.,*- Puducherry, Karaikal, Mahe and Yanam. Puducherry is the Capital of this Union Territory and one of the most popular tourist destinations in South India. Puducherry has been described by National Geographic as "a glowing highlight of subcontinental sojourn". The city has many beautiful colonial buildings, churches, temples, and statues, which, combined with the systematic town planning and the well planned French style avenues, still preserve much of the colonial ambience.

PUNJAB

The state of Punjab is renowned for its cuisine, culture and history. Punjab has a vast public transportation and communication network. Some of the main cities in Punjab are Amritsar, Chandigarh, and Ludhiana. Punjab also has a rich religious history incorporating Sikhism and Hinduism. Tourism in Punjab is principally suited for the tourists interested in culture, ancient civilization, spirituality and epic history.

Some of the villages in Punjab are also a must see for the person who wants to see the true Punjab, with their beautiful traditional Indian homes, farms and temples, this is a must see for any visitor that goes to Punjab. India-Pakistan border at Wagha is also a popular tourist attraction.

RAJASTHAN

Rajasthan, literally meaning "Land of the Kings", is one of the most attractive tourist destinations in Northern India. The vast sand dunes of the Thar Desert attract millions of tourists from around the globe every year.

SIKKIM

Originally known as Suk-Heem, which in the local language means "peaceful home", Sikkim was an independent kingdom till the year 1974, when it became a part of the Republic of India. The capital of Sikkim is Gangtok, located approximately 105 kilometers from New Jalpaiguri, the nearest railway station to Sikkim. Although, an airport is under construction at Dekiling in East Sikkim, the nearest airport to Sikkim would be Bagdogra.

Sikkim is considered as the land of Orchids and mystic cultures and colourful traditions. Sikkim is well known among trekkers and adventure lovers, as West Sikkim has a lot to give them. Places near Sikkim include Darjeeling also known as the Queen of hills and Kalimpong. Darjeeling, other than its world famous "Darjeeling tea" is also famous for its refined "Prep schools" founded during the British Raj. Kalimpong is also famous for its flora cultivation and is home to many internationally known Nurseries.

TAMIL NADU

Tamil Nadu is the top state in attracting the maximum number of foreign tourists in India. Tamil Nadu. Marina Beach, Carnatic music, Bharata Natyam dance and country's largest Shopping locality. This city is also famous for Medical tourism and houses Asia's largest hospital. Archaeological sites with civilization dating back to 3800 years are found in Tamil Nadu. With more than 34000 temples this state also holds the credit of having maximum number of UNESCO heritage sites in India which includes Great Living Chola Temples and Mahabalipuram.

Country's largest temple srirangam and Pichavaram the world's Second largest Mangrove forest are located in this state. Tamilnadu has some great temples like Madurai Meenakshi Amman Temple, Tanjore Brihadeeswarar Temple, Srirangam Ranganathaswamy Temple and all the mentioned temples has world class architecture that really mesmerize everyone. Kanyakumari is the southernmost tip of India provides sceneic view of sunset and sunshine over the Indian ocean.Hill stations like Yercaud, Kodaikanal, Ooty, Valparai, Yelagiri are widely visited. Velankanni Church and Nagoor Dharga are visited by people of all religion.Water Falls and Wildlife sanctuaries are located across the state.

UTTARAKHAND

Uttarakhand, the 27th state of the Republic of India, is called "the abode of the Gods". It contains glaciers, snow-clad mountains, valley of flowers, skiing slopes and dense forests, and many shrines and places of pilgrimage. Char-dhams, the four most sacred and revered Hindu temples: Badrinath, Kedarnath, Gangotri and Yamunotri are nestled in the Himalayas. Haridwar which means Gateway to God is the only place on the plains. It holds the watershed for Gangetic River System spanning 300 km from Satluj in the west to Kali river in the east. Nanda Devi is the second highest peak in India after Kanchenjunga.

Dunagiri, Neelkanth, Chaukhamba, Panchachuli, Trisul are other peaks above 23000 Ft. It is considered the abode of Devtas, Yakashyas, Kinners, Fairies and Sages. It boasts of some old hill-stations developed during British era like Mussoorie, Almora and Nainital.

UTTAR PRADESH

Situated in the northern part of India, Uttar Pradesh is important with its wealth of monuments and religious fervour. Geographically, Uttar Pradesh is very diverse, with Himalayan foothills in the extreme north and the Gangetic Plain in the centre. It is also home of India's most visited site, the Taj Mahal, and Hinduism's holiest city, Varanasi. The most populous state of the Indian Union also has a rich cultural heritage, and at the heart of North India, Uttar Pradesh has much to offer. Places of interest include Varanasi, Agra, Kanpur, Lucknow, Mathura, Jhansi, Prayag, Sarnath, Ayodhya, Dudhwa National Park and Fatehpur Sikri.

WEST BENGAL

Kolkata, one of the many cities in the state of West Bengal has been nicknamed the City of Palaces. This comes from the numerous palatial mansions built all over the city. Unlike many north Indian cities, whose construction stresses minimalism, the layout of much of the architectural variety in Kolkata owes its origins to European styles and tastes imported by the British and, to a much lesser extent, the Portuguese and French. The buildings were designed and inspired by the tastes of the English gentleman around and the aspiring Bengali Babu. Today, many of these structures are in various stages of decay.

Some of the major buildings of this period are well maintained and several buildings have been declared as heritage structures. From historical point of view, the story of West Bengal begins from Gour and Pandua situated close to the present district town of Malda. The twin medieval cities had been sacked at least once by changing powers in the 15th century. However, ruins from the period still remain, and several architectural specimens still retain the glory and shin of those times. The Hindu architecture of Bishnupur in terracotta and laterite sandstone are renowned world over. Towards the British colonial period came the architecture of Murshidabad and Coochbehar.

NATURE TOURISM

India has geographical diversity, which resulted in varieties of nature tourism.

- Water falls in Western Ghats including Jog falls.
- Western Ghats
- Hill Stations
- Wildlife reserves
- Deserts

WILDLIFE IN INDIA

India is home to several well known large mammals including the Asian Elephant, Bengal Tiger, Asiatic Lion, Leopard and Indian Rhinoceros, often engrained culturally and religiously often being associated with deities. Other well known large Indian mammals include ungulates such as the domestic Asian Water buffalo, wild Asian Water buffalo, Nilgai, Gaur and several species of deer and antelope. Some members of the dog family such as the Indian Wolf, Bengal Fox, Golden Jackal and the Dhole or Wild Dogs are also widely distributed. It is also home to the Striped Hyaena, Macaques, Langurs and Mongoose species.

India also has a large variety of protected wildlife. The country's protected forest consists of 75 National parks of India and 421 Sanctuaries, of which 19 fall under the purview of Project Tiger. Its climatic and geographic diversity makes it the home of over 350 mammals and 1200 bird species, many of which are unique to the subcontinent. Some well known national wildlife sanctuaries include Bharatpur, Corbett, Kanha, Kaziranga, Periyar, Ranthambore, Manas and Sariska. The world's largest mangrove forest Sundarbans is located in southern West Bengal. The Kaziranga National Park,Manas National Park, Sundarbans and Keoladeo National Park is UNESCO World Heritage Site.

HILL STATIONS

Several hill stations served as summer capitals of Indian provinces, princely states, or, in the case of Shimla, of British India itself.

Since Indian Independence, the role of these hill stations as summer capitals has largely ended, but many hill stations remain popular summer resorts.

Most famous hill stations are:

- Mount Abu, Rajasthan
- Pachmarhi, Madhya Pradesh-It is also known as The Queen of Satpura.
- Araku, Andhra Pradesh
- Gulmarg, Srinagar and Ladakh in Jammu and Kashmir
- Darjeeling in West Bengal
- Munnar in Kerala
- Ooty, Yercaud and Kodaikanal in Tamil Nadu
- Shillong in Meghalaya
- Shimla, Kullu in Himachal Pradesh
- Nainital in Uttarakhand
- Gangtok in Sikkim
- Mussoorie in Uttarakhand
- Manali in Himachal Pradesh
- Tawang in Arunachal Pradesh
- Mahabaleshwar in Maharashtra
- Haflong in Assam

In addition to the bustling hill stations and summer capitals of yore, there are several serene and peaceful nature retreats and places of interest to visit for a nature lover. These range from the stunning moonscapes of Leh and Ladhak, to small, exclusive nature retreats such as Dunagiri, Binsar, Mukteshwar in the Himalayas, to rolling vistas of Western Ghats to numerous private retreats in the rolling hills of Kerala.

BEACHES

India offers a wide range of tropical beaches with silver/golden sand to coral beaches of Lakshadweep. States like Kerala and Goa have exploited the potential of beaches to the fullest. However, there are a lot many unexploited beaches in the states of Andhra Pradesh, Gujarat, Maharastra, Tamil Nadu and Karnataka. These states have very high potential to be develop them as future destinations for prospective tourists.

Some of the famous tourist beaches are:

- Beaches of Vizag, Andhra Pradesh
- Beaches of Puri, Orissa
- Beaches of Digha, West Bengal
- Beaches of Goa
- Kovalam Beach, Kerala
- Marina Beach, Chennai
- City Beach, Puducherry

- Beaches of Mahabalipuram
- Beaches in Mumbai
- Beaches of Diu
- Beaches of Midnapore, West Bengal
- Beaches of Andaman and Nicobar Islands
- Beaches of Lakshadweep Islands

ADVENTURE TOURISM

- River rafting and kayaking in Himalayas
- Mountain climbing in Himalayas
- Rock climbing in Madhya Pradesh
- Skiing in Gulmarg or Auli
- Boat racing in Bhopal
- Paragliding in Maharashtra

NATIONAL TOURISM POLICY

A national policy on tourism highlighting the importance of the sector and the objectives of tourism development in the country was presented in the Parliament in 1982. The policy was formulated in an environment of a closed economy with rigid licensing procedures.

The policy did not emphasize the role of private sector, and foreign investment was not envisaged. The policy also did not lay adequate emphasis on domestic tourism and the need for product development. In the Chief Minister's Conference held on October 30, 2001, the Prime Minister of India Shri Atal Bihari Vajpayee had stated.

"Tourism is a major engine of economic growth in most parts of the world. Several countries have transformed their economies using the tourism potential the fullest. Tourism has great capacity to create large scale employment of diverse kind – from the most specialised to the unskilled and all of us know that generation of massive productive employment opportunities is what India needs the most". The Ministry of Tourism had prepared a draft National Tourism Development Policy with the objective of positioning tourism as a major engine of economic growth and to harness its direct and multiplier effects for employment and poverty eradication in an environmentally sustainable manner.

This draft was circulated to all the stakeholders in the Tourism sector, the Private sector, the industry Associations, the State Governments, Departments and Ministries of Government of India.

The draft on National Tourism Policy-2002 was also discussed at the three day Tourism Conclave comprising of:

- Meeting of all foreign and domestic officers of Tourism Ministry.
- Meeting of State Tourism secretaries and
- Meeting of the State Chief Ministers and Tourism Ministers.

The Policy rests upon the following basic principles:

- Account should be taken of the fact that for the last four decades or so, a tourism revolution has been sweeping the world. In 1964, the number of tourists leaving their homes, worldwide, was 100 million. This number increased to 200 million in 1974, 500 million in 1992 and 700 million in 2001. And this number is likely to swell to 1.5 billion by 2020 and receipts from it are estimated to cross $2000 billion.

  If India has to partake in this revolution in a meaningful way, it must change its strategies as well as the techniques and tools of its machinery of implementation. In this connection, it has to be noted with concern that during the last decade or so, India's share of world tourist traffic has remained static at 0.38 per cent.
- At the institutional level, a framework would have to be evolved which is Government-led, private-sector driven and community-welfare oriented. Government have to provide a legislative framework to regulate tourism trade and industry, ensure safety and security of the tourists and create basic infrastructure and health-care facilities. The private sector has to act as a main spring of the activities and impart dynamism and speed to the process of development as well as conservation. Both Government and the private sector would be required to safeguard the stability and also the social and economic advancement of the local communities and the communities in the neighbourhood.
- The deep-rooted relationship of tourism and our cultural assets should be fully recognised and provided for. Improvements and environmental upgradation of the protected monuments and the areas around them should be considered as a linchpin of the tourism industry.
- Effective linkages and close coordination should be established with such Departments as Civil Aviation, Environment, Forest, Railways, Home, etc.
- Sustainability should serve as a guiding star for the new Policy. The development and management strategies should be so worked out as to ensure that tourism largely acts as a smokeless industry and its ecological footprints remain as soft as possible. No one engaged, directly or indirectly, in the tourism industry, should be allowed to secure short-term gains by resorting to what has been called the darker side of tourism. Neither over-exploitation of natural resources should be permitted nor the carrying capacity of the tourist-sites ignored.
- Greater emphasis should be laid on eco-tourism whose parameters should be broader than those of nature tourism alone. It must help in eliminating poverty, in ending unemployment, in creating new skills,

in enhancing the status of woman, in preserving cultural heritage, in encouraging tribal and local crafts and in improving overall environment and facilitating growth of a more just and fair social order.

- Special thrust should be imparted to rural tourism and tourism in small settlements, where sizeable assets of our cultural and natural wealth exist.
- Due importance should be given to domestic tourism, particularly tourism connected with pilgrimage, and it should be so designed that the infrastructure created under it serves as a backbone of international tourism in times to come.
- A new class of young tourists, with marked preference for adventure and distant destinations, in hills, caves and forests, is emerging. This class is not looking for 5-star accommodation but only for simple and clean places to stay. The requirements of this class of tourists should be met and guest tourism encouraged through Panchayats and local bodies and associations.
- Special attraction of tourist for the Yoga, Siddha, etc., as well as for the Indian cuisine should be made use of and effectively encouraged.
- The tourist industry and travel agents should be persuaded to evolve and adopt voluntarily a Code of Ethics and its infringement should be firmly dealt with by Tour and Travel Associations.
- A section of the State police should be earmarked to act as tourist police and special training should be imparted to it.
- At the international level, India should play a dynamic role and make its presence felt at the World Tourism Organisation, World Tourism and Travel Council and Earth Council. Its unique cultural values and spiritual heritage should be projected with dignity and elevation befitting a great nation, whenever suitable opportunity comes our way.
- The civilizational issues as well as issues pertaining to civic administration and good governance must be attended to and made an effective part of the tourism policy. It should be ensured that good policies are not shipwrecked in the sea of half hearted implementation.

INTRODUCTION

The policy document seeks to enhance employment potential within the tourism sector as well as to foster economic integration through developing linkages with other sectors.

Broadly the policy paper attempts to:

- Position tourism as a major engine of economic growth;
- Harness the direct and multiplier effects of tourism for employment generation, economic development and providing impetus to rural tourism;

- Focus on domestic tourism as a major driver of tourism growth.
- Position India as a global brand to take advantage of the burgeoning global travel and trade and the vast untapped potential of India as a destination;
- Acknowledges the critical role of private sector with government working as a pro-active facilitator and catalyst;
- Create and develop integrated tourism circuits based on India's unique civilization, heritage, and culture in partnership with states, private sector and other agencies;
- Ensure that the tourist to India gets physically invigourated, mentally rejuvenated, culturally enriched, spiritually elevated and " feel India from within".

The policy document takes into consideration seven key areas that will provide the thrust to tourism development. These are: Swagat (Welcome), Soochana (Information), Suvidha (Facilitation), Suraksha (Safety), Sahyog (Cooperation), Samrachana (Infrastructure Development), and Safai (Cleanliness).

TOURISM AND NATIONAL DEVELOPMENT IN INDIA – CURRENT SITUATION AND PROSPECTS

In its modern form since the end of the Second World War, tourism has grown into one of the world's largest industries with a growth rate in excess of 5 per cent per annum over the past twenty years. International tourism flows across frontiers in the year 2000 reached 698 million while receipts from these flows reached US$ 595 billion (including receipts from international transport fares). Estimates prepared by the World Tourism Organization indicate that global domestic tourism flows are at least ten times greater than international tourism flows indicating that there were at least 6,980 million domestic arrivals in 2000. Globally, tourism accounts for 11per cent of the global GDP and 8per cent of the world trade employment

In most countries with a large population, domestic tourism is the foundation of a viable and sustainable tourism industry. Much of the growth of global tourism has been generated by domestic tourism, which tends to be more focused on rural destinations. With a growing interest in the intangible culture of different countries (*i.e.,* lifestyles, cuisine, ceremonies, music, religious beliefs, traditions, customs, and history), there is a strong potential to encourage international tourism to the rural areas as well. India's share of global international tourism at 2.64 million foreign arrivals through its borders in the year 2000 is relatively small in volume (about 0.38 per cent) but almost twice as high in terms of US$ receipts (about 0.69 per cent)

On the other hand, India's share of global domestic tourism is much higher (around 4.6 per cent of estimated global domestic tourism). While the proportion of global US$ receipts from international tourism increased from 0.57 per cent in 1990 to 0.69 per cent in 2000, this compares with a share of 1.37 per cent in 1981. In contrast, India's neighbours in South and South–East Asia have more effectively utilised tourism for economic growth and employment creation

A forecasting study undertaken by the World Tourism and Travel Council estimated that in 2001, tourism would account for 10.7 per cent of global Gross Domestic Product, 207.1 million jobs; US$ 1,063.8 billion in export value, and US$ 657.7 billion in capital investment. A study on the economic impact of tourism conducted by the World Tourism and Travel Council estimated that in 2001, the consumption activity arising from domestic and international tourism will contribute 5.3 per cent of India's Gross Domestic Product. Tourism will also sustain 25 million equivalent full time jobs or 6 per cent of India's workforce, and contribute more than US$ 3 billion in gross foreign exchange receipts. Separate estimates prepared by the Department of Tourism using a multiplier based on 1980 research suggests that the actual employment generation effect of (direct and indirect) tourism in India is around 42 million (includes full time/ part time/casuals).

The forecasting study undertaken by the World Tourism and Travel Council further indicates that between 2001 and 2011:

- Global Gross Domestic Product will increase from 10.7 per cent to 11 per cent;
- Global employment contribution will increase from 207.1 million to 260.4 million jobs or 9 per cent of total global employment;
- The global value of tourism related exports will increase from US$ 1,063.8 billion to US$ 2,538.3 billion or 12.8 per cent of global export value; and
- Global capital investment in tourism will increase from US$ 657.7 billion to US$ 1,434 billion or 9.3 per cent of global investment.

Forecast data from the World Tourism Organization shows that the share of tourism volumes and related receipts, Gross Domestic Product, employment, and export earnings is expected to move away from the developed countries towards the less developed countries as a result of favourable economic, motivational, technological, and policy factors. WTTC's status paper, "The India Imperative" has analysed India tourism in the light of the latest Tourism Satellite Accounting Research TSA (2001) and projections for the year 2011.

Subject to addressing key policy issues highlighted in the paper, WTTC has identified India as one of the foremost growth centres in the world in the coming decade:

- The development priorities of the Government of India up to 2012 are to place the economy on a significantly higher growth path that will deliver greater economic benefits in the context of the new global economic and security order, but also enhance human well-being, achieve social equity, sustainability, and efficiency. To achieve this overall development goal, the Government of India has embarked upon a strategy that involves a radical departure from past policies, and institutional arrangements in order to optimize and release the potential of its natural, human, financial, and technical resources.

- One of the sectors of the economy considered to have particular potential is tourism. Tourism is seen to be a priority sector because it is:
- Able to maximize the productivity of India's natural, human, cultural, and technical resources, and are sustainable development.
- Labour intensive and cottage or small industry based, providing employment that is of a high quality thus contributing to higher quality of life;
- Capable of being primarily focused on rural areas with appropriate and relatively low cost programmes;
- Has extensive forward and backward economic linkages that build overall income, employment (especially for women, youth, and disabled persons bringing greater social equity, and justice), investment, and raises central, state, and local government revenue;
- Is able to deliver significant levels of hard currency as an export industry;
- Able to promote understanding, peace, and contribute to national unity and regional stability.

There is great potential for creating enormous number of new jobs through travel and tourism. The employment potential is the highest in the tourism sector as compared to any other sector and India has the potential to more than triple its travel and tourism jobs.

The tourism industry has a very strong linkage to socio-economic progress of the country. It has a very high revenue capital ratio. It is estimated that an investment of ₹1 million creates 47 direct jobs and 11 indirect jobs, which far surpasses the employment potential from Agricultural and Industrial sector.

SWOT ANALYSIS

The tourism sector's contribution to the national development priorities and strategies has so far been relatively limited. A review of the sector's competitive strengths and weaknesses, opportunities, and threats indicates that it has considerable growth potential.

The main results of the analysis are:

- India's great competitive strength from a tourism point of view is its ancient and yet living civilization that gave rise to four of the worlds great religions and philosophies, and brought travellers and trade millennia ago. The rich natural and rural landscape of India is punctuated with the built heritage of its ancient past and more modern structures of the present and its hopes for the future. India's contacts with other civilizations is reflected in the rich cultural diversity of its people through its language forms, cuisine, traditions, customs, music, dance, religious practices and festivals, its holistic healing traditions, art, and craft.

- The main competitive constraints facing the tourism sector are the low priority that the sector has been given by government
- In the past it was unable to effectively link its role in relation to national development priorities, undue focus was laid on the international market at the expense of domestic tourism, the poor quality of the environments surrounding many of India's main tourist sites, the security scenario in the region that affects the perception of India as a safe and secure destination, the quality of facilities and services at attractions
- The quantity and quality of transportation service, and related infrastructure, facilitation of entry to India by international tourists, the multiplicity and high level of taxation
- Limited availability of tourist information in-source markets and at destination, limited scope, accuracy and reliability of market data for planning and management, insufficient marketing of India in its domestic and international markets, lack of attractive project financing, restrictive land use policies that limit the availability of suitable land for tourism development, limited and poor facilities and services outside the major cities, especially in rural areas, and the lack of community participation leading to in some cases hostility to tourism. The low priority accorded to tourism has meant that it has played only a marginal role in India's development programmes to date and this is reflected in the limited budgets, limited cooperation and coordination capabilities, and an inability to implement strategic initiative and projects.
- Notwithstanding the constraints (which themselves present opportunities), the key competitive opportunities are:- (1) leverage the huge potential of its domestic urban population to develop rural tourism
- The main internal threats to the development of the tourism sector are failing to effectively resolve the constraints identified above. These are security, safety and health situation; failing to involve communities in the decision making process for tourism development; and failure to adopt and implement sustainable development and management principles and practices at tourism sites, especially in the rural and natural areas of the country. From an external point of view, the main threats are not effectively addressing the fierce and ever-increasing competition from competing countries, over-reliance on a few well worn international and

domestic travel markets, unbridled growth of international tourism that is characterized by high volumes, low economic yields, and high levels of adverse socio-cultural, and environmental impacts, and further regional conflicts such as that resulting from the September 11 event of 2001.

India possesses a rich and diverse range of unique tangible and intangible cultural, natural, and man-made tourism resources, many of which are world class in quality, and most of which are located in rural areas. The tourism resources of the country have the potential to attract significantly higher levels of market demand from the domestic and international markets provided that sustainable site management practices and principles are adopted and applied, and the other constraints identified above are effectively resolved.

Provided that the identified constraints and opportunities are addressed, and appropriate plans prepared to handle the internal and external threats, then it is considered that India Tourism focus should be to:

- Substantially increase the proportion of the urban resident leisure and pilgrimage tourism to rural areas not just in terms of volume but also in terms of length of stay and expenditure. For example, the total urban resident leisure and pilgrimage domestic market is estimated to increase from 22.5 million in 2001 to 50.5 million by 2012 and it would be a key objective to encourage these to visit the rural areas through appropriate strategies; and
- Substantially increase the volume of high-yielding (high average per capita expenditure) international tourists from the priority regional and long haul source markets based on the identified travel interests.

TOURISM DEVELOPMENT GOALS, OBJECTIVES, AND STRATEGIES

The tourism industry, unlike many other industries is a composite of several service providers. These service providers are generally in the private sector. In, addition, public sector institutions such as the national or state departments of tourism are involved in the planning, development, and management of tourism. The participation of different private and public agencies makes tourism industry a complex phenomenon requiring a strong cooperation and coordination for it to be developed and expanded along lines that will contribute to the overall national development objectives.

Left to itself, the industry will develop naturally, but not necessarily optimally or sustainable, and without any clear links to the broad development objectives of the country. Uncontrolled tourism growth could damage India's socio-cultural structure, degrade its tangible and intangible cultural and natural heritage, and lead to adverse economic impacts such as high importation costs, and weakening inter-industry linkages. On the other hand, when the industry is properly planned, developed and managed at all levels of government in partnership with the private sector, it will strengthen India's socio-cultural structure. It would valorize its tangible and intangible cultural and natural heritage, and lead to positive economic impacts including enhanced employment and income opportunities in rural areas, lower importation costs, and stronger inter-industry linkages.

The vehicle for achieving the positive benefits of tourism, mitigating the negative effects, and delivering sustainable industry development framework of India's national development priorities is the preparation and implementation of a comprehensive national tourism policy. The overall goal and strategy for the development of the tourism industry is to ensure that its development is closely tied to the national development priorities of the country. In this context the Government of India's vision for the development of the tourism sector is: "Achieve a superior quality of life for India's peoples through Tourism which would provide a unique opportunity for physical invigouration, mental rejuvenation, cultural enrichment and spiritual elevation".

KEY OBJECTIVES

To achieve the overall vision for the development of tourism, five key strategic objectives need to be achieved.

They are:

1. Positioning and maintaining tourism development as a national priority activity;
2. Enhancing and maintaining the competitiveness of India as a tourism destination.
3. Improving India's existing tourism products and expanding these to meet new market requirements;
4. Creation of world class infrastructure
5. Developing sustained and effective marketing plans and programmes.

POSITIONING TOURISM AS A NATIONAL PRIORITY

- Inclusion of Tourism in the concurrent list of the constitution of India. This will provide a constitutional recognition to the tourism sector, help in channeling the development of tourism in a systematic manner and enable central government to legislate for tourism development. The proposal for including tourism in the concurrent. List was circulated to the State Governments and discussed at the Chief Ministers' Conference. Majority of the States have agreed to the proposal.
- To provide effective linkages and close coordination between Departments, a Group of Ministers on Tourism has already been constituted.
- Constitution of a Tourism Advisory Council with key stakeholders to act as a "think tank".

- Prepare the basis for the adoption of the Tourism Satellite Account system based on SN3 protocol for the national accounts;
- Plan, and implement a professionally managed integrated communications strategy to be called the 'National Tourism awareness campaign';

ENHANCING INDIA'S COMPETITIVENESS AS A TOURIST DESTINATION

- Visa on Arrival-Implement visa on arrival and consider strategies for the fast issuance of visas and permits including electronic visa approaches, and improved processing of arrivals by customs and immigration officials.
- Computerization of the system of issue of visas by Embassies/High Commission.
- Air capacity available to India is woefully short during peak travel months ranging from October to March and specially from main tourism originating destinations like North America, Western Europe and South East Asia. Additional seat capacity from the major destinations would provide a major impetus to tourism and economic development. An analysis by Indian Council for Research on International Economic Relations (ICRIER) reveals that the benefits of the additional seat capacity whether provided by the national carrier or any other international carrier would have a significant benefit for national economy.
- The model strengthens the argument for opening India's sky for enhancing tourism through increased capacity.
- Improve the standard of facilities and services at the nations international and major domestic airports by employing professional property management agencies to manage the physical premises on an outsource basis, and speeding up the privatization/leasing of airports.
- There is a need for creation of special tourism police force for deployment at major tourism destinations. This will provide travellers security through a sprit of courtesy and hospitality.

IMPROVING AND EXPANDING PRODUCT DEVELOPMENT

In relation to the development of products that are related to the special interests of the target markets, the product development strategy should be to:

- India has a unique cultural heritage. It has a vast array of protected monuments spread throughout the length and breadth of the country. India has 22 world heritage sites (16 are monuments). The conservation, preservation and integrated development of the area around these monuments provides a rare opportunity for growth and *expansion of cultural tourism* in India.

- Develop sustainable *beach and coastal tourism* resort products based on a more flexible approach to developments in the coastal zone. There is a need for identifying a series of government sites on the West Coast of India, free of encroachments, for the development of beach resorts by the private sector, with sites to be offered on long term lease at preferential terms. These sites should primarily be in the regions of Goa, Kerala, and North Karnataka, for reasons of air access.
- Develop and position the Cochin and Andaman and Nicobar Islands as *international cruise destination*. This positioning is supported by their proximity to international cruise routes, their exotic appeal and the need for high quality, low impact eco-tourism activities in the islands, and develop a dedicated cruise terminal;
- Capitalize by packaging India's unmatched variety of *traditional cuisines* that are today becoming increasingly popular in the world. The linkages and ripple effects created by a rapidly expanding restaurant sector can have dramatic implications for the Indian economy, implement private public partnership of the Culinary Institute of India that will research and document ancient culinary traditions, create a highly skilled workforce of culinary professionals that can populate not only hotel and catering establishments in India, but also internationally, serving to promote India internationally through a non-traditional medium, and encourage Indian entrepreneurs to establish restaurants of Indian ethnic cuisine internationally, by conceiving a innovative incentive scheme;
- Actively promote the development of *village tourism* as the primary tourism product to spread tourism and its socio-economic benefits to rural and new geographic areas. Key geographic regions for the development and promotion of endemic tourism. The optimum locations appear to be: Northeast states, Uttaranchal, Rajasthan, Ladakh, Kutch, Chattisgarh, and the Plantation regions (tea, coffee);
- India has some of the greatest variety of fauna in the world that has perhaps not been exploited to its full potential for tourism. In this context, the wildlife sanctuaries and national parks needs to be integrated as an integral part of the India tourism product, and priority needs to be given to the preparation of site and visitor management plans for key parks, after a prioritization of parks. Tentatively, these would be: Corbett National Park, Kanha National park, Bandhavgarh National park, Ranthambhore, Mudumalai, Nagarhole, Kaziranga, Periyar, Bharatpur, Little Rann of Kutch, Chilka, and Sundarbans. The

quality of tourist facilities available at the parks should be enhanced, in particular improve visitor information/interpretation centres, and the tiger and the elephant should be the 'brands' if Indian wildlife tourism;

- India perhaps has one of the greatest *adventure tourism* assets in the world in the form of the *Himalayas*, as well as in its mighty rivers. Mountain based adventure (soft and hard) activities in the Himalayas, creating the 'Himalayas' as the brand and icon of Indian adventure tourism should be developed and promoted. White water and more sedate great river rafting offers a unique tourism product, while regulations and certification for adventure tourism operators should be introduced so they meet minimum safety and conservation standards;
- That the domestic tourism market is mostly local or regional in nature and prefers recreational pursuits and that recreation and leisure is a vital component of the quality of life, particularly in urban areas, and needs to be recognized.
- India, despite its size, significance and attributes with world cities such as New Delhi and Mumbai, receives a minuscule proportion of the global *meetings, incentives, convention, exhibition* market with only 97 international conventions bringing approximately 25,000 people in the previous year. It is imperative not just for India's tourism development, but also for the development of international and domestic trade and commerce, that India construct a world class international convention centre in Mumbai.
- India is a region of the world's greatest bio-diversity, with a variety of unique natural locales, and is therefore, a perfect candidate for ecotourism. In this context, ecotourism should be made a priority tourism product for India with the focal points located in the Himalayas, Northeastern states, Western Ghats, Jharkhand, Andaman and Nicobar Islands, and the Lakshadweep Islands. Tour operators needs to be encouraged to promote ecotourism, which should also be made a grassroots, community based movement, though awareness, education and training of the local community as guides and interpreters;
- India is today being 're-discovered' by the world at large for the depth of its understanding of the physical, mental, emotional and spiritual manifestations of the world and humankind. In particular, India has traditions that focus on the holistic healing of individuals and on elevating the individual to a higher plane of consciousness and awareness. This can be India's most unique tourism product – *holistic healing and rejuvenation* of the individual from every dimension –

physical, mental, emotional and spiritual, and in doing so, it will capture the essence of the best of Indian philosophy and culture for international and Indian visitors alike.

- India has come to have a series of unique lodging products that can become one of India's immediate unique selling propositions (USPs). In this context, steps should be taken to eestablish a scheme for providing seed capital to entrepreneurs for the development of such unique accommodation products to be funded and administered at the State level, with adequate controls;
- India is a veritable *shopper's paradise* and the retail trade provides enormous forward and backward linkages throughout the economy. In this context, shopping should be recognized as an integral part of the tourism experience and a most valuable contributor to revenues. The development of dedicated shopping centres for traditional crafts, designed along the lines of ethnic village *haats* such as Dilli Haat and Shilpagram needs to be encouraged, the availability of information on where to procure specific crafts and produce reliable, unbiased shopping guides enhanced, funding support to reputed NGOs promoting the handicrafts sector should be provided, a directory of traditional crafts persons should be produced and promoted, touting should be controlled through regulation and legislation, and the "Made in India" brand should be promoted;
- India has unique events, fairs and festivals, some of which are well established, such as Pushkar, Desert Festival at Jaisalmer, Kumbh Mela, etc. In this context, this sector should be promoted as a unique product of India, the "Festivals of India" programme should be reintroduced in the top 12 future markets for India. Initially, there should be an annual event in UK and USA, followed by triennial events in each of the other markets;
- Business travel is also a form of tourism and typically occurs in urban environments and should be recognized accordingly. Urban quality along the lines specified for regional and site master plans, including tourism interests and requirements in the urban planning process should be improved, and New Delhi and Mumbai should be positioned as "World Cities" and the level of physical infrastructure, urban ambience, and public services developed befitting such a status; and
- A series of themed cultural attractions should be developed based on outstanding site planning and design, a National Register of key cultural sites for tourism should be prepared and published, and Delhi should be positioned as the cultural capital of India supported by an ongoing and vibrant calendar of cultural events.

The development of this recommended niche based special interest product mix will position India as a unique world-class destination.

CREATION OF WORLD-CLASS INFRASTRUCTURE

India's physical infrastructure is the very foundation on which tourism is to be built, and this ranges from ports of entry, to modes of transport to destinations, be they airways, roads, railways, or waterways, to urban infrastructure supporting tourism facilities such as access roads, power and electricity, water supply, sewage, and telecommunications amongst others. In this context, the strategic actions in relation to road, railways, waterways, and airport facilities are identified below.

DEVELOPMENT OF INTEGRATED CIRCUITS

Ministry of Tourism's financing assistance to the states has not been able to create an impact in terms of creation of international standard tourism infrastructure. The emphasis therefore has to be on identifying up travel circuits and converging all resources and expertise for development of these circuits as International Standard destinations.

ROADS

The road network is particularly vital to tourism, for almost 70 per cent of passenger travel in India is by roads. Many tourist circuits too, are entirely dependent on roads. The current government plan for the road system in the country, covering both inter-state highways and improvements to rural roads directly supports tourism development. There is an urgent need to construct and improve highways linking the World Heritage Sites and places of tourism significance. Ministry of Road Transport and National Highways will collaborate with Ministry of Tourism in this effort.

RAILWAYS

The Indian Railway system can be an enormous asset in the development of the tourism and hospitality industry in the country. India has 7,000 railway stations and 11,000 trains. The railways have a special fascination for foreign tourists who wish to experience the country both at leisure and close personal contact with the indigenous people.

The unqualified success of the "Palace on Wheels" substantiates the contention. For the vast majority of domestic tourists it is the railways, which is the main affordable means of travel linking the length and breadth of the vast and often enhancing sub-continent.

Railway services are equipped not only to meet the travel needs of domestic and foreign tourists, but also have the infrastructure and land resource to contribute significantly to the growth of hotel accommodation in the country.

The following measures are necessary:

- Introduction of Special Tourist Trains with a preset itinerary and with private sector participation.
- *Tourist Trains* – experienced private sector organizations need to be encouraged to introduce special tourist services between important destinations. In concept these special coaches may be privately owned by organizations who will design, build manage and market the product. To improve the financial viability and promote investment, accelerated depreciation should be allowed on such investments.
- *Railway Hotels* – the Indian Railways have a plan for establishing 100 hotels at railway stations serving specific tourist centres. The Private Sector should be incentivised to operate these hotels on long-term leases. These hotels could provide clean inexpensive accommodation for the budget tourists. The proposal to construct 100 hotels of 100 rooms in three years will add 10,000 rooms and help significantly to reduce the gap between supply and demand for hotel rooms.
- *Heritage Railway Buildings* – the Indian Railways owns a number of heritage structures. Effectively maintained and marketed these would not only serve as railway stations but also as places of tourist attractions. Some of these structures are Mumbai CST and Chruchgate and Lucknow railway station.
- *Hill Railways* – India is the proud possessor of five hill railways, which can compare with the best hill railway system in the world. These railways (Darjeeling, Nilgiri, Matheran, Kangra and Shimla) are slated to be encrypted by UNESCO as world heritage. It is essential to tap the enormous tourist potential of these products by developing these special tourist trains.
- *Railway Heritage Tourism* – Special tourism trains like Royal Orient, Budh Parikrama, Palace on Wheels and Fairy Queen are extremely popular with tourists, as they are steam hauled tourist trains. Stem traction is still operative in India and for special tourist segment it should be continued in perpetuity, otherwise skills to operate this kind technology could die.
- *Other Trains* – More trains like Shatabdhi and Rajdhani with a special tourism and hospitality focus should be planned both for the foreign and domestic tourists.

WATERWAYS

India's 7,000 kms coastline remains untapped for the promotion of cruises. There is immense potential for this activity in the East, South and West of India. Apart from Ocean-going Cruise Lines (a circuit being contemplated by potential Indian operators in Mumbai – Goa – Lakshadweep – Cochin – Colombo

– Maldives), the potential for River cruises in India needed to be developed for the North-Eastern States, (Brahmaputra and Ganges) and Kerela.

India is blessed with a vast coastline as well as several navigable rivers that have extreme tourism significance.

To capitalize on this, the strategic actions are to:

- Liberalise after due study the regime governing operation of passenger services along India's coastline, as this can form both a means of transport as well as a tourist attraction.
- Harness the potential of India's mighty rivers, especially the Ganges and the Brahmaputra as a means of transport as well as unique tourism products.

STRATEGIES FOR EFFECTIVE MARKETING

The competition for travellers from the source markets identified for India is fierce, and to effectively compete in these markets, India will have to shift its current traditional marketing approach to one that is more aggressive and competitive.

In this context, India will have to use an array of marketing tools and strategies to:

- Differentiate itself from the competing destinations including developing a unique market position, image, and brand that cannot be held by a competitor;
- Undertake an extensive qualitative and quantitative market research programme in the target source markets;
- Identify and assemble a highly attractive product offering tailored to the interests of each source market, and develop and implement on-going cost-effective promotion programmes in each source market in partnership with the States and the private sector of the tourism industry in India and the source markets. Of special importance is the formulation and implementation of a village tourism programme that would be primarily targeted at the domestic urban market in India but which could also attract the international market;
- Establish an effective and on-going market representation presence with the travel trade in each source market; and
- Establish an Internet portal in various languages to service the information, product description, and product sales requirements of the target market segments in each source market, and to connect these directly with the preferred suppliers.

CREATING AN INDIA TOURISM BRAND POSITION

In the international market, India requires a positioning statement that captures the essence of its tourism product to convey an "image" of the product to a potential consumer and which will become the India "brand". A good example of this positioning approach is Thailand's "Amazing Thailand" brand, Malaysia's "Malaysia, Truly Asia" brand, The Philippine's "Festival Islands" brand, and Egypt's "The Land of the Pharos" brand. These more or less powerful positioning statements serve to effectively differentiate each of these destination countries from their competitors, and provide an effective umbrella under which the whole marketing effort may be organized and implemented on a partnership basis. The India's positioning statement and branding should focus on what makes India unique and unmatched in the tourism world.

This is almost certainly related to its great competitive strength, *i.e.,* its ancient Vedic civilization with a cultural heritage that continues to live in a largely unchanging and vibrant manner even today, especially in its rural areas. In the domestic market, where the focus of interest is rural or village tourism, a different positioning statement is required. This has to be related to the concept of "returning to or rediscovering ones roots" in order to escape the complexities and pressures of India's cities for the calm green of the rural countryside and the simplicity of the traditional village. The development of a powerful positioning image and brand position for India in its international and domestic markets requires adequate research by a professional agency, and industry "buy in" if it is to be successful. This research is being undertaken.

MARKET RESEARCH

An extensive programme of market research in India's primary source markets is an essential first step to:

- Establish the present image of India as a destination in relation to its competitors;
- The ensemble of products likely to be of interest to the markets in each primary source country;
- Issues such as pricing, concerns about security, health, safety, and quality, basic information on how to arrange a trip to India including visa issuances, currency, and telecommunications, transportation services; and
- The influence of media, Internet portals, and the buying behaviour of the customer.

The results of this market research will help to guide the formulation and implementation of the overall marketing strategy, the formulation and implementation of product development and promotion strategies, and the indicators that should be used to measure the success of the strategies.

DIGITAL TECHNOLOGY FOR MARKETING

The Internet is having a greater impact on the marketing of travel and tourism than any technology since the invention of television. It has already established itself as a crucial channel via which tourism organizations can promote their destinations and products offered by their service providers.

The implications of the Internet and other growing interactive multi-media platforms are far reaching. India Tourism would be utilising both the Internet and the other emerging interactive technologies and capitalising on these new channels. The benefits to be gained include cost-effective global distribution and new opportunities for closer and eventually self-financing partnerships between public entities and private operators.

SUMMARY

India's tourism industry through the capacity of it's tourism resource, facilities and services and as yet relatively untapped market potential has considerable scope for expansion and development. The Tourism Policy elucidated above aims at setting-up a framework that will allow the various stakeholders to fully develop the potential of tourism and to harness this to the national development priorities.

3

Globalization and Tourism: The New Age

In recent years, reference to globalization in the academic and professional world is constant. The notable interdependence between economies and the trend towards greater similarity of lifestyles are two conventional points of reference in the globalization concept. Nevertheless, globalization, under other names, is not a new concept but rather an acceleration of trends that have been active for decades and even centuries. In fact, in the twentieth century, apart from technological advances and the political and social transformations of the past few decades, there had not been a great advance of this trend. It can even be said that financial and economic institutions in the second half of the nineteenth century were more internationalized than at the beginning of the twentieth century.

What is often understood as globalization comprises diverse economic, social and political phenomena. The intensification of commercial exchanges, marked by the progressive dismantling of protectionist barriers, the growing integration of financial markets, the presence of new industrialized countries and technological developments, especially in the area of know-how and information, are affecting both the national economies and the lifestyles of societies. All of this is creating the basis for a global system or organization, distinctly characterized by a high level of economic, socio-cultural and environmental interdependence. In the latter area, some authors have pointed to the problems caused by the global warming, pollution and the danger of nuclear war as factors which accelerate globalization. The development of these and other phenomena on a global scale clashes with the entrenched policies and institutions designed for national frameworks, as public policies, debated and occasionally agreed upon in international fora as they may be, still lack the global dimension. In this context, it is not remarkable that tourism activity is both the cause and effect of accelerated globalization. It is useful to point out three essential elements of contemporary tourism:

- The extension of tourism demand throughout the world: the increase in intra- and inter-regional travel - although many strata of the population are still travelling only locally or are strangers to tourism.

- Similarity of tourism demand: convergence of consumer preferences, tastes and lifestyles - although the type of travel is segmented.
- Concentration and similarity of tourism supply: expansion of distribution systems, business mergers, etc. - although new specialists agents are appearing on the scene.

To all of this it must added without doubt the impact of new technologies on tourism, which is even more significant than that of changes in consumer taste or in institutional structures. The traditional tourism resources, the comparative advantages (climate, landscape, culture, etc.), are becoming less and less important compared with other factors in tourism competitiveness. Information (or rather, the strategic management of information), intelligence (innovative capacity of teams within an organization) and knowledge (know-how, or a combination of technological skills, technology and organizational culture - *humanology*) now constitute new tourism resources and key factors in the competitiveness of tourism organizations (enterprises, destinations and institutions).

The major (most-visited) tourism destinations of the world are no longer the famous beaches or traditional cultural capitals, but rather man-made products, such as Orlando or Las Vegas. In fact, the greatest foreseeable competition in the medium term for the present tourism activity is not the appearance of new exotic resorts, but instead the massive use of the increasingly accessible and efficient information and communication technologies for new leisure products: virtual travel and experiences.

Tourism thus finds itself in a situation, which Kuhn (1962) would clearly define as a paradigm shift, and which is not casually related to or far from the globalization process of economy and society in general. The concept of a business paradigm, understood as a set of theories, values, attitudes, methods and instruments, rules and practices, is useful when analysing business strategy in given framework conditions. Thus, it is increasingly seen that, in recent decades, mass tourism business strategies (the Fordian Era of Tourism) - and especially profit-making through economies of scale and the consequent standardization of rigid tourism packages - are giving way to a new paradigm shaped by the segmentation of the new consumer demands, new technologies, new forms of business production and management and new framework conditions.

This new post-Fordian business paradigm in tourism, which Fayos-Solà (1994) called the *New Age of Tourism*, has repercussions on business strategy, and also very profound ones on the policy and even the organization of tourism administrations. The main objective of tourism policy is to improve the conditions under which tourism activity is carried out. In the Fordian era, increase in tourism activity required a quantitative type of action - which goal was maximizing the number of visitors. In this paradigm, the emphasis on attracting demand corresponded well to the then traditional type of economic policy, based on Keynesian mainstream thinking. Tourism receipts enhanced foreign currency earnings and the creation of employment, so that the success of this sectoral tourism policy allowed other economic policy objectives to be reached, especially those related to economic growth and full employment.

The Keynesian-style policies are based on handling the components of aggregate demand: consumption, investment, public expenditure and net exports (exports minus imports). In this intervention framework, tourism expenditure is considered as an item within exports. The income multiplier - *i.e.,* the mechanism which explains how an increase of the variables of aggregated demand (investment, public expenditure and exports) creates an increase in income which exceeds the initial effort - has constituted the central explanatory and justifying mechanism of demand policies.

The transmissions and leakages in the multiplier chain depend on the marginal propensity to consume (the part of each increment in income destined to consumption), on the marginal propensity to import, and the average tax rate. These last two elements constitute leakages in the Keynesian model: the greater these two elements are, the less the multiplier effect in the domestic economy is. Interior tourism expenditure (domestic plus incoming - traditionally considered under exports) favours the initial effort in the chain. Outgoing tourism expenditure (national less domestic - usually considered under imports) diminish, cancel or make this initial effort negative. The capacity of the national economy to supply the needs of tourism activity affects the marginal propensity to import, increasing or diminishing the final effect of income creation.

Within this theoretical framework we should emphasize how Keynesian-style economic policy makes full sense within a framework of nation-states, where the effects of these policies are highly predictable and controllable. However, this model lost validity after the financial and economic crises at the end of the 1970s, its theoretical base weakened by the difficulty of applying Keynesian formulas when facing wage-price spiralling inflation - stagflation - and a growing internation-alization of the economy.

The dismantling of international trade restrictions (tariffs, import duties, etc.) stimulated by the GATT strongly modified the preconceptions on marginal propensity to import. Imports have become less expensive and the previously described chain of induced consumption was easily channelled towards 'foreign' products. 'National' economic areas are now more receptive to foreign products. The leakages of the model described have increased considerably.

In addition, in international tourism markets the emergence of new destinations and products with competitive prices has been constant since these years, and is a strong threat to traditional destinations. With growing competition, it has been necessary to undertake the restructuring of traditional offers.

Within this setting, it is logical that tourism admini-strations since the 1980s have switched their emphasis to supply policies. The main aim of aggregated supply policies is to increase and improve the productive capacity of a country. Without abandoning supply policies, it is necessary to point out the change in perspective caused by this shift, since it was no longer only a question of creating internal or external demand, of improving demand conditions, of fostering their increase or moderation in accordance with the current economic cycle; or of tourism administrations concentrating on promotion.

From this time, the need to improve tourism production to meet with an ever growing competition was felt. This implied the dismantling of sub-sectors, enterprises and unproductive products, a greater research and development (R&D) effort in education and training, in the business quality clusters, in the infrastructure, public services and goods for the sector, etc.

This change, from a tourism policy based on demand to supply models, takes into consideration that the basic problem is not tourism demand, which will continue to grow according to all forecasts. Globalization and the increased competition in tourism markets after the 1980s has required a consistent improvement in the price/product-characteristics ratio, that is to say, a continuous striving towards quality and efficiency. The Spanish case provides a good example of the new approach to tourism policies, which prioritizes action on the quantity and, especially, quality of tourism supply, making available to businessmen the necessary mechanisms to increase competitiveness:

- Improving know-how by fostering R&D, tourism education and training, and information management;
- Diversifying the supply, with new products and destinations;
- Physical modernization of installations and infrastructure;
- Improving business clusters, encouraging action by ancillary businesses, associations and the *coopetition* (cooperation-competition) between private agents and the public sector;
- Improving promotion, with greater quality (responding to promotion needs of the actual, existing supply) and efficiency;
- Conservation and regeneration of tourism areas; and
- Improving horizontal (interdepartmental) and vertical (local-regional-state-intergovernmental) coordination of public administrations for tourism policy.

Globalization, governance and the nation-state: implications for national tourism policies As several authors have pointed out, the discussion on globalization often covers up highly ideological visions of the future; there is no true evidence that globalization has gone beyond the acceleration of political, economic and cultural internationalization processes which began in many cases centuries ago, and in any case, it does not appear to be totally just to use this concept to defend a radically anti-political vision of the world in the twenty-first century. It is obvious that the debate on globalization has rekindled extreme right and left ideological points of view. For the former, globalization will offer new hope (after the failure of the monetary experiences of the 1970s and 1980s) for a world where free trade, world capital markets and transnational organizations can fully use productive resources without the clumsy interference of governments.

For the radical left (also affected by the fall of state socialism and the anti-imperialist movements of past decades), globalization of capitalism indicates the uselessness of social-democratic style 'welfare' initiatives carried out at a national level. If we examine the general role of the state at present before defining its tourism policy functions, it is quite obvious that its capacities have been redefined. The *sovereignty*, exclusive control (excluding other authorities) of a territory no longer exists. The capacity to 'defend' its citizens from macro-conflicts has been questionable since the era of nuclear arms.

The claim to standardize and control culture within borders is also no longer justifiable; citizens of the world establish cultural affinities and links through means of communications that escape the control of nation-states and almost any censoring attempt. Finally, and this has been remarked previously, economic internationalization makes it practically impossible to carry out autonomous economic policies. But all this does not signify either the disappearance of the political role of nation-states, or a great change in international relations. Perhaps it should be recalled that in the first place the very sovereignty of states, as defined in the seventeenth and eighteenth centuries, has always depended on their international recognition. The guarantee of non-intervention by other states allowed the consolidation of sovereignty in the state itself.

Also, although nation-states have seen their capacity for exclusive control of a *territory* enormously diminished, what is true is that they still have a central role in the control of the *population* of this territory, taking into account that it is much less mobile than either information or economic flows. For this reason, it seems that the issue under debate is not the avowed disappearance or reduction to a minimum of the role of the nation-state in a 'globalized' world, but rather the question of governance in a more integrated society at world level and the role of governments in this society.

There is no doubt that the nation-states have a vital role in this process: they still possess a great deal of the power and, in any case, maintain the legitimacy of representing the populations that live within their frontiers; and beyond having an unquestionable role as 'local' suppliers of certain public goods in the world context, they are the natural interlocutors in intergovernmental organizations that can possibly make advances in the task of designing, proposing and maintaining standards (voluntary, agreed or legislated) for the functioning of international and/or global systems. Although there may be other protagonists in the creation of framework conditions - multinational companies for example - it does not seem that they can claim a greater representation of the world's citizens, and the authentic multinational nature of many companies - which in reality are strongly established in one of the developed regions of the world and also have operations and subsidiaries in other countries and regions - is questionable.

In any case, it seems evident that the *second generation* tasks, to which the introduction of this chapter refers - the creation and strengthening of responsible international and global institutions in charge of these framework conditions - will in great part depend on the collaboration between nation-states and other major protagonists on a world level. Within the area of tourism activity, and, as has been previously indicated, the transition from national policies almost exclusively quantitative in dimension (maximizing the number of tourists through promotion), to others stimulating competitiveness (quality and efficiency) in an international context, entails a change of traditional functions in the tourism public sector.

This change can be summarized as follows:

- First, the transition from a situation where the public sector owns and operates all types of tourism facilities and intervenes customarily in the direct provision of goods and services, to a role of coordinator of private and public actions in tourism.
- Second, the opening up of the goals and means of tourism policy, from an almost exclusive promotional content (generic advertising, trade missions and exhibits, publications, etc.), to a broad range of instruments to foster and facilitate the activities of tourism decision-makers.
- Finally, the evolution, from a philosophy of rigid regimentation of entrepreneurial activities, to deregulation and privatization of tourism.

This ties in well with the new role of the nation-state: international representation of populations (and enterprises) located within its frontiers, concordance of interests which are not always in agreement - through the stimulation of associative and cooperative activity - and the improvement of the quality of life within its territorial limits.The implications for the formulation of national tourism policies are clear:

- The objectives of these policies must refer to the creation of competitive frameworks on a local-regional-national scale which, by improving the conditions of the economic, social and environmental framework, achieve contributions of the tourism sector to the well-being of the citizens.
- Although the use of promotional instruments by tourism administrations (communication, publicity, etc.) continues to be requested by decision-makers in tourism, its importance is decreasing. On the other hand, the need to coordinate promotion with a wider range of instruments in tourism policy has become evident.

- The new public instruments for tourism development and management are not fundamentally different from those used in sectoral industrial policy. Essentially, they foster the competitiveness of existing tourism clusters and the adoption of strategies for success in international markets of emerging destinations or those which are in the process of restructuring.

Although a study of the budgets of national tourism administrations indicates that public expenditure in tourism is still greatly concentrated in promotional instruments, in the area of competitiveness and strategy there is a growing dedication to Porterian-type instruments.

Specifically, the new tourism policies of countries such as France, Spain, Italy, Germany, Canada, Australia and South Africa concur in the use of the following instruments:

Strengthening supply conditions:

- Human resource development in tourism. Education and training which is more in line with the short, medium and long-term needs of the tourism employers. Awareness of the need to anticipate the upsurge of new tourism professions and the continuous training of professionals in the sector.
- Fostering innovation and development (R&D) specifically for use by tourism enterprises. Awareness of the need to give priority to the R&D of tourism processes over the R&D directly applicable to products and services.
- Modernization of the productive plant, installations and infrastructure in tourism. Awareness of the need to make compatible the modernization of the supply of public and private goods and services, and to create lasting mechanisms to permanently (and not on a one-time basis) carry out this task.
- Impetus of diversification and specialization in tourism destinations, products and services, although taking into account that the competitive advantages are more easily achieved in the realm of tourism processes.
- Stimulus to the conservation of natural, cultural, urban or rural areas in which tourism is carried out, and of heritage sites sensitive to tourism use. Awareness that these areas form part of the consumer *tourism experience* and that there is no tourism product and destination quality without eco-tourism quality.
- Fostering a more even geographical distribution of tourism supply and demand, in support of other more generic objectives of public policy (*e.g.,* an incomes policy for farming in disadvantaged areas). This has to be tightly coordinated with the responsible regional and local governments.

Strengthening the business fabric:

- Fostering of associative and cooperative initiatives between tourism enterprises and destinations. Awareness of the need to cooperate and not only compete at the intra-cluster and inter-cluster level in the context of a national tourism policy.
- Stimulus to give tourism activities an adequate dimensional scope. Awareness that this dimensional scope depends on the nature of niche-markets and the (changing) state of available technology. New information and communication technologies allow for new solutions in this respect.
- Public and cooperative contributions to sectoral and sub-sectoral information management, useful for decision-making at the enterprise, sectoral association, *cluster*, tourism destination level or even at a macro-national level.
- Adaptation of the judicial and institutional framework to give confidence and greater efficiency to business decision-making. Awareness of the need to make this framework flexible so that it continuously adapts to rapidly changing circumstances.
- Contribution of the tourism administration and sectoral cooperation institutions to *strategic*decision-making, beyond considerations of short-or medium-term quality and efficiency and the search for excellence in established market niches.

Strengthening demand conditions:

- In the context of the Porterian paradox that a better informed, exigent and sophisticated demand favours competitiveness and strategic positioning of enterprises.
- Obtaining and disseminating market information on consumer groups typology and communication channels for this purpose.
- Improving the promotion policy, from an instrument based on passive information on the positive characteristics of products, destinations and cultural and environmental amenities, to a means of forming and modulating the expectations and even the perceptions of the clients.
- Support to marketing efforts of tourism enterprises and destinations. Awareness of the role of new technologies and stimulus to innovation in tourism marketing processes.
- Improving the tourism information milieu in which consumers, workers, enterprises and tourism administrations move. Awareness that the cost of obtaining this information for the individual decision-maker may be high and that it is therefore preferable to approach this matter as the provision of a public good.
- To strengthen tourism training and qualifications, not only within the business context, but also in that of the consumer and host societies.

- Protection of the consumer-tourist, improving the applicable standards and the inter-administrative coordination. Awareness that today's tourist demands a high degree of confidence in the quality of the product and in his personal safety as an essential condition to increasing his loyalty to tourism products, services and destinations.
- Integral management of tourism quality to increase the level of consumer satisfaction and the well-being of receiving societies. Awareness that it is essential to have existing client loyalty to be competitive in tourism destinations, and that this cannot be achieved only through aggressive commercial promotion aimed at new clients.

Strengthening of linked industries and services:

- Stimulus to the creation and adequate functioning of related industries and services in tourism clusters and destinations. Awareness of their relevance, both in the horizontal (complementary) and vertical (suppliers, sub-contractors and client companies) sense to achieve competitiveness.
- Coordination of public administrations concerned with tourism, both in the horizontal (departments within an administration) and vertical (local, regional and national administrations) sense. Awareness that the public administration in general (and not only the *tourism* departments of the same) constitutes part of this institutional and business milieu essential for competitiveness in tourism.
- Stimulus to the re-engineering of the macro-processes within the tourism clusters and destinations. Awareness that it is possible to achieve the necessary quality objectives by improving the efficiency of the optional useable processes. Re-engineering of public administrative processes and their coordination with the private sector, improving their quality and dedication to service, usually is an important part of this instrument.

THE ROLE OF INTERGOVERNMENTAL ORGANIZATIONS IN TOURISM

In spite of abundant references in professional and academic literature to globalization in tourism, the fact is that the tourism business fabric is mainly made of sub-sectors with a large number of medium, small and micro industries, often of a marked local character.

The most notable exceptions are the air transport sub-sector in itself and the existence of some large enterprises in the hospitality (hotel chains), travel agency (certain tour operators) and entertainment (macro theme parks) sub-sectors. In fact, though, one of the best-known business lobbies in the sector, the World Tourism and Travel Council (WTTC), which defines itself as comprising the chairpersons and highest executives (CEOs) of the largest companies in the world, has only seventy-five members. In addition, even when considering these large tourism enterprises, there is reason to question their status as *global* enterprises. Most frequently, they are strongly identified - by origin, business culture, major operations and decision-making strategies - with one of the countries of the G3 triad (North America, Europe and Japan), with their presence in other countries being as subsidiaries, franchises, etc.

For these reasons, it is difficult to agree with the statement that 'tourism is one of the most globalized industries'. The fact that many of the industry's clients have to cross borders to travel and that there are suppliers with products in several countries can grant it, at the most, a partially *international* character. According to WTO estimates, only one in ten tourist movements is international, while the rest are domestic. Thus, although international tourism demand is already more than 650 million trips annually and is growing at an accumulative yearly rate of 4.3 per cent, most travel takes place within world-regions (Europe, North America-Caribbean, East Asia-Pacific) and within national borders.

Additionally, tourism, unlike financial transactions or information flows, requires the physical transport of people, a characteristic which makes it highly controllable by the sovereignty, albeit residual, of nation-states. Thus, it seems reasonable to defend the premise that the tourism industry is still in a phase of international activity, although it is also true that tourism is, on the other hand, contributing to the worldwide dissemination of cultural and social habits, and is therefore in this regard, a *factor* in the globalization process.

However, the importance and growing expansion of international tourism, its contribution to the development of regions and countries, to income and employment creation, its status, which has already been mentioned, as a transmitter of cultural identity images, all justify the attention it has merited and still merits from institutions on a worldwide scale as well as the existence of an intergovernmental organization (WTO) specifically dedicated to international tourism policy. Neither an analysis, nor an exhaustive inventory of the international institutions, which have had or do have influence, either direct or indirect on tourism flows, is attempted here; the list is too long and the analysis complex. Many international organizations and agencies, from the OECD, with a tourism committee whose existence is now at risk, to the World Bank, have given attention to some of the most relevant functions of tourism activity.

The European Union, in 1989 for the first time, granted responsibility for tourism policy to a specific department - its General Directorate XXIII - although the budgetary provisions given to the tourism unit were always minimal and the main part of the European budget had a much stronger impact on tourism activity through the structural funds, programmes for innovations and training or, in the case of third world countries, through development aid programmes. Perhaps the most relevant issue, in the context of this chapter, is the substance of supranational intergovernmental action in tourism, *i.e., international tourism policy*, and the viability and pertinence of hypothetical global tourism policy.

Justification of an international tourism policy, apart from the arguments already indicated, is also based on the growing importance of the knowledge factor in the production of tourism services and *experiences*. Perhaps, somewhat paradoxically, the tourism industry, the origins of which tied it geographically to nature resources and/or historical or cultural heritage, has freed itself from these conditioning factors, to the extent where the most sought after tourism destinations at present are often totally artificial (man-made). The use of communication in tourism, often tied to the leisure-entertainment industry, has shaped new consumer needs and created a demand for new tourism destinations in a process where communication-entertainment (the film industry, computerized games, the internet, television, publishing, etc.) has created expectations in potential tourists which are later satisfied (theme parks, theme hotels, dramatized tourism experiences, etc.) with major contributions from information-communication technology and the entertainment industry.

It is in this context, where one can see a rapid tendency towards globalization in the tourism industry, standardizing supply and demand and freeing them from the confines of stationary cultural or natural realities, and making it almost indistinguishable from the leisure industry, advancing towards a future of *virtual experiences* that could easily escape the control of the sovereignty of states. What should the substance of a contemporary international tourism policy be, and in what direction should this policy move, taking account of the previously mentioned tendencies towards future globalization?

The first issue should, without doubt, be to identify the players in tourism policy. If the globalization of tourism is not considered to have already happened, there is still time and the opportunity to identify those players who are more desirable and those who are less so. There is also time to favour the most sensible future scenarios, seen from the perspective of the contribution of tourism to the well-being of citizens, and their participation in the decisions as to what type of well-being they truly desire. Far from accepting extreme positions on globalization - *i.e.,* that it is already determined, that the decision-making power of multinationals/transnationals is above that of the traditional sources of governance - it is possible to determine explicitly the current players, and possibly future ones, of governance in general and tourism policy in particular:

- *Regional and local administrations*: Although their area of competence falls within the framework of higher level administrations, they have the effective advantage of being close to the citizen and the entrepreneurial units. They constitute the ideal public players to implement sectoral policies, which can be decided on occasion within the local and regional context or coordinated with the administrations having a wider scope of action. In the democratic context they are validated by the vote of their citizens.

- *National administrations*: They still have a wide magnitude of sovereignty. On occasion, they have devolved part of this to regional and local administrations and/or relinquished part to institutions or administrations with an international mandate. In the democratic context, they are endorsed by the vote of their citizens and frequently discharge this representation within international institutions. The consequent limitations (free circulation of capital, elimination of tariffs, etc.) are accepted in view of the benefits expected from a better distribution of resources on an international/world scale, but other objectives of national economic policies can be in contradiction with this self-limitation.
- *Supranational administrations*: Their historical origin lies in commercial agreements. The European Union is the most significant experience in this sense. The size of this type of administration enables economic, social, environmental and sectoral policy objectives to be set, which are out of the reach of national administrations, and they can more successfully confront the undesirable aspects of the globalization process.
- Agreements between countries or even between blocks of countries (G3 or G7 type). These are established to confront specific problems (financial speculation, international crime, etc.) and sometimes lead to the creation of international legislation.
- International agencies and organizations created by a group of states to permanently handle specific issues arising from economic, social or environmental activities. In the field of tourism, the paradigmatic player in this category is the World Tourism Organization (WTO).

This final type of player is the one whose decisions on tourism policy are considered here, although the substance of the tourism policy which can evolve should be analysed within the context of other players in international governance. Non-governmental organizations (NGOs) and private sector businesses and institutions are excluded here as principal players in governance, since they lack democratic representation, although their important role as partners or associates in governance by the previously mentioned players is obvious.The instruments which are useful to the international organizations usually belong to one of the following categories:

- *Legislation*: Agreements with a judicial scope to standardize the laws of member states and even of other states which may join the initiative. These agreements are directed at remedying the non-extraterritoriality of national laws and/or the lack of international legislation and/or the lack of enforcing bodies.

- *Agreements without a judicial scope*: Aimed at eliminating or lessening the repercussions of frontier restrictions by creating a framework for greater security in international transactions. These agreements have a technological, economic, social and/or ethical content. They are generally enforced through specific mechanisms to penalize infractions.
- *Voluntary quality standards*: These are proposed without the need of previous consensus, at the initiative of the organization in question or by a group of member states. They propose a model for conduct with regard to technological, economic, sociological and/or ethical matters. They do not usually have authority to penalize, but are intended rather to oversee or coordinate. They are accepted voluntarily due to the added value they give in terms of promotional image, facilitation in communication with other players in the market, interspatial and inter-temporal measurements, etc.

Given the demonstrated difficulty in establishing and developing the tourism policy instruments indicated in the first two categories, it can be said that international organizations specialized in tourism, and concretely WTO, are showing a growing tendency to use voluntary quality standard instruments.

This signifies, without doubt, an advance over the previous situation, where the insistence to establish legal agreements, or even simply enforceable agreements, led to a general impasse given the inability to achieve consensus or wide majorities because of:

- The diverse economic, social, cultural and political situations of the member states;
- The frequently heterogeneous nature of the member state's representation in the organization: Departments of Foreign Affairs, of Commerce and Tourism, of Culture and Tourism, of the Economy (Tourism Department), of Industry and Tourism, of Tourism, etc.;
- The variable importance of departments of tourism and of tourism affairs within governments of member states, where on occasion they play a minor role;
- With regard to legislative instruments, the difficulty that departments with competence in tourism have to influence sufficiently the deliberations and decisions of the national legislative powers.

The instruments in the voluntary quality standards category can point to models, of varying types, for flexible and rapid action, which can be gradually adopted by member states and even as a global voluntary standard. These models can successfully bring added value to international markets, which are potentially global, and can be adapted to different national situations. Although the explicit adoption of a voluntary standard by a sovereign state facilitates its global establishment, this can be expedited, in the case of delay or a lack of will, if the standard is *de facto* adopted by the industry and/or citizens of the country in question. Furthermore, the standards proposed can also fail when their format is rejected or ignored by potential users.

Thus, in this context, it should be noted that the role of international organizations in tourism, and specifically that of WTO, is rapidly evolving, from the traditional one of a forum where countries meet, to that of serving as an information broker between the countries and of being responsible for carrying out economic development projects and giving specific assistance to countries, up to the present role of also serving as an institution where voluntary quality standards are created and implemented in such key areas of tourism as:

- The development of human resources for tourism - education, training, strategy, management and labour conditions;
- Statistical information;
- Market intelligence;
- Know-how in products, services and processes;
- Infrastructure, collective services and urban environments;
- Cultural and environmental aspects of tourism;
- Economic and social effects of tourism;
- Facilitation of international movements of travellers and tourists;
- Financing of tourism;
- Quality of products, services and tourism environments;
- Communication in tourism;
- Ethical aspects of tourism activity;
- Legislative processes and contents in tourism; and
- Coordination of administrations with competence in tourism - intra-administration, inter-administrations, and with the private sector.

The content of the tourism policy instruments being used in contemporary action is justified by the two major reasons for the existence of international organizations specialized in tourism (and that of the WTO itself):

- International and global public goods, externalities, market imperfections and merit and demerit goods.

To analyse the contemporary scope of this justification it must be realized that the foundations - *i.e.,* the so-called resources - of tourism activity are rapidly changing.

In principle, as has already been indicated, cultural and natural resources were those backing tourism development. The addition of financial capital and work efforts to these resources created tourism products. The comparative advantages of tourism destinations were based on the abundance and correct combination of these elements.

At present, the relevance of natural and cultural resources has diminished - except for world-class resources and in specialized niche markets - while the importance of financial capital and above all that of information, intelligence-creativity and know-how - used by human teams in business and organizational cultures prepared for competiveness and strategic success - has increased.

Given these circumstances, the role of international organizations specializing in tourism is clear:

- The provision of public goods which previously were the domain of the states, such as quality education and training, strategic information and basic know-how;
- The internalization of externalities in the planetary context, such as the costs of pollution or possible climate changes;
- The correction of imperfections in international markets such as the costs of information or the appearance of highly monopolized tourism operations; and
- The introduction of ethical criteria in carrying out tourism activity on an international scale (working conditions in tourism, sexual exploitation in tourism and the like).

This first justification of the activity of WTO or other international organizations clearly shows the differences between intergovernmental agencies or organizations - created by and responsible to a (large) group of states, and occupied with international governance - and other international organizations (such as NGOs, motivated by more specific aims), international business lobbies or large enterprises, whose objectives differ from, and on occasion are in conflict with, those mentioned above.

- The benefit to member states of exercising their sovereignty in optimal conditions and of supplementing it when it is questioned or proves inefficient in the globalization process.

This is where the traditional role of international organizations is evolving towards greater technical contents, which give depth and relevance to the member states' fora of discussion. Without assuming a conceptual breach with this traditional role, it is obvious that the use of a voluntary standard type of instruments, already mentioned above, gives greater flexibility and scope to the resolutions discussed and adopted in these fora, which are later subjected to a validation process - through an appraisal of their value in the market and society and their acceptance or not by businesses, institutions and the citizen.

The acceptance and establishment of these standards, when it takes place, represents a real step towards international and global governance for:

- It makes it possible to have truly global rules (standards), backed by states, which are more representative than businesses or other types of organizations;
- This acceptance happens only when the standards create added value for a large enough number of social and economic players;
- It reinforces the role of the organizations creating and overseeing these standards as well as the capacity of such organizations to adapt them to changing circumstances with greater democratic legitimacy.

Although the concept of globalization is broadly used in academic and professional literature, its exact definition, its measurement and its effects are far from being clear. The mere reference to phenomena affecting the world is still conceptually weak and cannot be used as evidence of globalization without being qualified. Economic, technological or cultural internationalization processes are not new, and their present acceleration does not imply that globalization is inexorable. Historically these processes have stopped and reversed several times.

It is also not evident that these processes and their future culmination in globalization imply the disappearance or impotence of the sovereignty of nation-states. This assumption on occasion responds to a highly ideological view of world society. States still have mechanisms to control large enterprises and to create new instruments for governance, guaranteeing democratic control of future scenarios compatible with the well-being of a majority of the citizens. Multinational/transnational enterprises are not necessarily global, since their cultural and strategic bases and the greater part of their business volume are generally found in only a few countries, normally located in the area of the G3 (North America, Europe or Japan).

The phenomena related to globalization affect tourism differently, depending on whether demand or supply are being considered. Demand shows clearer globalization tendencies as consumer preferences and expectatives converge, even though the *type* of holidays sought is becoming more diverse. On the other hand, tourism supply is still far from being global; thus, multinationals in tourism have not permeated the markets, with a few exceptions such as airlines, and hotel chains. The business fabric in almost all tourism sub-sectors is formed by hundreds of thousands of small and micro enterprises. In addition, international tourism, although significant and rapidly growing, only represents a minor part of the total volume of the tourism business, in the most part domestic. As tourism implies the physical movement of people, the capacity of the states to exercise their sovereignty in this activity is obvious.

National tourism policy will remain a key factor in the development of tourism in a majority of countries for at least the next decade, although devolution to regional and local governments may change its role in some areas. The importance of tourism and its economic, social and environmental implications, which affect governance and broader scope economic policy, speak in favour of establishing explicit national tourism policy frameworks. This sectoral policy may then be implemented by regional and local administration, which is closer to concrete tourism destinations and business clusters. The question is therefore one of reassigning tasks and it does not imply the automatic weakening of national tourism administrations. The substance of tourism policy in key countries has been broadly in line with other economic sectoral interventions, particularly industrial policy. Emphasis has shifted, from almost exclusive concern with promotion, to a wider range of instruments acting on productive conditions as well. However, the specific characteristics of tourism supply ask for special attention being put in certain elements of competitiveness.

The comparative advantages (natural and cultural resources) which used to be the base for the success of tourism destinations are giving way to *competitive* advantages in a new business paradigm (the New Age of Tourism) where information, inteligence and know-how play a vital role.

These national tourism policies increasingly have a central theme: the use of Porterian style instruments to foster the competitiveness of tourism clusters (destinations, sub-sectors and/or groups of enterprises).

These instruments belong to one or several of the following types:

- Strengthening the supply conditions;
- Strengthening the business fabric;
- Strengthening the demand conditions;
- Strengthening of linked industries and services.

Even though it may be premature thinking of tourism as an already globalized activity, the importance and expansion of international tourism does justify the treatment of tourism matters in international-scope organizations and the existence of an intergovernmental institution (the WTO) specifically dedicated to international tourism policy.

The work programme of any intergovernmental institution committed to tourism, and, in particular, that of WTO, must respond to two types of rationale:

- The importance in tourism of international and global public goods, externalities, market imperfections and merit and demerit goods; and
- The benefit to member states of exercising their sovereignty in optimal conditions and of supplementing it when it is questioned or proves inefficient in the globalization process.

When in this context, tourism policy implemented by an intergovernmental organization represents a real step towards international and global governance. International legislation or enforceable agreements are rather rigid instruments for international tourism policy. The evolution of national tourism policies - towards deregulation, privatization and a role coordinating public-private partnerships - leads the way to a more participative and less coercive kind of tourism policy. The preferred type of instruments of such a policy is found in the realm of voluntary standards of quality; they can be very flexibly adopted by countries, destinations or the industry. These types of instruments adapt best to the difficulties found in developing international tourism policy given:

- The heterogeneous nature of government departments competent in tourism;
- The diverse economic, social, cultural and political conditions in nation-states;

- The variable importance of departments of tourism within governments of nation-states, where on occasion they play a minor role; and
- The difficulty that departments with competence in tourism have to sufficiently influence the deliberations and decisions of the national legislative powers.

The threats and opportunities characterizing the internationalization and globalization processes in contemporary society require, in tourism as well, responses beyond *ad hoc* legislation, treaties or agreements. International and global matters need international and global *institutions*. The liberalization of trade and tourism, the removal of obstacles and the consequent improvement in the allocation of resources make for big improvements in the well-being of the peoples of the world.

However, it is important to pay attention to the *actors* of the globalization processes. Multinational/transnational companies and non-governmental organizations are without doubt very relevant decision-makers in the new realities - but they cannot play the leading role in representative governance, which is a question of increasing concern at world level. Tourism, because of its importance in the development of regions and countries and its capacity to convey images of cultural identity - so deeply needed in the configuration of global society - requires international and global *representative* organizations, to play a key role in world governance.

INFORMATION TECHNIQUES IN TOURISM

World renowned space scientist, Mr. Arthur C. Clarke, addressing the first meeting of the inter-governmental Council of the international programme for the development of communication in Paris in the year 1981, said, "In many ways and for many purposes, printed matter-books, newspapers and wallpapers will always be the best and the cheapest form of communication. But now electronics has given us tools that can perform miracles impossible to the printed word and which, of course, can reach millions who are unable to read. The newest and most powerful of these communication devices depend upon pace technology, a fact that is not generally recognised."

What Mr. Arthur C. Clarke had said almost a decade ago may seem to be a history as so much has been done in so little a time that one really wonders about the various changes that have taken place since then. In fact there has been a revolution in the various techniques in the field of information. The electronics have performed miracles in the last decade. Today we find ourselves in the middle of a new era, an era of information revolution. New techniques of data processings, mainly transmission of data and telecommunication, have already formed a new field of activity characterised by an enormous potential for growth. These developments have greatly facilitated rational management of the business world. Telecommunication devises are in use today in almost all fields of economy. Be it in industry, agriculture, medicine, travel or any other field these telecommunication devises are extensively used for the benefit of both the industry as well as the consumer. In this information revolution the new means of public telecommunication such as telex, telecopy or videotex have given a very tough competition to pioneer public communication means like newspapers, magazines, etc. At the same time, however, the new communication-means also offer great possibilities for improvement, rationalization and the expansion of the existing facilities for data collection and transmission.

NEW INFORMATION TECHNIQUES

The modern mass media techniques are as follows:

- Satellite Television
- Cable Television
- Videotex (in the framework of transmissions from individual television stations)

Since the above means ate very widespread ad they are very important. However, because of their wider coverage and their technical methods of transmission, they have one shortcoming. The short coming is that they cannot be directed to one specific person. In addition the person receiving the information is only partially informed. The receiver of the information also cannot start a dialogue or communicate. On the other hand, unlike the mass media, the following means give the possibility of direct transmission of information:

- Teletex
- Telecopy
- Telebox
- Videotex
- Telefax

Teletex

Teletex is an improvement over telex and has in fact developed from it The receiver for teletex is an electronic "typewriter, which can send electronically enriched "letters" to owners of Ordinary telex equipment. The transmission of message time is usually shorter in comparison with time taken with telex. Besides, it is also possible to transmit more office typewriter symbols. A normal electronic typewriter can be used as a receiver for teletex.

Telecopy

Telecopy provides the possibility of exchanging photocopies through a data network. Information in the form of either written document or technical drawing is remote copied. This means that two facilities for copying are connected. One at the sender's end and the other at the receiver's end. Transmission time is only a few minutes.

Videotex

Videotex occupies a special Position among the "new media". It plays a key role in the link between telecommunication and the computer sciences. It's advantages lie in the possibility it provides for linking computers, and also in its interactive dialogue capabilities. Using videotex, information and communication systems can be converted into interactive systems capable of communicating with one another. In fact, videotex is a multipurpose instrument with multiplicity of uses.

It serves as:

- An instrument for data processing
- An information medium
- An organizational aid
- A communication system, and
- A marketing instrument

This relatively new service connects various forms of use of the above-mentioned facilities and at the same time offers some other possibilities. To operate the service, a television set with a decoder and telephone is necessary without which the service cannot operate. In Europe, nearly all the households have television sets and a telephone and with the help of videotex. Separate households can be reached in large areas. Members of German BTX service as well as Members of France Telecom Service can now obtain all kinds of information from external computers Or use data bank all through their television sets. In many other countries in Europe, USA, etc., similar systems are in use. The use of videotex (VTX) is prevalent today in many fields. In addition to its use in the field of business because it allows fast message transmission, fast and inexpensive data collection and up-to-date information which are crucial for advertising, the system is also used by specialised groups of users for collecting orders in the field. It is also used in the field of tourism as a one-way system, for receiving bookings. Because of its low unit costs, it is used extensively mainly in connection with personal computers. It has been found that videotex (VTX) is the most advantageous means of communication, taking into account its low cost and the wider range of its application.

Telefax

Telebox is an electronic post office box system. Each member of the system has his or her "post office box" in the computer, where other members can leave their message. The owner of each box can electronically contact the others. All the above means discussed permit the exchange of information electronically through a data "network". The exchange of information between the members with the assistance of electronic transmission is very fast. The data are also available in written form in printouts. "Network" is a system of transmission linking facilities for automatic data processing. In this way different computers are connected, permitting data exchange and processing over long distances. Telecommunication is possible only when there is such a network available. Telephone is the simplest and the best known network.

In addition there is also a separate clear data network for the exchange of data which works digitally. In this way a high transmission speed is achieved and there is a very low ratio of errors during transmission. There are different types of networks which can be used for telecommunication purposes either separately or combined,. Text on the screen is provided by telephone network or any other network. Communication with other members or computers in any place by anyone can be achieved by combining the telephone network with additional facilities provided. The new communication techniques discussed above are extensively used today by a large number of enterprises as well as individuals. In tourism, in addition to travel agents, tour operators, hoteliers, airlines, travel journalists, etc. use these techniques.

Journalists who especially travel extensively use the following facilities:

- Telecopy (for sending previously prepared texts as originals)
- Teletex (for collecting and sending texts)
- Data banks (for collecting information).

The use of telecommunication techniques offers basic facilities and advantages in the following areas of work:

- Collection of information
- Processing of information, and
- Transmission of information.

The data bank is like a "master book" in which mass of books, newspapers, and materials from different meetings and all kinds of published work are stored. All the relevant information can be collected in no time by means of electronic data bank Collecting the same information from a book and a visit to a library would be time consuming and rather expensive. The journalist seeking information on any subject for an article on tourism can order the articles which are of interest to him, though the record room of his own editorial office, or directly through the data bank and these are recorded on the screen. He can also acquire a article through a directly connected printing machine. In this way, in a matter of minutes, he can finish his search and the collection of data for his article. A lot of time and expenditure is saved.

Processing of Information. Information processing is an original and most crucial part of a journalist's work. A journalist has to evaluate collected information, combine the same with his new ideas and summaries the same in the compact from of an article. As can be done only to a limited extent by means of telecommunication devices. For collecting data, the personal computer can offer, new applications without much difficulty, a journalist can process articles collected with the help of electronics. The wordings of an article or the get-up can be changed as often as a journalist desires and it can be transmitted easily.

Transmission of Information. When the article is prepared on the basis of collected data, the same is to be transmitted to the editorial office or directly to the printers in their office. Journalist can do this personally by a telephone call or in a written form. But the quickest and simplest method is to transmit the information with the assistance of telecommunication devices. If the article is written in the normal way on a typewriter, then it can reach the editorial office in no time if the journalist uses telecopy facilities. The process of writing can be speeded up if the article-is written using a personal computer as this will not require additional printing. The article then can be transmitted directly to the computer available in the printing office.

Use of Computer Technology

The computer technology has made its entry in the field of tourism in a big way. In fact, computers are in use in some way or other in various branches of tourism since the early sixties. Be it a travel agency, hotels, airlines or recently the railways, computers have played a key role in making thc task of providers of travel services an easy affair. Not only this, through home terminals, computers, is undertaking among other Jobs the planning of vacations for an individual and his family. Let us first of all understand the meaning of a computer.

Computer. A computer is a managerial tool capable of processing large amounts of data rapidly. A computer can perform arithmetic functions (addition, subtraction, division, and multiplication) and logical operations (sorting and ranking and assembling) in a fraction of a second. It dispenses results in a large variety of formats. The computers are capable of repeating programmed instructions almost endlessly without error, and maintaining a vast data base of stored information. The computer can be put too great number of uses in the day-to-day activities of human endeavor. In the travel industry, computers are extensively used today and they perform innumerable functions. The principal users of computers are:

- Airlines
- Hotels
- Travel Agents
- Railways

Computers in Airlines. The sudden growth about thirty years ago in the global travel meant a huge pressure on the existing handling of air traffic, especially the passenger traffic for the airlines. It was then that need was felt to computerise passenger reservation systems in major airlines. Growth patterns in passenger traffic had begun to indicate that handling reservations manually could not be sustained long without affecting the efficiency in the customer service. It was in the early 1960s, that IBM took the initiative and developed a computerised reservation system known as Programmed Airlines Reservation System, PARS. The system was not developed for or with any one airline. It was designed as an all-purpose software package that would fit the requirements of any domestic airline. The system was designed around IBM's new hardware range system 360, which was later to revolutionise the entire computer industry. Continental Airline was the first United States Airlines to use, the PARS System in the year 1967. Most major US airlines followed and used the system making PARS, a most successful software product of the time. It was an achievement for the IBM. The system was later expanded to meet the needs of several other airlines outside the United States of America resulting in the creation of International Programmed Airlines Reservation System, IPARS. Initially this system was a joint venture between IBM and British Overseas Airways Corporation, BOAC, and aimed at adapting PARS to the needs of airlines that had mainly international operations. In the following years many airlines adopted the system.

The international package became almost as much of a standard as PARS. Although many airlines modified the system extensively, PARS was at the base of most international airlines system. By the late 1960s, however, it became obvious that the system was too costly for smaller international airlines. These airlines developed their own IBM oriented reservation systems in early 1970s. The system developed was known as CPARS (C for Compact). This system was followed by a system known as Univac Standard Airline System, USAS. With the passing of the years more and more systems developed incorporating more functions to enable the airlines to have more transactions and instructions. The popularity of any system to a large extent also depends its coverage and online reservation network. The number of terminals which a system has is also an important consideration. The more the terminals a system has, the larger will be the online reservation network. The number of reservation transactions carried out by a system in a given time is yet another important aspect to be considered by an airline before using a system. To sum up the following main aspects are important to make a system perfect and universally acceptable:

- Number of reservation transaction to be handled
- Data links with other airlines
- Number of terminals
- Information processing capacity
- Data volume capacity

Recently a major advance has been made, in the airline reservation system in West Germany. A computer system capable of carrying out as many as 1000 reservation transactions every second, involving data links with 28 airlines, a host of car hire agencies and hotels and about 20,000 travel agencies in Europe alone has been set up at Erding in the Southern part of Germany. The system known as "Amadeus", has been developed jointly at a cost of DM 350 million by four airlines, Air France, Iberia, SAS and Lufthansa. The information processing capacity of the mainframe IBM and Unisys computers installed at Erding, the world's largest computer centre, involves a data volume equivalent to a library of 3,50,000 books.

Computer in Cargo. Most of the airlines are now using computers for cargo handling operations as well. The handling of cargo shipments on ground is a costly affair and the cost has been increasing over the year. Almost 50 per cent of the handling of cargo, shipment reflects the cost of manual information processing. Freight rate increases have not kept pace with cost increases, so airlines had either to accept reduced margins or take steps to reduce overheads. Computerization of cargo has helped reduce costs as this speeds up the handling of information related to consignments and also reduces the time the cargo spends on the ground. The pioneer in cargo computerization was Alitalia, whose PO 4-cargo system was adopted and modified by many major airlines, such as Swissair, TWA and British Airways. Univac's USA has a fully developed cargo module. Almost all major airlines in the world have now adopted one or another system of cargo computerization. To sum up, computerization in airlines has the following major advantages.

- High profile applications like reservations
- Applications of departure, control and cargo
- Accounting and budgeting,
- Forecasting and planning
- Engineering management
- Revenue accounting
- Fare construction and fare quotations
- Ticket printing
- Crew scheduling
- Crew management; and
- Yield optimization

In addition to the above, airlines have several other advantages from the use of computers. Each airline is developing its own system to suit its requirements. In addition to the airlines, the computer industry itself has also benefited a lot with the introduction of computerization in the airlines. The computer industry in general has directed considerable attention to the lucrative airline market and has reaped the profits. Hardware manufacturers saw the potential and produced special airlines terminals to meet their needs.

SITA. The role of SITA, 'Societe International de Tele Communications Aeronautiques' in airlines automation has been very crucial. Automation is the key to achieving a higher level of productivity in any industry, especially in the airlines industry and automation of airline functions will continue with more emphasis being put towards achieving short term benefits. SITA is responsible for providing Data Processing Services. In fact, SITA is the major supplier of information handling services for the airline industry. SITA's aims are to foster efficient telecommunications, data processing and transmission means for all categories of information required in the operation of air transport enterprises with the specific aim of promoting safe and regular air transport in all countries. There has always been a continued high growth of demand for the services offered by SITA. SITA provides data processing services in the following areas.

- Passenger Reservations
- Departure Control
- Meteorological Data
- Volcanic Ash Reports
- Credit Authorization and Document Verification
- Baggage Tracing (BAGTRAQ)
- Share Cargo Service
- Shared Flight Operations Data Base
- Flight Planning
- Baggage Handling and management Service
- Common Customs Interface System
- Fuel Management
- Airline Schedules and Flight Availability Data Base
- IATA Passenger Tariff Conference Support

From the above, it is observed that SITA is providing a valuable service to the airlines. Almost all the information required in the operation of air transport in the world is being provided to the airlines industry. The range of services offered by SITA is very extensive and new services are being added as and when these are required.

Computers in Hotels. The computer technology has entered the hotel industry in a big way. A hotel's most crucial internal resource is information and with the use of computers the information is available in a way that saves labour and ultimately increases the profits. Although computers in the hotel industry started being used as far back as in the late 1960s, it was only in the 1970s that the technological advances in the computer technology made possible the right combination of compactness and versatility for different sizes of hotels. The lower cost encouraged many individual hotels to install the system. Today computers are installed in large numbers and are widely accepted in the hotel industry. One of the most important factors for its large scale acceptance in the industry has been its reliability. The computer system has been found to be very reliable in the dissemination of the right kind of information at a push of the button. Hotel Industry today is a major market for the computer manufacturers and the software vendors. It has been increasingly realized that the hotel computer systems achieve better internal and external control and, through the use of analysis methods, provide the opportunity to improve the overall profitability of the unit. Like in the airlines, the computers offer substantial advantages for reservation systems in terms of speed and accuracy. The errors are almost negligible.

Application Areas. Hotel systems all over the world have traditionally been divided into the following two main areas:

- Front Office Application Areas.
- Back Office Application Areas.

Front Office Application Areas incorporate the following:

- Reservations
- Registration
- Guest accounting
- Night auditing
- Communication operations (telephones, telex, fax

Back Office Application Areas incorporate the following:

- Financial management
- Inventory control systems accounts
- Profit/loss accounts
- General ledger
- Credit card verifications.

The computer system streamlines the functioning of all the above areas in a hotel set-up. It helps in the smooth functioning of the hotel, better guest relations, increased efficiency of staff and the overall profitability of the hotel. The key to successful operation of a hotel lies in the information system with the introduction of computers in the hotel the information system has become more accurate and efficient. The guest has an access to the required information with push button convenience.

Since the computer is used as a communication medium, there is better coordination between various departments. The computer has relieved the staff of many routine jobs enabling them to devote more time and attention to the needs of the guests. The computers have made guest accounting systems more sophisticated and reliable. It automatically collects and calculates agents receipts and payments and consolidates and verifies credit card payments and cash controls.

The sales outlets like restaurants automatically record the guest's expenditure at the point of sale, while direct electronic links to the telephone system in the guest rooms can monitor guest calls for instant charging to their accounts. The computers have eliminated cumbersome accounting machines often seen at the cashier's desk giving a front office system a modern and sophisticated look, resulting in greater guest satisfaction and adding to the prestige of a hotel. Back office systems have a large number of areas having great potential for cost control where computers are used to a great advantage for the hotel. With the use of computers, management can, monitor the progress of individual restaurants and other sales outlets against targets and budgets which may be set for various items. Daily reports on inventory usage become available by way of organizing input from each centre collected at regular intervals throughout the day.

Computer Terminals. Modern day business traveller is increasingly getting used to have a computer in his hotel room. In fact, many such business travellers in countries like USA, Belgium, Holland, France, Germany, Japan, Canada and many other countries are enquiring before booking a room as to whether guest rooms where they are planning to stay have an in room computer terminal. The computer has thus entered the guest room of many hotels in the west and has become the latest novelty of a luxury hotel.

A number of individual hotels as well as hotel chains have introduced in-room terminals that are hooked by television and telephone into a data system that includes official airline guides, news agencies, stock market agencies, weather bureaus, shopping services, travel, club, entertainment guide, electronic games and even job listing features. Access to the computer terminal is gained by the guest by way of punching a credit card number which is charged for their time at the terminals on sliding rates roughly equivalent to those for long distance telephone calls. Computer systems in hotels have, in fact, revolutionised the hotel information systems resulting in ever increasing satisfaction for the guests and profitability for the management.

Computers in Travel Agency. As compared to the airlines and hotels, travel agents have rather been slow to computerise their operations. It was in the year 1983 Thomson Holidays first used computers. With the success of Thomson's Top (Thomson Open-line Programme) in introducing reservations via Prestel several more big tour operators introduced similar systems to sell their 1984 summer programmes. A Prestel set allows travel agents to make reservations with as many principals as agree to it. The videotex technology which allows tour operators to open reservations through Prestel sets is applied to airlines through British Telecom's Skytrack.

Today there are several airlines whose reservations are now open to Skytrack. Skytrack, an automated airline reservations system, enables travel agents to make booking on hundreds of world's airlines, using a standard Prestel television set and a keyboard. Prestel is being used for the basics required in the travel industry finding out airline schedules and fares, making reservations and getting information on a tour operator's holiday packages. The advantage of the system over travel books and brochures is that information is automatically updated and only flights or packages that are available are shown. Today many new systems have been developed which are being used by the travel agents and tour operators the world over. The advantages which the use of computers has given to agents are far more than the investments made in installing and using a system. Such advantages as knowing the availability of airline and railway reservations, hotel accommodation, amendments and cancellations, processing of documents such tickets, processing, account and management information etc., immediately just by pushing a button has proved to be a boom to the travel industry.

Videotex System. Videotex system has been a great help to travel agents and tour Operators in their functioning. The system invented by British Telecom is a way of providing computerised information without expense of supplying a computer terminal. All that is required is a telephone line and a standard colour television receiver with an adapter to link it to a keyboard and a decoder.

Videotex provides efficient, low cost information and reservation facilities which allows direct communications between agents and principals throughout the industry. Information is transmitted quickly and accurately via ordinary telephone lines to be visually displayed on a television type screen. At the touch of a button it displays information on holiday packages, airfares, accommodations, cruises, car rentals, insurance, and many other travel-related services.

Videotex system provides the following services to the travel agents/ four operators:

- Fast and efficient means of obtaining accurate, up-to-date information on every aspect of the travel industry with excellent visual capacity
- Direct access to the information supplied by industry principals, thereby speeding up transactions and increasing both the efficiency of selling and the quality of customer service.
- Information on new product developments, fare changes, special offers and any other information put into the system
- Display of tour itineraries, graphic illustrations of hotels, resorts and tourist attractions by selling staff.

Other videotex system benefits to users include:

- *Key word:* Immediate access to a specific piece of information
- *Increased sales:* More sale conversations due to immediate access of information
- *Increased productivity:* More efficient customers servicing
- *Cost efficient:* Reduced costs due to greater efficiency of communication
- *Up-to-date information:* Continued access to an entire library of travel-related information

The various systems in operation in travel agencies and tour operating companies have made a world of difference in their operations. In addition to the supply of immediate instant information the systems are also designed to supply printouts of itineraries, ticket vouchers, flight manifests, confirmations and a host of other relevant documents for both the customers as well as principals.

Computers in Railways. Railway systems in Europe and some other countries have now been using computers extensively. In countries like France, Germany and Belgium, to name a few, computers have been in use for over a decade. The most important use of computers in railways, however, is in the area of ticket reservation. The information regarding availability of seats is now available instantly in various networks.

In addition to the use of computers by railway retail agents, travel agents and tour operators, these are also being used directly by the railway systems. Railway systems use the computers for route planning, engineering, accounting, inventory planning and control, purchase and a host of other functions. The most remarkable use of computer in railways has, however, been made by France.

The metro system in Paris is one of the best in the world. France has been making great advances in the technology in its metro system. The latest technological marvel has been achieved beneath the surface of the earth through a concrete cylinder. No one on board is at the controls because there are no controls on board. Instead the sleek good-looking aluminium and steel train is being guided by a computer from a distant command centre. Moving at 100 kilometers an hour the train suddenly stops as soon as bright lights appear ahead. Glass doors slide open and the passengers step on an immaculate platform awash in filtered daylight tastefully decorated with mosaics and sculptures.

4

Tourism and Economic Development

This chapter seeks to introduce some of the important concepts and concerns associated with expanding the economic benefits of tourism through investment in infrastructure. It is adapted from previous work by the author and colleagues, and was presented in part in a World Tourism Organization publication. There is growing recognition that innovative approaches must be adopted in order to maintain the economic health of many countries, communities and regions. While conditions vary from region to region, tourism has been seen as an important form of economic development. It has also been promoted as a somewhat benign agent of economic and social change, a promulgator of peace through interaction and dialogue, and a service-based industry capable of creating employment and income.

The perception that tourism has only positive economic benefits has lessened in recent years, due to the growing awareness and knowledge of the more intangible and indirect economic costs of tourism. While it can be argued that tourism does offer an important alternative form of economic activity, it must be seen as only one component of a larger series of development initiatives within any economic system. That is not to say that tourism in selected circumstances cannot be the major source of income and jobs in a community or region, but rather that the impact and role of tourism will vary from region to region.

Experience has shown that tourism may take many forms and meet a number of tourist motivations. Experience has also shown that destinations can rise and fall in popularity, driven by various factors in the destination's internal and external environment. A destination that is entirely dependent on tourism is much more vulnerable to these shifts than an economy that is well diversified and has tourism as just one of its industries.

THE ECONOMICS OF TOURISM

In a tourism context, the economics of tourism has been defined by one writer as being. The concerned with the use of scare resource, labour, capital, land, and environmental resources, to produce the product, tourism, and with the distribution of this product between different.

It should be noted that in this definition, environmental resources are differentiated as a separate resource (rather than included as part of the 'land' resource.) In so doing, the underlying critical importance to the tourism product of the environment in terms of air and water quality and the aesthetic beauty of nature and the landscape is recognised.

Indeed, Bull (1995) argues that the basis for tourism lies in building upon these 'free' resources (or 'renewable resources' as they are sometimes termed), with a mixture of public sector and private sector resources. These free resources, together with the other scarce resources, are combined to form what most tourists perceive as the tourist 'product' they consume and which suppliers produce. As Bull (1995) points out, in today's world there are few truly free resources since any human activity makes demands on the world's resources and, as a consequence, ultimately someone will have to pay a price. All the resources have competing demands made upon them so that, if they are used for one form of development, they cannot be used in others ways. For example, a large flat land coastal area might be suitable for the development of a resort area for tourism or as a site for heavy industry.

If tourism is chosen ahead of heavy industry, an opportunity to develop heavy industry on this site has been lost and the cost of this choice is known as the 'opportunity cost', which represents the potential economic returns that are being given up in favour of developing tourism.

Economics, then, can be viewed at two levels. The *micro* level considers individual business and consumers and the *macro* level considers the economy as a whole in a particular area or in relation to the national or international economy. *Microeconomics* in tourism is therefore, concerned with how economic decisions are reached at the level of the individual tourism business or the individual tourism consumer. Key questions to consider include:

- What makes consumers decide which tourism products they are going to buy, and in what quantities?
- How do specific tourism businesses, decide with tourism products are going to be sold and distributed to consumers and in what quantities?
- How are the market prices for buying and selling tourism products arrived at?

Microeconomics in tourism is concerned with the study of the total (usually termed aggregate) effects of economic phenomena affecting the local, national or international economy. Key questions include:

- What factors determine the level of aggregate tourist spending?
- What is aggregate economic effect of tourism on the economy through the so-called 'multiplier' effect?
- In this chapter we will consider some of these questions first at the micro level and thereafter at the macro level.

ECONOMIC CHOICES

The cornerstone of economic analysis at the micro level is the consideration of supply and demand and the interaction between them. Every individual demands goods and services (products) and, when all these demands are put together, the resulting aggregate demand is what the industry must supply if all consumers are to achieve satisfaction.

The interaction of the forces of supply and demand determine the price of a product. Products have a price because they are useful (or have *utility* to use the economists' jargon), and because they are scarce. Their usefulness is shown by the fact that consumers demand them and scarcity is revealed by the unwillingness of firms of provide unlimited amounts of a product. Neither demand nor supply are static but vary with changing condition. Furthermore, the nature of demand and supply will vary according to the nature of the product in question. Before going on to consider the nature of demand and supply in tourism, it is necessary to consider briefly where the interaction of these forces takes places in a market. Markets are situations where buyers and sellers of products come together in order to exchange. To an economist, the term 'market' does not represent the geographical place where buyers and sellers meet buy instead, refers to all those buyers and sellers who exert an influence on the price of a product. Some markets are worldwide, such as the markets for oil, gold or foreign exchange, whereas others are more localised, such as the markets for holidays or transportation.

In analysing markets, economists distinguish between *perfect* and *imperfect* competition in markets. All markets have some imperfections, but economics often study perfect markets as they provide useful insight to the theoretical behaviour of markets and demonstrate what would happen if all the imperfections were to be removed.

A perfect market exists where there are a large number of buyers and sellers and no individual buyer or seller has enough market power to influence the market price. In a perfect market:

- Individual firms must sell at the prevailing market price.
- All buyers and sellers have the same information about prices.
- The consumer will act rationally by purchasing at the lowest available price.
- The product is uniform across the market (*i.e.,* it is homogeneous).
- There is freedom of entry into the market for new sellers.
- It is easy and cheap of transfer purchases from one seller to another.

These conditions, outlined above, ensure that price difference in the market are rapidly eliminated and that one market price is established for each product. In the world, of course, perfect markets do not exist, although some markets such as the market for foreign exchange, come close. All markets exhibit some degree of imperfection. Reasons for this include:

- Suppliers creating the impression that their products are different or better than those of their competitors.
- The loyalty of consumers to particular products preventing rational buying decisions being made.
- Buyers and sellers not having complete access to information on prices.
- An individual buyer or seller (or a group of buyers and sellers) being powerful enough to influence the price of the products on offer.

At the opposite end of the spectrum of market types from perfect markets are monopolistic markets where there is only one seller in the market, and the seller thereby has a very large influence on the price (unless the market is regulated by outside bodies). For example, the aviation market is heavily regulated by government agencies. Having briefly considered the nature of markets, we can now move on to consider demand and supply and how they interact in markets through the *price mechanism.*

THE CONCEPT OF DEMAND

Demand represents the quantity of a product buyers are willing and able to buy at a particular price over a specified period of time. Demand to an economist is not quite the same as wants. Everyone might want to go on a round-the-world cruise, but not everyone has the ability to pay for it. Thus, wants are unlimited, but demand is limited by the ability to pay. Several factors influence the total market demand for a product such as:

- The price of the product.
- The price of competing products.
- The size and distribution of household incomes.
- Fashion and tastes.
- Opportunities for consumption (*e.g.,* leisure time).

Central to a consideration of demand is the theory of demand which states that: Other things being equal, the quantity of a good or service demanded is inversely related to its price. In other words, as the price goes down the quantity demanded goes up and, conversely, as the price goes up the quantity demanded goes down.

The Demand Curve

This relationship between demand and price is usually shown graphically as a demand curve. A demand curve can be drawn:

- For an individual consume.
- A *market* demand curve which represents the aggregate quantity of a product demanded by all consumers together, at a given price.

A demand curve is constructed from a *demand schedule,* which shows the quantities of a product that are demanded at different prices. The market demand curve generally slopes downwards to the right because:

- As prices fall the product becomes cheaper relative to other products and, therefore, expenditure will shift to the product whose price has fallen. That is, a fall in the relative price of a product increases the demand for it—*the substitution effect.* (An increase in the relative price of a product decreases the demand for it).
- A fall in the product's price means that people with lower incomes will be able to afford it and the overall demand therefore increase. That is, a fall in the absolute price of a product increases in the demand for it—*the price effect.* (The converse is also true if the product's price rises).

Analysis of a given demand curve gives a great deal of information about the nature of demand for a particular product. In particular two factors are of interest:

1. The shape or slope of the demand curve.
2. The position of the demand curve.

The shape or slope of the curve is a reflection of its steepness, and tells us how sensitive demand is to changes in price; that is, the *elasticity of demand.* The position of the curve refers to its position in relation to each axis. As already established, changes in price result in movements along the curve.

ENVIRONMENTAL MANAGEMENT OF TOURISM DEVELOPMENT

Tourism plays an important role in economic development at community, national, regional and global levels by using natural resources and environments as key physical inputs. In making use of the environment and natural resources, the negative impacts have to be minimized to assure sustainable use, as well as generate enough tourism revenue to reinvest a certain portion of funds. The reinvestment should aim at enhancing the quality of the resources and build the management capacity at various levels. There is a complex relationship between tourism and the environment, such that tourism has inevitable and important environmental impacts, including: resource use, consumption, waste, pollution and effects from tourism-related transport. At the same time, beaches, mountains, rivers, forests and diverse flora and fauna make the environment a basic resource that the tourism industry needs in order to thrive and grow. While the viability of tourism could be threatened by negative environmental impacts, tourism could also contribute significantly to environmental protection.

This shows that tourism and the environment are interrelated and interdependent in complex ways, and together they could provide a sustainable economic base for development. In light of these observations, tourism policy-makers, managers and planners must address the issues of environmental management of tourism development in a sustainable manner. The adverse impact of tourism on the environment relates to pressure on natural resources, harm to wildlife and habitats, creation of pollution and waste and related social and cultural pressures.

Among the environmental issues that need to be addressed are:

- Deterioration of natural resources (fresh water, land and landscape, marine resources, atmosphere and local resources), which may be resilient, but can deteriorate rapidly if impact exceeds tolerable limits;
- Disruption of wildlife and habitats, including vegetation, endangered species, use of forest resources, intrusion into fragile areas with sensitive ecosystems;
- Creation of pollution and waste contaminating the land, fresh water sources, marine resources, as well as causing air and noise pollution.

There has been growing recognition that traditional tourism management practices have led to such undesirable social and environmental impacts, thus threatening the tourism industry's prospects for continued prosperity. The Environment Committee of the World Tourism Organization (WTO) has taken action through its Tourism and Environment Task Force by developing indicators of sustainability that are relevant to the tourism industry and accepted internationally. Tourism managers and planners can use these indicators to address concerns about sustainability. The ecological aspects of environments that become tourist destinations should be seen as ecosystems that are life-creating natural networks. Ecosystems temper climate, purify and store water, recycle wastes, produce food and support all other living things.

There are five categories of ecosystem, of which four are natural:

1. Coastal and marine,
2. Fresh water
3. Grasslands and
4. Forests; plus
5. Man-made ecosystems based on agriculture or aquaculture.

All five ecosystems can be viewed as tourism resources. The main issue for all categories is whether they can absorb negative impacts and remain sustainable. The notion of carrying capacity can indicate whether an ecosystem can sustain itself or whether it has become irreparably damaged. At the international level, attention to ecosystems and environmental threats to tourism has come from the World Tourism Organization through its ten-point Global Code of Ethics for Tourism approved in 1999, Agenda 21 agreed at the United Nation's Conference on Environment and Development, and the 1992 Rio Declaration on the Environment and Development.

Major environmental threats to the tourism industry have been identified as:

- Global warming,
- Loss of biological diversity and
- Deterioration of the abiotic environment (climate, soil, water and air) that nurture biotic components of ecosystems.

All of these issues make it evident that formulating policies to preserve the environment are decisive and must be made while meeting economic development goals, especially eradicating poverty, at the community, national, regional and global levels. Making effective policies require that the roles of different stakeholders be considered. The major stakeholders involved with issues of sound environmental management are: the community, the tourism industry, non-governmental organizations (NGOs), the government and international communities.

Each type of stakeholder should be actively involved and aware in managing the sustainable development of tourism, and they must also work in partnership. If all stakeholders work in partnership to sustain tourism development plus protect the environment, then the present generation will provide a meaningful legacy for future generations. Understanding the limits to economic growth, the carrying capacity of natural resources and the need for sustainable action should be the guiding forces in the management of tourism development.

COMMUNITY-BASED SUSTAINABLE TOURISM

Thailand's rich historical, cultural and natural attractions have contributed to the development of mass tourism, which has had both positive and negative effects on development. Small-scale tourism development projects that are community-based, focus on an ethnic group at a remote location and involve NGOs are less well known. For three years, a community-based sustainable tourism project has been implemented at the ethnic Karen village of Baan Huay Hee in the northwestern Thai province of Mae Hong Son. The project has been carried out with the help of a small NGO, the Project for Recovery of Life and Culture (PRLC).

The aims have been to:

- Improve the overall quality of village people's lives,:
- Preserve and reinforce the importance of Karen culture,
- Empower villagers to make their own decisions about their way of life and
- Contribute to the conservation of natural resources and the environment.

Tourism development in Thailand has spead from Bangkok to almost all parts of the country. Since the 1970s, the natural, cultural and historical attractions and friendly people of northern Thailand have made it a popular destination, first with trekking tourism followed by hilltribe tourism. Six major hilltribe groups make their home in the North: Akha, Hmong, Karen, Lahu, Lisu, Shan, Mien and Haw Chinese. By the 1990s, hilltribe tourism had become highly organized. However, the number of visitors has not been monitored systematically by the Tourism Authority of Thailand. Over the past ten years, the northern province of Mae Hong Son has become a major tourist destination due to its mist-covered mountains, dense forest areas and the cultural and ethnic diversity. While most hilltribe communities have maintained their way of life, some have become vulnerable to the negative aspects of tourism, especially giving a false image of the people as exotic and primitive based on lack of knowledge and communication among the tourists and the local people. Uncontrolled access to many remote areas has caused problems with waste management and has threatened the ecology in general.

The concept of community-based sustainable tourism (CBST) was developed as a way to overcome or minimize negative effects of tourism in a remote, rural area. CBST was developed as a form of tourism aimed at empowering local communities to be self-reliant, use a group process for local decision-making, support people's human rights and capabilities and help people raise incomes and improve standards of living on their own terms. Local knowledge, community participation, support for local capabilities and cultural exchange with tourists would help to sustain both cultural and natural resources. The NGO (PRLC) helped the Karen village at Huay Hee become the first site for CBST. The village became a successful model for over 60 villages and communities. The project for CBST became holistic in its approach and included natural resource management, sustainable tourism development, strengthened civil society, prevention of HIV/AIDS and drug abuse and youth leadership development. The people of Huay Hee developed a land classification system and cooperation model to work with government agencies responsible for a nearby national park in order to prevent deforestation and degradation of watersheds.

The village has been receiving tourists for about three years with the help of PRLC and another Thai NGO, Thai Volunteer Service-Responsible Ecological Social Tours (TVS-REST). Villagers could explain how they protect the forest and follow their own traditions, while adding to their incomes and improving their standard of living. Villagers became more aware of environmental issues, especially when tourists left garbage behind and picked rare orchids as they trekked on the mountains.

Men in the village received guide training and increased their understanding about how tourists should behave during treks. Women in the village provide meals, sell items made with traditional Karen weaving and take care of tourists during home stays. Home stays and guiding were shared among the families on a rotation basis, which meant both responsibility and income were shared.

Some of the earnings from tourism activities were saved in a village fund that was used to conserve the forest, grow orchids, buy equipment for hosting tourists and support education and travel related to their tourism training. Well-informed exchanges with tourists helped prevent cultural degradation and created more respect for Karen traditions. Equally important, the people at Huay Hee were empowered to see that tourism should provide supplementary income, especially since it was a seasonal activity. With training and support from the CBST project, people used their knowledge of traditional agricultural methods of subsistence farming to be self-reliant in food and to show tourists the role of agriculture in their everyday way of life.

The community-based sustainable tourism project implemented by Karen villagers at Baan Huay Hee in Mae Hong Son Province can serve as a model for other communities. They can be empowered to control the impact of tourism, avoid degrading the environment and create a stronger, empowered community. NGOs can help spread the concept and provide training, but then they must step back as villagers work together to find ways to make the CBST project succeed. The most sustainable form of tourism will be achieved when local people take control of their lives and determine to live according to their traditions on their own terms.

ECONOMIC EFFECTS OF TOURISM

The ability of a tourism destination to attract tourism revenues and investment in infrastructure is influenced by a complex number of characteristics, such as:

- Political constraints and incentives;
- The resources and conveniences offered;
- Market characteristics;
- Political stability;
- The ability of the destination to market and promote itself effectively.

The primary and secondary effects of tourism expenditures are discussed later in this chapter. In its simplest form, the economic impact of tourism can be measured as the difference in economic well-being between the income levels that would have existed without tourism activity and the income levels after tourism activity. There are a number of potential tangible and less tangible economic benefits and costs; these are summarized below.

The potential economic benefits of tourism development include:

- Increased resources for the protection and conservation of natural and cultural heritage resources;
- Increased income and improved standard of living from tourist expenditures;
- Increased induced income from tourism expenditures;
- New employment opportunities;
- Increased community visibility leading to other economic development opportunities;
- New induced employment opportunities;
- Increased tax base;
- Improved infrastructure and facilities;
- Development of local handicrafts.

The potential costs include:

- Seasonal employment;
- Low status/paying jobs;
- Inflation;
- Increased costs;
- Pollution;
- Increased traffic/congestion;
- Negative impacts on cultural and natural heritage resources;
- Increased crime;
- Increased taxes;
- Leakage of revenues and external domination;
- Over-dependence on tourism as a prime economic activity.

There are other costs that may have an indirect or long-term impact on the economic contributions of tourism. For example, land values may change as high-priced projects replace traditional and less profitable land uses. If agricultural landowners choose to sell or develop their land for tourism purposes, the tourism economy may have to rely on some food imports to feed the tourists and locals. The loss of traditional land values can also have an impact on the local heritage and sense of place. Moreover, conflict may arise between those landowners who do not wish to see the loss of the historic character of their community and area, and pro-tourism proponents.

Residents and speculators who suffer or benefit from rising land prices might join in the fray. Such conflict could escalate as tourism pressures increase, and the resulting scars on the community might take a long time to heal.

This short example helps to illustrate that understanding and measuring economic impacts is more complex than simply measuring direct impacts. It is also important to view economic impacts from a long-term perspective. Environmental degradation and pollution will result in short-term environmental costs and associated economic costs incurred in repairing the damage caused by the pollution. There could also be considerable long-term economic costs to the local, regional, and national economies if the destination is no longer desirable due to the effects of degradation and pollution.

MEASURING ECONOMIC IMPACTS OF TOURISM

A major objective of any tourism planning and development process should be to minimize negative impacts and ensure that the benefits are realised in an equitable manner. While there are significant problems on the road to achieving this objective, there is growing recognition that sustainable tourism approaches will help in reaching this goal. There are a number of methods for measuring the economic impacts of tourism activity, some of which are discussed below. Measuring the economic impact and employment creation activities of tourism should be carried out in an integrated fashion, taking into account direct and indirect job creation as well as the economic well being of the community.

While employment creation is seen as an important objective, concern for the overall local economy must also be a major consideration. As has been discussed, this implies that jobs and economic benefits may be realised from a number of sources other than tourism. It may also imply that jobs are created as the result of private sector entrepreneurial activity as well as community initiative.

SUPPLY-DEMAND AND PRICE ELASTICITIES

The economic contribution of tourism activity to a community or region is influenced by a diverse number of factors within and outside the destination. Given that diversity, it is difficult to calculate impacts due to the wide range of effects associated with tourism economic activities, the diverse number of participants involved in those activities, and the complex interrelationships between various sectors. Tourism economic activity is often explained using the concept of supply and demand. A number of variables influence the demand and supply of a tourism product or service. For example, if the price of a hotel room increases, demand may decrease, as visitors seek other locations or accommodation sources, and the supply of available hotel rooms therefore increases.

The supply-demand relationship of tourism goods and services can be influenced by factors such as the price elasticity of demand for tourism. When demand is price elastic, a lower price could generate a higher demand and hence higher revenues. Similarly, if demand is price inelastic, a lower price could result in lower overall revenues. Knowing the price elasticity of demand can aid tourism service providers in designing their product mix. However, a number of factors affect price elasticity, making it difficult to calculate.

ECONOMIC IMPACT ANALYSIS

A variety of economic analyses are carried out to support tourism decisions. As these different kinds of economic analysis are frequently confused, let's begin by positioning economic impact studies within the broader set of economic problems and techniques relevant to tourism. These same techniques may be applied to any policy or action, but we will define them here in the context of tourism. Each type of analysis is identified by the basic question(s) it answers and the types of methods and models that are appropriate. Benefit cost analysis and economic impact analysis are frequently confused as both discuss economic "benefits".

There are two clear distinctions between the two techniques. B/C analysis addresses the benefits from economic efficiency while economic impact analysis focuses on the regional distribution of economic activity. The income received from tourism by a destination region is largely off-set by corresponding losses in the origin regions, yielding only modest contributions to net social welfare and efficiency. B/C analysis includes market and non-market values (consumer surplus), while economic impact analysis is restricted to actual flows of money from market transactions.

While each type of economic analysis is somewhat distinct, a given problem often calls for several different kinds of economic analysis. An economic impact study will frequently involve a demand analysis to project levels of tourism activity.

In other cases demand is treated as exogenous and the analysis simply estimates impacts if a given number of visitors are attracted to the area. A comprehensive impact assessment will also examine fiscal impacts, as well as social and environmental impacts. Be aware that an economic impact analysis, by itself, provides a rather narrow and often one-sided perspective on the impacts of tourism.

Studies of the economic impacts of tourism tend to emphasize the positive benefits of tourism. On the other hand environmental, social, cultural and fiscal impact studies tend to focus more on negative impacts of tourism. This is in spite of the fact that there are negative economic impacts of tourism (*e.g.*, seasonality and lower wage jobs) and in many cases positive environmental and social impacts (*e.g.*, protection of natural and cultural resources in the area and education of both tourists and local residents). An economic impact assessment (EIA) traces changes in economic activity resulting from some action.

An EIA will identify which economic sectors benefit from tourism and estimate resulting changes in income and employment in the region. Economic impact assessment procedures do not assess economic efficiency and also do not generally produce estimates of the fiscal costs of an action. For many problems economic impact analysis will be part of a broader analysis. Environmental, social, and fiscal impacts are often equally important concerns in a balanced assessment of impacts. An economic impact analysis will assess the contribution of tourism activity to a region's economy.

The basic questions an economic impact study usually addresses are:

- How many jobs in the area does tourism support?
- How much tax revenue is generated from tourism?
- How much do tourists spend in the area?
- What portion of sales by local businesses is due to tourism?
- How much income does tourism generate for households and businesses in the area?

An economic impact analysis also reveals the interrelationships among economic sectors and provides estimates of the changes that take place in an economy due to some existing or proposed action.

The most common applications of economic impact analysis to tourism are:

1. To evaluate the economic impacts of changes in the supply of recreation and tourism opportunities. Supply changes may involve a change in quantity, such as the opening of new facilities, closing of existing ones, or expansions and contraction in capacity. Supply changes may also involve changes in quality, including changes in,
   - The quality of the environment,
   - The local infrastructure and public services to support tourism, or
   - The nature of the tourism products and services that are provided in an area.
2. To evaluate the economic impacts of changes in tourism demand. Population changes, changes in the competitive position of the region, marketing activity or changing consumer tastes and preferences can alter levels of tourism activity, spending, and associated economic activity. An economic impact study can estimate the magnitude and nature of these impacts.
3. To evaluate the effects of policies and actions which affect tourism activity either directly or indirectly. Tourism depends on many factors at both origins and destinations that are frequently outside the direct control of the tourism industry itself. Economic impact studies provide information to help decision makers better understand the consequences of various actions on the tourism industry as well as on other sectors of the economy. For example, increased air pollution standards have been opposed in some regions due to the predicted economic consequences of the closing of plants that cannot meet the new standards. Tourism interests counter these arguments with estimates of the potential gains in income and jobs in tourism industries that depend on good air quality and visibility.
4. To understand the economic structure and interdependencies of different sectors of the economy. Economic studies help us better understand the size and structure of the tourism industry in a given region and its linkages to other sectors of the economy. Such understandings are helpful in identifying potential partners for the tourism industry as well as in targeting industries as part of regional economic development strategies. Issues such as economic growth, stability, and seasonality may be addressed as part of these studies.
5. To argue for favourable treatment in allocation of resources or local tax, zoning or other policy decisions. By showing that tourism has significant economic impacts, tourism interests can often convince decision-makers to allocate more resources for tourism or to establish policies that encourage tourism. Tax abatements and other incentives

frequently given to manufacturing firms have also been granted to hotels, marinas and other tourism businesses based on demonstrated economic impacts in the local area.

6. To compare the economic impacts of alternative resource allocation, policy, management or development proposals. Economic impact analyses are commonly used to assess the relative merits of distinct alternatives. The economic contribution of expanded tourism offerings may be compared for example with alternatives such as resource extraction activities (mining, timber harvesting) or manufacturing. Impacts of alternative tourism development proposals may also be evaluated, *e.g.,* tourism strategies that emphasize outdoor recreation, camping development, a convention facility, or a factory outlet mall.

Tourism has a variety of economic impacts. Tourists contribute to sales, profits, jobs, tax revenues, and income in an area. The most direct effects occur within the primary tourism sectors—lodging, restaurants, transportation, amusements, and retail trade. Through secondary effects, tourism affects most sectors of the economy. An economic impact analysis of tourism activity normally focuses on changes in sales, income, and employment in a region resulting from tourism activity.

A simple tourism impact scenario illustrates. Let's say a region attracts an additional 100 tourists, each spending $100 per day. That's $10,000 in new spending per day in the area. If sustained over a 100 day season, the region would accumulate a million dollars in new sales. The million dollars in spending would be distributed to lodging, restaurant, amusement and retail trade sectors in proportion to how the visitor spends the $100.

Perhaps 30per cent of the million dollars would leak out of the region immediately to cover the costs of goods purchased by tourists that are not made in the local area (only the retail margins for such items should normally be included as direct sales effects). The remaining $700,000 in direct sales might yield $350,000 in income within tourism industries and support 20 direct tourism jobs. Tourism industries are labour and income intensive, translating a high proportion of sales into income and corresponding jobs.

The tourism industry, in turn, buys goods and services from other businesses in the area, and pays out most of the $350,000 in income as wages and salaries to its employees. This creates secondary economic effects in the region. The study might use a sales multiplier of 2.0 to indicate that each dollar of direct sales generates another dollar in secondary sales in this region. Through multiplier effects, the $700,000 in direct sales produces $1.4 million in total sales.

These secondary sales create additional income and employment, resulting in a total impact on the region of $1.4 million in sales, $650,000 in income and 35 jobs. While hypothetical, the numbers used here are fairly typical of what one might find in a tourism economic impact study. A more complete study might identify which sectors receive the direct and secondary effects and possibly identify differences in spending and impacts of distinct subgroups of tourists (market segments). One can also estimate the tax effects of this spending by applying local tax rates to the appropriate changes in sales or income. Instead of focusing on visitor spending, one could also estimate impacts of construction or government activity associated with tourism. There are several other categories of economic impacts that are not typically covered in economic impact assessments, at least not directly.

For example:

- *Changes in prices*: Tourism can sometimes inflate the cost of housing and retail prices in the area, frequently on a seasonal basis.
- *Changes in the quality and quantity of goods and services*: Tourism may lead to a wider array of goods and services available in an area (of either higher or lower quality than without tourism).
- *Changes in property and other taxes*: Taxes to cover the cost of local services may be higher or lower in the presence of tourism activity. In some cases, taxes collected directly or indirectly from tourists may yield reduced local taxes for schools, roads, etc. In other cases, locals may be taxed more heavily to cover the added infrastructure and service costs. The impacts of tourism on local government costs and revenues are addressed more fully in a fiscal impact analysis.
- *Economic dimensions of "social" and "environmental" impacts*: There are also economic consequences of most social and environmental impacts that are not usually addressed in an economic impact analysis. These can be positive or negative. For example, traffic congestion will increase costs of moving around for both households and businesses. Improved amenities that attract tourists may also encourage retirees or other kinds of businesses to locate in the area.

INDUCED EFFECTS

A standard economic impact analysis traces flows of money from tourism spending, first to businesses and government agencies where tourists spend their money and then to:

- *Other businesses*: Supplying goods and services to tourist businesses,
- *Households*: Earning income by working in tourism or supporting industries, and
- *Government*: Through various taxes and charges on tourists, businesses and households

Formally, regional economists distinguish direct, indirect, and induced economic effects. Indirect and induced effects are sometimes collectively called secondary effects. The total economic impact of tourism is the sum of direct, indirect, and induced effects within a region. Any of these impacts may be measured as gross output or sales, income, employment, or value added. Direct effects are production changes associated with the immediate effects of changes in tourism expenditures. For example, an increase in the number of tourists staying overnight in hotels would directly yield increased sales in the hotel sector. The additional hotel sales and associated changes in hotel payments for wages and salaries, taxes, and supplies and services are direct effects of the tourist spending.

Indirect effects are the production changes resulting from various rounds of re-spending of the hotel industry's receipts in other backward-linked industries (*i.e.,* industries supplying products and services to hotels). Changes in sales, jobs, and income in the linen supply industry, for example, represent indirect effects of changes in hotel sales.

Businesses supplying products and services to the linen supply industry represent another round of indirect effects, eventually linking hotels to varying degrees to many other economic sectors in the region. Induced effects are the changes in economic activity resulting from household spending of income earned directly or indirectly as a result of tourism spending.

For example, hotel and linen supply employees supported directly or indirectly by tourism, spend their income in the local region for housing, food, transportation, and the usual array of household product and service needs. The sales, income, and jobs that result from household spending of added wage, salary, or proprietor's income are induced effects.

By means of indirect and induced effects, changes in tourist spending can impact virtually every sector of the economy in one way or another. The magnitude of secondary effects depends on the propensity of businesses and households in the region to purchase goods and services from local suppliers. Induced effects are particularly noticed when a large employer in a region closes a plant.

Not only are supporting industries (indirect effects) hurt, but the entire local economy suffers due to the reduction in household income within the region. Retail stores close and leakages of money from the region increase as consumers go outside the region for more and more goods and services. Similar effects in the opposite direction are observed when there is a significant increase in jobs and household income.

Final demand is the term used by economists for sales to the final consumers of goods and services. In almost all cases, the final consumers of tourism goods and services are households. Government spending is also considered as final demand. The same methods for estimating impacts of visitor spending can be applied to estimate the economic impacts of government spending, for example, to operate and maintain a park or visitor centre.

REGIONAL MODELS

An input-output model (I-O model) is a mathematical model that describes the flows of money between sectors within a region's economy. Flows are predicted by knowing what each industry must buy from every other industry to produce a dollar's worth of output. Using each industry's production function, I-O models also determine the proportions of sales that go to wage and salary income, proprietor's income, and taxes.

Multipliers can be estimated from input-output models based on the estimated re-circulation of spending within the region. Exports and imports are determined based upon estimates of the propensity of households and firms within the region to purchase goods and services from local sources (often called RPC's or regional purchase coefficients). The more a region is self-sufficient and purchases goods and services from within the region, the higher the multipliers for the region. Input-output models make a number of assumptions.

The basic ones are that:

- All firms in a given industry employ the same production technology (usually assumed to be the national average for that industry), and produce identical products.
- There are no economies or diseconomies of scale in production or factor substitution. I-O models are essentially linear—double the level of tourism activity/production and you double all of the inputs, the number of jobs, etc.
- The model doesn't explicitly keep track of time, but analysts generally report the impact estimates as if they represent activity within a single year.
- One must assume that the various model parameters are accurate and represent the current year.

I-O models are firmly grounded in the national system of accounts, which relies on a standard industrial classification system (SIC codes) and various federal government economic censuses, in which individual firms report sales, wage and salary payments and employment. I-O models will generally be at least a few years out-of-date, although this isn't usually a major problem unless the region's economy has changed significantly. An I-O model represents the region's economy at a particular point in time.

Tourist spending estimates are generally price adjusted to the year of the model. Multiplier computations for induced effects generally assume that jobs created by additional spending are new jobs, involving new households in the area. Induced effects are computed assuming linear changes in household spending with changes in income. Estimates of induced effects may be inflated due to the violation of these assumptions. Induced effects tend to account for the vast majority of the secondary effects of tourism, and therefore should be used with caution.

MULTIPLIERS EFFECTS OF TOURISM

Multipliers capture the secondary economic effects (indirect and induced) of tourism activity. Multipliers have been frequently misused and misinterpreted in tourism studies and are a considerable source of confusion among non-economists. Multipliers represent the economic interdependencies between sectors within a particular region's economy. They vary considerably from region to region and sector to sector. There are many different kinds of multipliers reflecting which secondary effects are included and which measure of economic activity is used (sales, income, or employment).

For example,

- The Type I sales multiplier = direct sales + indirect sales direct sales.
- The Type II or III sales multiplier[1] = direct sales + indirect sales + induced sales direct sales.

Multiplying a Type I sales multiplier times the direct sales gives direct plus indirect sales. Multiplying a Type II or III sales multiplier times the direct sales gives total sales impacts including direct, indirect and induced effects. The multipliers defined above are called ratio type multipliers as they measure the ratio of a total impact measure to the corresponding direct impact. Comparable income and employment ratio type multipliers may be defined by replacing sales with measures of income or employment in the above equations. Ratio multipliers should be used with caution.

A common error is to multiply a sales multiplier times tourist spending to get total sales effects. This will generate an inflated estimate of tourism impacts. The problem is that tourism spending or sales is not exactly the same as the "direct effects", appearing in the multiplier formula. Tourist purchases of goods (vs. services) are the primary source of the problem. To properly apply tourist purchases of goods to an input-output model (or corresponding multipliers), various margins (retail, wholesale and transportation) must be deducted from the "purchaser price" of the good to separate out the "producer price".

In an I-O model, retail margins accrue to the retail trade sector, wholesale margins to wholesale trade, transportation margins to transportation sectors (trucking, rail, air etc.) and the producer prices of goods are assigned to the sector that produces the good. In most cases the factory that produces the good bought by a tourist lies outside of the local region, creating an immediate "leakage" in the first round of spending and therefore no local impact from production of the good.

Before applying a multiplier to tourist spending, one must first deduct the producer prices of all imported goods that tourists buy (*i.e.,* only include the local retail margins and possibly wholesale and transportation margins if these firms lie within the region). Generally, only 60 to 70per cent of tourist spending appears as final demand in a local region. While all tourist purchases of services will accrue to the local region as final demand, only the margins on goods purchased at retail stores should be counted as local final demand. The ratio of local final demand to tourist spending is called the capture rate. Capture rate = local final demand/tourism spending in local area.

Capture rates, like multipliers, will vary with the size and nature of the region as well as the kind of tourist spending included. One must therefore be cautious in taking a multiplier or capture rate cited in one study and using it in another. Another way of calculating a multiplier (generally the preferred approach among economists) is as a ratio of income or employment to sales. This kind of multiplier is sometimes called a Keynesian multiplier or response coefficient.

- Type III Income multiplier = Total direct, indirect, and induced income direct sales
- Type III Employment multiplier = Total direct, indirect, and induced employment direct sales

This income (employment) multiplier produces total income (employment) impacts when multiplied by the direct sales. One must still be careful in distinguishing between tourism spending/sales and direct sales effects. Some studies may embed the capture rate in the multiplier, expressing the ratio in terms of tourism spending rather than direct sales.

The economic impacts of tourism are typically estimated by some variation of the following simple formula:

Economic Impact of Tourism = Number of Tourists × Average Spending per Visitor × Multiplier

The formula suggests three distinct steps and corresponding measurements or models:

1. Estimate the change in the number and types of tourists to the region due to the proposed policy or action. Estimates or projections of tourist activity generally come from a demand model or some system for measuring levels of tourism activity in an area. Economic impact estimates will rest heavily on good estimates of the numbers and types of visitors. These must come from carefully designed measurements of tourist activity, a good demand model, or good judgement. This step is usually the weakest link in most tourism impact studies, as few regions have accurate counts of tourists, let alone good models for predicting changes in tourism activity or separating local visitors from visitors from outside the region.
2. Estimate average levels of spending (often within specific market segments) of tourists in the local area. Spending averages come from sample surveys or are sometimes borrowed or adapted from other studies. Spending estimates must be based on a representative sample of the population of tourists taking into account variations across seasons,

types of tourists, and locations within the study area. As spending can vary widely across different kinds of tourists, we recommend estimating average spending for a set of key tourist segments based on samples of at least 50-100 visitors within each tourism segment. Segments should be defined to capture differences in spending between local residents vs. tourists, day users vs. overnight visitors, type of accommodation (motel, campground, seasonal home, with friends and relatives), and type of transportation (car, RV, air, rail, etc.). In broadly based tourism impact studies, it is useful to identify unique spending patterns of important activity segments such as downhill skiers, boaters, and convention and business travellers. Multiplying the number of tourists by the average spending per visitor (be careful the units are consistent) gives an estimate of total tourist spending in the area. Estimates of tourist spending will generally be more accurate if distinct spending profiles and use estimates are made for key tourism segments. The use and spending estimates are the two most important parts of an economic impact assessment. When combined, they capture the amount of money brought into the region by tourists. Multipliers are needed only if one is interested in the secondary effects of tourism spending.

3. Apply the change in spending to a regional economic model or set of multipliers to determine secondary effects. Secondary effects of tourism are estimated using multipliers or a model of the region's economy. Multipliers generally come from an economic base or input-output model of the region's economy. In many cases multipliers are borrowed (often improperly) or adjusted from published multipliers or other studies. One should not take a multiplier estimated for one region and apply it in a region with a quite different economic structure. Generally, multipliers are higher for larger regions with more diversified economies and lower for smaller regions with more limited economic development. A common error is to apply a statewide multiplier (since these are more widely published) to a local region. This will yield inflated estimates of local multiplier effects. Multipliers can also be used to convert estimates of spending or sales to income and employment. Simple ratios can be used to capture how much income or jobs are generated per dollar of sales. These ratios will vary from region to region and across individual economic sectors due to the relative importance of labour inputs in each industry and different wage and salary rates in different regions of the country. Be aware that job estimates are generally not full time equivalents, making them difficult to compare across industries with different proportions of seasonal and part time jobs. Income or

value added are generally the preferred measures of the contribution of tourism to a region's economy.

THE TYPICAL APPROACHES FOR AN ECONOMIC ASSESSMENT

At the simple, "quick and dirty" end of the spectrum are highly aggregate approaches that rely mostly on judgement to determine tourism activity, spending and multipliers. Such estimates can be completed in a couple hours at little cost and rest largely on the expertise and judgement of the analyst. At the other extreme are studies that gather primary data from visitor spending studies and apply the spending estimates to formal regional economic models for the area in question. In between are a wide range of options that employ varying degrees of judgement, secondary data, primary data, and formal models.

Different levels of detail and corresponding expense (time and money) and accuracy are possible for each of the three steps—estimating tourist volume, spending, and multiplier effects. Four typical approaches illustrate the levels of detail that are possible and the associated methods to sales estimates. With sound judgement in choosing the parameters, the MGM model can yield reasonable ballpark estimates of economic impacts at minimal cost. This approach, however, provides little detail on spending categories or which sectors of the economy benefit from either direct or secondary effects. The aggregate nature of the approach also makes it difficult to adjust recommended spending rates or multipliers to different applications. The Bureau of Economic Analysis's (BEA) RIMS II user handbook illustrates how to apply published multipliers to estimate economic impacts. This approach starts with visitor spending (from survey or secondary sources) divided into a number of spending categories and makes use of sector specific multipliers to estimate the direct and total sales, income and employment effects. Multipliers from the BEA's RIMS II models are used to estimate secondary effects. Multipliers are reported for 39 sectors for each state in the second edition of their report.

This method uses margins to properly account for retail purchases of goods and makes use of disaggregate sector-specific multipliers for each state. Multipliers for sub-state regions are not as readily available, but can be acquired from BEA or other sources. Secondary effects cannot be disaggregated to individual sectors using the BEA approach.

The MI-REC/IMPLAN System: Stynes and Propst have developed a fairly complete micro-computer-based system for estimating economic impacts of recreation and tourism. The system combines spreadsheets for estimating spending with the IMPLAN input-output modeling system. IMPLAN uses county level data to estimate 528 sector input-output models for regions down to account level. IMPLAN generates a complete set of economic accounts for the region including multipliers and trade flows. MI-REC spreadsheets estimate visitor spending within up to 33categories based on the number and types of visitors attracted to an area. Spending is then bridged to the IMPLAN model sectors to estimate direct, indirect and induced effects in terms of sales, income and employment. Users may estimate spending via visitor surveys or use the MI-REC database of spending profiles, compiled from previous studies. The system also includes price indices to easily update spending data to a current year.

Two other systems for estimating economic impacts of tourism should be noted. The TEIM or Travel Economic Impact Model developed by the U.S. Travel Data Centre has been widely used to estimate tourism and travel impacts at state and national levels. A more recent development is the satellite accounting approach developed by the World Travel and Tourism Council. Both of these systems are primarily designed for estimating the overall economic significance of tourism at national or state levels. They are not readily applied to estimate the impacts of particular policies and actions at the local level.

The TEIM relies on national travel surveys to estimate trip volume and spending on a state-by-state basis. Local estimates of impacts are obtained using simple allocation formulas to distribute statewide impacts to counties and cities within the state. These local estimates do not account very well for the distinct types of tourism activity or spending patterns in different sub-regions of a state. The WTTC effort also focuses on national and statewide accounting of tourism's economic significance. Their satellite tourism account identifies the contribution of travel and tourism to gross national product (GNP) or gross state product (GSP). Using the standard national system of accounts, they identify the portion of sales, taxes and investment attributable directly to travel and tourism. The WTTC system does not use multipliers or attempt to estimate secondary effects. It does, however, capture a great deal of travel-related economic activity, not covered by visitor trip spending, such as durable goods purchases (boats and RV's), construction and investment in tourism, and government expenditures.

An economic impact study involves four basic:

1. Define the problem
2. Estimate the change in final demand (tourism spending).
3. Estimate the regional economic effects of this change
4. Interpret, apply, and communicate the results

The most important part of any study is the first step—clarifying the nature of the problem being addressed and intended uses of the results. Before launching an economic impact study, be sure this is the kind of study that is needed rather than one or more of the other kinds of economic analyses. Stynes and Propst (1996) identify seven factors that should be specified as part of defining a problem for an economic impact assessment:

- Define the action to be evaluated. Begin by clarifying the action or actions involved in the problem. Actions may include construction, government investment, changes in marketing, management, or policies, or changes in the quality or quantity of tourist facilities. If evaluating impacts of existing tourism activity, be sure to define what is to be included as "tourism".

- Identify the change in the amount and kinds of recreation/tourism activity resulting from the action. The action must be defined precisely enough in step one to be able to estimate the changes in the number and types of visitors to the area and/or their spending patterns. As a general rule, the analysis should be with vs. without the action rather than simply before vs. after. Thus, if tourism has been growing by 5per cent per year and a new promotional programme increases this to 10per cent this year, only half of the 10per cent growth can likely be attributed to the promotional programme. Identifying the net changes in activity that are attributable to an action can be a complex and difficult task. Assessments of economic impact, however, rest firmly on such estimates, so attention to these details is very important. In situations of some uncertainty, we recommend evaluating impacts using a range of estimates in order to establish rough confidence intervals around your estimates. Evaluating a range of alternatives also helps to evaluate the sensitivity of the results to your initial estimates of changes in activity levels.
- Identify the kinds of spending to be included. Tourism may impact the local economy through visitor trip spending, durable goods purchases, government spending, or investment and construction. Which to include in a given analysis depends on how the problem is defined, and again, on attributing given spending changes to the proposed action.
- Identify the study region. Perhaps the most important, yet often neglected part of a recreation and tourism impact assessment is the definition of a study region. The region defines the area for which impacts are desired, as well as the portions of visitor spending that are relevant. An impact assessment evaluates the impacts on households, businesses, and organizations within the given region. Spending that visitors make outside of a study region either at home or en route are not included in assessing impacts of spending on the designated region. For an economic impact analysis, the study region should be large enough to constitute a viable economic region. Since little economic data exists below the county level, the county is generally the smallest region one should consider for a tourism impact assessment.
- Identify key economic sectors and desired sectoral detail. The proposed action and anticipated uses/users of the results should

suggest the key sectors that will be impacted. Recreation and tourism activity typically impact the lodging, restaurant, amusements, retail, transportation and government sectors most directly. In the problem definition stage consideration of impacted sectors helps to identify relevant categories of spending. The desired sectoral detail plays an important role in structuring the presentation of results. In some cases only an aggregate measure of impacts may be desired. In other cases, clients may be interested in which particular sectors are most heavily affected and will want estimates of sales and jobs broken down by sector. If formal input-output models are used, impacts may be estimated in considerable sectoral detail. This is not possible if an aggregate spending estimate or multiplier is used.

- Identify the most important measures of economic activity. Tourism impacts may be reported in terms of visitor spending, business receipts/sales/production, wage and salary income, proprietors income and profits, value added, and employment. The direct effects are the most important and are captured well by estimates of visitor spending. Simple ratios can be used to convert direct spending or sales to the associated income and jobs. Input-output models and multipliers are needed only if one is interested in secondary effects.
- Identify the tolerable levels of error in the results. Although confidence intervals and estimates of error are rare in economic impact studies, this doesn't mean they are not important. You should have at least a ballpark idea of how much error you can tolerate in the analysis, as this will dictate how much effort and expense you must put into it. The more accuracy you demand, the greater the requirements to gather up-to-date local data on visitation, spending and economic activity. These data allow you to fine tune the spending estimates and input-output models or multipliers. Such fine tuning will require time, knowledge, and money that must be weighed against the benefits of the improved estimates. Estimates of impacts are based on three components: visits, spending, and multipliers. You should try to balance the errors across these components.
- What are some questions to ask when evaluating or interpreting a tourism economic impact study? Evaluating, interpreting and applying an economic impact study requires a clear understanding of the findings and at least some knowledge of the underlying concepts and methods. Judging the accuracy or quality of a study can be based on the reputation of the author or the quality of presentation, although a careful evaluation of the methods that were used is the best approach. Here's some questions to ask when reading or evaluating a tourism economic impact study.

- *Impact of what?* The report should identify the action being evaluated. An economic impact assessment is most useful when evaluating the effects of a particular action or policy. If so, the action and assumptions about alternatives should be spelled out in presenting a with vs. without scenario. If the study reports impacts of existing tourism activity, identify how tourism is defined (if at all). What kinds of tourism activity and spending are included? Which trip expenses are included? Does the study include all visitor spending or only spending of tourists who live outside the local region? Does the study address impacts of visitor trip spending, durable goods purchases, operational expenses of a programme, or construction and investment?
- *On what region?* The study region should be defined (preferably with a map). It should be viable both economically and as a distinct tourism destination area. Spending that is included should be restricted to spending in this region and multipliers should represent the given region of interest. A short profile of tourism and economic activity in the region provides useful background for an economic impact study.
- *Sources and quality of the data:* The report should identify the sources of the data for estimating visits, spending, and regional economic multipliers/models. The methods that were used to estimate impacts should be clear. Judgements of the quality of the estimates must be based largely on an understanding of the data and methods that were used. A more disaggregate analysis reporting spending within at least six categories, visitors for two or more distinct segments, and multipliers and results broken down by sector will generally be more accurate and meaningful than a study that only uses aggregate data. Disaggregation is particularly helpful when adjusting secondary data taken from government reports or other studies to a new situation. The fundamental question is whether the visit estimates, spending profiles and multipliers adequately represent the intended population and study area.
- *Quality of methods:* There are a number of issues to watch for in evaluating methods.
- *Visits:* Has the study clearly defined which visits/visitors will be affected by the proposed action, separated local visitors from tourists, and identified which visitors would be lost or gained due to the action (with vs. without the action)? Are secondary sources of visitation reliable? If models are used, how good are they and do the assumptions hold for the intended application? Has the study handled potential double counting problems in estimating visits?
- *Spending:* How accurate are the spending estimates? Do the spending averages or totals seem reasonable? If spending averages are taken

from a secondary source, evaluate the source, as well as how well these averages may apply to the intended application. What year does the spending represent? Has the data been price adjusted to the current (or model) year? If spending data come from a visitor survey, evaluate the survey methods-how was spending measured, what was the sample size, the response rate, soundness of the analysis? Are variances and confidence intervals reported for the spending estimates? Are visitors divided into distinct segments to reduce variances? Also make sure the units for which spending is reported match the units for visits, *i.e.,* the study doesn't multiply a per party spending average times the number of person visits. If adjustments are made in units of analysis, evaluate the assumed or estimated average length of stay or party size assumptions.

- *Multipliers:* If "off-the-shelf" or borrowed multipliers are used, investigate the source. Does the study clearly define what type of multiplier is being used (Type I, Type III, income, sales or employment, ratio or Keynesian) and use the multiplier appropriately? In particular, watch for studies that multiply tourism spending by a multiplier taken from an input-output model. They should adjust for the capture rate either by reducing spending, only using retail margins on goods purchased by tourists, or using a "tourist spending" multiplier that takes the capture rate into account. If an input-output model is used, the report should summarize where it came from, what year it represents, the levels of sectoral aggregation, and the basic assumptions of the model.
- *Communication and reporting of results:* The study should communicate the study results in terms that are understandable to the intended audience. For most audiences, a summary and glossary of economic terms is helpful. Most readers will not fully understand terms like indirect and induced effects, Type I and Type III multipliers, and input-output models. Formal definitions of the measures of sales, income, and jobs that are reported are also needed to clarify what each of these terms include and the measurement units. For example, is income only wage and salary income or does it also include proprietors income, rents and profits? Study limitations and errors should be indicated.

DIRECT AND INDIRECT EFFECTS OF TOURISM EARNINGS

The economic benefits of travel and tourism can be derived directly or indirectly. The primary effect is direct benefits that result from direct tourist expenditures for goods and services in the destination. These are realised through business receipts, income, employment and government receipts from the sectors that directly receive the tourism expenditure. Indirect benefits are generated by the circulation of tourism expenditures in the destination country through domestic inter-business transactions. For example, indirect benefits can be generated from the investment and spending by the businesses that benefit directly from tourism expenditures. The direct business receipts, when re-funneled as investments or used to purchase other goods and services from domestic suppliers, stimulate income and employment in other sectors. In addition, tourism spending within the destination area can create induced benefits.

As income levels rise due to the direct and indirect effects of change in the level of tourism expenditure, some of the additional personal income is spent within the destination. This results in induced benefits, such as local income and jobs in the local goods and service sector. Hence, the spending by tourists at the destination can create direct benefits in tourism-related services and sectors such as accommodation, hospitality, attractions, events and transportation. This spending can also create a significant amount of indirect and induced benefits in other sectors such as agriculture, construction and manufacturing. Indirect and induced benefits are also referred to as the secondary effect.

MULTIPLIER MODEL OF TOURISM REVENUE TURNOVER

Multipliers measure the effect of expenditures introduced into an economy. Tourism multipliers are used to determine changes in output, income, employment, business and government receipts, and balance of payments due to a change in the level of tourism expenditures in an area. For example, if tourism expenditures increase by 15 per cent due to attendance at a special event in the destination, some of this added revenue may be used by the event to purchase food and other goods from the local economy, as well as on payment of wages, salaries, government taxes etc.

The suppliers to the event may then spend the money received from the event on other goods, services, taxes etc., thus generating yet another round of expenditures. Employees from the events and local suppliers to the events may use the additional personal income, derived from the direct and indirect effects of the increase in tourism expenditures, to consume local goods and services.

Some of the added revenues from the increase in tourism expenditures may, however, undergo leakage. For example, revenues may leak out of the local economy in the form of payment for imports or monies saved. Import payments can take several forms, such as repatriation of profits to foreign corporations and salaries to non-local managers, as well as payment for imported goods and promotion and advertising by companies based outside the destination.

Tourism-related commodities and services could be purchased from within the destination, thereby reducing leakages through the creation of economic interrelationships among the goods and service providers in the destination. The net effect of the successive rounds of spending of added tourism expenditure is the multiplier effect. In essence, tourism multipliers attempt to describe the relationship between direct tourism expenditure in the economy and the secondary effect of that expenditure upon the economy. Some of the factors that affect the multiplier are the size of the local economy, the propensity of tourists and residents to buy imported goods or services, as well as the propensity of residents to save rather than spend. In mathematical terms.

Some common multipliers are:

- The income multiplier, which measures the extra domestic income generated by an extra unit of tourism expenditure;
- The employment multiplier, which measures the increased number of primary and secondary jobs created by an extra unit of tourism expenditure;
- The government multiplier, which measures the extra government revenue created by an extra unit of tourism expenditure.

Multipliers can be calculated for a country, region or community. However, the information provided by tourism multipliers has to be very carefully evaluated. Factors such as the size of the destination can significantly affect the multiplier. A smaller economy may have a much smaller multiplier than a larger one since more goods and services might be imported to meet the tourists' needs, resulting in a greater leakage of revenues out of the destination. Hence, multipliers may vary greatly among communities within a country or region. Furthermore, since tourism multipliers can be calculated in a number of different ways, care must be taken when comparing the multipliers of different countries. Multipliers should be examined together with other measurements and indicators in order to determine the positive and negative economic impacts of tourism on the community.

INPUT-OUTPUT ANALYSIS

Studies of the economic impacts of tourism generally include inputoutput analysis. This kind of analysis helps to demonstrate how economic sectors are related, the number of linkages and the effect of these linkages. This form of analysis is, therefore, a means of analyzing inter-industry relationships in the flow of goods and services in an area's economy, through the chain of producers, suppliers and intermediaries to the final buyer.

Input-output analysis commences with the development of a table that illustrates, in matrix form, how transactions flow through the economy over a given time period. The rows of the matrix show the sales of the total output by each sector to every other sector. The columns demonstrate the inputs required by every sector from the other sectors. When assessing tourism accommodation, the rows in the table would demonstrate the output, *i.e.,* the revenues generated by each industry from the sale of products or services, including accommodation, meals, tour guides and related services such as laundry, medical services etc.

The columns would allow us to see the inputs that go into the output of the accommodation sector, including food, utilities, paper products, advertising and promotion services, wage and salary levels etc. Using a combination of matrix manipulations, multipliers can be calculated to provide an assessment of the effects of different sectors on each other. While input-output tables are helpful in understanding the linkages of the sectors in the economy, it must be remembered that the information obtained provides a snapshot of inter-industry economic actions at only one point in time.

TOURISM SATELLITE ACCOUNTS

Satellite accounts provide comprehensive information on a field of economic activity, and are generally tied to the economic accounts of a nation or region. The Tourism Satellite Account is a relatively new phenomenon. For example, the British Columbia Ministry of Development, Trade and Tourism has developed a Tourism Satellite Account as a separate input-output model designed to display tourism's contributions to the province related to the overall input-output model of the province. A Tourism Satellite Account has also been developed by Statistics Canada in order to assess the significance of tourism to Canada. The account uses concise definitions of tourism and attempts to provide a clear and real measure of tourism-related economic activity. Both direct and indirect tourism activities are accounted for in areas such as, but not limited to, demand, supply, employment, taxes etc. Such a tool is crucial in determining the complex spending patterns of visitors as well as the goods and services that cater to their needs.

Some of the advantages of the Tourism Satellite Accounts can be summarized as follows:

- They help governments and businesses determine the value of tourism to the economy, and thereby develop strategies for ensuring competitive advantage;
- They identify the amount of benefit enjoyed by various sectors, and the employment, income, taxes and other benefits that flow from those sectors;
- They provide a comprehensive picture of the size and scale of tourism in a country, and can help to gather support for ensuring adherence to the principles of sustainable tourism development.

COST-BENEFIT EVALUATION

By applying a number of economic tools and methods, destinations are able to obtain a large array of economic information on tourism; this information can then be used to make decisions. In assessing this information, analysts, planners, and managers have to determine not just whether jobs and wealth are created, but also how the benefits are distributed, what costs result from the development process, and whether the benefits of tourism outweigh the economic, social and cultural costs. It is clear that economic analysis needs to be integrated with other data in order to provide a reasonable indication of whether tourism is a good strategy for the destination.

Cost-benefit analysis is an important activity to perform, but is also difficult to carry out, since a number of the costs are very difficult to quantify. How does one measure the "sense of place" or "spiritual happiness" of a population? How does one quantify the loss value of habitat fragmentation to ecological integrity? While strides are being taken to develop full-cost, environmentally-based accounting, some measures may need to remain qualitative rather than quantitative. Full-scale cost-benefit analysis, while recommended, can therefore be time consuming, expensive and difficult to conduct. Another challenge of cost-benefit analysis lies in identifying who benefits from, and who pays the costs of, tourism. Smaller cost-benefit analyses can be conducted on specific issues to provide information related to tourism.

OBSTACLES TO CREATING ECONOMIC DEVELOPMENT FROM TOURISM

There are a number of obstacles to creating economic development through tourism. These obstacles are discussed below.

Market Obstacles

The potential for a region or municipality to attract tourists on a long-term basis is a key factor. Tourism activities, to a very large degree, are dictated by what is considered "popular" at a given point in time. In addition, the ability and interest of tourists to travel and how far they are willing to travel is dependent on a variety of factors, such as income levels, cost of fuel, job security, physical condition and mobility, and travel motivations.

The ability of a destination to conduct a reliable market survey, identify a positioning strategy and promote itself is essential. However, this requires skill and knowledge that is often lacking in many areas. In addition, cooperation in the marketing effort is important but difficult to achieve in many urban and rural settings.

Community Obstacles

Negative perceptions of tourism are often found at the local level. Tourism activities are not generally viewed as "viable" or "appropriate" business ventures. Generally, tourism is viewed as a short-term activity until more appealing and profitable employment can be found, since many tourism positions pay low wages and are seen as low-status occupations. These perceptions act as a deterrent to local people participating in tourism-related employment.

Lack of Infrastructure

As is discussed later in this study there are a number of infrastructure elements that are crucial to the success of tourism at all levels of a country or region. As tourism tastes change and become more sophisticated, and as the competitive environment further develops, countries and destinations will require adequate infrastructure to meet market demands as well as environmental regulations.

Environmental Obstacles

The emphasis in most tourism activities tends to be on attracting larger numbers of tourists to a region or site, posing problems for environmentally sensitive areas. It is clear that some environments may have to generate high-yielding tourist activities to generate sufficient income while protecting social and natural environments. This is difficult to accomplish in the highly competitive tourism market.

Lack of Integration

There is limited integration and cooperation between many tourism businesses given that, for the most part, the local tourism industry tends to be fragmented or lacking in tourism expertise.

Institutional Obstacles

There is very little coordinated governmental support and promotion for tourism development and initiatives. In addition, governmental activities are often poorly structured to help plan and manage tourism. In other instances, political and other ideologies make tourism planning and management difficult to implement.

Employment and Training Obstacles

There is a serious lack of training and education opportunities in tourism planning and management. The training that is available is often very narrow in focus, and does not address the broader context of tourism and the range of potential opportunities. The scarcity of employment equity and opportunities for women is a serious obstacle in ensuring an equitable distribution of the benefits of tourism activity. In addition, access to education and training is limited for a number of disadvantaged groups. It is clear from this discussion that there are a number of factors and obstacles that need to be considered in the expansion of tourism. It is essential that an integrated approach be taken. The role of infrastructure in that particular process will be explored in the remaining portion of this study.

RESTRICTIONS ON FOREIGN INVESTMENT

The Emergency Decree of 1944 granted extensive discretionary control over foreign capital to the Ministry of Foreign Relations and was intended to avert disruption of the economy by temporary investments of flight capital. The decree introduced restraints on the "creation, modification, liquidation and transfer of stock" of Mexican companies that might have foreign shareholders and were organized subsequent to its enactment. While it originally affected few and relatively insignificant activities, the Emergency Decree was nonetheless the precursor of present legal restraints on foreign investment in Mexico.

Two years later, the Interministerial Committee was created to coordinate national and foreign investment. Composed of representatives of the President and several ministries, it was established to make "a systematic and continuing study" of foreign investment in Mexico so that "a proper balance" between foreign and domestic capital could be maintained.

The committee, however, "largely ratified the practices already adopted by the Ministry of Foreign Relations under its discretionary powers." Since 1953, the committee has functioned haphazardly, and its significance has depended upon the conduct of the incumbent administration. Nevertheless, the committee's inaction did not deter enforcement of the Emergency Decree, which the Ministry of Foreign Relations in fact expanded beyond its literal provisions. Even though the Emergency Decree applied only to specifically delineated activities, the Ministry instructed notaries and public registry officials that licenses were required for the incorporation or amendment of the articles of any company, regardless of the purpose or nature of the business. At the same time, beginning in the early part of World War II, Mexico's attitude towards foreign capital shifted in an effort to improve the economy.

Between 1940 and 1965, direct foreign investment almost quadrupled, and by 1969, it exceeded two billion dollars. This increase, however, was accompanied by pressure from Mexican industrialists to limit the inflow of foreign capital.

Extensive foreign investment was noted to result in decapitalization and to increase the country's balance-of-payments problems. Government economists also were concerned and recommended that "the pattern of investment in assembly and processing operations, characteristic of the 1940's... be broken and greater use of domestically produced intermediate materials encouraged to stimulate import substitution." Efforts were increasingly made to displace foreign investment. Joint ventures of Mexican and foreign capital were promoted, as were industrial integration programmes, and foreign participation was excluded from certain industries and severely limited in others.

In 1966 the Ministry adopted another significant policy: to deny licenses for the acquisition of majority interests in existing Mexican companies. The mélange of restricted industries suggests that there was no overall planning or general policy concerning foreign participation in the Mexican economy. Some of the restrictions related to national security and the public welfare, while others seem to have been imposed in response to pressure from ad hoc private groups fearful about foreign competition.

Furthermore, although special laws were enacted that expressly limited foreign investment in certain industries, other industries were added to the restricted list "solely on the basis of policy decisions by the Ministry of Foreign Relations, acting either on its own initiative or, more likely, on the initiative of, or at least with the concurrence of, other governmental agencies." By 1970, the only legal restrictions on the amount of foreign participation in industrial activities were those resulting from the application of the Emergency Decree of 1944 and the exclusion of private participation, both domestic and foreign, in nationalized industries.

The Government used other techniques, however, to divest foreigners of control and ownership, including tax incentives and the selective application of import controls.

As one author has noted, the administration "seemed to prefer the flexibility in shaping its policies to individual investment projects that was allowed by the absence of a general law on foreign investments," and it adopted "specific statutory restraints in selected industries as it felt the need or desirability [to arise]." The resultant overall attitude towards foreign investment was "one of cautious acceptance," although many perceived it to be excessively protective and nationalistic. Foreign investment was encouraged as a complement to domestic investment, and the Ministry of Commerce and Industrial Promotion increasingly insisted on Mexicanization and industrial integration. Businesses dependent upon imports of raw or intermediate products or materials, or of machinery or equipment learned that procurement of the necessary import licenses might depend on whether they had become Mexicanized.

The Ministry of Commerce and Industrial Promotion supervised not only the issuance of such licenses, but also industrial integration programmes. In return for a guarantee by the Ministry that the necessary licenses would be granted, that imports of competing products would be excluded or that Mexican competitors would need to meet the same conditions, new and existing companies agreed to increase the Mexican content of their products, limit prices and payments abroad, observe quality control standards and divert 51 per cent of their capital stock to Mexicans over a specified period of time. Furthermore, foreign investors learned that the availability of tax concessions depended upon Mexicanization.

As a result, an informal process of clearing investment projects with the Ministry of Commerce and Industrial Promotion developed, as prospective foreign investors sounded out the administration for assurances that their projects would be favourably received. The position of the foreign investor also changed. Tax and other concessions were offered to concerns with majority Mexican ownership under the 1972 Law for the Promotion of New and Necessary Industries, to manufacturing businesses in the border zones and areas outside Mexico City, and to enterprises exporting Mexican manufactured products; but the administration was no longer receptive to the establishment of firms for the final processing or mere assembly of imported parts or intermediate products.

Also, enterprises that were heavily dependent on imports were subjected to strong pressure to develop domestic production. The informal process of clearing proposed new investments and important expansions of existing facilities was "virtually institutionalized," and although still not required by law, the Ministry usually insisted that the projects be underwritten with a majority of Mexican capital.

Between 1972 and 1976, Mexico extended the controls over foreign investment. Of utmost importance was the Law for the Promotion of Mexican Investment and for the Regulation of Foreign Investment (the Foreign Investment Law or FIL), enacted in 1973. Its purpose was to codify existing laws, regulations and policies, and it established the National Foreign Investment Commission (FIC) to exercise significant discretionary powers created by law, and the National Registry of Foreign Investment (FIR).

THE FOREIGN INVESTMENT LAW AND THE FOREIGN INVESTMENT COMMISSION

Since 1973, the FIL has been the principal source of foreign investment restrictions. It applies to capital investments in Mexican businesses, to investments in the acquisition of Mexican real or personal property, and to other specified transactions, including the pledging of Mexican corporate shares to foreigners and foreign participation in a real property trust. It is restrictive, however, only with regard to direct investment; it does not explicitly regulate indirect investment such as loans. Actually, the FIL set forth only two major changes in the restriction of foreign investment. It limited foreign participation in the management of a corporation to the proportion of foreign capitalization and established the 49-51 per cent concept as a general rule.

This was the first time legislation required majority Mexican participation in a broad spectrum of activities and not in just a single activity. Although the FIL does not explicitly define either foreign investment or foreign investors, it does provide a list of activities and individuals that will be considered as such. It stipulates those economic activities exclusively reserved to the Government, those reserved to Mexican individuals or corporations without foreign participation and those in which foreign participation is specifically limited to less than 49 per cent.

It also contains a general provision limiting foreign participation in new businesses whose activities are otherwise not regulated to a maximum of 49 per cent. Furthermore, the FIL requires governmental authorization for investments acquiring more than 25 per cent of the equity or more than 49 per cent of the fixed assets of an existing Mexican company, and for any transaction resulting in the transfer of management to a foreign investor. Unless a foreign investor is interested in establishing a business with more than 49 per cent foreign equity, the business may simply be registered with the FIR.

However, the final decision on whether a foreign investor may hold a majority of foreign capital and control rests with the FIC. Since the 1973 law vested the FIC with broad discretionary powers, the commission could increase the "maximum" 49 per cent foreign equity whenever it deemed the project beneficial to the Mexican economy. The burden, though, now fell on the foreign investor to show that majority foreign equity and control would "stimulate a balanced and equitable development" and "consolidate the economic independence of the country." The FIC consists of representatives of the President and seven ministries, and meets on a monthly basis.

Pursuant to its statutory powers, it may:

- Increase or reduce the percentage of foreign participation in geographical areas or economic activities when there are no required definite percentages and establish the terms and conditions under which the investment will be received;
- Resolve on specific percentages and conditions for those projects which "may justify special treatment";
- Resolve on projected foreign investment in companies established or to be established in Mexico;
- Resolve on the participation of existing foreign investors in new areas of economic activities or in new product lines; and
- Establish "requirements and criteria" for the application of foreign investment laws and regulations.

Pursuant to the FIL, the FIC issues General Resolutions setting forth standards and requirements for applying the law, although there are no "regulations" *per se*. Applications submitted to the FIC for approval of majority foreign equity are first analysed by a technical committee and then submitted to the FIC for formal acceptance. Invariably, applications undergo a process of negotiation, ranging from 4 to 16 months in duration.

Investment with majority foreign equity has had several disadvantages: the length of time required to obtain approval for either the formation or expansion of a company, and the restricted sources of tax and other investment incentives. In contrast, an investment of 49 per cent or less foreign equity can be organized immediately, may be expanded into different areas or used for new product lines, qualifies automatically for tax and other incentives, and usually will provide easier access to administrative agencies and the various licenses required for imports.

Furthermore, Mexican laws protect minority shareholders, whether Mexican or foreign, against decisions by a majority group of shareholders, and additional protection may be secured by provisions inserted into the bylaws or articles of incorporation. Since the enactment of the 1973 FIL, exceptions to the 49-51 per cent concept have been granted rarely and only under special circumstances. Foreign equity in excess of 49 per cent has tended to be approved in such sectors as tourism, priority industries, advanced technology, capitalization and investments preserving employment, and for priority activities of Mexican corporations with severe economic problems. Furthermore, the overwhelming majority of these exceptions have been contingent upon agreement eventually to Mexicanize.

The FIC bases its decisions on the criteria set forth in the National Industrial Development Plan (NIDP) and the FIL. The foreign investment allowed should always be complementary to the Mexican economy; there should not be substitution of fields covered; the company should be ready to export; it should commit itself to a precise plan to train Mexican personnel; a high percentage of the financing should come from abroad; there should be diversification of the sources of investment; the company should have a significant positive effect on local employment; the project should preserve the cultural and social values of Mexico; it should be located in an underdeveloped geographical area; and it should contribute to the technological development of the country. Two of the most significant criteria considered by the FIC in determining exceptions under the FIL are whether the proposed activity is an industry or is in a geographical area encouraged under the NIDP. Although each presidential administration adopts its own NIDP, the underlying premise remains constant.

The 1983-1988 NIDP incorporates criteria set forth in the FIL. Moreover, the 1983 NIDP contains detailed political and economic policies governing "the Mexican State, the diagnosis of the national problems, the purposes and strategies of solutions in a national and international context, and the bases for implementation of those strategies." Each NIDP, therefore, provides indicators of the attitude and direction to be taken by the incumbent administration towards foreign investment. In February 1983, the Constitution was amended, enabling "the federal government to adopt measures of great scope in economic matters, and reorienting the principles governing the actions of the state and private individuals."

The amendments embody principles consistent with the present administration's philosophy of la Rectoría del Estado (the state as sovereign and the sole conductor of the economy). The amendments identify activities reserved exclusively to the Government, but they also provide for the development of the private sector. In view of the increasing restrictions on the amount of allowable foreign equity in various activities, the formidable effort required to obtain an exception to the 49-51 per cent "rule" and the few exceptions granted, the FIC's announcement in February 1984 that it would consider up to 100 per cent foreign capital investment in a significant number of activities ran completely counter to the expectations of the investment community. Mexico's present policy on foreign investment is in the process of evolution and finds support in the FIL, the NIDP, resolutions of the FIC, and declarations by the Executive Secretary of the FIC and the Secretary of Commerce and Industrial Promotion. It focuses primarily on the selective promotion of new or necessary industries. No longer amenable to the acceptance of foreign investment in an indiscriminate manner, it does, however, encourage activities that will further the economic development of the country.

The primary objective of the 1984 Guidelines for Foreign Investment is the active, systematic and selective promotion of foreign investment in specific activities considered the most important for "a fair and balanced growth of the Mexican economy." That promotion is to focus on those areas which will generate a positive foreign exchange balance, produce competitive exports and import substitution, contribute to national scientific and technological development, advance Mexico's further integration into the international community, involve large investments, and create employment and geographical decentralization of industry. In analysing the basis of foreign investment policy, the FIC acknowledges that, "[a]lthough an adequate Law exists for direct foreign investments, a systematic policy has not always been followed for an effective utilization of its potential for the country's development."

The FIC has found that, in reality, "the effective use of investments to promote national technological development, to efficiently replace imports or generate exports for a positive trade surplus" has been hindered by multinational corporations that "frequently tend to seek benefits through equipment and technologies already obsolete in their own countries, protectively, and obtain excessive gains at the expense of national consumers." Similarly, the FIC concedes that, while past practices have quantitatively limited foreign investment, such practices have not induced a "favourable direction." Instead, foreign investment policy "has been limited to a simple check of investment propositions, set forth in accordance with international production strategies, or marketing of foreign companies' products, not always adequate to local, or national priorities or those of certain sectors." The FIC also recognizes that negotiations regarding foreign investments have been "limited to imposing local integration requirements or filling export quotas," with "[t]he latter in many cases hav[ing] been difficult or impossible to follow." The Guidelines represent the FIC's attempt to correct these deficiencies by adjusting Mexico's policies on foreign investment and its regulation. While foreign investment will remain a "complement" to domestic investment, the "policy will cease to be merely defensive and [will] turn active and systematic, promoting the formation of foreign investment alternatives, just as to needs derived from national development priorities."

The Guidelines list priority activities that may receive up to 100 per cent direct foreign investment. Priority undertakings, as delineated in the Guidelines, include the production of non-electric equipment and machinery, electric machinery and appliances, electronic equipment and devices, and equipment and material for transportation; metal mechanics; the chemical industry; other manufacturing industries; advanced technology services; and the hotel industry. The Guidelines state, however, that the enumerated activities are of an "indicative character" and that the list may be expanded by the Ministry of Commerce and Industrial Promotion "as a result of specific proposals or through the various groups of the national productive sectors."

Certainly, one of the most important goals of the Guidelines is to encourage national technological development. As the FIC recognizes, however, preference will need to be given to "coinvestment" in order to "guarantee a real transference of technology." Nevertheless, compared to large firms, small and medium-sized foreign companies are to receive "more flexible treatment" since it is presumed that their "investments and transference of technology carry lesser risks of dependency and may be valuable in agricultural and livestock sectors and certain branches of capital equipment and consumers' items." Increases in the percentage of foreign equity in Mexican companies by capitalization of debt, sale of stock or waiver of stock subscription rights of first refusal by Mexican shareholders may be granted for financially troubled industries on the list of national priorities.

Alternative measures, however, must first prove unworkable, and the increase of capital must be indispensable to the survival of the company. Furthermore, provision is made for the expansion of existing foreign companies in priority areas where such expansion will lead to the "modernization of the plants, the commitment of greater volumes of exports and increase the level of national integration in the production process." Another significant aspect of the Guidelines is the absence of a requirement to Mexicanize within a specified time period. Although the FIL does not deal with this issue, almost every exceptional allowance of majority foreign equity that was granted before the Guidelines were issued required Mexicanization, usually within 10 years.

The FIC has acknowledged, however, that "the process of Mexicanizing companies in which foreigners participate has in many cases resulted [in] an illusion with undesirable effects on industrial concentration, pricing policies and available investment resources." Some reports announcing the Guidelines have viewed them as an open invitation to any and all foreign investment. The Guidelines very clearly state, however, that only certain activities will be promoted. Although other activities are generally welcome, the requirement of minority foreign equity will continue to apply. The activities promoted under the Guidelines are strategic in nature, in conformity with the goals of the NIDP, and even those activities will be analysed by the FIC in terms of the criteria set forth in both the NIDP and the FIL.

On August 30, 1984, the FIC published five new resolutions pursuant to the Guidelines. Their purposes are twofold: to update the FIC's General Resolutions in accordance with the economic priorities of the NIDP and the Guidelines, and to improve and expedite the application process for majority foreign investments. For example, the resolutions eliminate the need for FIC authorization for certain foreign investment activities in in-bond companies; for the substitution of foreign directors, provided the ratio of domestic and foreign capital is not changed; and, under certain circumstances, for the opening or relocation of specified establishments. Additionally, the resolutions enlarge the powers of the Executive Secretary of the FIC, and he may authorize certain actions without prior FIC approval. The resolutions also include provisions that are expected to decrease significantly the amount of time required to complete an application for majority foreign capitalization.

Pursuant to the resolutions, applications to the FIC are to be negotiated through the Executive Secretary, who is then to submit them to the FIC for its formal acceptance within 30 business days of completion of the file. Announcement of the Guidelines has resulted in much speculation and misunderstanding. Research for this object included interviews that were graciously extended by bankers, corporations, the FIC and foreign investment legal practitioners. Their perceptions of the Guidelines assisted invaluably in the following analysis of Mexico's changing position on foreign investment.

PATTERN OF GLOBAL ECONOMIC DEVELOPMENT

While there are many details that are the subjects of ongoing research, the large-scale pattern of business and economic development through the 20th century is not the subject of significant dispute. One of the most fundamental underlying trends is that as poorer countries develop economically they progressively 'take over' industries in which low labour costs are a significant advantage, and export their products to richer countries. Employment in these relatively low-productivity activities is thereby lost from the rich countries. In parallel, the familiar processes of automation and improving business practices continually reduce the number of employees needed to produce a given quantity of goods and services. However, these trends have not caused rising unemployment overall because the displaced employees are re-employed in new industries which are continually being created.

The process of global economic development is thus one of continuous change, involving the decline and failure of companies as well as the birth and growth of new ones. As a consequence, for most people it is not possible to improve their standard of living without accepting change in their working lives. In addition, the timing of economic booms and recessions depends on many factors including chance discoveries leading to innovation, the whims of entrepreneurs and the vagaries of political decisions. Although economic growth can be hindered by government policies, the underlying process cannot be stopped-at least not without preventing people from trying to improve their standard of living which is not desirable. In the simplest terms, some people use their heads to work out ways of achieving the same results with less effort. This human creativity, specifically in inventing machines improving business practices (including expanding trade), and developing new popular services makes the productivity of work grow continuously, decade after decade, enabling everyone's incomes and standards of living to rise progressively.

World economic growth also requires international flexibility and agreement on rules of 'fair play'. For example, the rapid economic growth achieved by Japan from the 1960s until the 1980s caused considerable trade friction with the then more advanced countries as it changed the pattern of global specialisation-even leading the French Prime Minister Cresson to describe Japan as "France's number one enemy". Thus Japan's rapid growth depended on the richer countries' willingness to make adjustments to facilitate it, which Japan in turn is now required to show towards later developing countries.

However, as a measure of how much more adjustment in the structure of the world economy is going to be required, note that the combined populations of India and China are 20 times the population of Japan, and their average wages are just a small percentage of Japanese wages today. Consequently the adjustments in the pattern of global specialisation that will be required to accommodate the growth in these countries' shares of world trade will be proportionately many times larger than was required for Japan. The recent rapid growth of exports of clothing from both countries, and of food products, light manufactured goods and motorcycles from China, and bicycles and software from India, is just the beginning of this long process of adjustment. In principle the growth of exports resulting from such differences in labour costs will not end until average incomes in these countries reach broadly the same level as in the richer countries.

(The current loss of competitiveness of certain industries in Korea Taiwan and other southeast Asian countries, as their average incomes rise relative to those in China, are examples of this process.). For humanitarian reasons, as well as from the wish to reduce friction between richer and poorer countries, we must hope that poorer countries' economic development continues successfully. But, as an inescapable corollary, to the extent that these countries' participation in the world economy grows through the 21st century, proportionately greater innovation of new industries will be required in the currently more advanced countries. If this is insufficient, unemployment will increase very substantially, and/or average incomes will fall proportionately because of inexorable competition from countries with lower average incomes.

Overall, as the human effort needed to produce the same output of goods and services becomes less and less through technical and managerial progress, and unless humans generate more total output and consume more goods and services, the total amount of work needed will fall. In this case, unless the remaining work is shared out through shortening average working hours (and reducing wages proportionately), more and more people will become unemployed. During the 20th century demand did not reach such a limit; instead, although employment in many older industries shrank drastically in the richer countries, the continuation of economic growth was stimulated by the creation of new industries.

CREATION OF NEW INDUSTRIES

During the 20th century, as the number of people in economically more advanced countries who worked in such fields as agriculture, horse-drawn transport, steam-engines, mining, textiles, clothing and many other traditional activities declined, a wide range of new industries arose which re-employs those displaced. These included car manufacturing and associated activities (such as oil production, refining and distribution and road construction and maintenance), electricity generation and distribution, the film, radio, television and video industries, aircraft manufacturing and operation and associated activities (such as airport construction and operation and air traffic management), telecommunications, computers, tourism and an ever-growing range of leisure industries, including many sports activities.

During the 20th century also, government activities expanded from <10per cent of GNP to some 40per cent-though this trend has more-or-less stopped or even begun to reverse in most countries with the recent moves towards privatisation. This new trend has been stimulated by work in the field of 'Public Choice' economics, which has provided the theoretical explanation for the fact that, in general, government activities are economically very inefficient, as outlined for instance in.

It is a sine qua non for continuing economic growth in the 21st century that the rich countries continue this process of creating new industries which will employ people displaced from older industries as they progressively automate and migrate to lower-cost countries. During the 20th century this process created high-productivity employment for hundreds of millions of people around the world, and enabled many more people in developing countries to gain employment in exporting and importing businesses, thereby facilitating their economic growth. It is a key desire of companies in poorer countries today to be allowed to increase their exports to richer countries, but these are restricted by international treaties designed to protect relatively uncompetitive activities in the richer countries, in order to reduce local unemployment. For example the governments of the USA and the EU subsidise the production of many agricultural products, thereby reducing the market for imports from cheaper countries, and they also subsidise the export of agricultural surpluses, providing a second blow to poorer countries' price-competitive agricultural industries. The G7 countries also limit clothing and textile imports from poorer countries.

The development of new industries has another important aspect, namely the 'leading sector' effect: as investors anticipate the future profits that they expect to be earned in new industries, market prices of relevant companies' shares rise. This attracts more investment to these companies, helping them to grow faster, while the 'wealth effect', whereby shareholders spend their new (anticipated) wealth, spreads the benefits of expansion to other sectors of the economy.

This process was seen particularly clearly in the late 1990s in the USA, when share prices of many companies related to the major innovations of the Internet and World Wide Web grew by hundreds and even thousands of percent. As shareholders became wealthy, at least 'on paper', they increased their spending on a wide range of goods and services including houses, cars, restaurants, travel and leisure, thereby greatly stimulating the general economy. Unfortunately, in this particular case, much of the rise in share prices of 'new economy' companies was distorted in an economic 'bubble' in which investors had become unrealistically optimistic. Consequently the companies in question did not achieve the high level of profits that stockbrokers' analysts were predicting, and their share prices have since fallen steeply to date, destroying several trillion dollars of the 'wealth' that had been anticipated. (Controversy continues over the relative blame attributable to failures of business ethics, stockbrokers' conflicts of interest, auditors' standards, market regulation, media reporting, economic policy and investor caution.)

Today the need for new industries is particularly urgent because of the serious imbalances in the world economy. These include the decade-long recession that has led to the highest unemployment in Japan for 50 years, with continuing deflation and negative economic 'growth'; continuing double-digit unemployment in much of continental Europe-as well as in Russia, Southeast Asia, South America and many other countries; and a deepening recession combined with an unsustainably high trade deficit and private indebtedness in the USA. The fundamental reason for this deflationary condition of the world economy is the excess capacity in many older industries and insufficient investment in the establishment and growth of profitable new industries, which alone can create new employment for those no longer needed in mature industries. The record US trade deficit of more than $1 billion per day, first reached during the 'Clinton bubble', is a measure of many US industries' lack of economic competitiveness: toys, clothing, electrical goods, steel, televisions, personal computers and mobile telephones are just some of the industries in which fewer and fewer US-based manufacturers can match global competition. The only way in which the currently richer countries can maintain higher average incomes than currently less-developed countries is through working with higher productivity: people earning higher incomes cannot compete with people using the same technology and know-how but working at significantly lower incomes. The solution to enabling those in already rich countries to maintain or increase their standards of living while also enabling poorer countries to grow rapidly, is for companies in G7 countries to work at newer activities that poorer countries cannot yet perform. The need for this was explicitly recognised in a 2001 article in the Washington Post: "What this country needs is a really good $500 billion technology-something to reignite popular enthusiasm and the economy".

What, then, are the new industries that are expected to generate new fields of large-scale high-productivity employment? It is important to note first that commentators' inability to predict future industries is no evidence that they will not arise: almost no-one in 1902 could even imagine, let alone predict, the rise of passenger air travel, nor a fortiori its growth to its current world-changing scale. Economic commentators today predict growth in employment in many areas of the information industry (although it is important to recognise that the growth of the Internet is also eliminating work in many related fields); in biotechnology, including the use of genetic information in agriculture and medicine; and in activities aimed at environmental preservation.

Many new opportunities could also arise through restructuring the incentives created by the government-imposed pattern of taxation and subsidies. For example, in many countries employment is heavily taxed and large companies are subsidised, while the use of non-renewable resources and environmentally damaging activities are lightly taxed or even subsidised. Reversing these undesirable distortions could increase the quantity of employment in many different fields, including particularly recycling activities. An important clue to the identity of other fields in which new jobs will arise in rich countries can be found in the 'Engel coefficient', which is defined as the proportion of peoples' income spent on food (although alternative definitions based on expenditure on 'necessities' are also used). The average Engel coefficient in any country falls progressively as it develops economically; in G7 countries it is now typically <25per cent. Further economic growth in such rich countries depends less on providing for consumers' real 'needs' and more on satisfying their 'wants'. Broadly speaking, this explains the relatively rapid growth of leisure-related industries. Although many people feel that there are more 'important' things in which to invest than leisure industries, once average productivity reaches the level in the G7 countries, most basic needs of the society can be satisfied by a fraction of the workforce-for example agriculture typically employs <5per cent of the workforce. Thus there is no longer enough 'essential' work to employ more than a fraction of the population in richer countries.

One problem that arises in low-Engel-coefficient societies is that the demand for non-essential goods and services is relatively unstable, since by definition their consumption can readily be cut if necessary. This inherent instability is seen clearly in the demand for tourist air travel which periodically falls sharply as a result of heightened concern about the risk of terrorism. Another example of this instability is that as the number of two-, three-and four-car families increases, sales of used cars can grow rapidly at times of recession, leading to dramatic falls in the demand for new cars.

The truth of the 'human condition' at the start of the 21st century is that economic development has progressed so far in the G7 countries that, if the average standard of living is to continue to rise, there is an urgent need for the growth of major new industries, most of which will probably be leisure services broadly defined. The reason for this is that in order for a new industry to grow to large scale it must provide services that will be purchased by a large proportion of the middle-class population-most of whom already possess most of the goods they 'need'. Arguably the most significant industrial development of the 20th century was the development of passenger air travel from zero in 1900 to 1.5 billion passengers per year in 2000. Among other effects, this development has helped the hotel and restaurant industries to reach their present scale, employing some 60 million people or 3per cent of the world's total labour-force, and some 6per cent in Europe. As a pointer to the future growth potential, a survey performed in 2001 showed that the majority of middle-aged and older Japanese do not wish to purchase any more goods; the main service they wish to buy is foreign travel-which has notably been booming even during the current recession.

Until 2001 the aviation industry was predicting 100per cent growth over the next 20 years, although airlines' increased costs for security and customers' fears of terrorism may reduce this. However, it should be noted that tourism is already having damaging environmental impacts as a result of ever-growing numbers of tourists visiting popular destinations. It is not clear that this activity can reasonably grow by a factor of 1000per cent as would be necessary by the time-perhaps 2100?-when most of the world population attains a middle-class lifestyle which includes foreign travel.

Some commentators, mostly in the richer countries, take the view that most of those living in the presently poorer countries will remain poor forever. However, living standards are rising in every country, and the desire for material comfort is strong everywhere that living standards are low. While attaining a 'middle-class lifestyle' in the same form as seen today in G7 countries for a world population of perhaps 10 billion people would cause many industries-energy, construction, cars, agriculture, waste disposal-to degrade the environment severely, it must be anticipated that technological progress will greatly ease currently foreseeable problems. The application of even only presently foreseeable advances in already existing fields-such as genetic engineering and hydroponics in agriculture, energy efficiency and non-fossil (solar) energy, city planning, and Internet-based tele-commuting, to name but a few-holds such clear promise that simple extrapolations based on multiplying existing economic activity by increased population numbers without allowing for technological improvements are unrealistically pessimistic. As a result it may be that the main limits to the potential for terrestrial economic growth are political ones. It is clearly in the self-interest of the already-rich countries to try harder to help overcome these in order to reduce the friction that would be inevitable in a globalized world with continuing gross inequalities in living standards.

Whatever the longer term future, assuming that economic growth will continue for at least a few more decades, the popularity of leisure travel in low-Engel-coefficient societies raises the question of what other newer destinations people could travel to. Tourist destination development is proceeding rapidly around the world, but a new possibility which has received ever-increasing attention is passenger travel to space, or 'space tourism'. It is now clear that this idea is not only not fantasy, but it is a promising candidate to grow into a major new activity as economically valuable and socially significant as passenger air travel.

ECONOMIC POTENTIAL OF PASSENGER SPACE TRAVEL

On the 'demand side' of passenger space travel, market research performed in Japan, Canada, the USA, Germany and the UK, and summarised in has shown that there is enormous pent-up consumer demand. It is sometimes suggested that this demand is fictitious; for example a recent letter to Aviation Week and Space Technology stated: "People were already travelling in the early days of aviation-by trains boat and car. They had a reason for travelling and infrastructure to support them when they reached their destination. The aeroplane became another mode of transportation. The reasons for travelling do not exist for space. No one is visiting relatives, emigrating nor going to business meetings. And there is no infrastructure in space".

However, it is a mistake to have preconceived ideas about people's reasons for wishing to travel to space, which are obviously different from reasons for travelling on Earth. The market research referred to above shows consistently that a large proportion of the middle class population of the richer countries does want to go to space, and that their major reason for wanting to do so is to be able to look back at the Earth. The fact that all of the 400 people who have been to space to date say that it was the greatest experience of their lives probably has some connection with this immense popularity. While there is a great need for more market research, and it will remain uncertain how many people will actually travel to space until the service becomes widely available, there is no justification for denying facts shown by market research.

Furthermore, contrary to what the above letter states, there is infrastructure to support travellers-a partly assembled space station which was sufficient for the first customer, Dennis Tito, to describe the Russian section as "paradise". The second piece of infrastructure for space travellers, Mir Corp's 'Mini-Station', is due to become operational for an investment of $100 million. And as launch costs fall to a few hundred dollars/kg as passenger traffic grows, it will be possible to assemble even very large accommodation facilities in orbit at a cost acceptable to hotel companies.

On the 'supply side' of passenger space travel technical studies by the Japanese Rocket Society (JRS), Dietrich Koelle, Ivan Bekey, Bristol Spaceplanes, Buzz Aldrin and others have shown that the cost of developing the required vehicles and infrastructure would be a small fraction of the $25 billion that G7 taxpayers already pay every year for government space activities. The great potential of passenger space travel for 'space commercialisation' has also been acknowledged in reports published by Nasa; the American Institute of Aeronautics and Astronautics (AIAA) which concluded: ''In light of its great potential public space travel should be viewed as the next large new area of commercial space activity''; and the Japan Federation of Economic Organisations, among other organisations.

One particularly interesting conclusion of the Nasa report namely that "generally available trips to orbit and weeklong stays in low Earth orbit hotels now can be seen as certainly feasible" gives a further indication of how large the economic impact of space tourism may become. This is because in all market research to date most people say they would like to spend several days or a week or more in orbit, rather than only a few hours or a day. Thus in addition to economical launch vehicles the demand for space tourism will also drive the construction and operation of accommodation in orbit-that is space hotels.

The only detailed professional study of the potential development of passenger space travel published to date is that of the Japanese Rocket Society (JRS) briefly reviewed in. (A large number of other papers from the pioneering JRS study are available in the library of the six major JRS reports published as of 2002 are available only in Japanese.)

According to the JRS scenario, the number of customers would reach 700,000 per year 17 years after starting the development of the ' Kankoh-maru' passenger vehicle, with a return flight price of some $20,000 per passenger.

The JRS cost estimates are in line with those of Koelle and Bekey. Extrapolating from this, when the number of guests reaches one million per year after perhaps 20 years, there will need to be accommodation for more than 10,000 people in orbit, and several thousand staff will work in orbit. Since no one has identified any other space activity that offers anything approaching this level of demand, we reach a conclusion that is still not widely appreciated-the hotel industry will probably become the largest employer in space.

From the economic point of view it is very significant that the development of orbital accommodation will lead to the participation of a wide range of associated industries, thereby greatly expanding the number of different industries involved in space activities including particularly such consumer-oriented activities as construction, interior design, hotel management, catering, fashion, entertainment and sports. This will have the effect of bringing the economic energy of the consumer economy to bear on space activities, which are cutoff from this source of economic growth, except for certain information services.

In addition to stimulating innovation in these many different fields, the growth of space tourism in this way could also exert a 'leading sector' effect, whereby an expansionary economic influence will diffuse through the economy as direct investment and optimism lead to increased shareholder wealth. Furthermore, the increase in employment and economic growth which the development of passenger space travel causes directly in more advanced economies will in turn reduce the pressure for protection against imports from less developed economies. Such a scenario is strikingly different from the effect of existing governments' non-science space activities which, sadly, contribute very little to the economy or employment, despite the very large financial resources they consume.

LOW ECONOMIC VALUE OF SPACE AGENCIES' ACTIVITIES

The desirability of initiating passenger space travel might be less if space agencies were engaged in work that was of great economic value or urgency-but they are not. Some 20per cent of their budgets are typically used for scientific research, including astronomy and Earth observation, which can be assumed to have value per se. However, the remaining 80per cent, some $20 billion per year, is used for the development of technological systems and technologies for such purposes as "space infrastructure development". The economic value of the results of this expenditure can be considered in two parts, direct and indirect.

Direct Economic Value

The definition of economic value is the present value of future profits to which an activity gives rise. Since space agencies' investment mostly does not lead to commercially profitable activities, it has far less economic value than normal business investment. The difference between commercial activities and space agencies' activities. In round figures when a company invests $1 billion it typically generates commercial sales revenues of some $1 billion per year, from which the cumulative profits over several years exceed the initial investment by a sufficient margin to satisfy investors and increase the assets of the company. (For example, $1 billion investment might generate profits of $3 billion over 10 years, from which $2 billion would be repaid to investors, and $1 billion would add to the company's assets.) By contrast, the expenditure of some $20 billion per year by government space agencies on non-science activities generates little or no increase in commercial space activities: employment in space activities is currently shrinking, rather than growing cumulatively, as would result from commercial investment on this scale.

For example, the development and operation of expendable launch vehicle systems are heavily loss making; such launchers never repay their development costs, and depend in many cases on continuing government funding of periodic 'upgrades'. At the time of writing, the most recent of many articles describing the lack of demand for satellite launch services states that, of the three main launch vehicle manufacturers: "Arianespace, the only company that discloses its annual earnings, posted a loss in 2001 for the second straight year..." and predicts that because "the market could remain flat for the next 10-20 years..." one of the three companies may disappear in the anticipated 'shake-out'.

Following the conventional definition of economic value given above, the ' International Space Station' (ISS) project has very little economic value: almost no companies want to pay to use its facilities, and their total contribution will represent a small fraction of its running costs alone, let alone repaying taxpayers' investment of some $50 billion. The probability of researchers on board the station making a valuable scientific discovery must also be judged to be low: research in microgravity has been underway for more than 30 years, and there is little expectation of any major discoveries in the near term, particularly since the microgravity environment on board the station will be of low quality.

This and the station's very high cost led many science research bodies, including the US National Science Foundation and the British Science Research Council, not to support the project. In 2001, as the latest step in the ISS's ever-growing cost and ever-shrinking capabilities, Nasa's announcement of further 'cost growth' of $5 billion led to it becoming the subject of a special investigation by the US government's General Accounting Office.

Upon the departure of its then administrator it was decided to appoint the deputy director of the Office of Management and Budget (OMB) as his replacement. (It is perhaps worth noting that accounting is not a mysterious activity. When the managers of a $15 billion per year organisation choose to use accounting systems that allow them to be 'surprised' by cost over-runs as large as $5 billion, this is surely not accidental-it is done because it is in their economic interest to obscure the truth.

In this, space agency managers' behaviour is entirely consistent with the economic analysis of government bureaucracy pioneered by Niskanen. Because of the incentives which a bureaucratic organisation creates for its staff, they are motivated primarily to increase their budget; they have no motivation "either to know or seek out the public interest or to act in the public interest". Until the 'crisis' of 2001, successive Nasa administrators' policy of having such inadequate accounting information was successful in preserving its budget; and it seems very unlikely that Nasa or its management will suffer any significant cost-certainly nothing approaching that experienced in commercial companies when their accounts are revealed to be untrustworthy, such as the 'carnage' among 'new economy' companies in the USA in 2001-2002.)

Indirect Economic Value

Advocates of larger budgets for government space agencies frequently argue that government spending on space is much more beneficial for the economy than other forms of economic activity, thanks to the useful inventions arising from the development of space-related technology. The original source of this idea was a study performed during the 1970s by Chase Econometrics, which claimed to find such an effect. In a recent citation members of the US Congressional Research Service in 1998 wrote: "Studies by Chase Econometrics Inc., and the Midwest Research Institute in the late 1980s determined that every Nasa R&D dollar produced $5-$9 in economic activity".

However, it is rarely reported that when Chase Econometrics tried to reproduce their work in 1980 they concluded that: "productivity changes from Nasa R&D spending proved not to be statistically different from zero". Hertzfeld studied the issue in detail and concluded: "due to theoretical and data problems with the macroeconomic model and data sets available, this approach to finding aggregate economic returns to R&D expenditure is difficult at best, and probably impossible". Other studies of particular technologies developed at Nasa which have subsequently been used in new products are said to have shown reasonable rates of return. However, such studies do not enable any conclusions to be drawn concerning the relative value of alternative innovations that would have arisen if the same funding had been applied in other fields, such as marine engineering, electrical engineering etc.

In this context the bar chart presented to the US Congressional Science Committee by Sean O'Keefe, when Deputy Director of the OMB during 2001, is of interest. This shows that Nasa's budget of $15 billion per year is twice the combined research budgets of the US National Science Foundation (NSF) and the US National Cancer Institute (NCI). Since scientific research funded by these organisations has contributed to many of the Novel prizes and scientific advances which US researchers generate, the lack of Novel prizes or major technological advances arising from Nasa's work-let alone twice the annual output of the NSF and NCI combined-is striking. Seen in this light, the claim that US government spending on Nasa projects (including the $5 billion cost-growth during 2001) is particularly valuable for the economy is not credible. It appears rather to be a convenient myth that serves the economic interests of the government-funded space industry. Much more credible is the 'common sense' view that Nasa's expenditure of more than $100 billion during administrator Goldin's 1992 2001 tenure, during which employment in the space industry grew not at all and passenger space travel was starved of research funding (as discussed below), was a serious misuse of economic resources which could have been used much more productively on other activities.

SPACE AGENCIES' ANTI-SPACE TOURISM POLICY

In view of the low economic value of space agencies' current activities, it is very unsatisfactory that they are making no attempt to realise or even evaluate passenger space travel. In this the agencies do not simply show a lack of enthusiasm-they appear to have deliberately delayed progress towards this economically valuable objective, and even to have concealed valuable information from the public. For example, the largest government space agency, Nasa, is required by US federal law to "encourage, to the maximum extent possible, the fullest commercial use of space". In its 1998 report, 'General Public Space Travel and Tourism', Nasa confirmed that space tourism is a realistic objective; that most people will be able to take a trip to space; that suborbital space travel (similar to that experienced by the first American to travel to space, Alan Shepard) is easily feasible using long-available technology; and that passenger space travel is likely to grow into a major commercial use of space. The report also included a long list of recommendations as to how to encourage this commercial use of space. However none of the recommendations in this report have been implemented, and no funding at all was allocated to advance the possibility-out of the $56 billion that Nasa has spent between that report's publication and time of writing. This behaviour is clearly contrary to Nasa's obligation to "encourage, to the maximum extent possible, the fullest commercial use of space".

It is worth noting that Nasa's 'space tourism report' can be judged the most economically valuable report Nasa has ever published, since it describes what is likely to become the largest commercial activity in space, and steps to realise it. It is therefore of particular interest that the then Nasa administrator Goldin refused to allow the report to be made available via Nasa's web site for over 3 years. The author spoke to both Goldin in 1999 and then deputy associate administrator Graver in 2000 at public meetings at which they both stated (in recorded sessions) that NP-1998-03-11-MSFC would be put upon the Nasa web site. However, this simple step did not take place until 2002. Early in 2001 Nasa administrator Goldin attempted unsuccessfully to prevent the US citizen Dennis Tito visiting the international space station; his high-profile campaign was widely reported in the media. Yet the 80per cent popular support shown for Dennis Tito in US opinion polls provides a good indication of the great popularity of passenger travel and the misguidedness of Nasa's stance on this matter. Subsequent events during 2001 included the announcement that Goldin would not continue as Nasa administrator; testimony requested by the Subcommittee on Space and Aeronautics of the Congressional Science Committee from Nasa deputy associate administrator W. Michael Hawes on 26 June concerning Nasa's work relating to space tourism; and the appearance on Nasa's internet web site of its space tourism report after over 3 years delay.

Also during 2001 newly appointed Nasa Chief of Staff Courtney Stand drafted a plan for the agency under which it was proposed that Nasa would "provide commercial projects with engineering support for private-sector development of commercial manned spaceflight vehicles for commercial space tourism". (It is perhaps worth noting that the main supporter of space tourism in the US government today is the associate administrator for Commercial Space Transportation in the FAA. As the first head of the then Office of Commercial Space Transportation within the Department of Transportation Stand could be expected to take a more commercial approach.)

The selection of Nasa during 2001 as the fourth-worst-managed activity within the US government, and the recently initiated probe into its extraordinary mismanagement of the ISS project provide further testimony to the very poor value-for-money that US taxpayers receive in return for $15 billion per year-over and above Nasa's deliberate delaying of the development of passenger space travel services. The growing political disenchantment with this behaviour is reflected in the recent comment that "space spending is moving from the back burner to completely off the stove".

Other Countries' Activities

Other countries' government space agencies also have responsibility for commercialisation of space activities, but they take a similar stance towards passenger space travel. For example the European Space Agency (Esa) joined Nasa's unsuccessful attempt to prevent Dennis Tito visiting the international space station, and has likewise provided almost no funding whatsoever for research on the economic potential of passenger space travel. The senior staff of Esa and their political paymasters do not want to know about the commercial potential of passenger space travel, any more than their counterparts in Nasa and the US Congress, exactly as Niskanen's work describes.

Uniquely among G7 countries' space agencies, the British National Space Centre (BNSC) invests in neither expendable launch vehicles (such as the

European Ariane) nor the international space station, since it is required to focus on space science research and activities with potential to be commercialised. However, in 2000 it was criticised by the UK Parliamentary Trade and Industry Committee for investing some 1 billion Sterling over the past decade in remote sensing systems that have generated far less commercial revenue than planned, and for actively discouraging any British government investment in research aimed at realising passenger space travel. The BNSC staff responsible for this stance, Director-General Colin Hicks, Deputy Director-General David Leadbeater and Director of Policy and Finance Alan Cooper, ignored the Committee's suggestion to perform some analysis of its feasibility. They have still provided no justification for their decade-long prevention of funding of work towards passenger space travel-which is clearly contrary to the BNSC's stated objective "to help industry maximise profitable space-based business opportunities".

Space agencies' negative behaviour towards the largest commercial opportunity in space can be termed a 'Conspiracy of Silence'. The economic reasons for their acting so strongly against the public interest in this matter are discussed in, and some of the 'cultural' reasons why the heads of space agencies unanimously refuse to permit any work to facilitate passenger space travel. Because of government space agencies' organisational structure making them responsible for commercialisation presents a conflict of interest with their own economic interest in survival and expansion, since it would mean handing over some of their operations to private companies.

They resolve this conflict, predictably, in their own interests by suppressing the most promising commercial application, which is ipso facto also the most threatening to their own interests. Nasa, Esa and other countries' national space agencies also exert a strong influence on the news media, being a near-monopoly source of information about space activities. This has helped to delay, though not to prevent, the growth of interest in passenger space travel in the mass media. By contrast, Russian companies have now already profitably carried two space tourists to orbit, and are currently planning an orbiting 'mini-station' for tourism accommodation at a cost of $100 million. This is particularly noteworthy since, at the time of writing, Nasa's mobile exhibition 'Starship 2040' is publicising the idea of a small module being feasible for space tourism in 2040. 'Starship' is smaller than the first US space station 'Skylab' that operated 70 years before this date. Together with the suppression of the 1998 Nasa space tourism report until July 2001, this can only be seen as deliberate 'disinformation' designed to mislead the US public, media, government and others about the potential for space tourism. In view of the potential for passenger space travel described above, it is clearly greatly against the public interest that space agencies are knowingly resisting progress in these ways in favour of continuing their existing activities despite their low economic value.

5

Prospects of E-Tourism

E-COMMERCE TOURISM

Tourism is growing fastest in the developing countries, where it is a major component of most economies. Tourism is one of the world's largest industries, and it is a natural partner for the Internet, where it is also the world's largest on-line industry. Community-based tourism (CBT) has been shown to foster local development in developing countries, particularly in the poorer rural areas. At the same time, Information and Communication Technologies are being deployed within poor communities in developing countries and are beginning to demonstrate their potential for inducing local development. This chapter describes an action research initiative for introducing electronic commerce for community based tourism (e-CBT) in three Asian rural communities in order to reveal its potential for community development.

E-CBT targets an important and growing market segment in the developing world, consisting of individual travellers for whom travel is an essential component of their life-style and who seek new and authentic experiences that are not directed towards a mass market. The proposal describes strategic partnerships between a University in Hong Kong and three other Asian universities who will work with local communities and tourism authorities for the eventual propagation of the development benefits of e-CBT among wider rural populations in their countries.

The WTO forecasts that international arrivals are expected to reach over 1.56 billion by the year 2020. The total expected tourist arrivals by region shows that by 2020 the top three receiving regions will be Europe (717 million tourists), East Asia and the Pacific (397 million) and Americas (282 million). East Asia and the Pacific, South Asia, the Middle East and Africa are forecasted to record growth at rates of over 5per cent per year, compared to the world average of 4.1 per cent. By 2010, WTO forecasts that the Americas will lose its number two position, behind Europe, to East Asia and the Pacific, which will receive 25 per cent of world arrivals. Tourism offers huge opportunities for developing countries to increase incomes from the growing number of arrivals that land on their shores. However, it has been recognized that many tourism policies developed from central governments without local involvement fail to cater for the sensibilities and aspirations of the communities that tourists visit. The conference on Community Based Ecotourism in Southeast Asia agreed that local communities should have the right to self-determination and to decide whether to accept or not accept the policies that affect their livelihood.

As tourism is essentially a micro- enterprise, tourism lends itself to local entrepreneurial activity, and community-based tourism has emerged as a mechanism for fostering locally based tourism operations, as opposed to those whose financial interests are often located away from the tourist destination. Moreover, as Information and Communication Technologies (ICTs) are beginning to be deployed in rural communities for the purpose of fostering local development, communities are able to implement electronic commerce in support of their CBT operations, and engage in e-CBT. Furthermore, it will be shown that the Internet is not only a natural partner for tourism, it also a natural partner for the market segment that e-CBT should target. With more than 600 million people on-line by September 2002, and more than 60per cent of them residing in Europe or North America, even small and remote communities with an Internet connection can address huge global markets.

The purpose of this chapter is to introduce the concept of electronic commerce for community based tourism, e-CBT, as a mechanism for local development. E-CBT involves the operation of local tourism activities which are promoted across the internet by a community using a community based telecentre, which provides community access to information and communication technologies. The concept is presented as a method for fostering rural development in developing countries.

Tourism is a principal export for developing countries and the least developed countries (LDCs). It is growing rapidly and is the most significant source of foreign exchange after petroleum (WTO, 2002). There is a general shift of tourism arrivals towards developing countries. Growth rates of international tourism receipts during the 1990s were, on average, 50per cent higher in the major developing country destinations than in comparison with the major developed country destinations. By far the largest single developing country international tourism destination is China.

The People's Republic accounted for US$10 billion in international tourism receipts in 1996, receiving 22.7 million international visitors, experiencing 19per cent annual growth rates of receipts since 1980. Together with earnings generated by the Hong Kong Special Administrative Region, China's 1996 receipts surpass US$20 billion. In 2001, China ranked fifth in the world's top tourism destinations, measured both by the number of international arrivals and by international tourism receipts. Yet in terms of Gross National Income per capita, China ranks 108 out of 173 countries in the World Bank's statistical indicators for 2001. China, Thailand and Indonesia together generated 40per cent of all international tourism receipts accruing to developing countries in 1996.

The World Tourism Organisation says there is a strong economic case for promoting tourism in developing countries, suggesting that affirmative action and pro-poor policies are able to go beyond trickle down and multiplier affects by unlocking opportunities for the poor within tourism (WTO 2002). Success in poverty alleviation through tourism depends, says the WTO, partly on effective community-public-private partnerships that serve to reduce financial leakages and increase economic linkages to the local economy.

Financial leakages occur where a disproportionately low percentage of tourism revenues stays in the local market, and they reduce the development impact of tourism. Linkages with the local economy foster revenue retention from tourism activities, and they depend on quality, reliability and competitiveness of local products.

WTO suggest various steps that can be taken to increase the benefits to the local economy in tourist destination areas, by;

- Facilitating local community access to the tourism market,
- Minimising the financial leakages from the local economy,
- Maximising the linkages of tourism to the local economy,
- Building on and complimenting existing livelihood strategies through employment and small enterprise development,
- Ensuring that tourism products contribute to local economic development not just to national revenue generation.
- Tourism is a principal export for 83per cent of developing countries and it is the principal export for one third of them.
- Developing countries had 292.6 million arrivals in 2000, an increase since 1990 of nearly 95per cent. The 40 least developed countries had 5.1 million international arrivals in 2000; they achieved an increase of 75per cent in the decade.
- 80per cent of the world's poor, those living on less than US$1 per day, live in 12countries. In 11 of these countries, tourism is significant and growing
- The developing countries are attracting an increasing share of global international tourist arrivals up from 20per cent in 1973 to 42per cent in 2000.

The developing countries and particularly the LDCs secured a larger increase in the income per international arrival between 1990 and 2000 than did the OECD or the European Union countries. The LDCs secured an increase of 45per cent between1990 and 2000 and the developing countries nearly 20per cent. This compares with18per cent for the OECD countries and 7.8per cent for the EU. In 2000, tourism ranked third among the major merchandise export sectors for both developing countries and LDCs. If petroleum industry exports are discounted (and they are significant in only three) tourism is the primary source of foreign exchange in the 49 LDCs.

COMMUNITY BASED TOURISM

Community-based tourism provides alternative economic opportunities, which are in essence in rural areas. Community-based tourism is regarded as a tool for natural and cultural resource conservation and community development and it is closely associated with ecotourism, sometimes referred to as community-based ecotourism. It is a community-based practice that provides contributions and incentives for natural and cultural conservation as well as providing opportunities for improved community livelihood.

It has the potential to create jobs and generate entrepreneurial opportunities for people from a variety of backgrounds, skills and experiences, including rural communities and especially women. Community-based tourism has been implemented in many developing countries, often in support of wildlife management, environmental protection and/or development for indigenous peoples.

Community tourism should;

- Be run with the involvement and consent of local communities. (Local people should participate in planning and managing the tour.)
- Give a fair share of profits back to the local community. (Ideally this will include community projects (health, schools, etc).)
- Involve communities rather than individuals. (Working with individuals can disrupt social structures.)
- Be environmentally sustainable. (Local people must be involved if conservation projects are to succeed.)
- Respect traditional culture and social structures.
- Have mechanisms to help communities cope with the impact of western tourists.
- Keep groups small to minimise cultural/ environmental impact.
- Brief tourists before the trip on appropriate behaviour.
- Not make local people perform inappropriate ceremonies, etc.
- Leave communities alone if they don't want tourism. (People should have the right to say 'no' to tourism.)

Community based tourism occurs when decisions about tourism activity and development are driven by the host community. It usually involves some form of cultural exchange where tourists meet with local communities and witness aspects of their lifestyle. Eco-tourism also emphasises observation and learning by the tourist, alongside economic and cultural conservation, and the delivery of benefits that ensure long-term sustainability of communities and natural resources. In Nepal, the Tourism for Rural Poverty Alleviation Programme began in 2001, jointly funded by the United Nations Development Programme (UNDP), the UK Department for International Development (DFID) with advisory services from SNV (Stichting Nederlandse Vrijwilligers) a Dutch development organisation.

Operating in six remote locations, the programme employed social mobilisation and tourist awareness programmes in villages to empower local communities to manage their own tourism development. In Vietnam, the International Union for Conservation of Nature and Natural Resources (IUCN) or World Conservation Union, is operating a community based tourism pilot in Sa Pa, a highly visited area with colourful ethnic minorities. Funded mainly by the Ford Foundation, the goal of the project is to assist local stakeholders to achieve an environmentally, culturally and socio-economically sustainable form of tourism, establishing mechanisms that support the active participation of the community in tourism decision-making and implementation.

The Nam Ha ecotourism project in Lao PDR uses community-based tourism as a vehicle to integrate environmental and cultural conservation with sustainable socio and economic development. Working closely with local villagers, limits were set on the number of trekking tourists allowed each year so as not to overwhelm the communities and to ensure that tourist incomes supplement rather than replace other economic activities.

Typically, with community-based tourism, the community runs all of the activities that a tourist engages in; lodging, food, guiding and craft sales. Benefits include; economic growth in rural regions; the distribution of tourism revenue, which can foster improved welfare and equity in the industry; improved resource conservation by local people; and diversification of the regional and national tourism product.

Intertwined with community-based tourism in developing countries is the concept of pro-poor tourism. In most counties with high levels of poverty, tourism is a significant and/or growing component of the economy. Governments and aid agencies acknowledge that whilst economic growth is essential for poverty reduction, of itself, it is insufficient to ensure a significant reduction. Growth that is specifically pro-poor is a pre-requisite for significant progress towards agreed targets for poverty reduction.

Tourism has many characteristics that make it potentially pro-poor;

- It is a diverse industry, which increases the scope for wide participation,
- The customer comes to the product, providing important opportunities for linkages(*e.g.,* souvenir sales),
- It is highly dependent on natural capital (wildlife, scenery) and culture, assets that some of the poor have in abundance, even if they have few financial resources,

- Tourism can be more labour intensive than manufacturing,
- A higher proportion of benefits (jobs, trade opportunities) go to women.

Pro-poor tourism is defined as tourism that generates net benefits for the poor. It maximises the potential for eradicating poverty by developing appropriate strategies in co-operation with all major groups, indigenous and local communities. Benefits may be economic, but they may also be social, environmental or cultural. Pro-poor tourism is not a specific product or sector of tourism, but an approach to the tourism industry. The core activity is to increase access of the poor to economic benefits. Pro-poor tourism strategies unlock opportunities for the poor; whether for economic gain, other livelihood benefits, or participation in decision- making.

Early experience shows that pro-poor tourism strategies do appear able to 'tilt' the industry at the margin, to expand opportunities for the poor and have potentially wide application across the industry. Poverty reduction through pro-poor tourism can therefore be significant at a local or district level. Moreover, the poverty impact may be greater in remote areas, though the tourism itself may be on a limited scale. Most examples of community-based in tourism in developing countries qualify as pro-poor tourism as they are designed to foster development at grassroots levels.

MODERN ACCOUNTANCY IN HOTEL

The first book on accounting was written by a Croatian merchant Benedetto Cotrugli, who is also known as Benedikt Kotruljeviæ, from the city of Dubrovnik. During his life in Italy he met many merchants and decided to write, Della Mercatvra et del Mercante Perfetto in which he elaborated on the principles of modern, double-entry book-keeping. He finished his lifework in 1458. However, his work was not published until 1573, as a result of which his contributions to the field have been overlooked by the general public. For this reason, Luca Pacioli, also known as Friar Luca dal Borgo, is credited for the "birth" of accounting. His Summa de arithmetica, geometrica, proportioni et proportionalita, a synthesis of the mathematical knowledge of his time, includes the first published description of the method of keeping accounts that Venetian merchants used at that time, known as the double-entry accounting system. Although Pacioli codified rather than invented this system, he is widely regarded as the "Father of Accounting".

The system he published included most of the accounting cycle as we know it today. He described the use of journals and ledgers, and warned that a person should not go to sleep at night until the debits equalled the credits! His ledger had accounts for assets, liabilities, capital, income, and expenses — the account categories that are reported on an organization's balance sheet and income statement, respectively. He demonstrated year-end closing entries and proposed that a trial balance be used to prove a balanced ledger. His treatise also touches on a wide range of related topics from accounting ethics to cost accounting.

The first known book in the English language on accounting was published in London by John Gouge in 1543. It is described as A Profitable Treatyce called the Instrument or Boke to learn to know the good order of the keeping of the famous reconynge, called in Latin, Dare and Habere, and, in English, Debitor and Creditor.

A short book of instructions was also published in 1588 by John Mellis of Southwark, in which he says, "I am but the renuer and reviver of an ancient old copy printed here in London the 14 of August 1543: collected, published, made, and set forth by one Hugh Oldcastle, Scholemaster, who, as appeareth by his treatise, then taught Arithmetics, and this booke in Saint Ollaves parish in Marko Lane."

John Mellis refers to the fact that the principle of accounts he explains is "after the forme of Venice". A book described as The Merchants Mirrour, or directions for the perfect ordering and keeping of his accounts formed by way of Debitor and Creditor, after the Italian manner, by Richard Dafforne, accountant, published in 1635, contains many references to early books on the science of accountancy. In this book, headed "Opinion of Book-keeping's Antiquity," the author states, on the authority of another writer, that the form of book-keeping referred to had then been in use in Italy about two hundred years, "but that the same, or one in many parts very like this, was used in the time of Julius Caesar, and in Rome long before."

An early Dutch writer appears to have suggested that double-entry book-keeping was even in existence among the Greeks, pointing to scientific accountancy having been invented in remote times. There were several editions of Richard Dafforne's book - the second edition in 1636, the third in 1656, and another in 1684. The book is a very complete treatise on scientific accountancy, beautifully prepared and containing elaborate explanations.

The numerous editions tend to prove that the science was highly appreciated in the 17th century. From this time on, there has been a continuous supply of literature on the subject, many of the authors styling themselves accountants and teachers of the art, and thus proving that the professional accountant was then known and employed. The requirements for entry in the profession of accounting vary from country to country.

Accountants may be licensed by a variety of organisations, such as the British qualified accountancy bodies including Association of Chartered Certified Accountants and Institute of Chartered Accountants, and are recognized by titles such as Chartered Certified Accountant and Chartered Accountant, Certified Public Accountant, Certified Management Accountant, Certified General Accountant, or Certified Practising Accountant. Some Commonwealth countries often recognise both the certified and chartered accounting bodies. The majority of "public" accountants in New Zealand and Canada are Chartered Accountants; however, Certified General Accountants are also authorized by legislation to practise public accounting and auditing in all Canadian provinces, except Ontario and Quebec, as of 2005. There is, however, no legal requirement for an accountant to be a paid-up member of one of the many Institutes and other bodies which are effectively a form of professional trade union. Unlike the Law Society, which can legally stop a solicitor from practising, accountancy institutes do not have such authority. However, auditors are regulated.

Before the Enron and other accounting scandals, there were five large firms and were called the Big Five. Since Arthur Andersen's assurance practice split with a plurality joining KPMG in the US and Deloitte and Touche outside of the US, Arthur Andersen left from the group. Previous to this there were also groupings referred to as the "Big Six" and the "Big Eight". Enron turned out to be only the first of a series of accounting scandals that enveloped the accounting industry in 2002.

This is likely to have far-reaching consequences for the U.S. accounting industry. Application of International Accounting Standards originating in International Accounting Standards Board headquartered in London and bearing more resemblance to UK than current US practices is often advocated by those who note the relative stability of the UK accounting system. Accounting reform of a far more comprehensive sort is advocated by those who see issues with capitalism or economics, and seek ecological or social accountability.

According to Accountancy Age's 2005 league table, fee income amongst the Top 50 accounting firms in the UK rose from £6.3bn to £7.0bn. This followed two successive years in which fee income had declined, largely a result of the sale by some of the larger firms of their consultancy arms. Fee income in most business areas - audit, tax, corporate finance and consultancy - rose in the 2005 survey, with insolvency and wealth management being the only segments where revenue fell. Price water house Coopers remains the largest firm with fee income totalling £1,780m followed by Deloitte, KPMG and Ernst and Young.

The combined revenue of the Big Four accounted for £5.0bn, 72per cent of the fee income of the Top 50, down from 78-79per cent in the years up to the 2002 survey and the third year in succession a decline in their share has occurred.

Ernst and Young's fee income is the smallest of the largest four firms, but still over three times that of the next largest firm, Grant Thornton. The amount of fee income tapers off amongst the mid-tier firms so that in total there were only 25 firms that each generated more than £15m of revenue in the 2005 survey. For more details regarding British qualified accountancy professionals, please refer to the page of British qualified accountants.

Management Accounting

Management accounting is concerned with the provisions and use of accounting information to managers within organizations, to provide them with the basis in making informed business decisions that would allow them to be better equipped in their management and control functions.

Unlike financial accountancy information, management accounting information is used within an organization and is usually confidential and access to which is only available to a select few. According to CIMA, The Chartered Institute of Management Accountants, Management Accounting is "the process of identification, measurement, accumulation, analysis, preparation, interpretation and communication of information used by management to plan, evaluate and control within an entity and to assure appropriate use of and accountability for its resources. Management accounting also comprises the preparation of financial reports for non- management groups such as shareholders, creditors, regulatory agencies and tax authorities".

Aims:

- Formulating strategies;
- Planning and constructing business activities;
- Making decisions;
- Well use of resources;
- Supporting financial reports preparation; and
- Safeguarding assets.

In the late 1980s, accounting practitioners and educators were heavily criticized on the grounds that management accounting practices had changed little over the preceding 60 years, despite radical changes in the business environment. Professional accounting institutes, perhaps fearing that management accountants would increasingly be seen as superfluous in business organizations, subsequently devoted considerable resources to the development of a more innovative skills set for management accountants. The distinction between 'traditional' and 'innovative' management accounting practices can be illustrated by reference to cost control techniques. Traditionally, management accountants' principal technique was variance analysis, which is a systematic approach to the comparison of the actual and budgeted costs of the raw materials and labour used during a production period.

While some form of variance analysis is still used by most manufacturing firms, it nowadays tends to be used in conjunction with innovative techniques such as life cycle cost analysis and activity-based costing, which are designed with specific aspects of the modern business environment in mind. Lifecycle costing recognizes that managers' ability to influence the cost of manufacturing a product is at its greatest when the product is still at the design stage of its product lifecycle, since small changes to the product design may lead to significant savings in the cost of manufacturing the product. Activity-based costing recognizes that, in modern factories, most manufacturing costs are determined by the amount of 'activities' and that the key to effective cost control is therefore optimizing the efficiency of these activities. Activity-based accounting is also known as Cause and Effect accounting.

Both lifecycle costing and activity-based costing recognize that, in the typical modern factory, the avoidance of disruptive events is of far greater importance than reducing the costs of raw materials. Activity-based costing also de-emphasizes direct labour as a cost driver and concentrates instead on activities that drive costs, such as the provision of a service or the production of a product component. The most significant recent direction in managerial accounting is throughput accounting, which recognizes the interdependencies of modern production processes and provide managers with a tool that will allow them to measure the contribution per unit of constrained resource for any given product, customer or supplier. A seldom expressed alternative view of management accounting is that it is neither a neutral or benign influence in organizations, rather a mechanism for management control through surveillance. This view locates management accounting specifically in the context of management control theory.

There are several related professional qualifications in the field of accountancy including:

- Management Accountancy Qualifications
  - CIMA
  - MA
  - Institute of Cost and Works Accountants of India
  - AAFM
- Other Professional Accountancy Qualifications
  - Chartered Certified Accountant,
  - Chartered Accountant,
  - Certified Public Accountant,

Accounting Management is the practical application of management techniques to control and report on the financial health of the organization. It involves the analysis, planning, implementation, and control of programmes designed to provide financial data reporting for managerial decision making. This includes the maintenance of bank accounts, developing financial statements, cash flow and financial performance analysis. Accounting management is a mandatory knowledge module of any MBA programme. Accounting is often referred to as billing management. The goal is to gather usage statistics for users. Using the statistics the users can be billed and usage quota can be enforced.

Examples:

- Disk usage
- Link utilisation
- CPU time

For non-billed networks, 'Administration' replaces 'Accounting'. The goals of Administration is to administer the set of authorized users, by establishing users, passwords and permissions; and to administer the operations of the equipment such as by performing software backup and synchronization.

Activity-Based Costing

Activity-based costing is a method of allocating costs to products and services. It is generally used as a tool for planning and control. This is a necessary tool for doing value chain analysis. The concepts of ABC were developed in the manufacturing sector of the U.S. during the 1970s and 80s.

During this time, the Consortium for Advanced Manufacturing-International, now known simply as CAM-I, provided a formative role for studying and formalizing the principles that have become more formally known as Activity-Based Costing. Robin Cooper and Robert Kaplan, proponent of the Balanced Scorecard, brought notice to these concepts in a number of articles published in Harvard Business Review beginning in 1988.

Cooper and Kaplan described ABC as an approach to solve the problems of traditional cost management systems. These traditional costing systems are often unable to determine accurately the actual costs of production and of the costs of related services. Consequently managers were making decisions based on inaccurate data especially where there are multiple products.

Instead of using broad arbitrary percentages to allocate costs, ABC seeks to identify cause and effect relationships to objectively assign costs. Once costs of the activities have been identified, the cost of each activity is attributed to each product to the extent that the product uses the activity. In this way ABC often identifies areas of high overhead costs per unit and so directs attention to finding ways to reduce the costs or to charge more for costly products. Activity-based costing was first clearly defined in 1987 by Robert S. Kaplan and W. Bruns as a stage in their book Accounting and Management. They initially focused on manufacturing industry where increasing technology and productivity improvements have reduced the relative proportion of the direct costs of labour and materials, but have increased relative proportion of indirect costs. For example increased automation has reduced labour, which is a direct cost, but has increased depreciation, which is an indirect cost.

Traditionally cost accountants had arbitrarily added a broad percentage onto the direct costs to allow for the indirect costs. However as the percentages of overhead costs had risen, this technique became increasingly inaccurate because the indirect costs were not caused equally by all the products. For example one product might take more time in one expensive machine than another product, but since the amount of direct labour and materials might be the same, the additional cost for the use of the machine would not be recognised when the same broad 'on-cost' percentage is added to all products. Consequently, when multiple products share common costs, there is a danger of one product subsidising another. Like manufacturing industries, financial institutions also have diverse products which can cause cross-product subsidies. Since personnel expenses represent the largest single component of non-interest expense in financial institutions, these costs must also be attributed more accurately to products and customers. Activity based costing, even though developed for manufacturing, can therefore be a useful tool for doing this. This extended use of ABC to financial institutions was presented in 1990 in an article appearing in the Journal of Bank Cost and Management Accounting by Richard Sapp, David Crawford and Steven Rebishcke.

Direct labour and materials are relatively easy to trace directly to products, but it is more difficult to directly allocate indirect costs to products. Where products use common resources differently, some sort of weighting is needed in the cost allocation process. The measure of the use of a shared activity by each of the products is known as the cost driver.

For example, the cost of the activity of bank tellers can be ascribed to each product by measuring how long each product's transactions takes at the counter and then by measuring the number of each type of transaction. Even in activity-based costing, some overhead costs are difficult to assign to products and customers, for example the chief executive's salary. These costs are termed 'business sustaining' and are not assigned to products and customers because there is no meaningful method. This lump of unallocated overhead costs must nevertheless be met by contributions from each of the products, but it is not as large as the overhead costs before ABC is employed.

Although some may argue that costs untraceable to activities should be "arbitrarily allocated" to products, it is important to realise that the only purpose of ABC is to provide information to management. Therefore, there is no reason to assign any cost in an arbitrary manner. Management accountants can be creative in finding other ways to represent these costs on internal reporting statements.

MANAGING BUDGET

Budget generally refers to a list of all planned expenses and revenues. A budget is an important concept in microeconomics, which uses a budget line to illustrate the trade-offs between two or more goods. A personal budget is among the most important concepts of personal finance. In a personal or family budget all sources of income are identified and expenses are planned with the intent of matching outflows to inflows. There are a wide variety of personal budgeting methods and tools that can be employed to help individuals and families with the budgeting process. Also the level of planned finance available to a person, corporation or government, as set by a certain person. The budget of a government is a summary or plan of the intended revenues and expenditures of that government. In the United States, the federal budget is prepared by the Office of Management and Budget, and submitted to Congress for consideration. Invariably, Congress makes many and substantial changes. Nearly all American states are required to have balanced budgets, but the federal government is allowed to run deficits. In the UK the budget is prepared by the Chancellor of the Exchequer, the second most important member of the government, and must be passed by Parliament. The Parliament seldom makes changes to the budget. The budget of a company is compiled annually. A finished budget usually requires considerable effort and can be seen as a financial plan for the new financial year.

While traditionally the Finance department compiles the company's budget, modern software allows hundreds or even thousands of people in the various departments to contribute their expected revenues and expenses to the final budget. If the actual numbers delivered through the financial year turn out to be close to the budget, this will demonstrate that the company understands their business and has been successfully driving it in the direction they had planned.

On the other hand, if the actuals diverge wildly from the budget, this sends out an 'out of control' signal and the share Cost-plus pricing is a pricing method commonly used by firms. It is used primarily because it is easy to calculate and requires little information. There are several varieties, but the common thread in all of them is that you first calculate the cost of the product, then include an additional amount to represent profit. Cost-plus pricing is often used on government contracts, and has been criticized as promoting wasteful expenditures.

Calculating Price Using the Cost-plus Method

There are several ways of determining cost, and the profit can be added as either a percentage markup or an absolute amount. One example is:

P = (AVC + FCper cent) × (1 + MKper cent)

where:

- P = price
- AVC = average variable cost
- FCper cent = percentage allocation of fixed costs
- MKper cent = percentage markup

For example: If variable costs are 30 yen, the allocation to cover fixed costs is 10 yen, and you feel you need a 50per cent markup then you would charge a price of 60 yen:

P = (30 + 10) × (1 + 0.50)

P = 40 × 1.5

P = 60

An alternative way of doing a similar calculation is:

P = (AVC + FCper cent)/(1 " MKper cent)

To make things simpler, some firms, particularly retailers, ignore fixed costs and just use the purchase price paid to their suppliers as the cost term. They indirectly incorporate the fixed cost allocation into the markup percentage. To simplify things even further, sometimes a fixed amount is applied rather than a percentage.

This fixed amount is usually determined by head-office to make it easy for franchisees and store managers. This is sometimes referred to as turnkey pricing. Another variant of cost plus pricing is activity based pricing. This involves being more careful in determining costs. Instead of using arbitrary expense categories when allocating overhead, every activity is linked to the resources it uses. Cost will need to be recalculated and the percentage markup will likely need to be adjusted as the product goes through its life cycle. This is sometimes referred to as product life cycle pricing, although it is seldom done deliberately or in a planned and organized manner. Price skimming and penetration pricing are also types of product life cycle pricing but they are demand based pricing methods rather cost based.

Advantages of Cost-plus Pricing:

- Easy to calculate
- Minimal information requirements
- Easy to administer
- Tends to stabilize markets - insulated from demand variations and competitive factors
- Insures seller against unpredictable, or unexpected later costs
- Ethical advantages

Disadvantages:

- Tends to ignore the role of consumers
- Tends to ignore the role of competitors
- Use of historical accounting costs rather than replacement value
- Use of "normal" or "standard" output level to allocate fixed costs
- Inclusion of sunk costs rather than just using incremental costs
- Ignores opportunity costs
- Contractors may not focus on performance because the cost is always covered by the client

In microeconomics, Production is simply the conversion of inputs into outputs. It is an economic process that uses resources to create a commodity that is suitable for exchange. This can include manufacturing, storing, shipping, and packaging. Some economists define production broadly as all economic activity other than consumption.

They see every commercial activity other than the final purchase as some form of production. Production is a process, and as such it occurs through time and space. Because it is a flow concept, production is measured as a "rate of output per period of time".

There are three aspects to production processes:

1. The quantity of the commodity produced,
2. The form of the good produced,
3. The temporal and spatial distribution of the commodity produced.

A production process can be defined as any activity that increases the similarity between the pattern of demand for goods, and the quantity, form, and distribution of these goods available to the market place. A production process is efficient if a given quantity of outputs cannot be produced with any less inputs. It is said to be inefficient when there exists another feasible process that, for any given output, uses less inputs. Some economists use the term X-efficiency to indicate that production processes tend to be inherently inefficient due to satisfying behaviour.

The "rate of efficiency" is simply the amount of outputs divided by the amount of inputs. If a production process uses 50 units of input to produce one unit of output it is more efficient than a process that uses 55 units of input to produce the same level of output. It is said to be 10per cent more efficient. The inputs or resources used in the production process are called factors by economists. The myriad of possible inputs are usually grouped into four or five categories.

These factors are:

- Raw materials
- Labour services
- Capital goods
- Land.

Sometimes a fifth category is added, entrepreneurial and management skills, a subcategory of labour services. Capital goods are those goods that have previously undergone a production process. They are previously produced means of production. Some textbooks use "technology" as a factor of production.

In the "long run" all of these factors of production can be adjusted by management. The "short run" however, is defined as a period in which at least one of the factors of production is fixed. A fixed factor of production is one whose quantity cannot readily be changed. Examples include major pieces of equipment, suitable factory space, and key managerial personnel. A variable factor of production is one whose usage rate can be changed easily. Examples include electrical power consumption, transportation services, and most raw material inputs. In the short run, a firm's "scale of operations" determines the maximum number of outputs that can be produced. In the long run, there are no scale limitations. The total product of a variable factor of production identifies what outputs are possible using various levels of the variable input. This can be displayed in either a chart that lists the output level corresponding to various levels of input, or a graph that summarizes the data into a "total product curve". The diagram shows a typical total product curve. In this example, output increases as more inputs are employed up until point A. The maximum output possible with this production process is Qm. If there are other inputs used in the process, they are assumed to be fixed. The average physical product is the total product divided by the number of units of variable input employed. It is the output of each unit of input.

If there are 10 employees working on a production process that manufactures 50 units per day, then the average product of variable labour input is 5 units per day. The average product typically varies as more of the input is employed, so this relationship can also be expresses as a chart or as a graph. A typical average physical product curve is shown.

It can be obtained by drawing a vector from the origin to various points on the total product curve and plotting the slopes of these vectors. The marginal physical product of a variable input is the change in total output due to a one unit change in the variable input or alternatively the rate of change in total output due to an infinitesimally small change in the variable input. The discrete marginal product of capital is the additional output resulting from the use of an additional unit of capital.

The continuous marginal product of a variable input can be calculated as the derivative of quantity produced with respect to variable input employed. The marginal physical product curve is shown. It can be obtained from the slope of the total product curve. Because the marginal product drives changes in the average product, we know that when the average physical product is falling, the marginal physical product must be less than the average. Likewise, when the average physical product is rising, it must be due to a marginal physical product greater than the average. For this reason, the marginal physical product curve must intersect the maximum point on the average physical product curve. MPP keeps increasing till it reaches its maximum. Up until this point every additional unit has been adding more value to the total product than the previous one. From this point onwards, every additional unit adds less to the total product compared to the previous one.

But the average product is still increasing till MPP touches APP. At this point, an additional unit is adding the same value as the average product. From this point onwards, MPP starts to reduce and so does APP because every additional unit is adding less to APP than the average product. But the total product is still increasing because every additional unit is still contributing positively.

Therefore, during this period, both, the average as well as marginal products, are decreasing, but the total product is still increasing. Finally we reach a point when MPP crosses the x-axis. At this point every additional unit starts to diminish the product of previous units, possibly by getting into their way. Therefore the total product starts to decrease at this point. This is point A on the total product curve.

Diminishing returns can be divided into three categories:

1. Diminishing Total returns, which implies reduction in total product with every additional unit of input. This occurs after point A in the graph.
2. Diminishing Average returns, which refers to the portion of the APP curve after its intersection with MPP curve.
3. Diminishing Marginal returns, refers to the point where the MPP curve starts to slope down and travels all the way down to the x-axis and beyond. Putting it in a chronological order, at first the marginal returns start to diminish, then the average returns, followed finally by the total returns.

These curves illustrate the principle of diminishing marginal returns to a variable input. This states that as you add more and more of a variable input, you will reach a point beyond which the resulting increase in output starts to diminish. This point is illustrated as the maximum point on the marginal physical product curve. It assumes that other factor inputs are held constant. An example is the employment of labour in the use of trucks to transport goods. Assuming the number of available trucks is fixed, then the amount of the variable input labour could be varied and the resultant efficiency determined. At least one labourer is necessary.

Additional workers per vehicle could be productive in loading, unloading, navigation, or around the clock continuous driving. But at some point the returns to investment in labour will start to diminish and efficiency will decrease. The most efficient distribution of labour per piece of equipment will likely be one driver plus an additional worker for other tasks. Resource allocations and distributive efficiencies in the mix of capital and labour investment will vary per industry and according to available technology. Trains are able to transport much more in the way of goods with fewer "drivers" but at the cost of greater investment in infrastructure.

With the advent of mass production of motorized vehicles, the economic niche occupied by trains has become more specialized and limited to long haul delivery. There is an argument that if the theory is holding everything constant, the production method should not be changed, *i.e.,* division of labour should not be practiced. However, the rise in marginal product means that the workers use other means of production method, such as in loading, unloading, navigation, or around the clock continuous driving. For this reason, some economists think that the "keeping other things constant" should not be used in this theory. The total, average, and marginal physical product curves mentioned are just one way of showing production relationships. They express the quantity of output relative to the amount of variable input employed while holding fixed inputs constant. Because they depict a short run relationship, they are sometimes called short run production functions. If all inputs are allowed to be varied, then the diagram would express outputs relative to total inputs, and the function would be a long run production function. If the mix of inputs is held constant, then output would be expressed relative to inputs of a fixed composition, and the function would indicate long run economies of scale.

Rather than comparing inputs to outputs, it is also possible to assess the mix of inputs employed in production. An isoquant relates the quantities of one input to the quantities of another input. It indicates all possible combinations of inputs that are capable of producing a given level of output. Rather than looking at the inputs used in production, it is possible to look at the mix of outputs that are possible for any given production process. This is done with a production possibilities frontier. It indicates what combinations of outputs are possible given the available factor endowment and the prevailing production technology. You can use a lot of labour with a minimal amount of capital, or you could invest heavily in capital equipment that requires a minimal amount of labour to operate, or any combination in between. For most goods, there are more than just two inputs.

For example in agriculture, the amount of land, water, and fertilizer can all be varied to produce different amounts of a crop. An isoquant, in the two input case, is a curve that shows all the ways of combining two inputs so as to produce a given level of output. In the three input case it will be a surface. Iso is Latin for equal and quant is short for quantity. Movement along an isoquant depicts a constant rate of output, but a changing input ratio.A unique isoquant can be constructed for every level of output, and a family of isoquants can be created to represent various output levels. Isoquants further from the origin represent greater amounts of output. Isoquants are usually considered to be everywhere dense, meaning an infinite number of them could be plotted in any two input space. A typical isoquant is illustrated in the diagram to the right. At point A in the diagram Ka units of capital are combined with La units of labour to produce 100 units of output.

It is downward sloping, convex to the origin, and non-intersecting. A complete isoquant is actually a closed curve, but only the "down sloping to the right" portion makes economic sense. The upward sloping parts of isoquants, for example, indicate that level of output could be produced by less of both inputs so this section is of little interest to decision makers. The economic section of the isoquants is defined by a pair of lines called ridge lines. The "downward to the right" slope of the economic region of an isoquant is due to the possibility of substituting one input for another in the production process while keeping the level of output constant. Isoquants are typically convex to the origin reflecting the fact that the two factors are substitutable for each other at varying rates.

This rate of substitutability is called the "marginal rate of technical substitution" or occasionally the "marginal rate of substitution in production". It measures the reduction in one input per unit increase in the other input that is just sufficient to maintain a constant level of production. For example, the marginal rate of substitution of labour for capital gives the amount of capital that can be replaced by one unit of labour while keeping output unchanged.

To move from point A to point B in the diagram, the amount of capital is reduced from Ka to Kb while the amount of labour is increased only from La to Lb. To move from point C to point D, the amount of capital is reduced from Kc to Kd while the amount of labour is increased from La to Lb. The marginal rate of technical substitution of labour for capital is equivalent to the absolute slope of the isoquant at that point. It is equal to 0 where the isoquant becomes horizontal, and equal to infinity where it becomes vertical.

The opposite is true when going in the other direction. In this case we are looking at the marginal rate of technical substitution capital for labour. It can also be shown that the marginal rate of substitution labour for capital, is equal to the marginal physical product of labour divided by the marginal physical product of capital. In the unusual case of two inputs that are perfect substitutes for each other in production, the isoquant would be linear. If, on the other hand, there is only one production process available, factor proportions would be fixed, and these zero-substitutability isoquants would be shown as horizontal or vertical lines.

Fixed Assets Management

Fixed assets management is an accounting process that seeks to track fixed assets for the purposes of financial accounting, preventive maintenance, and theft deterrence. Many organizations face a significant challenge to track the location, quantity, condition, maintenance and depreciation status of their fixed assets. A popular approach to tracking fixed assets utilizes serial numbered Asset Tags, often with bar codes for easy and accurate reading. Periodically, the owner of the assets can take inventory with a mobile barcode reader and then produce a report. Off-the-shelf software packages for fixed asset management are marketed to businesses small and large. Some Enterprise Resource Planning systems are available with fixed assets modules.

Free Cash Flow

Free cash flow measures a firm's net increase in:

- Cash from operations,
- Less the dividends paid to preferred shareholders, and
- Less expenditures necessary to maintain assets.

Increases in non-cash current assets may, or may not be deducted, depending on whether they are considered to be maintaining the status quo, or to be investments for growth.

Problems with Capx

- The expenditures for maintenance of assets is only part of the capx reported on the Statement of Cash Flows. It must be separated from the expenditures for growth purposes. This split is not a requirement under GAAP, and is not audited. Management is free to disclose maintenance capx or not. Therefore this input to the calculation of free cash flow is easy to manipulate. Since it is a very large number, maintenance capx's questionable validity is the basis for some people's dismissal of 'free cash flow'.
- A second problem with the maintenance capx measurement is its intrinsic 'lumpyness'. By their nature, expenditures for capital assets that will last decades are infrequent, but costly when they occur. 'Free cash flow', in turn, will be very different from year to year. No particular year will be a 'norm' that can be expected to be repeated.

Uses of the Metric

- Free cash flow measures the ease with which businesses can grow and pay dividends to shareholders. Even profitable businesses may have negative cash flows. Their requirement for increased financing will result in increased financing costs reducing future income. It is easier to grow with organic cash flows than with additional financing.
- According to the discounted cash flow valuation model, the intrinsic value of a company is the present value of all future free cash flows, plus the cash proceeds from its eventual sale. The presumption is that the cash flows are used to pay dividends to the shareholders. Bear in mind the lumpyness discussed.
- Some investors prefer using free cash flow instead of net income to measure a company's financial performance, because free cash flow is more difficult to manipulate than net income. The problems with this presumption are itemized at cash flow and return of capital.
- The payout ratio is a metric used to evaluate the sustainability of distributions from REITs, Oil and Gas Royalty Trusts, and Income Trust. The distributions are divided by the free cash flow. Distributions may include any of income, flowed-through capital gains or return of capital.

This metric is used only by shareholders. Debt holders are not concerned with maintaining the operating capital assets, or with growing the business. Nor are they concerned with taxes paid since their payments come first. The appropriate metric for debt holders is EBITDA.

Change Management

There are several phrases regarding organizational change and development that look and sound a lot alike, but have different meanings. As a result of the prominence of the topic, there seems to be increasingly different interpretations of some of these phrases, while others are used interchangeably. Without at least some sense of the differences between these phrases, communications about organizational change and development can be increasingly vague, confusing and frustrating. There are different overall types of organizational change, including planned versus unplanned, organization-wide versus change primarily to one part of the organization, incremental versus transformational, etc.. Knowing which types of change you are doing helps all participants to retain scope and perspective during the many complexities and frequent frustrations during change. Successful change efforts often include several key roles, including the initiator, champion, change agent, sponsor and leaders. Organization-wide change in corporations should involve the Board of Directors. Whether their members are closely involved in the change or not, they should at least be aware of the change project and monitor if the results are being achieved or not. As the change agent, you might be performing different roles during the project.

Appreciative Inquiry is a recent and powerful breakthrough in organizational change and development. It's based on the philosophy that "problems" are often caused as much by our perception of them as problems as by other influencing factors. The philosophy has spawned a strong movement that, in turn, has generated an increasing number of models, tools and tips, most of which seem to build from the positive perceptions of those involved in the change effort. There are numerous well-organized approaches from which to manage a change effort. Some of the approaches have been around for many years — we just haven't thought of them as such. For example, many organizations undertake strategic planning. The implementation of strategic planning, when done in a systematic, cyclical and explicit approach, is strategic management. Strategic management is also one model for ensuring the success of a change effort.

There are numerous, major methods and movements to regularly increase the performance of organizations. Each includes regular recurring activities to establish organizational goals, monitor progress towards the goals, and make adjustments to achieve those goals more effectively and efficiently. Any or all of the following approaches will improve organizational performance depending on if they are implemented comprehensively and remain focused on organizational results. Some of the following, *e.g.,* organizational learning and knowledge management, might be interpreted more as movements than organization performance strategies because there are wide interpretations of the concepts, not all of which include focusing on achieving top-level organizational results. However, if these two concepts are instilled across the organization and focus on organizational results, they contribute strongly to organizational performance. On the other hand, the Balanced Scorecard, which is deliberately designed to be comprehensive and focused on organizational results, will not improve performance if not implemented from a strong design.

THE USE OF THE INTERNET IN TOURISM AND HOSPITALITY

The internet is being used by the tourism and hospitality industry to perform six key functions: direct e-mail marketing, advertising, providing information, distribution and sales, customer service and relationship marketing and marketing research.

DIRECT E-MAIL MARKETING

One of the most promising applications in online advertising is direct e-mail marketing, in which a user chooses to receive messages from a particular advertiser. In 2004, over 36 million online travellers in the US signed up with travel suppliers to receive e-mail offers and promotions. Of these, 11 million said they booked trips based solely on an e-mailed travel promotion. This form of advertising is relatively inexpensive, has high response rates and is easy to measure, and is targeted at people who want information about certain goods and services. Unlike banner advertising in its various forms, sending sales messages by e-mail seems quite acceptable to internet users, since they agree to accept the message.

The success of an e-mail campaign - like that of a direct mail campaign - depends on the quality of the list, which can be created in-house or be rented from a list broker. Typically, these lists include opt-in names and addresses. 'Opt-in' means that the people on the list have agreed to receive direct e-mail. E-mail advertisements sent to lists that are not opt-in are called spam. Spam refers to the inappropriate use of a mailing list or other networked communications facility as a broadcast medium. It is unsolicited 'junk' e-mail. One of the problems with e-mail is its low cost, which results in users receiving an increasing number of unwanted messages. The consequence is that more and more e-mail goes unopened, and gaining permission to send someone a message is becoming more important.

Establishing first contact is the toughest goal of any e-mail marketer. The most obvious place to find prospects is via other web sites, newsgroups and mailing lists. This can work, but many mailing lists and newsgroups have settled on their own set of experts. It is harder to penetrate market share this way. E-mail marketing is still in its infancy online, and many of the so-called lists are not tested or even targeted. The best means of survival is still endorsed mailing to a group of interested customers, which is why it is important to allow people to remove themselves from lists.

The goal is to have customers make first contact, and then have the marketer follow up. This can be encouraged by giving customers something of real value, such as a good special report or newsletter. Yukon Tourism in Canada had major success in 2006 reaching brand new audiences with an e-mail campaign promoting the 'Yukon Alaska Ultimate Adventure Contest'. Yukon Tourism rented two types of lists: one owned and operated by TELUS, made up of Canadians who had previously requested other types of travel information, and the second a Forge Marketing database of people who had already indicated an interest in Yukon travel. The 'click thru' rate (those who viewed the messages) was almost 19 per cent, and 69 per cent of people on the second list asked for more information.

Advertising

These days, the internet is an important part of the media mix, and internet advertising is seen by some as the convergence of traditional advertising and direct response marketing. Online advertising holds four distinct advantages:

1. Targe tability. Online advertisers can focus on users from specific companies, geographical locations and nations, as well as categorize them by time of day, computer platform and browser. They can target using databases, a tool that serves as the backbone of direct marketing. They can even target using a person's personal preferences and actual behaviour.
2. Tr ac k ing. Marketers can track how users interact with their brands and learn what is of interest to their current and prospective customers. Advertisers can also measure the response to an ad (by noting the number of times an ad is clicked on, the number of purchases or leads an ad generated, etc.). This is difficult to do with traditional television, print, and outdoor advertising.
3. Deliverability and flexibility. Online, an ad is deliverable 24 hours a day, 7 days a week, 365 days of the year. Furthermore, an ad campaign can be launched, updated or cancelled immediately. This is very different from print or television advertising.
4. Interactivity. An advertiser's goal is to engage the prospect with a brand or a product. This can be done more effectively online, where consumers can interact with the product, test it, and, if they choose, buy it.

Online marketers can advertise via e-mail (as discussed earlier) and by sponsoring discussion lists and e-mail newsletters. But a common form of advertising on the internet is the banner ad – an advertisement placed as a narrow band across the top of a web page. In terms of appearance and design, banner ads are often compared to outdoor posters. The content of the ad is minimal. Its purpose is to stir interest, so that the viewer clicks the ad for more information. Once the banner ad is clicked, the viewer sees the advertisement in its entirety, usually via a link to the advertiser's home page. The design characteristics of the ad are critical, since the goal is to encourage clicking. The web site the ad links to must be interesting, or the surfer will quickly return to the previous page. A recent study of internet strategies used by resorts showed that well-placed and appropriate use of banner ads can be highly effective. Advertising money is also increasingly being spent on search-engine advertising, which allows companies to target consumers as they research a holiday. The growth of search engine use for online travel research or booking is staggering, and has been facilitated by the introduction of newer 'travel-specific' search engines such as Kayak, Sidestep and Yahoo's Farechase. In Britain, seven out of ten people use Google when they trawl the internet for flights, for instance. The search engine delivers the results and alongside them displays about a dozen 'sponsored links' from companies that have paid to appear on the page. Each time a consumer clicks on one of these links, Google gets a fee.

Marketers are also using the internet to place ads that may or may not be shown on television at a later date, taking advantage of internet users' insatiable appetite for online content. The Case Study at the end of this chapter shows how an ad created by Tourism Australia was downloaded by over 100,000 people in the UK alone before being aired on television. BMW expanded the boundaries of advertising formats on the web with its short films featuring BMW automobiles, which were an attraction in themselves, rather than an advertising distraction. The company launched its first round of films online in the summer of 2001 and the short film *The Hire,* featuring its Z4 and X5 models, also spawned its own comic book collection. Advertising in online virtual worlds is another opportunity for marketers. An example is Second Life, an online world with a million registered users and a thriving virtual economy. Second Life allows its users to create a new, and improved, digital version of themselves. 'Residents' can buy land, build structures and start businesses. The service is fast becoming a three-dimensional test bed for corporate marketers, including Sony BMG Music Entertainment, Sun Microsystems, Nissan, Adidas, Toyota and Starwood Hotels. Retailers have set up shops to sell digital as well as real-world versions of their products, and even musicians can promote their albums with virtual appearances. In October 2006, performer Ben Folds promoted a new album playing at the opening party for Aloft, an elaborate digital prototype for a new chain of hotels planned by Starwood Hotels and Resorts. Projects like Aloft are designed to promote the venture but also to give its designers feedback from prospective guests before the first real hotel opens in 2008.

According to marketing experts, the success factors for marketing tourism on the web include the following: attracting users, engaging users' interest and participation, retaining users and ensuring that they return, learning about user preferences, and relating back to users to provide customized interactions. Learning about user preferences would appear to be the most important element of this model, as it affects the remaining elements, and yet very few studies have attempted to understand the behaviour of tourists online. Although statistical measures can be obtained through log files, it is difficult to ascertain the meaning behind the results (*e.g.,* whether clicking on a link was an accident or an intended behaviour). Surveying visitors might be a better way to understand consumer preferences and to establish the effectiveness of a site.

Research that has looked at content of web pages suggests that it is crucial that content is accurate, attractive and easily searchable. Interactivity is also an imperative, as the behaviour of consumers changes when they log onto the internet: they not only search for information but also expect interaction and entertainment.A positive experience on the web site increases the time spent there, and therefore increases the dollar amount spent (Hoffman and Novak, 1996). Offering virtual tours is one way of providing interactivity, and many destinations offer these for an extensive selection of places. Virtual tours of hotels on the corporate web site have proven to be a major sales asset for some hotel chains. Live video is another way of allowing visitors to interact with web sites. For example, the Wavehouse web site (www.wavehouse.com) allows users to view live video of surfers using the San Diego attraction.

It is also important for tourism operators and destinations to consider the language of their online visitors. The New York tourism bureau had added Chinese language pages to its web site in order to take advantage of the growing Chinese market. Outrigger Hotels and Resorts has also recognized that it holds an international presence and needs to disseminate information about its properties in several languages. Its locations in the Pacific and South Pacific receive a lot of business from Korea and Japan, so the company has built portals to address these markets. In recent years, there has been much discussion of Web 2.0. The phrase Web 2.0 was first coined in 2005 by Tim O'Reilly, a web pioneer, as a way to mark a turning point in web development. It takes into account a fundamentally different point of view, where a web site is built around a rich user experience, not a product or service. Customer-centric 2.0 web sites require that a company puts itself in the shoes of a web site visitor and sees its organization as it appears through that. A recent study of ski area web sites concluded that those that take the time to design their site with the needs of their customers as the primary focus will not only be rewarded with more visitors on the web, but on the slopes too (Rufo, 2006). The survey found the most user-friendly ski area web sites had four things in common:

1. They provided current information in a simple, clear, and attractive way;
2. They gave visitors a good reason to come back again (in technical web terms, they have 'stickiness');
3. They involved the visitor. Not only did they provide interactive tools, they openly encouraged guests to contribute comments, content or images to their site;
4. They made sure the web site matched other branding materials such as brochures and ads.

A major challenge for tourism organizations selling via the internet is converting surfers into buyers. A 2006 study of North American consumers found that the top three reasons for those who research but hesitate to continue with an online booking are concern over credit card security, web site performance issues and limits on the actions that can be taken online, and frustration with web site performance. Interestingly, and worryingly from an internet marketing point of view, the number of consumers concerned with submitting their credit card information nearly doubled from 9 percent in 2005 to 16 percent in 2006. The Snapshot below provides some advice to tourism marketers on how to convert hits into sales.

PROVIDING INFORMATION

Online users are often divided between those that plan and those that book. In the US, some 78 per cent of travellers can be described as online travel planners, since they consulted the internet to get travel and destination information. The most popular sources of travel information in 2005 for the Americans were online travel agencies such as Expedia and Yahoo (67 per cent); search engine sites (64 per cent); travel company sites (54 per cent) and destination sites (46 per cent). One in three online planners checked web sites and then called a supplier's toll-free number. The most popular planning activities conducted on the internet are: searching for maps and driving directions (50.6 million), searching for airfares (49 million) and looking for places to stay (48 million). The internet is also the preferred method of obtaining travel information amongst internet users in the UK, with some 65 per cent of UK internet users in 2005 using the web to research travel. A major trend affecting web usage for travel planning in the UK is the arrival of such meta-search engines as www.kayak.com and www.allcheckin.com, which enable customers to compare instantly details for flights, hotels and rental cars.

The internet is also an important source of information for tourism practitioners. A new international tourism portal set up for the travel trade is Tourism-Review.com. Launched in 2006, this web site provides daily, weekly and monthly tourism news as well as an online TV newscast that communicates relevant information between professional organizations and industry practitioners worldwide. Several synoptic directories list festivals, conferences and travel destinations, as well as travel trade companies and organizations. 'With so much information overloading travel trade professionals, there is a demand for more relevant and focused sourcing,' said the site's project head, Igor Fes. 'Our final target is providing the users with customized information in all rich media formats available with the latest developing technology.' Another online source of information for the travel trade, travel media or researchers is WorldTourismDirectory.com. The site has detailed information on countries and territories listed and organized by the following categories: Government Tourism Agencies; Tourism Schools and Institutes; Travel Associations and Services; Transport; Outdoor and Recreational Activities; Publications and

Information Sources; Immigration and Foreign Affairs; Chambers of Commerce; Regional and Local Tourist Information Offices; Miscellaneous Information Offices; Information Offices Abroad; and Embassies/Consulates. Besides the comprehensive country directory there is also a visitor's guide, country profile and a country map.

Another trend is the importance of travel blogs in gathering travel information. Rather than passively viewing a collection of static pages, today's internet user is becoming an active participant and, as the Opening Vignette highlighted, there is a growth in social networking – the creation and sharing of free content made by individual users. It is changing the way people consume media. For example, home video nights have been replaced by YouTube.com, and flipping through photo albums is now done via Flickr.com. Ease of use is the biggest factor driving this trend, both for users and creators. Jupiter Research in New York tracked a dramatic growth of internet users who read blogs, from 11 per cent in 2005 to 23 per cent in 2006. In September 2006, YouTube was recording 100 million views a day, and receiving 60,000 new videos a day. One of the major reasons for the success of Australia's 'Where the bloody hell are you?' advertising campaign was the number of people viewing the ads on YouTube.

DISTRIBUTION AND SALES

In 2005, the share of online travel planners who also book online continued to grow worldwide. The purchase of airline tickets continues to dominate the booking activity, closely followed by accommodation reservations. Ticket sales for all kinds of events and attractions are also showing steady growth. In the US, while the major online travel agencies attracted the most online bookers (29.6 million Americans used either Expedia, Travelocity and Priceline at least once in 2005), search engine sites experienced the fastest growth (from 11.6 million bookers in 2004 to 18.7 million in 2005) closely followed by destination sites – up to 12.6 million bookers. In Europe, the enthusiasm for the internet in the UK made it the largest online travel market in 2004, accounting for 36 per cent of the European travel market. It is believed that one of the reasons for this is the high volume of airline tickets purchased online via UK low-cost carriers, which lifts internet usage overall. In Europe, fragmentation in the online travel agency market is high compared to the US. Of the European online travel agency market, 60 per cent is in the hands of the top five agencies, whereas in the US, the three companies referred to above serve 93 per cent of the online agency market. One growing competitor for these agencies is Orbitz.com, created when five airlines – American, Continental, Delta, Northwest and United – came together to develop a state-of-the-art travel web site. Orbitz is now one of the largest online travel companies in the world, selling airfares, lodging, car rentals, cruises and vacation packages. Orbitz's inventory includes 455 airlines, 500,000 lodging properties, 25 car rentals, 30 vacation package providers and 18 airlines.

Hotels, in particular, are turning to the internet to increase sales. High-tech investments in web sites and other facilities already have paid off for many participants in the hospitality industry. A survey of hotels in 2005 found that online sales represented 44 per cent of business for those questioned (Green and Warner, 2006). Their average spend on online marketing was US$50,000 per year, and respondents rated their own web site as more effective than any other online channel of distribution. The greatest challenge for hotels was setting prices of optimized revenue and having consistency between prices in different distribution channels. Online agencies and non-hotel sites have also been building up their hotel business as a way to diversify from low-margin air sales.

Southwest, for example, launched a hotel reservations service in 2001 using the Galileo global distribution system. Expedia is also having tremendous success online. In March 2001, it announced that it had sold more than one million room nights in less than three months. In comparison, it took the company three years to sell its first million room nights. Through its Travelscape division, which operates on the merchant model, Expedia contracts for special room blocks to resell to consumers at a margin, thus guaranteeing revenue for the hotel. Hotels can sign on to become an 'Expedia Special Rate Hotel' through Travelscape, to help fill unsold inventory. Travelscape helps hotels maximize revenue during peak, shoulder and off-peak travel periods; it also offers hotels an Extranet tool that allows them to manage inventory and rates online. However, tensions between hotels and online agencies have led to some hotels pulling inventory from web sites. For example, InterContinental Hotels pulled its 3,500 hotels from Expedia and hotels.com in 2004. IHG said the online agencies would not comply with business guidelines it had issued, and sought to have more control over how its rooms were sold. Many companies are forming online partnerships in order to distribute their travel products or services. An example is Luxurylink.com. Following the lead of auction sites such as Priceline, Luxurylink.com is an alliance of tourism companies around the world that lets visitors bid on sumptuous accommodation and vacation packages. Properties are sorted into nine geographic sections – such as the Caribbean or Europe – and can be accessed by browsing or by conducting a customizable search based on destination.

Listings include photos and a thorough description of the package; pricing and auction details such as 'retail value'; the minimum bid for the package; the start and close dates of the auction; and the smallest bid increments that the listing accepts. Before visitors can bid on listings that pique their interest, they must first register at the site. Winning bidders receive notification by e-mail, followed by a personal phone call within 20 minutes to collect payment information. The Global Spotlight below highlights a customer-driven pricing strategy for travel that has increased in popularity due to the internet – the reverse auction. Priceline is one of a number of companies that act as intermediaries between prospective buyers, who request quotations for a product or service, and multiple suppliers who quote the best price they are willing to offer. Buyers can then review the offers and select the supplier that best meets their needs.

Customer Service and Relationship Marketing

The internet is moving marketers much closer to one-to-one marketing. The web not only offers merchants the ability to communicate instantly with each customer, but it also allows the customer to talk back, and that makes it possible for companies to customize offers and services. It is now relatively easy for customers to check on the status of their bookings or their frequent flyer/visitor programmes at any time of the day. The Snapshot below presents the key motivating factors behind consumers' planning and booking travel online. The main reason consumers have adopted the internet is that it enables them to shop 24/7 in the comfort of their home. Ease of navigation is then the primary reason for variations in purchase decisions between different online products.

Many consumers, too, are looking to build relationships on the web. Godin introduced the concept of permission marketing, in which online consumers volunteer to be marketed to in return for some kind of reward. This type of marketing uses the interactivity offered by the web to engage customers in a dialogue and, as a consequence, in a long-term interactive relationship. Permission marketing is based on the premise that the attention of the consumer is a scarce commodity that needs to be managed carefully. Its emphasis is on building relationships with consumers instead of interrupting their lives with mass-marketing messages. About two-thirds of hotels are using their online channels to collect information on their customers, and then use that information to drive marketing campaigns (Green and Warner, 2006). Selective marketing, whereby consumers are shown advertising and promotions related to their browsing interests, is also on the increase. For example, the use of online coupons is rising rapidly, by more than 50 per cent a year, as internet giant Google, joins companies like ValPak and CoolSavings to bring new technology to the business of marketing national or local coupons over the internet. Digital coupons typically must be printed and physically turned in at a store so there is still some paper handling. The next stage, according to marketing experts, will come with the spread of digital cell phones with location tracking and automatic short-range communication technology. Electronic coupons will be delivered to cell phone owners on demand and redeemed by whisking the phone past a cash register, eliminating all the paper (Lohr, 2006).

6

Recreation and Tourism Marketing

Earlier it was mentioned that a product can be "ideas, goods, or services." Since tourism is primarily a service based industry, the principal products provided by recreation/tourism (R/T) businesses are recreational experiences and hospitality. These are intangible products and more difficult to market than tangible products such as automobiles. The intangible nature of services makes quality control difficult but crucial. It also makes it more difficult for potential customers to evaluate and compare service offerings. In addition, instead of moving the product to the customer, the customer must travel to the product (area/community).

Travel is a significant portion of the time and money spent in association with recreational and tourism experiences and is a major factor in people's decisions on whether or not to visit your business or community. As an industry, tourism has many components comprising the overall "travel experience." Along with transportation, it includes such things as accommodations, food and beverage services, shops, entertainment, aesthetics and special events. It is rare for one business to provide the variety of activities or facilities tourists need or desire. This adds to the difficulty of maintaining and controlling the quality of the experience. To overcome this hurdle, tourism related businesses, agencies, and organizations need to work together to package and promote tourism opportunities in their areas and align their efforts to assure consistency in product quality.

TOURISM MARKETS

Tourists makeup the third, and perhaps most important subsystem. Successful tourism Programme require a strong market orientation. The needs and wants of the tourists you choose to attract and serve must be the focus of much of your marketing and development activity. Therefore, it is important to clearly understand which tourism market segments you wish to attract and serve. Tourists fall into a very diverse set of categories with quite distinct needs and wants. You should identify the different types of tourists, or market segments that you presently serve or would like to serve. This may involve one or more tourism market surveys. A visitor survey identifies the size and nature of the existing market and asks the following questions:

- What are the primary market segments you presently attract?
- Where do they come from?
- What local businesses and facilities do they use?
- What attracted them to the community?
- How did they find out about your community?
- How satisfied are they with your offerings?

A market survey (usually a telephone survey) also can be conducted among households in regions from which you wish to attract tourists. This type of study helps identify potential markets, and means of attracting tourists to your area.

Tourism Market Segments

In a general tourism plan, some clear target tourism market segments should be identified. You might begin by defining the market area from which you will draw most of your visitors. The size of your market area depends upon the uniqueness and quality of your "product", transportation systems, tastes and preferences of surrounding populations, and your competition.

Identifying the market area will help target information and promotion and define transportation routes and modes, competition, and characteristics of your market.

Next, divide your travel market into the following trip length categories:

- Day trips from a 50 mile radius,
- Day trips from 50 to 200 miles away,
- Pass-through travelers,
- Overnight trips of 1 or 2 nights (most likely weekends), and
- Extended overnight vacation trips.

After you have an idea of your market area and kinds of trips you will be serving, begin defining more specific market segments like vehicle campers, downhill skiers, sightseers, family vacationers, single weekenders, and the like. These segments can be more clearly tied to particular resources, businesses, and facilities in your community.

What kinds of products and services are likely to attract each of these groups? Tourist needs as well as their impact on the local community are quite different for day tourists versus overnight tourists.

Areas catering primarily to weekend traffic will experience large fluctuations in use. In deciding the relative importance of these different segments, communities need to assess both their ability to provide required services (do you have enough rooms?), as well as the demand for different types of trips relative to the supply and your competition.

The Environment

A tourism plan is significantly affected by many factors in the broader environment. Indeed, one of the complexities of tourism planning is the number of variables that are outside of the control of an individual tourism business or community. These include such things as tourism offerings and prices at competing destinations, federal and state policy and legislation, currency exchange rates, the state of the economy, and weather. These factors are discussed more fully in Extension bulletin E-1959 as part of the market environment analysis. Local populations also must be considered in tourism planning. As they compete with tourists for resources, they can be significantly affected by tourism activity, and they are an important source of support in getting tourism plans implemented. A survey of local residents can be conducted to assess community attitudes towards tourism development, identify impacts of tourism on the community, and obtain local input into tourism plans. Public hearings, workshops, and advisory boards are other ways to obtain public involvement in tourism planning. Local support and cooperation is important to the success of tourism Programme and should not be overlooked.

Step three: Generating Alternatives. Generating alternative development and marketing options to meet your goals requires some creative thinking and brainstorming. The errors made at this stage are usually thinking too narrowly or screening out alternatives prematurely. It is wise to solicit a wide range of options from a diverse group of people. If tourism expertise is lacking in your community, seek help and advice outside the community.

Tourism planning involves a wide range of interrelated development and marketing decisions. The following development questions will get you started:

- How much importance should be assigned to tourism within a community or region?
- Which general community goals is tourism development designed to serve?
- Which organization(s) will provide the leadership and coordination necessary for community tourism planning? What are the relative roles of public and private sectors?

Tourism marketing decision questions include

- *Segments*: Which market segments should be pursued; geographic markets, trip types, activity or demographic subgroups?
- *Product*: What kinds of tourism products and services should be provided? Who should provide what?
- *Place*: Where should tourism facilities be located?
- *Promotion*: What kinds of promotion should be used, by whom, in which media, how much, when? What community tourism theme or image should be established?

- *Price*: What prices should be charged for which products and services. Who should capture the revenue?

Step four: Evaluating Alternatives. Tourism development and marketing options are evaluated by assessing the degree to which each option will be able to meet the stated goals and objectives. There are usually two parts to a systematic evaluation of tourism development and marketing alternatives: (1) Feasibility analysis, and (2) Impact assessment. These two tasks are interrelated, but think of them as trying to answer two basic questions: (1) Can it be done?, and (2) What are the consequences? A decision to take a specific action must be based both on feasibility and desirability.

Feasibility Analysis

First, screen alternatives and eliminate those that are not feasible due to economic, environmental, political, legal, or other factors. Evaluate the remaining set of alternatives in more detail, paying particular attention to the market potential and financial plan. Make a realistic assessment of your community's ability to attract and serve a market segment or segments. This requires a clear understanding of the tourism market in your area and how this market is changing. Also carefully identify your competition and evaluate your advantages and disadvantages compared to the competition. Plan towards the future because it takes time to implement decisions and for your actions to take effect. Therefore, look at the likely market and competition for several years to come. Review forecasts for the travel market in your area, if available. Careful tracking of tourism trends in your own community can help identify changes in the market that you will have to adapt to.

Impact Assessment

When evaluating alternative development and marketing strategies it is important to understand the impacts, both positive and negative, of proposed actions. The types of impacts and their importance vary across different communities and proposed actions. Generally, the size, extent, and nature of tourism impacts depend upon:

- Volume of tourist activity relative to local activity
- Length and nature of tourist contacts with the community
- Degree of concentration/dispersal of tourist activity in the area
- Similarities or differences between local populations and tourists
- Stability/sensitivity of local economy, environment, and social structure
- How well tourism is planned, controlled, and managed.

Look at both the benefits and costs of any proposed actions. While tourism development can increase income, revenues, and employment, it also involves costs. Evaluate benefits and costs of tourism development from the perspectives of local government, businesses, and residents.

Impacts on Local Government

Local government provides most of the infrastructure and many of the services essential to tourism development, including highways, public parks, law enforcement, water and sewer, garbage collection and disposal. Evaluate tourism decisions with a clear understanding of the capacity of the local infrastructure and services relative to anticipated needs, and take into account both the needs of local populations and tourists.

A fiscal impact analysis evaluates the impact of tourism on the community's tax base and local government costs. It entails predicting the additional infrastructure and service requirements of tourism development, estimating their costs, deciding who will pay for/provide them, and how. Will tourism generate increased local government revenue through fees and charges, local sales or use taxes, increased property values or property tax rates, or larger local shares of federal and state tax revenues?

Impacts on Business and Industry

Businesses that are directly serving tourists benefit from sales to tourists. Through secondary impacts, tourism activity also benefits a wide range of businesses in a community. For example, a local textile industry may sell to a linen supply firm that serves hotels and motels catering primarily to tourists. A local forest products industry sells to a lumberyard where local woodcarvers or furniture makers buy their supplies. They in turn sell to tourists through various retail outlets. All of these businesses benefit from tourism.

If most products and services for tourists are bought outside of the local area, much of the tourist spending "leaks" out of the local economy. The more a community is "self-sufficient" in serving tourists, the larger the local impact.

Impacts on Residents

Local residents may experience a broad range of both positive and negative impacts from tourism development. Tourism development may provide increased employment and income for the community. Although tourism jobs are primarily in the service sectors and are often seasonal, part time, and low-paying, these characteristics, are neither universal nor always undesirable. Residents may value opportunities for part time and seasonal work. In particular, employment opportunities and work experiences for students or retirees may be desired.

Residents may also benefit from local services that otherwise would not be available. Tourism development may mean a wider variety of retailers and restaurants, or a better community library. It may also mean more traffic, higher prices, and increases in property values and local taxes. The general quality of the environment and life in the community may go up or down due to tourism development. This depends on the nature of tourism development, the preferences and desires of local residents, and how well tourism is planned and managed.

Steps five and six: Implementation, and Monitoring and Evaluation. We will not attempt a complete discussion of decisionmaking, plan implementation, and monitoring, but these are critical steps in the success of a tourism plan. A set of specific actions should be prescribed with clearly defined responsibilities and timetables. Monitor progress in implementing the plan and evaluate the success of the plan in meeting its goals and objectives on a regular basis. Plans generally need to be adjusted over time due to changing goals, changing market conditions, and unanticipated impacts. It is a good idea to build monitoring and evaluation systems into your planning efforts.

Successful tourism planning and development means serving both tourists and local residents. The bulletins in this series stress the importance of a market orientation for attracting and serving tourists. This market orientation must be balanced with a clear view of how tourism serves the broader community interest and an understanding of the positive and negative impacts of tourism development. Remember, tourism should serve the community first and the tourist second. Tourism development must be compatible with other activities in the area and be supported by the local population. Therefore, the tourism plan should be closely coordinated with other local and regional planning efforts, if not an integral part of them.

THE MARKETING PLAN

One of the most important steps a business or community can take to improve the effectiveness and efficiency of their marketing efforts is to develop a written marketing plan. This plan will guide their marketing decisions and assist them in allocating marketing resources such as money and personnel time.

The plan should include:

- The overall business objectives—what you want to accomplish;
- An assessment of the market environment—what factors may affect your marketing efforts;
- A business/community profile—what resources are available,
- Market identification (segmentation)—the specific groups or clientele most interested in your product;
- The marketing objectives for each segment;
- The marketing strategies (or mixes) for different markets you target—the best combination of the 4 Ps (product, price, place, promotion) for each segment;
- An implementation plan—how to "make it work;"
- The marketing budget-how much you have to spend; and
- A method for evaluation and change.

A framework which can be used to develop a marketing plan. Each component will be briefly discussed in the remainder of the bulletin. For more information regarding different components of the plan be sure to consult other bulletins in this series.

OVERALL BUSINESS OBJECTIVES

Businesses, agencies, and communities should develop overall objectives and regularly monitor their progress. The objectives should provide guidance for all decisions including finances, personnel and marketing. They should be quantitative and measurable statements of what the business or community wants to accomplish over a specified period of time. Business objectives are often stated in terms of sales, profits, market shares and/or occupancy rates. Communities frequently establish objectives relating to such things as increasing the number of tourists, developing or changing their image, facility and activity development, cooperation among tourism related businesses and increasing length of stay and local expenditures. It is important that the objectives be reasonable given the market conditions and the firm's or organization's resources. Establish a few reasonable objectives instead of a long, unrealistic "wish list." This is especially true for new businesses or communities which do not have much experience in tourism development and/or marketing.

MARKET ENVIRONMENT ANALYSIS

The next step in developing a marketing plan is to assess the impact of environmental factors (such as economic, social and political) on present and future markets. Changes in these factors can create marketing opportunities as well as problems.

DEMOGRAPHIC AND LIFESTYLE TRENDS

Changing demographics and lifestyles are having a major impact on R/T participation. An assessment of these trends is important to understand how they will likely affect your business or community.

Some of the important trends that bear watching:

- Population growth and movement;
- Rural community growth compared to metropolitan areas;
- Number of adult women employed outside the home;
- The number of households is growing, especially non- family and single parent households, but family size is decreasing;
- The impact of two wage earner households on real family income;
- The number of retired persons with the financial ability to travel;
- Better health to an older age; and
- Continued aging of the population (we are becoming a middle aged society).

ECONOMIC CONDITIONS

Overall economic conditions can have significant impacts on recreation and tourism markets. A marketing strategy that is effective during periods of low unemployment rates may have to be significantly adjusted if unemployment increases. Businesses and communities should monitor and assess the likely impact of factors such as unemployment rates, real family income, rate of inflation, credit availability, terms and interest rates.

Consideration should also be given to the prices of complementary products, such as lodging, gasoline and recreation equipment.

LAWS AND GOVERNMENT ACTIONS

As a complex industry, tourism is significantly affected both positively and negatively by laws and by actions of governmental agencies. For instance, rulings on such things as liability issues or decisions regarding building and health codes may change or possibly prevent the construction of a proposed facility. If a public facility changes the prices of its services, this could affect the service offerings of associated private businesses. These actions may have both positive and negative effects on the marketing efforts of the business and community. To avoid wasting valuable resources it is important that R/T businesses, agencies, and communities continually monitor and evaluate governmental actions.

TECHNOLOGY

Technological developments are increasing rapidly. New recreation products, such as all-terrain vehicles and wind surfers, provide new ways for people to satisfy their recreational preferences. New production technologies and materials offer recreation and tourism businesses ways to reduce costs and improve the quality of their products/services. Advances in telecommunications have and will continue to create new promotional opportunities. Technological innovations, in relation to jobs and the home, have resulted in increased leisure time for many people.

COMPETITION

Businesses and communities must identify and analyse existing and potential competitors. The objective of the analysis is to determine the strengths and weaknesses of the competition's marketing strategies. The analysis should include the competition's:

- Product/service features and quality;
- Location relative to different geographic markets;
- Promotional themes and messages;
- Prices; and
- Type of customer they are attracting.

BUSINESS AND COMMUNITY PROFILES

Too many communities attempt to market themselves as tourist destinations without accurate information about their resources (facilities, services, staff), image (projected vs. Actual), and how well their customers are satisfied. Without this information, it is difficult to make other decisions in the planning process.

Included should be such things as recreational and entertainment facilities, cultural and historic sites, overnight accommodations, restaurants, shopping opportunities, special events and activities, staff size, and transportation. Each item of the "inventory" should also be assessed in terms of quality and availability.

DEVELOPING A MARKETING PLAN

The Opening Vignette highlights the importance of successful positioning and planning in today's marketing environment. Through careful planning, G.A.P Adventures has become one of the largest adventure companies in the world. In its principles, marketing planning is no more than a logical thought process in which all businesses should engage. It is an application of common sense, as relevant to a small bed and breakfast as it is to an international airline.

The term marketing plan is widely used to mean a short-term plan for two years or less. This chapter is devoted to the development of such plans. A strategic marketing plan, on the other hand, is different, as it covers three or more years. A marketing plan serves a number of purposes within any tourism organization. It provides a road map for all future marketing activities of the firm; it ensures that marketing activities are aligned with the corporate strategic plan; it forces marketing managers to review and think through all steps in the marketing process objectively; it assists in the budgeting process to match resources with marketing objectives; and it creates a process to monitor actual against expected results.

A systematic marketing planning process consists of eight logical steps. For the strategic marketing plan, the first four stages may be more detailed, but any short-term marketing plan should also include an assessment of these steps. Each step feeds into the next one. A marketing plan is not a stand-alone tool, so the first stage is examining the goals and objectives of the organization as a whole and then developing a marketing plan that will support the company's mission statement, corporate philosophy, and corporate goals. Once the corporate connection has been clarified, the next stage is defining the current situation, reviewing the effectiveness of current activities, and identifying opportunities.

This is the 'analysis and forecasting' stage. The third stage is concerned with defining marketing goals and objectives derived logically from the previous stages of the planning process.

At the fourth stage, target markets should be selected from the previously developed list of available segments, and once the market has been segmented and a target market identified, the next step is positioning. Market positioning is ultimately how the consumer perceives the good or service in a given market, and is used to achieve a sustainable competitive advantage over competitors. The fifth stage involves selecting and developing a series of strategies that effectively bring about the required results.

This part of the plan shows how the organization intends to use the 7 Ps. The marketing plan needs to address the resources required to support the strategies and meet the objectives, and resource requirements are the focus of the plan's sixth stage. The seventh stage is concerned with marketing control and how objectives will be achieved in the required time, using the funds and resources requested. Finally, at the eighth stage, the plan should be communicated both internally and externally to achieve maximum impact. Most marketing plans will contain an executive summary of the whole, and this should be no more than a few pages in length. A good approach is to sum up each section and present them in the order in which they appear.

THE CORPORATE CONNECTION

A good marketing plan begins with the fact that the only purpose of marketing is to support the enterprise. Marketing planning should therefore reflect the goals and objectives of the organization as a whole. The mission or vision statement reflects the organization's philosophy, and the goals and objectives as set out in the business plan become the basis of planning for all departments. Marketing's responsibilities in relation to the corporate vision are usually outlined in one or more separate marketing-specific documents.

Goals can be defined in terms such as sales growth, increased profitability and market leadership, whereas objectives are the activities that will accomplish the goals. A vision statement usually answers the question, 'What do we want to be?', whilst the mission statement will answer the question, 'What business are we in?' Whereas the vision describes where the organization wants to be in some future time, the mission is a broader statement about an organization's business and scope, goods or services, markets served and overall philosophy.

Vision and mission statements can vary. G.A.P Adventures has the following mission statement that focuses on service: 'Our priority is to satisfy every customer, every time, through outstanding, personalized service! We are dedicated to the customer experience and are constantly evaluating how we can improve this experience.' Cheddar Caves and Gorge in the UK, however, has a mission statement based on social values and sustainability: ' To make the Caves accessible to visitors in a way which increases visitor awareness of their value, while responding to the social needs of our visitors and protecting the natural environment for future generations.'

ANALYSIS AND FORECASTING

The next stage of the marketing plan is defining the current situation. It is essential that each component of the business be reviewed in order to ensure that resources can be allocated efficiently. Several models exist for reviewing effectiveness and identifying opportunities but those proven by time and practical application across a range of industries include portfolio analysis, competitor analysis, segmentation analysis, SWOT (strengths, weaknesses, opportunities and threats) analysis, and forecasting.

PORTFOLIO ANALYSIS

Portfolio analysis first became popular in the 1960s, when many organizations sought to improve their profitability by diversifying their activities so as not to keep all their eggs in one basket. The Boston Consulting Group (BCG) model was one of the most popular approaches to evaluating a very diverse group of goods and services, based on long-term planning and economic forecasts.

The model adopts the view that every product of an organization can be plotted on a two-by-two matrix to identify those offering high potential and those that are drains on the organization's resources. High market share means that a business is a leader in that good or service; low market share indicates that either the marketplace is heavily competitive or a good or service has not had widespread market acceptance. A good or service can then take up one of four theoretical positions within the model. A cash cow is a product that generates cash and turnover, but has limited long-term prospects. A dog provides neither cash flow nor long-term opportunities and does not hold great promise for improved performance. In the illustration, the company has three dogs.

Stars are products that have a dominant share of a fast-growing market. Although they may not generate a large amount of cash at present, they have potential for high returns in the future. Question marks are fairly speculative products that have high-risk potential. They may be profitable, but because they hold a small market share, they may be vulnerable to competition. Goods or services go through the product life cycle, which can affect where they are positioned within the BCG model. A new product may be in the 'question mark' cell; as it becomes successful it moves into the 'star' category, and then moves on to become a 'cash cow' before starting to decline and becoming a 'dog'.

A good example of a tourism product that has taken up all four positions in the BCG model is the Concorde jet airplane. Beginning as a question mark, the delta-winged marvel, a product of 1960s technology and optimism, quickly became a star as business executives and famous stars asserted their status by happily spending thousands of dollars to save a few hours' travelling time. The product soon became a cash cow, and more than 2.5 million passengers flew on

British Airways' Concordes after they entered service in 1976. However, filling the 100 seats on a Concorde became increasingly difficult, and between 2000 and 2003, Concorde could be classified as a dog. In April 2003 it was announced that the supersonic airline run by British Airways and Air France would be retired that year because of slumping ticket sales. As part of a portfolio analysis, an organization should assess each good and service in terms of its position on the product life cycle.

COMPETITOR ANALYSIS

Information on the number and type of competitors, their relative market shares, the things they do well and things they do badly all assist in the planning process. Competitor analysis also highlights market trends and the level of loyalty of consumers. Competitors can be divided into four broad categories: direct competitors offer similar goods and services to the same consumer at a similar price; product category competitors make the same product or class of products; general competitors provide the same service; and budget competitors compete for the same consumer dollars. In addition to the existing competition, there is also the threat of potential competition in the form of new entrants.

In China recently, a number of new foreign entrants has led to a very competitive hotel sector, particularly in the budget inn category. Ambitious players like US-based Wyndham Worldwide Corp.'s Super 8 chain entered China in 2004, and by 2006 had 33 hotels. It plans to increase that to 110 hotels by 2009. Local players in this sector, like Home Inns and Hotels Management Inc., and Jinjiang International, are also expanding aggressively. Other organizations are planning for the growing Chinese travel market.

Michael Porter (1980) suggests that there are only three generic strategies for dealing with competition: low-cost leadership, differentiation, and focus. Low-cost leadership is the simplest and most effective strategy, but it requires large resources and strong management to sustain. A low-cost leadership strategy is used when a firm sets out to become the low-cost producer in its industry. Low-cost producers typically sell a standard, or no-frills, product and place considerable emphasis on reaping scale or absolute cost advantages from all sources. It may be short lived, as it is easy for competitors to match a low price in an attempt to drive off the challenge. The low-cost airlines that are springing up all over the world are examples of companies following such a strategy.

Differentiation is a strategy that consists of an innovative technological breakthrough, which can take competitors a long time to imitate. A competitive advantage can be gained with a product that is newer, better and/or faster. The improvement can be in performance, durability, reliability, or service features. Airbus's new 560-tonne jet, the A380, carries up to 800 passengers and has differentiated itself from competitors by becoming the world's biggest commercial airliner. A focus strategy concentrates on designing a good or service to meet the needs of one segment of the market better than the competition does. Bruce Poon Tip from GA.P Adventures follows such a strategy in the adventure tourism business.

All three of these generic strategies are based on the organization's creation of a unique position for itself, which distinguishes its offerings from those of its competitors by price, product features, or the way in which it serves the needs of a particular segment. This process, known as 'positioning'. The Global Spotlight below shows how a Mexican resort is differentiating itself from other all-inclusive resorts by targeting the overweight tourist.

TARGETING THE OVERWEIGHT: SIZE-FRIENDLY VACATIONS AT FREEDOM PARADISE

'Live Large – Live Free, At Any Size, At Any Age' is Freedom Paradise's motto. Dutchman Jurriaan Klink opened the 'size-friendly' resort in the Mexican Riviera in June 2003 after observing that overweight holidaymakers did not seem comfortable in traditional resorts, and discovering that no other specific facilities existed for this growing niche market – despite the fact that an estimated 61 per cent of the US adult population is considered overweight by the Centres for Disease Control.

The former Cancun hotel manager spent three years researching the plus-size community to determine both needs and concerns. With over 300 million obese people worldwide, and, in particular, over 60 per cent of his target American customers overweight, the market was ripe. Klink, along with General Director Julio Rincon was amazed that no one else had tapped into this lucrative niche and set about developing the resort from two existing bankrupt hotels.

The project was kept secret while US$2 million of renovations were completed at the Riviera Maya site, near Tulum, Mexico, about 70 miles south of Cancun. Its close proximity to the US was paramount in choosing the site, as Americans were to be the key target market for the 112-room resort.

In order to cater for the needs of the larger consumer, walls were ripped out and doorways were widened; constricting bath tubs were removed and bathrooms were reconstructed with benches in the showers and hand-held nozzles; furniture was custom-designed with larger sizes in mind. Dining chairs, for example, are twice the standard 26-inch size and without restricting arms. The king-sized beds were reinforced to encourage uninhibited romance.

Sturdy wooden, four-foot wide loungers plus thick benches with tree trunk legs were produced for poolside comfort and gradual inclines with grab bars were added to the pools, rather than flimsy ladders. In the hibiscus- and palm-filled gardens, wider and flatter walking spaces were created. Three restaurants were also added to the existing two, featuring different themes: Mexican, Italian, international, a steak-house and a Hawaiian-style seafood room.

Menus were created with healthy eating as well as plentiful, good quality food in mind, all of which is included in the resort tariff. A large mural in the reception area depicts the 'King and Queen of Paradise', a large couple feasting on a picnic rug in a beautiful tropical setting, designed to make larger visitors feel welcome. Staff are hired in all sizes and given sensitivity training by psychologist and human resources director Martha Bueno, who emphasizes that size acceptance goes beyond physical accommodations.

Klink's creed is that oversized people should not 'postpone their lives' because of their size, always putting off fun until they manage to lose weight. All resort activities, including snorkelling, scuba diving, beach volleyball, fishing and sailing, have been customized to be safe and comfortable for the guests. There are also cultural tours to nearby ruins and beauty spots plus a well-ness centre that promotes yoga, meditation and Tai Chi without pressurizing weight loss programmes. A children's club, bird-feeding, flower and astrology workshops are also featured. Pricing ranges from US$125 to $195 per person per night depending on season and based on double occupancy. Klink gained huge media attention prior to opening his innovative resort, resulting in a flood of potential plus-size customer inquiries. With a plethora of TV and newspaper articles and features, even negative publicity such as crude jokes made by late night television show hosts did not deter people from making reservations. Bookings could be made directly or through tour wholesalers and travel agencies. Travel agent orientation trips were also arranged to enlighten sales forces about the differentiation of the product and to help them assess and advertise the new concept. Cross-promotions were also eventually established with fashionable, plus-size clothing company, Lane Bryant and Figure magazine.

Competitions were set up with the two partners, offering an all-expenses-paid holiday at Freedom Paradise for the winners. Figure magazine also featured articles and ads for the resort. These partnerships enabled Freedom Paradise to reach target market customer databases for further promotions. Klink intends to open more size-friendly resorts in North America if the market permits. He is concerned that some oversized individuals who have already been put off travelling because of hardship and mental and physical discomfort will not easily be convinced to try another beach vacation. However, brand awareness was created quickly for the first resort due to its uniqueness as well as its humanitarian aspects. Says Klink, 'From a business standpoint, this is a smart idea. From a humanity standpoint, it's really beautiful.'

SEGMENTATION ANALYSIS

Segmentation analysis refers to the way in which organizations identify and categorize customers into groups defined by similar characteristics and similar needs or desires. The Global Spotlight above showed how the owner of Freedom Paradise spent three years researching the plus-size community to determine both the needs and concerns of his target market. The concept of segmentation is widely adopted in tourism marketing, as few companies in the industry attempt to appeal to an entire market.

The core advantage of segmentation is that customers will be more satisfied with the product because it has been designed with their needs in mind. Their social needs are also satisfied because they will be mixing with people like themselves and avoiding incompatible types. If an organization knows exactly which segments it wishes to reach, it can select the media most likely to be read, heard, or seen by those consumers, and so spend less on general mass-market advertising. If it knows the lifestyles and attitudes of that segment and the benefits they are seeking from the product, the advertising message can be made more persuasive. It shows the major European customer travel segments, their characteristics, and the tour operators that serve each segment.

SEGMENTATION ANALYSIS

The practice of dividing total markets up into groups on the basis of similar characteristics

The criteria used most often by tourism and hospitality suppliers to segment the market are as follows:

1. Demographic segmentation uses the primary variables of age, gender, family life cycle, and ethnicity to segment the markets. Club 18–30, for example, uses age and lifestyle stage variables to attract young singles interested in a vibrant night life.
2. Psychographic segmentation divides buyers into different groups based on social class, lifestyle and personality characteristics. Psychographics and lifestyle segmentation are based on personality traits, attitudes, motivations, and activities. People in the same demographic group can have very different psychographic profiles.
3. Geographic segmentation is the division of markets according to geographical boundaries, such as countries, provinces/states, regions, cities, or neighbourhoods. In the past, for most destination marketing organizations (DMOs), market segmentation was often limited to understanding the more lucrative international tourist market. However, since the terrorist attacks of 11 September 2001, destination marketers have recognized the significance of local and provincial residents and the impact that they have on tourism receipts (Hudson and Ritchie, 2002).
4. Benefit segmentation divides customers based on the benefits they desire, such as education, entertainment, luxury, or low cost. Customers weigh different features of a service, and these are evaluated to form the basis of benefit segmentation. Customers of Freedom Paradise would value benefits such as large walking spaces

and large dinner portions, whereas for most sport tourists these services would be irrelevant.

5. Behaviour segmentation divides the market into groups based on the various types of buying behaviour. Common bases include usage rate (light, medium, and heavy), user status (former users, non-users, potential users, first-time users, and regular users of a product), loyalty status (many people stay in five-star hotels as much for the status it confers on them as for the additional comfort), buyer-readiness stage, and occasions. On special occasions, people are prepared to pay more for special treatment, so many restaurants now have deals for children's birthday parties, while hotels and cruise lines have special honeymoon suites.
6. In sum, the heart of any marketing plan is careful analysis of available market segments and the selection of the appropriate target markets. A common mistake within tourism and hospitality is the selection of inappropriate segments. Las Vegas tried unsuccessfully to rebrand itself as a family destination, providing pirate- and circus-themed hotels, funfairs, rides, amusement and games arcades, and animal attractions. They have since reverted to attracting more appropriate market segments, with the help of their 'What Happens in Vegas, Stays in Vegas' advertising campaign. When developing a marketing plan, marketers can gather information concerning market segments from two sources. Internal data can be analysed by looking at business cards, guest registrations, credit card receipts, customer surveys, direct observations and staff perceptions. External data can be gathered from published industry information, marketing research, or by making guesstimates after talking with competitors, vendors, and others in the industry.

Market segmentation is a dynamic process because customer trends are not static. It is thus important to carry out regular – preferably continuous – tracking studies to monitor changes happening in the market. One of the most recent trends in tourism and hospitality has been a 'demassification' of the market, in which a greater number of niche markets are replacing the mass ones of the past. As a result, niche marketing is increasing, whereby products are tailored to meet the needs and wants of narrowly defined geographic, demographic, or psychographic segments. The Snapshot below highlights how an Australian wine tourism company has successfully targeted the Generation X market.

SWOT ANALYSIS

SWOT is an acronym for strengths, weaknesses, opportunities and threats. A SWOT analysis provides scope for an organization to list all its strengths (those things it does best and its positive product features) and its weaknesses (problems that affect its success). These factors are always internally focused. For hotels and visitor attractions, location may be a major strength, or the strength may lie in the skills of certain staff members.

Strength may also lie in historical artifacts or architectural style, or having a particularly favourable consumer image. Once identified, strengths are the basis of corporate positions and can be promoted to potential customers, enhanced through product augmentation, or developed within a strategic framework. In the Snapshot profiling Four Seasons in this chapter, several strengths of the Four Seasons Hotels and Resorts can be identified, including their reputation, brand equity and global positioning. Weaknesses, ranging from aging products and declining markets to surly customer contact staff, must also be identified. Once identified, they may be subject to management action designed to minimize their impact or to remove them where possible. Weaknesses and strengths are often matters of perception rather than 'fact', and may be recognized only through consumer research. Again, using Four Seasons as an example, weaknesses could include not being diversified enough and therefore being vulnerable to negative external environmental impacts.

Opportunities are events that can affect a business, either through its reaction to external forces or through its addressing of its own weaknesses. An opportunity identified recently by Four Seasons Hotels and Resorts is in private charters and general cruises, a move that may improve the group's weakness of not being diversified enough. Threats are those elements, both internal and external, that could have a serious detrimental effect on a business. After 11 September 2001, the subsequent downturn in the economy had a devastating impact on tourism and by the end of 2002, Four Seasons had not recovered. The subsequent Iraq war and concerns about sudden acute respiratory syndrome (SARS) led to a huge number of cancelled trips to North America and to thousands of dollars in lost tourism revenue for all hotels, including Four Seasons.

A SWOT analysis is usually best undertaken early in the planning process, and in large organizations a SWOT is often carried out for each division. For example, a convention hotel would conduct a SWOT on the property as a whole, but might also undertake a separate exercise for the functions area, restaurants, retail outlets and recreation facilities. To enhance their own foresight and bring to bear an independent, fresh vision, it is common practice in large market-oriented businesses for managers to commission consultants to carry out regular audits of all aspects of their business, including a SWOT analysis.

FORECASTING

Because information is never perfect and the future is always unknown, no one right conclusion can ever be drawn from the evidence gathered in the

SWOT process. As a result, forecasting becomes an important stage in the planning process to support a SWOT. Forecasting is market research based but future oriented, and it relies on expectations, vision, judgement, and projections for factors such as sales volume and revenue trends, consumer profiles, product profiles, price trends, and trends in the external environment.

The Snapshot below provides forecasts for the growing Chinese travel market based on reports by several market research companies. Because the future for tourism and hospitality products is subject to volatile, unpredictable factors and competitors' decisions, the goal of forecasting is not accuracy but careful and continuous assessment of probabilities and options, with a focus on future choices. Forecasting recognizes that most marketing-mix expenditure is invested months ahead of targeted revenue flows. Since marketing planning is focused on future revenue achievement, it is necessarily dependent upon skill, judgement, foresight and realism in the forecasting process.

There are two main sets of forecasting techniques: qualitative and quantitative. Qualitative techniques are those that seek to estimate future levels of demand, based on detailed subjective analysis. They include sales staff estimates, senior management opinions and buyers' intention surveys. Two more sophisticated qualitative techniques are the Delphi technique and scenario planning. The Delphi technique involves obtaining expert opinions about the future prospects for a particular market without the experts actually meeting or necessarily knowing at any stage the composition of the panel. Long-term scenario planning is undertaken by larger organizations such as hotel or airline companies. This is a systematic attempt to predict the composition of the future market environment in 10–25 years' time, and the likely impacts on the company.

Quantitative techniques rely on analysis of past and current data. In some instances this implies the simple projecting of future demand in terms of past trends; in other instances, unravelling causal determinants needs to be considered. A number of well-tested methods are used, but most require a degree of statistical ability. Time-series (non-causal) techniques involve the forecasting of future demand on the basis of past trends. Causal methods attempt to show, by using regression analysis, how some measure of tourism demand is influenced by selected variables other than time. Finally, computer simulations are becoming more popular – trend-curve analysis and multiple regressions are combined mathematically to generate a computer model that simulates tourism demand.

MARKET SEGMENTATION (IDENTIFICATION)

Recreation and tourism businesses and communities often make the mistake of attempting to be all things to all people. It is difficult, and risky, to develop marketing strategies for the mass market.

Strategies designed for the "average" customer often result in unappealing products, prices, and promotional messages. For example, it would be difficult to develop a campground that would be equally attractive to recreational vehicle campers and backpackers or promote a property to serve both snow mobilers and nature oriented cross country skiers.

Marketing is strongly based on market segmentation and target marketing. Market segmentation is the process of:

- Taking existing and/or potential customers/visitors (market) and categorizing them into groups with similar preferences referred to as "market segments;"
- Selecting the most promising segments as "target markets;" and
- Designing "marketing mixes," or strategies (combination of the 4 Ps), which satisfy the special needs, desires and behaviour of the target markets.

There is no unique or best way to segment markets, but ways in which customers can be grouped are:

- Location of residence—instate, out-of-state, local;
- Demographics—age, income, family status, education;
- Equipment ownership/use—RV's, sailboats, canoes, tents, snowmobiles;
- Important product attributes—price, quality, quantity; and
- Lifestyle attributes—activities, interests, opinions.

To be useful, the segment identification process should result in segments that suggest marketing efforts that will be effective in attracting them and at least one segment large enough to justify specialized marketing efforts. After segments have been identified, the business or community must select the "target markets," those segments which offer them the greatest opportunity.

When determining target markets, consideration should be given to:

- Existing and future sales potential of each segment;
- The amount and strength of competition for each segment;
- The ability to offer a marketing mix which will be successful in attracting each segment;
- The cost of servicing each segment; and
- Each segment's contribution to accomplishing overall business/ community objectives. It is often wiser to target smaller segments that are presently not being served, or served inadequately, than to go after larger segments for which there is a great deal of competition.

MARKETING OBJECTIVES FOR EACH SEGMENT

Marketing objectives which contribute to the accomplishment of the overall business objectives should be established for each target market.

Objectives serve a number of functions including:

- Guidance for developing marketing mixes for different target markets;
- Information for allocating the marketing budget between target markets;

- A basis for objectively evaluating the effectiveness of the marketing mixes (setting standards); and
- A framework for integrating the different marketing mixes into the overall marketing plan.

The target market objectives should:

- Be expressed in quantitative terms;
- Be measurable;
- Specify the target market; and
- Indicate the time period in which the objective is to be accomplished.

For example, increase the number of overnight stays by people from the Chicago market over the next two years by five per cent. Remember, rank objectives by priority and carefully evaluate them to ensure that they are reasonable given the strength of the competition and resources available for marketing.

TOURISM MARKETING STRATEGY

THE ACCIDENTAL TOURIST

"For Newfoundland and Labrador, there's no such thing as an accidental tourist. It takes deliberate planning and determined effort to visit here, compelled by curiosity and the promise of what's unique and different in our people, culture, lifestyle, and dramatic scenery."

BARRIERS AND OPPORTUNITIES

Travel distance, access, and cost continue to be significant barriers for visitors, and a competitive disadvantage for the tourism industry in Newfoundland and Labrador.

A short peak season, capacity constraints during peak season, and increasing problems and delays at border crossings and in airports make increasing tourism visitors and revenue even more difficult. Competing with well-known tourism destinations that are well-funded and heavily advertised makes the job even tougher. Despite these barriers, there are opportunities open to Newfoundland and Labrador Tourism.

Baby bloomers are entering the empty nest stage of the family lifestyle. They have money, time, and keen interest to explore destinations that are off the beaten track, unusual and unspoiled places where few have gone before. Places like Newfoundland and Labrador.

Ontario, our largest non-resident market, still remains largely underdeveloped for Newfoundland and Labrador tourism. Our greatest opportunity may lay in the launch of the new Tourism brand positioning and personality for Newfoundland and Labrador – and the creative strategy which we use to express it. Our coastline, rich history, unique culture, people, and natural environment remain our key strengths.

MARKETING OBJECTIVES

The marketing objectives for Newfoundland and Labrador Tourism are to increase non-resident visitation and expenditures from our core markets, thereby increasing the tourism industry's annual contribution to the economy. The strategies and campaigns created to achieve these marketing objectives will also be guided by the desire of government and the Tourism Board to extend the tourism season beyond the core summer season in order to increase the economic benefit and the long-term viability of the industry.

MARKETING STRATEGY

Newfoundland and Labrador Tourism will take a growth-strategy approach to marketing Newfoundland and Labrador as a tourism destination. Advertising will reach and persuade visitors to come to Newfoundland and Labrador, rather than to other destinations in their evoked set. Public and media relations will reinforce the key messages, delivering a consistent and relevant brand image of the province, while sales and online initiatives will "close the loop."

The tourism product – in the form of attractions, experiences, and infrastructure – has a larger role to play in increasing length of stay, amount of money spent per trip, and overall tourism revenues. To be successful in attracting customers from competitors, it's essential that we focus and concentrate our resources on the best opportunity – and create programmes and campaigns that are fully integrated.

TARGET MARKETS

Newfoundland and Labrador Tourism will focus and concentrate its resources against the target audiences and markets which offer the best opportunity and the highest return on investment. The target market is the non-resident touring and explorer market with concentration in Toronto, Ottawa, Calgary, Halifax and Montreal. Additional geographic markets include the Mid-Atlantic Region of the United States, California and the UK. Activity-based markets include Meetings, Convention and Incentive Travel market, the Hunting and Fishing market, the Hiking market and partnerships in Outdoor Adventure and Cruise markets.

TOURING AND EXPLORER MARKET

The touring and explorer group is a broad leisure market seeking sightseeing and soft-adventure experiences – from nature viewing to cultural experiences to hiking, birding, and whale-watching. Demographically, research reveals them to be singles and couples in the pre- and post-full nest stage of the family life cycle. Not surprisingly, they tend to be in two age groups: 25 to 34 and (skewed) 45+ years of age. They also tend to be well-educated and have a higher than average proportion who are university-educated and have higher than average household incomes. Psychographically, they see themselves as increasingly sophisticated and experienced travellers, seeking more unusual places and experiences 'off the beaten track'. They are looking for an antidote to the stress and plastic composition of urban life and modern times. They're interested in discovering and experiencing the unspoiled natural environment. They are curious people, more interested in unexpected and intriguing experiences than repeat trips to conventional 'tourist' destinations: "been there, done that."

Marketing efforts in the United States will shift from the New England region to the Mid-Atlantic region for Newfoundland and Labrador. These travellers are seeking adventure and cultural experiences in new destinations. To maximize our efforts, Newfoundland and Labrador works cooperatively with the Atlantic Canada Tourism Partnership (ACTP). ACTP is a nine-member, pan-Atlantic partnership comprising of the Atlantic Canada Opportunities Agency, the four Atlantic Canada Tourism Industry Associations, and the four provincial departments responsible for tourism. The international market is developmental for Newfoundland and Labrador, with low penetration but with long-term potential and high-spend per visitor.

Newfoundland and Labrador Tourism will continue to pursue this market in partnership with its Atlantic Canada Partners (ACTP), with primary focus being on the United States and the United Kingdom. Marketing activities include travel trade partnerships, familiarization tours, trade shows, media relations, and joint marketing with the Canadian Tourism Commission (CTC). The CTC and its industry partners have launched a new global advertising campaign in the UK, Germany, and France. ACTP is a partner in this UK programme to build more consumer awareness of the region.

MEETINGS, CONVENTIONS AND INCENTIVE TRAVEL MARKET

Newfoundland and Labrador Tourism provides consultation, materials support, and mailing assistance to international, national, and regional conference organizers hosting conventions and meetings in Newfoundland and Labrador. Incentive travel is a global management tool that uses an exceptional travel experience to motivate and/or recognize staff for increased levels of performance in support of organizational goals.

Newfoundland and Labrador Tourism provides consultation, marketing, and product development support to industry suppliers in this lucrative market. Trade shows and marketplaces are available through partnership opportunities in North American markets.

OUTDOOR ADVENTURE MARKET

Outdoor and nature activities such as hiking, birding and kayaking are core to our tourism experiences. These experiences appeal to outdoor enthusiasts and have a broad appeal to our touring and explorer market. Newfoundland and Labrador Tourism partners with the Newfoundland and Labrador Adventure Tourism Association at consumer and trade shows.

HUNTING AND FISHING MARKET

Newfoundland and Labrador offers hunters and sport fish enthusiasts some of the most amazing and rewarding outdoor recreation experiences in the world. Newfoundland and Labrador Tourism partners with the Newfoundland and Labrador Outfitters Association (NLOA) to develop a fully-integrated marketing programme for the hunting and fishing market.

TOURISM MARKETING INFORMATION SYSTEM

The major aim of Tour MIS is an optimal information supply and decision support for the tourism industry. The first step is to provide aniline tourism survey data, as well as evaluation programmes to transform data into precious management information. Tour-MIS predominantly comprises:

1. A database containing tourism market research data (declarative knowledge),
2. Various programme modules (method-base, procedural knowledge) converting acknowledged methods/models into simple surfaces, and
3. Various administrative programmes which assist the maintenance of the data- base and track and control the information search behaviour of users.

The internet supports the transport and presentation of animated and unanimated pictures, sound and video recordings and text and numerical data and is expandable. A high- performance SQL-database and a functionally designed user interface for Tour MIS based on hypertext and Perl permits the development of interactive applications.

The programme modules contained in the method-base are developed according to the specific requirements of tourism managers. The internet offers a number of advantages against the old PC-solution. Since changes in the database have immediate worldwide effect the speed of information transmission can be reduced to the availability of the information source.

For example, Tour MIS makes the monthly projections of Statistics Austria available within only a few seconds to all regional managers of the Austrian National Tourist Office regardless of whether they are located in New York, Sydney, Tokyo or Madrid.

Anybody provided with access to the internet and entitled to use Tour MIS may access data and information, make calculations or simulations send or receive data – without tiresome postal procedures, danger of loss, delays and costs. All these advantages have led to a significan expansion in the number of users.

Conditions for the Use of the System

In the beginning Tour MIS was provided with strict access control and used to be only accessible to certain users. In this respect the application did differ from traditional internet offers. However, the present concept is also not an Intranet. Unlike the Intranet which supports internal information management systems Tour MIS is not owned by a certain organization but is open to all authorized tourism organizations, societies, tourism consult- ants, companies, tourism training centres, pressure groups, etc. in Austria and abroad. By covering the maintenance costs, a consortium of 12 of the most important initiators of market research projects in Austria (Austrian National Tourist Office, nine provincial tour- ism organizations, the two special interest associations for Hotel Trade and Restaurant

Trade of the Federal Chamber of Commerce, Federal Ministry for Economic Affairs and Labour Tourism and Recreational Commerce Section) guarantee the continuous updating of the comprehensive database. Since 2000 this initiative has provided the Austrian tourism industry with free access to overall data and functions (with some exceptions) of Tour MIS. The necessary hardware resources are situated at the Institute for Tourism and Leisure Studies at the University of Economics and Business Administration in Vienna where a major part of the necessary maintenance work is carried out.

The Tour MIS Database

In the beginning Tour MIS contained data that was strongly influenced by the internal interests of its commissioner, the Austrian National Tourist Office. In this respect international tourism statistical data, empirical tourism studies and economic indicators for the most important markets of origin for the Austrian tourism industry have been collected in Tour MIS. The PC-version, developed in the early nineties, contained more than 10,000 time series. The periodicity of information was generally based on annual data, however the most significant time series have also been recorded for periods of less than a year.

Over the years the database has continually expanded. Due to the increasing importance of overseas markets further information has been required. Unequal needs of provincial tour- ism organizations led to additional statistics regarding the federal provinces and Vienna, being city and federal province at the same time, acquired an exceptional position. Furthermore data on the Austrian and international city tourism has been added. This information was collected at the branch offices of the Austrian National Tourist Office, transmitted by fax and data was entered manually into the marketing information system in order to be available to users. Later based on international cooperation (European Cities' Tourism, European Travel Commission) the first online maintenance agreements with local tourism organizations were initiated. The most important available data sources of Tour MIS are indicated in. Besides the basic information search functions the method-base has also been continually upgraded. In this respect the system more and more meets the requirements of an efficient decision support tool. In the next paragraphs the most important data sources and the facilities for analysis and reporting are discussed.

National Tourism Statistics Austria

One of the first data sources which was installed in Tour MIS was the official tourism statistics in Austria. Data generated from the registration with accommodation suppliers is one of the fundamental supports of the official inbound tourism statistics in Austria. Accommodation statistics are divided into two different kinds of survey: the accommodation for inbound travel and the accommodation capacity. The data on arrivals and over nights are surveyed for 50 generating countries related to 13 different accommodation types and 1,600 municipalities (= report communities) on a monthly basis.

Thus the official travel survey offers 25 million data points per annum which can be transformed into precious information for tourism managers. From the data material important information on tourism development, trends in markets of origin and accommodation types, evaluation of the competing situation can be derived. For example, for each of the 1,600 municipalities the database allows the user to regularly monitor the development of the average duration of stay, the seasonality, market shares, guest-mix structure, and, in connection with the capacity statistics, the occupancy rate. Tour MIS presently offers official tourism statistics only at the provincial basis which nevertheless requires maintenance work of 11,700 data sets per month. The necessary data transfer from the host system of Statistic Austria (ISIS) to Tour MIS takes place automatically each time after the arrival of new data segments and in accordance with various maintenance routines.

The information supply of Tour MIS users takes place by means of predominate tables and reports created for the user in real time operations. The content and design of tables or reports plays an important role in the user's perception of the system's usefulness and usability. Only if the information supply meets the users' needs will the system achieve its aim of providing a high-performance usage of market data and improve the information supply in tourism management.

7

Challenges and Opportunities for Sustainable Tourism Development

APPROACH OF SUSTAINABLE TOURISM

Many destinations are now pursuing strategies that aim to ensure a sensitive approach when dealing with tourism. Many of these strategies are based on a formal expression of principles for sustainable tourism. Planners and others can use these principles as basic guidelines when attempting to incorporate the broad vision of sustainability into local policies and practices.

The list of principles provided below are important for destinations and organizations that wish to be guided by the ethic of sustainable and responsible tourism. Residents of a community must maintain control of tourism development by being involved in setting a community tourism vision, identifying the resources to be maintained and enhanced, and developing goals and strategies for tourism development and management. Equally important, community residents must participate in the implementation of strategies as well as the operation of the tourism infrastructure, services, and facilities. A tourism initiative should be developed with the help of broad-based stakeholder input. Tourism development must provide quality employment.

The provision of fulfilling jobs has to be seen as an integral part of any tourism development. Part of the process of achieving quality employment is to ensure that, as much as possible, the tourism infrastructure (hotels, restaurants, shops, etc.) is developed and managed by local people. Experience has demonstrated that the provision of education and training for local residents and access to financing for local businesses and entrepreneurs are central to this type of policy. Broad-based distribution of the benefits of tourism must occur at the tourism destination. Local linkages and resident participation in the planning, development, and operation of tourism resources and services will help to ensure that a more equitable distribution of benefits will occur among residents, visitors, and other service providers. Sustainable tourism development has to provide for inter generational equity. Equitable distribution of the costs and benefits of tourism development must take place among present and future generations.

To be fair to future generations of tourists and the travel industry, society should strive to leave a resource base no less than the one we have inherited. Sustainable tourism development must, therefore, avoid resource allocation actions that are irreversible. A long-tend planning horizon needs to be adopted by businesses and destination tourism organizations to ensure that destinations are not used for short-tend gain and then abandoned as visitor tastes and business interests move elsewhere. A longer-tend horizon encourages the use of proactive strategies to ensure destination sustainability and the establishment of local linkages over time. Hannony is required between the needs of a visitor, the place, and the community. This is facilitated by broad stakeholder support with a proper balance between economic, social, cultural, and human objectives, and a recognition of the importance of cooperation among government, the host communities, and the tourism industry, and the non-profit organizations involved in community development and environmental protection. Tourism strategies and plans must be linked with a broader set of initiatives and economic development plans.

A need exists for more coordination at both policy and action levels among the various agencies involved and among different levels of government. This is particularly relevant to tourism and environmental policies. Service provisions such as transportation, parking, and water and sewer capacities must also be considered in conjunction with tourism plans and developments. Cooperation among attractions, businesses, and tourism operators is essential given that one business or operation can be directly affected by the performance or quality of another. There is a definite need for impact assessment of tourism development proposals. The capacity of sites must be considered, including physical, natural, social, and cultural limits and development should be compatible with local and environmental limits. Plans and operations should be evaluated regularly with adjustments as required. Guidelines have to be established for tourism operations, including requirements for impact assessment. There should be codes of practice established for tourism at all levels -national, regional and local. There is also a need to develop indicators and threshold limits for measuring the impacts and success of local tourism ventures. Protection and monitoring strategies are essential if communities are to protect the resources that form the basis of their tourism product.

Tourism planning must move away from a traditional growth-oriented model to one that focuses on opportunities for employment, income and improved local wellbeing while ensuring that development decisions reflect the full value of the natural and cultural environments. The management and use of public goods such as water, air, and common lands should include accountability on behalf of the users to ensure that these resources are not abused. Sustainable tourism development requires the establishment of education and training programmes to improve public understanding and enhance business, vocational and professional skills.

Sustainable tourism development involves promoting appropriate uses and activities that draw from and reinforce landscape character, sense of place, community identity and site opportunity. These activities and uses should aim to provide a quality tourism experience that satisfies visitors while adhering to the other principles of sustainable tourism. The scale and type of tourism facilities must reflect the limits of acceptable use that resources can tolerate. Small-scale, low impact facilitiec and services should be encouraged, for example, through financing and other incentives. The tourism process must also ensure that heritage and natural resources are maintained and enhanced using internationally acceptable criteria and standards.

Sustainable tourism marketing should include the provision of a high quality tourist experience which adheres to the other principles outlined above, and whose promotion should be a responsible and an ethical reflection of the destination's tourism attractions and services. These principles are ambitious, and it is fair to say very difficult to achieve so that tourism developments that will always adhere to all of these principles. However, these principles must be seen as targets for all tourism planning. Crategic integrated sustainable tourism planning The nature of sustainable tourism development requires a process of planning and management that brings together a series of interests and concerns in a sustainable and strategic form of planning and development. Tourism planning continues to be contentious and somewhat nebulous, because most government officials and tourism industry practitioners harbour their own definitions and parameters of the task. By its very nature, planning is multidimensional and is purposely integrative. Even in the less complex circumstances of some Asian and Pacific countries at early phases of tourism development, it is necessary for those with the responsibility to oversee- or administer tourism planning in the public interest to be cognizant of two special dimensions: strategic planning and integrated planning.

Need for integrated tourism planning Although there is evidence that some tourism destinations have been developed without conscious, strategic and integrated planning, many of them have experienced unforeseen consequences that have led to their deterioration.

THE NEED FOR PLANNING

Some managers and decision-makers argue that we are overwhelmed with plans and planning processes. Others argue that we require more regulation and planning in order to ensure that the goals of sustainable tourism can be met. There are others who maintain that we require less planning and possibly less regulation. There is no right answer to the level of planning that a particular situation calls for and clearly every society context will determine what is appropriate. Similarly, though sustainable tourism calls for a high level of local involvement in planning and developing tourism, the amount and quality of resident participation will vary depending on the cultural and political factors in the destination. It is obviously useless to develop a sophisticated planning system if there is no political or community support for it. In these cases, one might first have to create an appropriate setting or structure for a planning process that avoids the failures of past planning practices.

THE FAILURES OF TRADITIONAL PLANNING

Many people are sceptical about the effectiveness of planning. They see it as a waste of time since most plans never see the light of day and end up on a shelf. In many cases, planning in the past has tended to be very much based on developing regulatory procedures as opposed to creating suitable mechanisms for achieving the goals and objectives developed within the planning process. The failure of traditional and rational approaches to planning can be attributed to a number of factors as discussed below.

Lack of Flexibility

The logical, rational approach to planning, it has been argued, has made plans far too rigorous and unable to adapt to changing conditions. Unless the external environment is perceived to be quite static, a detailed step wise approach that is rigorously adhered to could make it very difficult for the organization or destination to create an optimal fit between its resources and the forces influencing tourism in its setting. A dynamic approach as provided through strategic planning principles enables a dynamic planning process, better able to adapt to changes.

Lack of Strategic Thinking and Vision

A major criticism has been launched against traditional, rational planning approaches by some researchers who argue that such plans lack leadership vision in the process of formulating strategies. The inclusion of "strategic vision" by leaders and decision-makers (not technical planning experts) ensures that the plan is not merely an operational plan, but provides direction and concepts for achieving the organizations broad goals and interests.

Ineffective Top-Down Planning

Planning by the destination's planning officials or by retaining planning experts from outside the destination results in a plan which is unable to effectively represent the diverse opinions, needs and attitudes of a range of tourism stakeholders. The chances of successful implementation of such a top-down plan is further inhibited by the lack of community support and involvement in the process, particularly inpolitical systems where residents seek greater participation in the decision- making of their community direction.

Poor Linking of Formulation and Implementation

Another major impediment to planning has been the inability to link formulation of the plan to the outcomes of implementation so as to ensure accountability and to measure the success of the planning exercise. The lack of clear, easy to implement actions and responsibilities to ensure accountability for carrying out the actions, has been a deterrent to effective implementation. A clearly defmed relationship between the planning and implementation of action steps must be present to ensure effective delivery of both the tourism experience and the sustainability of the destination's assets and resources. Strategic tourism planning -an action planning approach

A strategic planning approach is essential for sustainable tourism, where by the disparate planning and development activities related to tourism are linked to an overall, broad strategic tourism plan to provide an integrated framework for directing tourism. Strategic planning seeks an optimal fit between the system and its environment.

Hence, it: is long-term; contains vision; specifies goals (ends); specifies major actions (means) to achieve goals; specifies the major resource allocations to arrive at (ways); is dynamic, flexible and adaptable; ensures that formulation and implementation of the strategic plan are not discrete, but linked closely through constant monitoring, environmental scanning, evaluation and adjustment; and is not a linear process (*e.g.,* constant environmental scanning occurs throughout the process to enable proactive response and adjustment; monitoring can start as soon as target indicators and levels are established to provide base line information).

A strategic approach to a sustainable community tourism plan alsorequires: close coordination with local and regional legislative and political structures; community participation and support; a new role for planners as educators and providers of technical expertise, but not solely plan designers; the plan is designed primarily by those who have a stake in the outcome; an innovative and inclusive organizational structure for joint planning; a learning community that is informed, educated and aware; applying the principles of sustainable tourism development to ensure the long-term sustainability of the ecology, the local economy and the socio-cultural values of the host community, while distributing the benefits equitably among the stakeholders.

SUSTAINABLE TOURISM DEVELOPMENT: PRINCIPLES AND PRACTICES

When policy-makers, planners and investors decide to develop the tourism industry, they find that there are many different forms of tourism. The forms vary according to their location, the interests of the tourists and the tourism resources that are available.

Regardless of form, however, there are certain positive impacts of tourism that are expected to contribute to development.

For example, there is added support for the economy of a community, new employment is created, community stability can be maintained, amenities in the area are enhanced and the community can build a sense of pride and local identity. At the same time, planners and stakeholders have to take into account possible negative impacts from tourism. Sustainable tourism is one approach to development of the tourism industry designed to provide a context that can guide choices, bring together stakeholders so they act in the common interest and help decision-makers see more clearly how to balance the positive and negative impacts at present and in the future.

One definition of sustainable tourism states that it is tourism developed and maintained in an area (community, environment) in such a manner and at such a scale that it remains viable over an indefinite period and does not degrade or alter the environment (human or physical) in any way that might prohibit the successful development and well-being of other activities and processes.

This definition includes a number of imperatives that should serve as guides for action:

- Make prudent use of the earth's resources,
- Alleviate poverty and reduce gender inequalities,
- Enhance the quality of life,
- preserve biodiversity and life support systems for all natural habitats,
- Preserve indigenous knowledge and ways of life based on respect for different traditions, and
- Encourage bottomup responsibility for participation and enhanced capabilities for local level decisionmaking.

From these premises it is possible to set forth a number of principles for sustainable tourism development.

The main principles include the following:

- Residents must maintain control over tourism development and planning requires broad-based community input.
- Quality employment must be provided for the community along with education and training programmes.
- Distribution of the benefits must be broad-based and cooperation among local stakeholders is essential.
- Intergenerational equity must be provided and tourism businesses and other tourism agencies must adopt long-term planning horizons.
- Tourism strategies and plans must be linked to broader initiatives reflected in economic development plans of the community, region or nation and move away from the traditional growth-oriented model.

- Harmony is required between the needs of the visitor, the place and the community in order to promote appropriate uses and activities.
- The scale and type of tourism facilities must reflect limits of acceptable use, and this means guidelines are needed for tourism operations and impact assessments must be required.
- The community heritage and natural resources must be maintained and enhanced using internationally acceptable criteria and standards.
- Marketing for sustainable tourism must provide for a high quality tourist experience.

The practice of sustainable tourism development is based on management of capacities and sites. Simply put, carrying capacity measures the level of use that is sustainable. However, there are a number of issues to be addressed, which means that carrying capacity becomes quite complex in the management of tourism development. Every environment serves multiple purposes and sensitivity to different use levels depends on the values of all users. A range of valued products and services must come from the same environment and different types of use have different impacts. Carrying capacity can be useful because it draws attention to limits and thresholds beyond which a site should not be developed.

There are a number of ways to measure carrying capacity, including:

- Tangible resource limits,
- Tolerance by the host population,
- Visitor satisfaction,
- Rates of growth, and
- Other quantifiable indicators.

Site management involves managing visitors, educating visitors and having a visitor use plan. There are a variety of means that can be used to manage visitors by controlling or restricting access. Visitors can be educated through interpretation of local cultural values, by providing cultural guidelines, having discussions and briefings on arrival about appropriate behaviour and by using advertising and promotion campaigns. A visitor use plan can be prepared to indicate and control the physical access to sites.

While there are a set of principles and practices to help guide sustainable tourism development, stakeholders still face a number of challenges. Among the challenges are the following: Getting the public sector, including governments at all levels, actively involved in the process of conserving and developing cultural heritage sites; obtaining the funds needed to develop products and getting the government to serve as a joint venture partner where appropriate; ensuring that tourism strategies and plans are integrated and linked to broader development plans, especially at the community level; encouraging local businesses, tourism operators and other stakeholders to cooperate; requiring impact assessments, including monitoring and indicators, where tourism development involves heritage resources and communities; making interpretation an essential part of the development process; and finding creative financing appropriate to developing countries and areas of Asia and the Pacific where financial resources might be limited.

EXPECTATIONS OF TOUR OPERATORS FOR INCREASING TOURIST FLOWS TO MYANMAR

There are two key viewpoints involved when tour operators make decisions about selecting destinations for international tourists. First is the viewpoint of the tour operator who will be interested in: new destinations where there is less competition, good destinations that will be easy to promote and destinations that provide a high level of security for tourists. Second is the viewpoint of the client / potential tourist who will be influenced by lack of information on how secure the country is, bad images portrayed in the international mass media, the quality of infrastructure, the availability of international restaurants and whether shopping is unrestricted. It can be said that Myanmar has certain strengths and weaknesses according to the analysis of tour operators. Myanmar's strength as a tourist destination is that it is unspoiled and not overdeveloped, especially in terms of the marine and beach environment and the unique and rich culture and its heritage. This makes the country a strong tourism product that is relatively easy to sell. At the same time, however, there are a number of points that detract from Myanmar's attractiveness as a tourist destination. For example, the transportation infrastructure is not convenient or easily accessible and the sense of personal security is not strong.

Tourists are restricted to visiting only four places in the country and there is a compulsory charge in US dollars for all arriving international tourists. Tour operators can offer several suggestions about measures and actions that would increase tourist flows to Myanmar.

The government can play a direct role by:

- Improving the domestic infrastructure, particularly land transportation;
- Provide more tourism promotional programmes;
- Open Mandalay Airport and provide for more international flights;
- Open land routes at key border crossings with China and Thailand (Tachilek-Mae Sai); and
- Provide better levels of security to help improve the international image.

The national tourist organization needs more promotional programmes at the regional and international level and should actively organize its promotional programmes abroad. The tourism industry should work together with the national tourist organization to promote Myanmar as a destination. Some specific recommendations from the view of a tour operator that could be considered cover the following points.

First, flight connections need improvement in order to attract tourists. National air carriers can play a major role by connecting various international destinations to various domestic destinations. This is a prerequisite for making promotions successful. National carriers with flights to various domestic destinations should connect with regional carriers from Bangkok or Singapore, for example, either directly or via Yangon.

Second, national carriers should undertake joint marketing and promotion to help increase tourism flows, either individually or in cooperation with international airlines. The national carriers, plus international carriers should have joint marketing and promotion in cooperation with the Ministry of Tourism. Such collaboration could start with product promotion workshops.

Third, regular business contacts should be maintained. The Ministry of Tourism could assign the top domestic tour operators to give competitive rates and better services to travel agents and operators overseas. There should also be increased contacts between Myanmar tour operators and international operators at trade fairs, travel marts, regional workshops, etc. The main general point to keep in mind is that sustainable tourism development can be achieved only through teamwork and collaboration with a focus on the goal of prosperity for the whole country.

PUBLIC-PRIVATE PARTNERSHIP IN TOURISM DEVELOPMENT: EXPERIENCES OF THAILAND

In the tourism industry, partnerships will require some give and take, but overall they involve win-win situations when both sides work together for the larger good. In fact public-private partnerships and cooperation were the main reasons for the success of the Amazing Thailand campaign of 1998-1999. It is possible to see a new paradigm of partnership emerging that goes beyond marketing and promotion and now focuses on developing the tourism industry in a sustainable way. From 1982 to 1996, tourism was Thailand's top foreign exchange earner, and annual growth in visitor arrivals during 1998 and 1999 has been over 10 per cent.

In provinces with high tourism potential, it was found that development of tourism infrastructure had raised the overall standard of living. Nationwide, tourism has contributed to increased appreciation of Thailand's natural and cultural resources and led to stronger calls for protection and preservation. Among several factors contributing to Thailand's tourism growth, one is the effective use of the Amazing Thailand campaign by the Tourism Authority of Thailand (TAT) and Thai Airways International, the national airline; and the private sector.

In effect, this has been more than a promotional campaign. It has made the whole industry focus on the shared goals of increasing tourism revenue by attracting more visitors to stay longer and spend more. In 2001, the marketing campaign keeps the slogan of Amazing Thailand and positions the country as offering "Treasures for Pleasure of the World". At the same time, tourism policies seek to build stronger awareness about sustainable tourism among government agencies, especially at the grassroots level with related rural agencies.

It is important to keep in mind that TAT is more like a state enterprise mostly engaged in marketing activities and it does not have ministerial status. This makes it more imperative to have partnerships with the private sector in order to save costs, generate innovative ideas, oversee the implementation process and ensure that needs of the taxpayers are met.

Partnership with the private sector means that they participate in three major processes:

1. Planning,
2. Implementing and
3. Auditing and policy-making.

As part of the planning process, the private sector is represented on TAT' s Board of Directors, on the National Committee on Tourism Promotion and Development, as well as various committees and working groups of TAT. In addition, there are high-level industry think tanks that provide year-round, two-way information and help plan and synchronize public-private sector activities. The think tanks help TAT to plan future directions for the industry and help set plans for budget allocations. TAT partnerships with the private sector have been very successful in the implementation process.

This has included lobbying to liberalize the visa policy, providing matching promotional funds, promoting shopping and organizing shopping festivals, organizing joint tourism trade fairs and shows, and many other activities. Three examples of recent successful public-private sector partnerships were the light and sound presentation on the River of Kings (Chao Phraya River) to celebrate the King's sixth cycle birthday anniversary in 1999, the consortium of TAT and 77 domestic tour operators to promote the "Thais Tour Thailand" campaign and the ecotourism project, Kiriwong Tourism Development Project, in southern Thailand. Since 1995, the Kiriwong Tourism Development Project has involved the private and public sector and the local community as an ecotourism project aimed at environmental conservation, improving a tourist destination and creating better understanding and awareness in the southern province of Nakhon Si Thammarat.

In 1996, local people set up the Kiriwong Ecotourism Society to work with the local municipality, the Khao Luang National Park and TAT to conserve nature, preserve local traditions, increase local incomes and improve the quality of life. The project has made the area become a popular ecotourism attraction and has won several national awards. Auditing and policy-making require collaboration among government agencies and partnership with the private sector. As a marketing agency, TAT has to work with government agencies that have the legal authority concerning policies related to tourism and nature and cultural heritage conservation.

There is a Tourist Business and Guide Act for licensing tour companies and guides. However, TAT has no power of enforcement and must work with the Tourist Police. The private sector is also encouraged to take approaches that are self-enforcing for standards and membership. TAT encourages local officials, such as district and provincial authorities, to become more pro-active in sustainable tourism development. Local officials and communities can work together to make policies and plans based on their views about how tourism fits in with their environment and way of life.

Public-private partnership is a crucial element in sustaining tourism development, especially when governments face resource constraints. The exact nature of the balance between public and private responsibilities needs to be carefully worked out. In Thailand, the tourism industry has met the challenge of marketing, and now it has to address the challenge of managing sustainable tourism development.

HUMAN RESOURCES DEVELOPMENT IN THE TOURISM SECTOR

The rapid rates of growth of tourism in Asia and the Pacific have given cause for concern in the area of human resources development. It is important to recall that tourism is a labour-intensive industry and a major source of employment. The World Travel and Tourism Council recently estimated that tourism in Asia and the Pacific directly employed about 55 million people, and this makes issues of human resources development very significant at the regional level.

In most countries of the region there is not a shortage of manpower, but there is an acute shortage of trained manpower in the tourism sector. This has been found to be the case at all levels of the tourism industry. Most countries in the region have identified the main problems as a shortage of trained labour, lack of trainers, inadequate training materials and lack of tourism education strategies as part of the national tourism planning overall.

Other issues concerning human resources development in the tourism industry include: working conditions, availability of education and training, policy issues, information and technology and cultural issues particular to a country or a region. It is important to see tourism needs in the broader framework of national human resources development objectives. There are certain standard objectives, but there can be differences in emphasis depending on a country's level of development. More importantly, the objectives have to be linked to human resources development strategies that form part of an integrated plan.

For tourism human resources, the strategies for education and training should also be part of an integrated plan covering tourism development overall.

However, most countries in the region have not included human resources development strategies in their broad plans. Developing human resources in the tourism industry faces unique challenges, because customer preferences, travel patterns, information technology and conditions at destinations are changing rapidly. As a result, strong and flexible human resources development strategies are needed.

The strategy should mirror human resources needs and the corresponding recruitment, employment and training requirements. Usually, there are three separate government ministries involved in matters related to tourism education and training: education, labour and tourism. Coordination among these different agencies is important, as well as including other government organizations that might be involved.

One way to achieve meaningful coordination that could be proposed by the national tourism organization in any country is to establish a national committee or council for tourism education and training. Such a committee or council could be advisory and consultative and should bring the following together: ministries responsible for tourism, labour and education; workers organizations (unions); professional and trade associations (employers); the national association of hotel and tourism schools; and all other parts of the tourism sector. Such a national committee/council should set standards and review policies, set objectives and identify results.

The committee/council would be required to:

- Monitor labour market conditions and related trends
- Review existing and future needs for tourism personnel in management, supervisory positions, skilled and unskilled staff
- Review programmes of existing education and training institutions to evaluate the relevance to identified needs
- Liaise with the university system to promote development of appropriate programmes and activities
- Encourage the private sector to take initiatives to provide training programmes and facilities (perhaps recommending incentives)
- Advise and encourage in-service training programmes, establish guidelines and organize workshops
- Set guidelines for career development of vocational educators and trainers involved with tourism
- Encourage seminars and workshops about management and supervisory techniques, and teaching and training techniques for trainers
- Liaise with authorities involved in the development of occupational skill standards, testing and certification for designated occupations
- Enhance the image of tourism as an employer and improve recruitment

Strategies for human resources development in the tourism sector should highlight the role of the private sector, with the government acting as a catalyst to create conditions and guidelines. Most tourism employment is in the private sector, and it is thus crucial that the private sector participates, provides support and resources and gives consultation. The private sector also has to see that it will benefit from national objectives, strategies and policies for human resources development in the tourism industry. In fact, studies have shown that profits increase due to improved quality service and costs are reduced significantly when companies invest in training.

Trade associations can play an important role to encourage the private sector's direct contribution to tourism human resources development. There are a number of international and regional organizations that provide support in the area of human resources development in the tourism industry. For example, WTO's THEMIS Foundation offers standardized programmes and provides access to resources and has developed TEDQUAL and GTAT as tools for designing, defining and managing quality standards for tourism education and training. ESCAP has assisted member countries and areas to set up APETIT as a regional network for tourism training and education institutes to pool and share their resources and cooperate in human resources development in the tourism industry. While tourism policy-makers and practitioners face a number of issues concerning human resources development, coordinated actions at the national level and cooperation at the regional and international levels can help in the search for solutions.

FACILITATION OF TRAVEL

The tourism paradigm that focuses on tourists' needs and wants has undergone a major change that gives attention to security, sanitation and satisfaction. This has had a strong effect on many countries' tourism policies, in addition to the effects of greater global interdependence and regional integration, which have created a rapidly changing global tourism market. For Thailand, facilitation of travel involves attention to any impediments and obstacles that affect the flow of international tourists and the growth of tourism, which can be influenced by government policies.

Thailand has taken initiatives in seven main areas to decrease obstacles and thus facilitate travel and tourism. The first area is accessibility, and this includes access by air, land and sea. There are five international airports in Thailand, and the geographic location has made Thailand a hub for the region and subregion. About 80 per cent of all tourists arrive by air. Aviation policy regarding traffic rights remains an obstacle, but the Thai government has adopted an open skies policy by gradually liberalizing its bilateral air service agreements. Thailand has opened 26 permanent immigration checkpoints to facilitate land access at borders with Myanmar, Lao People's Democratic

Republic, Cambodia and Malaysia. At some points, there are still obstacles due to inadequate infrastructure. Access by sea has received less attention, although it is a growing segment of Thai tourist arrivals. International cruises that connect to Thailand do not operate regularly, and there is only one major connecting point at Phuket. Obstacles to the development of sea tourism and the sea cruise market are lack of infrastructure and low demand. The second area is visa facilitation, and removing many obstacles in this area has helped Thailand's tourism growth. Visa exemptions are given to tourists from 59 countries and visa on arrival is allowed for tourists from 97 countries.

Some changes have also been made to reduce time-consuming processes at immigration and customs checkpoints. The third area contributing to facilitation of travel is infrastructure development. This includes building a new international airport, expansion of Bangkok International Airport and highway expansions leading to border checkpoints. Other infrastructure projects have focused on port improvements and development in southern Thailand and mass transit systems for Bangkok.

The telecommunications infrastructure has been upgraded and expanded. The public health system gives nationwide coverage and the Tourist Police and Tourist Assistance Centres support the local police with security services for tourists. Deregulation and duty exemptions comprise a fourth area that helps facilitate tourism. The exit/departure tax was deregulated and the few currency restrictions pose no problems for tourists. Special regulations and conditions are intended to encourage imports of non-commercial goods for international conferences and exhibitions. Tourists can get refunds on the value-added tax as part of efforts to promote Thailand as a shopping destination.

Sustainable tourism development is a fifth area that contributes to facilitation of travel. The concept of sustainable tourism development has made both the private and public sector more aware about cultural and environmental conservation, ecotourism and agro-tourism. Many other government agencies have joined in efforts to upgrade destinations that reflect Thailand's natural diversity and cultural heritage. The sixth area contributing to facilitation is information technology development.

Promotional activities of TAT are being designed to make use of new information technology that gives tourists more channels of tourism information about Thailand. The seventh area for facilitating travel and tourism is privatization. The government is considering a number of steps to privatize certain parts of Thailand's aviation and airline industry. This should help improve efficiency of services and contribute to effective marketing activities for tourism in Thailand. It is clear that facilitation can produce both positive and negative effects for tourism in any country, including Thailand.

Tourism arrivals and revenues have increased over the last 20 years, and new business and employment opportunities have been created in the tourism industry. Tourism-related infrastructure in various parts of the country has improved the quality of life for local people and helped promote local arts and crafts. Tourism has contributed to increased awareness about conservation of the environment and the cultural heritage.

However, the carrying capacity has been exceeded at some popular tourist destinations, resulting in pollution, environmental degradation and rising living costs. There is a national plan for ecotourism, but it has not yet been implemented to take a practical reality. As a result, growth of tourism lacks a proper direction. Greater facilitation of travel might also create a negative image as some travellers might engage in various criminal activities in Thailand. The total picture of tourism development in Thailand or any destination goes beyond facilitation of travel and must include coordination among government agencies and between the public and private sector.

In addition, there are opportunities for regional and subregional cooperation that can contribute to tourism development. The use of modern information technology will become increasingly important for the tourism industry during the era of globalization as a part of remaining competitive and as part of reaching target markets. Most importantly, tourists will be attracted to destinations that make sustainable tourism development an achievable, realistic goal that produces results.

TOURISM DEVELOPMENT ALONG THE ASIAN HIGHWAY

Myanmar has a large number and wide variety of tourism resources that should give it a strong potential for tourism development. In addition, there are advantages of geographical location and large areas of environment attractive for ecotourism. These conditions make it worthwhile to consider road linkages with neighbouring countries as one way to attract greater numbers of tourists, especially by means of the Asian Highway as a part of regional and worldwide networking.

The Asian Highway project has been a part of ESCAP work for a number of years. In 1996, the Intergovernmental Meeting on Tourism Development in Bangkok and made a strong request for ESCAP to strengthen its activities for promotion of tourism along the Asian Highway. Tourism development along the Asian Highway involves utilizing the highway itself and linked roads to expand tourism flows by focusing on road transportation and related infrastructure. According to ESCAP studies in 1999, the Asian Highway network covered about 90,000 km and included 25 countries. Three out of five of the main Asian Highway routes pass through Myanmar. One section is between Yangon and Mandalay and has links with two national routes. Another section is between Payagyi and Myawadi and links with two other national routes. The Asian Highway also has links from Tamu to Mandalay. Another route needs to be upgraded or newly constructed. At its fifty-second session in 1997, the

Commission suggested that ESCAP should initiate activities to promote tourism along the Asian Highway. The secretariat sent a questionnaire to identify major tourism attractions along the Asian Highway, and the Government of Myanmar was one of member countries that responded.

Five attractions in Myanmar were selected as accessible or having the potential for access by the Asian Highway:

1. Shwedagon Pagoda in Yangon,
2. Bagan,
3. Mandalay,
4. Kyaikhtiyo Pagoda and
5. Inle Lake.

All five are the most well known destinations in Myanmar, and four are along the route of the Asian Highway, with Bagan accessible by feeder routes linked to the Asian Highway. While both Yangon and Mandalay are large cities characterized as urban destinations, they also have major attractions that show the cultural heritage as well as lakes and rivers that provide a unique natural environment. Kyaikhtiyo Pagoda is a major cultural attraction as a first destination for tourists traveling by road from Mae Sot, Thailand to Myawadi.

Inle Lake and neighbouring destinations could be considered as resort rest areas for enjoying the landscape and natural environment. Bagan and surrounding towns may be the most widely known unique cultural heritage sites in Myanmar, which also have a variety of natural attractions nearby. Road conditions may have to be upgraded, but the level of services for tourists using road transportation may be considered satisfactory.

The other areas along the Asian Highway may be developed as ecotourism or resort sites for tourists in view of the mountains and hills as natural attractions. Other areas that have potential for tourism development based on road transportation. One area is the mountain and hill area in the North and North-East near the border with China. This area has high potential for ecotourism and cultural tourism if some roads are upgraded and opened for general travel. A second area is the coastal area along the Bay of Bengal where there are several beaches opened as coastal resorts. There are also sites that show the cultural heritage of this coastal region of Myanmar.

Some feeder roads linking to the Asian Highway would have to be upgraded to attract more tourists. In addition to the physical aspect of road transport involving the Asian Highway in Myanmar, the government might also want to address several related issues as well. There is a need to provide more information and public relation services in the major home countries of tourists interested in Myanmar. Increased facilitation is another issue to be considered, such as issuing visas on arrival at all entry checkpoints, by air and road, in particular. Facilitation could also include greater access by allowing entry at one checkpoint and exit at another checkpoint. Services along the land routes, including the Asian Highway routes, should include road signs in English and facilities for travellers, such as restaurants, gas stations and tourist information centres.

Overall tourism development along the Asian Highway requires three types of actions:

- Construction and upgrading of road facilities,
- Planning and development of tourism infrastructure at tourist destinations and
- Improved services for tourists.

In most situations, the government is usually expected to implement projects involving infrastructure. However, resources may be limited and the scale of the projects may have to be large and integrated with each other for efficient implementation. It might be possible to consider public-private sector partnerships for such projects, but the government must make careful plans, set priorities and draw up a budget that includes some self-financing components. It is important to keep in mind that tourism infrastructure development is part of national infrastructure development, which can be expected to contribute to the overall social and economic well-being of everyone in the country.

ECOTOURISM: CHALLENGES AND OPPORTUNITIES

Over the past decade, tourism has become the largest industry worldwide in terms of employment and share of global gross domestic product. The tourism industry has been growing rapidly as well as changing at a fast pace. As more people are interested in spending leisure time in nature, ecotourism has become one of the fastest-growing segments of the tourism industry.

This creates opportunities in areas characterized by natural attractions, wildlife and wilderness habitats. Local communities may benefit in economic terms as well as create a commitment to conservation and sustainable development. At the same time, however, increased demands for ecotourism create pressure on carrying capacity. Greater numbers of visitors makes it more likely that habitats will be at risk and the wilderness and cultural heritage could be ruined.

It is expected that China will encounter many challenges, because it already ranks sixth worldwide in terms of tourist arrivals. In the next twenty years, China is forecast to be the top tourist destination and the fourth largest source of tourists in the world. This prospect for major tourism growth in China makes it important to quickly consider the environmental and social issues that are part of sustainable tourism development. Careful planning and assessment are important parts of sustainable tourism development. Officials responsible for national parks and other nature areas will have a major responsibility for handling the challenges and deciding which opportunities for tourism development can be sustained over the long term. Local communities will also have to participate in planning and assessment when culture and heritage are important parts of ecotourism. It has been noted that the principles for ecotourism have not yet been firmly established in order to guide planning and assessment. However, two basic principles of ecotourism that have been identified are: encourage conservation and provide benefits to the local populations.

However, planners and policy-makers must also keep in mind certain realistic truths about tourism: it consumes resources, creates waste and requires certain kinds of infrastructure; it creates conditions for possible over-consumption of resources; it is dominated by private investment with priority on maximizing profits; its multi-faceted nature makes control difficult; and it may be seen as simply entertainment services consumed by tourists.

The challenge of sustainable tourism development, therefore, is to balance the principles with these truths, and this can be done only through integrated, cooperative approaches involving all stakeholders and related economic activities in the area. There are certain tools that can be used to help achieve balance, such as assessment of carrying capacity, finding the limits of acceptable change and doing cost/benefit analysis.

Tourism policy-makers, planners and managers should consider these tools as helpful only if they take a holistic, coordinated approach, especially since benefits and costs in terms of sustainable tourism development are not easily defined in monetary terms. Furthermore, measuring the success of tourism involving nature and culture should not just be based on number of visitors or amount of income; rather measurement should include the length of stay, quality of the experience and whether natural and cultural resources have been conserved. Ecotourism can clearly create opportunities for spreading the economic benefits of tourism to villages, remote areas and national parks, as long as the government policy aims to have more tourism in these areas and the local people have participated in the process.

Along these lines, policy-makers should be aware that smaller-scale business operators are more appropriate for activities related to ecotourism and government policies need to support this level of tourism services.

The main challenges for policies and activities that develop ecotourism are:

- Ecology and the vulnerability of nature and wildlife;
- Aesthetics in terms of expectations held by the tourists and the local communities;
- Economic benefits, costs (including opportunity costs and externalities) and risks; and
- Social impact involving local communities and cultural heritage.

In China, the wealth of historical and cultural monuments, the vibrant and diverse cultures and the spectacular geographic variety already create a major tourism product. Ecotourism provides a possibility for small-scale, low-impact tourism that can be widely distributed throughout the country. With more than 56 ethnic groups, there is good potential for village-based tourism, especially in areas with natural, cultural and historical resources.

The level of investment would not be high, and the returns for villages can be significant to supplement regular incomes. Additional employment could be created through transport services, guide services, handicraft production, lodging and other logistical support. Carefully planned ecotourism, especially if it is village-based and includes local participation, can provide direct benefits that might offset pressures from other, less sustainable uses of natural and cultural resources. In many developing countries, including China, ecotourism can fulfill the need to view the environment and cultural heritage as resources to safeguard for future generations.

PROMOTION OF CULTURAL TOURISM AND HERITAGE SITE MANAGEMENT

The major contribution of the tourism industry as a vehicle for economic development in many countries around the world has been widely acknowledged. At the same time, tourism should be seen as an activity that contributes to a better understanding of places, people and their cultures. In the process of sharing and experiencing the culture and heritage of a country such as China, international tourists will also have a stronger positive image of the country at the present time.

The phenomenon of cultural tourism can be understood in terms of supply, demand, marketing and promotion. The issues concerning heritage site management can be considered by looking at the supply and demand sides. Many sites, artifacts and festivals in countries worldwide have special meaning and significance for local people and reflect the varied history of mankind. In fact, many places have been designated as world heritage sites. However, the creation of special events and arrangement of sites for the purpose of attracting tourists is a relatively recent phenomenon. The notion of supply with respect to cultural tourism relates to an assessment of how a cultural manifestation would be accepted by the market.

An objective, unbiased assessment would be needed, and it is usually best obtained from knowledgeable outsiders. Local culture may also have to be assessed in terms of suitability for tourism, and this means that it is important for local stakeholders to be identified, especially who will benefit more and who will benefit less. Considering cultural tourism from the demand side requires understanding that people become tourists for a variety of reasons and motives. Most of the time, tourists seek a variety of attractions at a location and cultural tourism products may be one of several factors that create a tourist attraction. There may be sites of cultural and historical significance that are so unique that they create their own demand, such as the Great Wall in China. Of course, demand for cultural tourism products will also depend on the adequacy of tourism infrastructure, quality of accommodations, state of the environment, etc. The possibility of overcrowding at a cultural site, especially during special holiday periods, will affect demand Evaluating tourists based on their country of origin can help to identify the different interests and expectations concerning visits to cultural and heritage sites. At the same time, it is important to be aware that most tourists travel for leisure, so that the culture has to be explained in ways that are easy to understand, including gestures of hospitality.

For most tourists, cultural experiences are embedded in other tourist experiences such as nature walks, shopping, dining and relaxing at the beach. There are several issues for marketers to keep in mind when marketing and promoting cultural tourism. Since tourism is a business for tour operators, principals and intermediaries, cultural products may have to be well known and contribute to making a package of tourist activities more attractive in revenue terms. A destination and its cultural attractions have to compete with other destinations offering similar experiences.

It could be best to have a marketing strategy that focuses on a small number of carefully selected target markets and targets appropriate travel writers and journalists to create a positive image. Procedures and related formalities must contribute to facilitating the movement of tourists and infrastructure at cultural sites should also focus on visitors' health and safety. When looking at heritage site management from the supply side viewpoint, it is important that sites be identified, registered and categorized in terms of their tourism potential.

The tourism potential of sites can also serve as an incentive for their restoration and protection. Another incentive is to have World Heritage designation for cultural sites, of which China has 23 World Heritage sites. The demand side viewpoint of heritage site management relates to the profiles and expectations of international tourists. It is important to know how long tourists will be staying, whether the heritage site is at a remote location, how developed is the transport infrastructure for reaching the destination, and what are some alternative, competing tourist activities that visitors might prefer. Management of the actual heritage site raises a number of issues that policy-makers, planners and managers in developing countries faced with limited resources (for protection and preservation) must consider.

A site may have started as a manifestation of the nation's cultural history, but it has been transformed into a tourist attraction. There must be adequate protection against removal of artifacts; there must be adequate funds and a long-term commitment to maintain and restore the site; there must be balance between site protection and accessibility to interested tourists; there must be knowledge and understanding through interpretation provided by well-educated and trained guides, guidebooks and signs; and the use of souvenirs and promotional products to maximize revenues must be carefully managed.

Promotion of cultural assets and heritage sites can help to attract certain segments of the tourist market, but it is important to understand that most international tourists have a variety of interests and expectations when they visit a country. Cultural attractions and heritage sites must be well managed and properly interpreted in order to gain the maximum tourism benefit for the local community, the tourists and the site managers. This will enhance the image of the country, as well as create greater international understanding of people, places and cultures.

PLANNING FOR SUSTAINABLE DEVELOPMENT

The underlying approach now applied to tourism planning, as well as to other types of development, is that of achieving sustainable development. The sustainable development approach implies that the natural, cultural and other resources of tourism are conserved for continuous use in the future, while still bringing benefits to the present society The concept of sustainable development has received much emphasis internationally since the early 1980s, although tourism plans prepared even before that period often were concerned with conservation of tourism resources.

The sustainable development approach to planning tourism is acutely important because most tourism development depends on attractions and activities related to the natural environment, historic heritage and cultural patterns of areas. If these resources are degraded or destroyed, then the tourism areas cannot attract tourists and tourism will not be successful. More generally, most tourists seek destinations that have a high level of environmental quality - they like to visit places that are attractive, clean and neither polluted nor congested. It is also essential that residents of the tourism area should not have to suffer from a deteriorated environment and social problems.

One of the important benefits of tourism is that, if it is properly developed based on the concept of sustainability, tourism can greatly help justify and pay for conservation of an area's natural and cultural resources. Thus, tourism can be an important means of achieving conservation in areas that otherwise have limited capability to accomplish environmental protection and conservation objectives.

A basic technique in achieving sustainable development is the environmental planning approach. Environmental planning requires that all elements of the environment be carefully surveyed, analysed and considered in determining the most appropriate type and location of development. This approach would not allow, for example, intensive development in flood plain and steep hillside areas.

An important aspect of sustainable development is emphasizing community-based tourism. This approach to tourism focuses on community involvement in the planning and development process, and developing the types of tourism which generate benefits to local communities. It applies techniques to ensure that most of the benefits of tourism development accrue to local residents and not to outsiders. Maximizing benefits to local residents typically results in tourism being better accepted by them and their actively supporting conservation of local tourism resources.

The communitybased tourism approach is applied at the local or more detailed levels of planning, but it can be set forth as a policy approach at the national and regional levels. The benefits accruing to local communities are also beneficial to the country, through the income and foreign exchange earned, employment generated and support that local communities give to national tourism development and conservation policies.

Also related to sustainable development is the concept of quality tourism. This approach is being increasingly adopted for two fundamental reasons - it can achieve successful tourism from the marketing standpoint and it brings benefits to local residents and their environment. Quality tourism does not necessarily mean expensive tourism. Rather, it refers to tourist attractions, facilities and services that offer 'good value for money', protect tourism resources, and attract the kinds of tourists who will respect the local environment and society. Quality tourism development can compete more effectively in attracting discriminating tourists. It is also more environmentally and socially self-sustaining. Achieving quality tourism is the responsibility of both the public and private sectors. This concept should be built into the tourism planning, development and management process.

LONG-RANGE AND STRATEGIC PLANNING

Long-range comprehensive planning is concerned with specifying goals and objectives and determining preferred future development patterns. Tourism development policies and plans should be prepared for relatively long-term periods - usually for 10 to 15 and sometimes 20 years - depending on the predictability of future events in the country or region. These may seem to be long planning periods, but it commonly requires this length of time to implement basic policy and structure plans. Even development of specific projects, such as major resorts or national park-based tourism, can require a long time.

A planning approach which has received considerable attention in recent years, and is applicable to some tourism areas, is strategic planning. While the outcomes of strategic and long-range comprehensive planning may be very similar, strategic planning is somewhat different. It focuses more on identification and resolution of immediate issues. Strategic planning typically is more oriented to rapidly changing future situations and how to cope with changes organizationally. It is more action oriented and concerned with handling unexpected events. Applied only by itself, strategic planning can be less comprehensive in its approach. By focusing on immediate issues, it may deviate from achieving such long-term objectives as sustainable development. But if used within the framework of integrated long-range policy and planning, the strategic planning approach can be very appropriate.

PUBLIC INVOLVEMENT IN PLANNING

Planning is for the benefit of people, and they should be involved in the planning and development of tourism in their areas. Through this involvement, tourism development will reflect a consensus of what the people want. Also, if residents are involved in planning and development decisions - and if they understand the benefits the tourism can bring - they will more likely support it. At the national and regional levels of preparing tourism plans, the common approach to obtaining public involvement is to appoint a steering committee.

This committee offers guidance to the planning team and reviews its work, especially the draft reports and policy and planning recommendations that are made. A planning study steering committee is typically composed of representatives of the relevant government agencies involved in tourism, the private sector, and community, religious and other relevant organizations. Also, open public hearings can be held on the plan. These hearings provide the opportunity for anybody to learn about the plan and express their opinions. Another common approach, when the plan is completed, is to organize a national or regional tourism seminar. This meeting informs participants and the general public about the importance of controlled tourism development and the recommendations of the plan. Such seminars often receive wide publicity in the communications media.

In a large country or region, the usual procedure is for the tourism plan to be prepared by the central authority with public involvement. This can be termed the 'top-down' approach. Another procedure sometimes used is the 'bottom-up' approach. This involves holding meetings with local districts or communities to determine what type of development they would like to have. These local objectives and ideas are then fitted together into a national or regional plan.

This approach achieves greater local public involvement in the planning process. But it is more time consuming and may lead to conflicting objectives, policies and development recommendations among the local areas. These conflicts need to be reconciled at the national and regional levels in order to form a consistent plan. It is important that the development patterns of the local areas complement and reinforce one another, but also reflect the needs and desires of local communities. Often a combination of the 'top-down' and 'bottom-up' approaches achieves the best results.

MODERN CONCEPT OF SUSTAINABLE DEVELOPMENT

The modern concept of sustainable development originates with the report of World Commission on Environment and Development (1987) (also known as the Brundtland Commission) and which offered the now-familiar definition of sustainability as 'develop-ment that meets the needs of the present without compromising the ability of future generations to meet their own needs'. According to Wall and Mathieson (2006: 289) the key elements in the Brundtland approach to sustainable development are that it should:

- Maintain ecological integrity and diversity;
- Meet basic human needs;
- Keep options open for future generations;
- Reduce injustice;
- Increase self-determination.

Sustainable development principles also support the empowerment of people to be involved in decisions that influence the quality of their lives and enable cultures to be sustained. By these means, developments that are truly sustainable will meet the essential criteria of being economically viable, environmentally sensitive and culturally appropriate.

From certain perspectives, the concept of sustainable development appears to offer little more than a new reading of some well-established practices, especially in so far as some of the principles that it espouses simply articulate a form of prudent resource management that has been widely and effectively practised in areas such as agriculture for many centuries. Butler (1991), for example, observes that royal hunting forests in twelfth-century England were managed in ways that we would now define as 'sustainable' whilst there is an interesting and compelling argument to be made that the growth of urban seaside resorts as centres of mass tourism after 1850 also represented a highly sustainable form of development that was not only able to absorb a rapidly expanding market, but also to both maintain and contain its activity over many decades.

However, the proponents of sustainable development will surely point to the modern concept as presenting a much more holistic vision of how development should be organised (embracing, in an integrated fashion, the political, social, cultural, economic and ecological contexts), and being informed both by a stronger ethical dimension and by possessing a clearer emphasis upon the adoption of long-term views of developments and their potential impacts. The concept implicitly recognises that there are basic human needs (*e.g.,* food, clothing, shelter) that processes of development must match and that these needs are to be set alongside aspirations (*e.g.,* to higher living standards, security and access to discretionary elements such as tourism) that it would be desirable to match.

But since there are environmental limitations that will ultimately regulate the levels to which development can actually proceed (and if principles of sustainability are also to embrace implicit notions of equity in access to resources and the benefits that they bring), then the achievement of sustainable development requires a realignment in attitudes and beliefs that mark this approach out as being fundamentally different.

Although there is inherent logic to the sustainable development approach, the concept has nevertheless been subject to some quite significant criticisms. The outwardly simple definition of sustainability provided by the Brundtland Commission conceals much controversy and debate over who defines what is, or is not, sustainable and what sustainable development might therefore mean in practice.

Whilst it is generally recognised that the term has become an essential item in the vocabulary of modern political discourse, it has also come to be used in 'meaningless and anodyne ways' (Mowforth and Munt, 2003: 80). For some critics the lack of conceptual clarity is compounded by a basic ambiguity in the term itself: the concept of 'sustainability' implying a steady-state, whereas 'development' implies growth and change (Page and Dowling, 2002). Wall and Mathieson (2006) suggest that the reconciliation of this apparent tension can only be achieved by placing an emphasis on one or other of the component words to help clarify the approach, and perhaps for this reason, the concept of sustainability has acquired a diversity of interpretations. These range from, at one extreme, a 'zero-growth' view that argues that all forms of development are essentially unsustainable and should therefore be resisted, to very different perspectives that argue for growth-oriented resource management based around the presumed capacities of technology to solve environmental problems and secure a sustainable future.

Such flexibility in interpretation whilst, at one level, constituting a weakness, may also be seen as a strength if it allows differing perspectives to co-exist under the broad umbrella of 'sustainability'. Imprecision can be easily translated into flexibility. Both Hunter (1997) and Sharpley (2000) have therefore suggested that the idea of sustainable development can be conceived as what they label 'an adaptive paradigm' that establishes a set of meta-principles within which contrasting development approaches may legitimately co-exist.

From the preceding discussion, the relevance of sustainable forms of development to tourism should be obvious, given that it is an industry with a high level of dependence upon 'environments' as a basic source of attraction but also one that has, as we will see, a considerable capacity to stimulate a significant degree of environmental change. Tourism therefore needs to be sustainable even though – as with the wider concept of sustainable development – there are difficulties of definition and, especially, significant challenges in turning a theory of sustainable tourism into practice.

A number of difficulties around the concept of sustainable tourism have been noted. First, Wall and Mathieson (2006) emphasise that since sustainable development is an holistic concept, any approach that deals with a single sector (such as sustainable tourism) raises the risk that one system is sustained at the expense of another. Hunter (1995) offers a similar criticism of many early sustainable tourism initiatives that, he asserts, failed to place tourism development into the wider contexts of development and environmental change.

In developing this point, second, Sharpley (2000) notes that holistic approaches are difficult to implement in sectors (such as tourism) that are characteristically fragmented and therefore dependent upon large numbers of small, independent enterprises (not to mention their customers) adopting sustainable principles and practices in a coordinated fashion. Perhaps for this reason, many sustainable tourism projects have been implemented only at a local level, characterised by Wheeller as 'micro solutions struggling with a macro problem' (cited in Clarke, 1997). Indeed, it is perhaps a more damning criticism of some sustainable tourism approaches that they implicitly seem to reject the notion that mass forms of tourism can be sustainable, even to the extent that mass and sustainable forms of tourism have been represented in some readings not only as polar opposites, but also as being characterised as – respectively – 'bad' and 'good' forms of tourism.

Third, and perhaps because of this type of dichotomised reading of sustainable tourism, the concept has become widely confused with a plethora of alternative forms of tourism and their associated labels. A diversity of alternatives – many of which are focused around the enjoyment of nature – have emerged over the last two decades or so and with which sustainable tourism has been widely confused. 'Responsible tourism', 'soft tourism', 'green tourism', 'ecotourism', 'nature tourism', 'ethical tourism' and, of course, 'sustainable tourism' are all epithets that have been applied to new styles of travel. But whilst many of these forms of tourism may indeed embrace most of the preferred attributes of sustainable tourism, sustainability is not confined to alternative travel, nor is it necessarily a characteristic, as the growing body of research literature on the unsustainable nature of alternative tourism makes clear.

Finally, it may be noted that one of the primary practical barriers to the development of sustainable forms of tourism is embedded in the nature of tourism consumption itself. The tourism is widely perceived by tourists as a means of escape from routines and typically as a hedonistic experience in which behavioural norms are frequently suspended in favour of excessive patterns of expenditure and consumption. In this context, the prudence and social responsibility that is implicit in most understandings of sustainability sits uneasily. This has prompted a number of writers, for example McKercher (1993a), to argue that there is little evidence of a widespread propensity amongst tourists to adopt sustainable tourism lifestyles, even though the encouragement of changed patterns of behaviour on the part of tourists is often an integral objective of sustainable tourism policies. However, although doubts about the true sustainability of tourism have been widely aired in the academic literature, the concept remains very much at the forefront of current thinking around the theme of tourism and environmental change and although there are divergent perspec-tives, there is still a consensus that proposes that a sustainable approach – one which manages growth within acknowledged resource conservation limits – offers the best prospects for continued tourism development. Sustainable tourism needs therefore to develop in ways that:

- Ensures that renewable resources are not consumed at a rate that is faster than rates of natural replacement;
- Maintains biological diversity;
- Recognises and values the aesthetic appeal of environments;
- Follows ethical principles that respect local cultures, livelihoods and customs;
- Involves and consults local people in development processes;
- Promotes equity in the distribution of both the economic costs and the benefits of the activity amongst tourism developers and hosts.

TOURISM AND ENVIRONMENTAL CHANGE

The challenge to tourism that is presented by the sustainable development agenda will become clearer if we move to consider in more detail how tourism relates to environmental change. It has already been intimated that the basic complexities of tourism–environment relationships are compounded by the diverse nature of those impacts and the inconsistencies through time and space in their causes and effects. But it is also important to note that the effects of tourism upon the physical environment are often partial, and one of the practical difficulties in studying those impacts is to disentangle tourist influences from other agencies of change that may be working on the same environment. So, for example, the beach and inshore water pollution that developed as a serious environmental problem along parts of the Italian Adriatic coast in the late 1980s was partly attributable to the presence of tourists but was also a consequence of the discharge of considerable volumes of urban, agricultural and industrial waste into the primary rivers that drain to this sea.

The diversity of environmental impacts of tourism and the seriousness of the problem vary geographically for a number of reasons. First, we need to take account of the nature of tourism and its associated scales of effect. Impact studies often make the erroneous assumption that tourism is a homogeneous activity exerting consistent effects, but, there are many different forms of tourism and types of tourist. The mass tourists who flock in their millions to the Spanish Mediterranean will probably create a much broader and potentially more serious range of impacts than will small groups of explorers trekking in Nepal, although paradoxically, where mass forms of tourism are well planned and properly resourced, the environmental consequences may actually be less than those created by small numbers of people visiting locations that are quite unprepared for the tourist. For example, depletion of local supplies of fuel wood and major problems of littering have been widely reported along the main tourist trails through the Himalayan zone in Nepal.

Second, it is important to take account of the temporal dimensions. In many parts of the world, tourism is a seasonal activity that exerts pressures on the environment for part of the year but allows fallow periods in which recovery is possible. So, there may be short-term/temporary impacts upon the environment that may be largely coincident with the tourist season (such as air pollution from visitor traffic) or, more serious, long-term/permanent effects where environmental capacities have been breached and irreversible changes set in motion (*e.g.,* reductions in the level of biodiversity through visitor trampling of vegetation).

Third, diversity of impacts stems from the nature of the destination. Some environments (*e.g.,* urban resorts) can sustain very high levels of visiting because their built infrastructure makes them relatively resilient or because they possess organisational structures (such as planning frameworks) that allow for effective provision for visitors. In contrast, other places are much less robust, and it is perhaps unfortunate that a great deal of tourist activity is drawn (by tastes, preferences and habits) to fragile places. Coasts and mountain environments are popular tourist destinations that are often ecologically vulnerable, and even non-natural resources can suffer. Historic sites, in particular, may be adversely affected by tourist presence and in recent years attractions such as Stonehenge in England, the Parthenon in Greece and the tomb of Tutankhamen in Egypt have all been subjected to partial or total closure to visitors because of negative environmental effects.

In exploring the environmental impacts of tourism, it is helpful to adopt a holistic approach to the subject. Environments, whether defined as physical, economic or social entities, are usually complex systems in which there are interrelationships that extend the final effects of change well beyond the initial cause. Impact often has a cumulative dimension in which secondary processes reinforce and develop the consequences of change, so treating individual problems in isolation ignores the likelihood that there is a composite impact that may be greater than the sum of the individual parts. As an illustration of this idea, the initial effects of trampling of vegetation by tourists become compounded through related processes of environmental change that may, in extreme circumstances, culminate in the collapse of local ecosystems.

A second advantage of a holistic approach is that it encourages us to work towards a balanced view of tourism–environment relationships. The temptation is to focus upon the many obvious examples of negative and detrimental impacts that tourism may exert, but, as the concept of a symbiotic relationship makes clear, there are positive effects too. These might be represented in the fostering of positive attitudes towards environmental protection/ enhancement or be reflected more practically in actual investment in environmental improvement that restores localities for resident populations as well as providing support for tourism.

The third advantage of a holistic approach is that it recognises the breadth (some might say the imprecision) of the term 'environment' and the fact that different types of impact are likely to be present. As is perhaps implicit in the preceding discussion, the term can embrace a diversity of contexts – physical ecosystems; built environments; or economic, social, cultural and political environments – and tourism has the potential to influence all of these, in varying degrees. The economic and socio-cultural dimensions of sustainability are discussed elsewhere in the book, so the discussion that now follows focuses upon the influences that tourism may have upon physical environments, ecosystems and the built environment, together with a consideration of ways in which symbiotic relationships between tourism and the environment may be sustained through managed approaches.

BIODIVERSITY

Under the heading of biodiversity are located a number of effects that broadly impact upon the flora and fauna of a host region. The potential areas of positive influence on environmental change through tourism mainly relate to the ways in which tourism provides both the impetus and the financial means to further the conservation of natural areas and the species they contain through the designation of protected zones and the implementation of new programmes of land management (Wall and Mathieson, 2006).

The scope for tourism to provide economic support for conservation has been illustrated in areas as diverse as, for example, Australia, Brazil, Greece and Kenya.

However, arguably the more commonplace patterns are those associated with varying forms of damage to biodiversity. Most widely, processes of tourism development (construction of hotels and apartments, new roads, new attractions, etc.) can result in a direct loss of habitats. In the Alps, extensive clearance of forests to develop ski-fields and the loss of Alpine meadows with particularly rich stocks of wild flowers to new hotel and chalet construction has significantly altered ecological balances and, in the case of deforestation, greatly increased risks associated with landslides and snow avalanches (Gratton and van der Straaten, 1994).

At a more localised scale, other impacts become apparent. Destruction of vegetation at popular visitor locations through trampling or the passage of wheeled vehicles is a common problem. Typically, trampling causes more fragile species to disappear and to be replaced either by bare ground or, where regeneration of vegetation is possible, by more resilient species. The overall effect of such change is normally to reduce species diversity and the incidence of rare plants which, in turn, may impact upon the local composition of insect populations, insectivorous birds and possibly small mammals for which plant and insect populations are key elements in a food chain.

Larger animals may be affected in different ways by tourism, even within environments that are protected. Reynolds and Braithwaite (2001) have developed a detailed summary of how tourist engagement with wildlife can initiate important behavioural changes in animals and alter the structure of animal communities. Some of the effects relate to modification of habitats through actions such as land development, reduction in plant diversity or pollution, but perhaps of greater importance is the potential to modify behaviours and introduce new levels of risk to animal communities. Behavioural modifications that Reynolds and Braithwaite associate with increased levels of tourist engagement include:

- Disruption of feeding and breeding patterns;
- Alterations to dietary patterns where animals are fed by tourists;
- Increased instance of animal migration;
- Increased levels of aberrant behaviour;
- Modification of activity patterns, such as a raised incidence of nocturnalism;

whilst noted risks include:

- Reduced levels of health and conditioning;
- Reduced levels of reproduction;
- Increased levels of predation, especially of young animals where parents are suffering frequent disturbance through the presence of tourists.

EROSION AND PHYSICAL DAMAGE

The impacts of tourism upon the diversity of flora and fauna link with the second area of concern, erosion and physical damage, and this illustrates how environmental problems tend to be interlinked. Erosion is typically the result of trampling by visitors' feet, and, whilst footpaths and natural locations are the most likely places for such problems to occur, extreme weight of numbers can lead to damage to the built environment. The Parthenon in Athens, for example, not only is under attack from airborne pollutants but also is being eroded by the shoes of millions of visitors. However, in such situations, tourism can have positive impacts, for although the activity may be a major cause of problems, revenue generated by visitors may also be a key source of funding for wider programmes of environmental restoration.

A more common problem is soil erosion, the systematic manner in which the environment operates actually transmits the initial impact of trampling to produce a series of secondary effects which may eventually exert profound changes upon local ecosystems, leading to fundamental change. Localised examples of such damage can be spectacular. In north Wales, popular tourist trails to the summit of Snowdon now commonly reveal eroded ground that may extend to 9m in width, whilst localised incidence of soil erosion and gullying has lowered some path levels by nearly 2m in a little over twenty years.

INFLUENCING CONSUMER BEHAVIOUR TO PROMOTE SUSTAINABLE TOURISM

PROBLEMS

At the 1998 World Travel Market, WTTC hosted, as a part of its Environmental Awareness Day, a seminar entitled "Does the Consumer Care?" At this event, MORI presented the latest findings from their Business and the Environment survey—an annual UK survey devoted to public attitudes to the environment.

The survey is now in its tenth year and illustrates the challenge facing the Travel and Tourism industry in influencing consumer behaviour to promote sustainable tourism. According to this survey, Travel and Tourism is now more associated with environmental damage than it has been in the past. Despite this decline in perception, the industry's economic success is not dependent on its green record—public sensitivity to environmental problems on holiday/ business trips has not increased and is no more of a deterrent to repeat travel than it was previously. There is a downward trend in the public's willingness to pay extra for environmental protection and environmentally friendly products, including "green" Travel and Tourism. Awareness of companies making environmental commitments is only marginally up.

Therefore, the challenge is to persuade the consumer that it is in their interests to adopt and promote a sustainable approach in their activities and purchasing decisions. Education programmes and the development and widespread acceptance of codes of conduct are useful tools in achieving this step. Once this message has been conveyed, it is then important to back this up with the necessary information to enable consumers to make informed choices. It is here that "ecolabels" and award programmes have value.

EDUCATION PROGRAMMES

The Foundation for Environmental Education in Europe (FEEE) seeks to promote environmental education by carrying out campaigns and improving awareness of the importance of environmental education. It is composed of a network of international organisations. The FEEE (headquarters in Denmark) runs three major campaigns in Europe for providing safe and clean beaches and marinas. The award itself is given annually to beaches and marinas that satisfy a number of essential criteria in three separate areas: water quality; beach management and safety; and environmental information and education.

"GREEN GLOBE"'s Dodo Campaign, is based on a cartoon character, who features in 65 Travel and Tourism videos. Dodo explains and promotes the actions that visitors can take to reduce the impacts of their travels. The videos are aimed at children and are designed to be fun, whilst conveying important messages about sustainable Travel and Tourism. The aim is to have these videos shown on in flight and in-room television channels to raise awareness and influence consumer behaviour.

CODES OF CONDUCT

Codes of conduct are also used to try and influence consumer behaviour. For example, "Guidelines for Responsible Environmental Tourism" are prepared and distributed by the American Society of Travel Agents to all customers who book holidays through their members' branches. The Guidelines aim to "encourage the growth of peaceful tourism and environmentally responsible travel" and include 10 recommendations to encourage tourists to act responsibly and show respect for their hosts and the environment of their destinations.

The Pacific Asia Tourism Association (PATA) is an industrial association, which promotes the Pacific Asia area's Travel and Tourism destinations, products and services. PATA also serves as a central resource of information and research, travel industry education and training, as well as quality product development with sensitivity for culture, heritage and environment. In 1992, PATA introduced its "Code for Environmentally Responsible Tourism" to strengthen the principles of preservation in the region.

Businesses, organisations and individuals wishing to affirm their support for the PATA Code are encouraged to participate in the PATA Green Leaf programme. The Africa Travel Association has produced "Responsible Traveller Guidelines"; the Japanese Association of Travel Agents has produced the "Declaration of Earth Friendly Travellers" and there are many more examples of industry codes aimed at educating and influencing their customers.

ECO LABELLING

There are numerous examples of industry sponsored labelling schemes, whose aim is to recognise good industry practice and influence consumer behaviour into purchasing the labelled products. For example, the "Green Key, Denmark" certificate operated by the Hotel, Restaurant and Leisure Industry Association (HORESTA) has 56 criteria that includes environmental information, water and energy consumption and waste management. Special features also include ecological food products, outdoor areas, non-smoking rooms, and adaptations for access by disabled persons.

There are a number of industries that runs and sponsors award programmes to highlight and promote examples of good practice. For example, British

Airways has run the "Tourism for Tomorrow" awards since 1992 to encourage action to protect the environment. The awards are directed at tour operators, hotels, national parks and heritage sites, and other activities associated with tourism. By selecting projects showing best practice in their field as role models, others are encouraged to follow suit and consider the environment in the everyday running of their tourism business.

The awards are run annually, with a winner selected from each of five regions and an overall winner. In addition, two special awards are made for mass tourism destinations. The awards are run in association with the British Tourist Authority, the Association of British Travel Agents, the Pacific Asia Travel Association and the American Society of Travel Agents. Entries to the awards have been increases every year. American Express also sponsors a variety of environmental awards for international tourism organisations.

AGENTS AND PARTNERSHIPS FOR CHANGE

- A broad based approach is called for which requires Travel and Tourism to work with: national governments to raise the profile of environmental and social issues within the education system;
- NGOs to raise awareness of tourism issues in their work and activities and provide feedback to the Travel and Tourism industry;
- Development organisations to communicate with host communities to understand their needs and requirements;
- Local authorities to engage local people through the inclusion of tourism issues in Local Agenda21 plans;
- National and international trade associations, labour representative organisations and training providers to increase awareness and training of staff in environmental and social issues;
- Travel and Tourism publications (such as travel guides);
- Travel and Tourism journalists to raise the profile of reporting environmental and social impacts of tourism among consumers and tourism businesses;
- The Internet as a source of information for potential travellers.

AREAS FOR FURTHER ACTION

The WTTC/MORI data shows the scale of the task still remaining. The industry has developed a number of initiatives to influence consumer behaviour. However, if consumers do not understand or are not aware of the issues involved and do not demand more sustainable products then, in the long term, it will not be in the industry's interests to move in that direction.

The priority for future action, therefore, should be to raise awareness among travellers of the issues associated with tourism and the impact their activities can have on local destinations and cultures.

BROAD-BASED SUSTAINABLE DEVELOPMENT THROUGH TOURISM

The Travel and Tourism industry has a vested interest in protecting the natural and cultural resources that are the core of its business. Travel and Tourism has less impacts on natural resources and the environment than other sectors and it has already done much to address the issues arising from its activities.

There are examples, however, from around the world where the impact of Travel and Tourism has been damaging to the local environment and people.

Some of the factors which contributes to the harmful impact of tourism are:

- A lack of awareness on the part of those making decisions about tourism development of the social, economic and environmental balance to be pursued in achieving sustainable development;
- A lack of commitment by tourism operators and travellers to contribute to the maintenance of the local environment and culture of the host destination;
- A weak institutional framework with inadequate controls can lead to tourism development which is both inappropriate and intrusive;
- Unfairly traded tourism, whereby local communities are unable to share in its benefits;
- Large flows of visitors in remote or sensitive locations can place considerable strains on local resources (particularly water) and supply systems. Travellers' expectations of the goods and services, which should be available, can lead to these items or services, being imported from outside or local supply chains, being distorted to meet demands; and
- Tourism can change a destination's cultural make-up and, if poorly developed, can increase crime, prostitution and other social problems.

In order for tourism to realise its potential to achieve broad-based sustainable development, an effective partnership between Government and all sectors of the industry will be required. The following illustrates what is being done:

INTERNATIONAL COOPERATION

IH&RA and the United Nations Organisation for Education, Science and Culture (UNESCO) have signed a cooperation agreement to encourage world-wide hotel chains to sponsor UNESCO cultural heritage sites and attract tourism to them via their marketing campaigns.

NATIONAL GOVERNMENTS

In India, the government is pump priming local "eco-tourism" activities, which are primarily driven by local women. In Mexico, the government is kick starting village development for "eco-tourism" lodges in the Chiapas region involving the whole community. In England, the government has recently held a national consultation on sustainable tourism and, as a result, is developing a new strategy for tourism, which incorporates the principles of sustainable development as a core component. The Caribbean Tourism Organisation has developed a comprehensive strategy to develop "eco-tourism" in the Caribbean region. This strategy is closely integrated with the goals of the Association for Caribbean States (ACE) for a green Caribbean.

"GREEN GLOBE" has developed a specific "Destinations" programme to recognise those tourist destinations where there is a concerted effort by all those involved in the local tourism industry to improve the quality of the environment. The Destinations process provides a framework to guide tourist locations towards achieving sustainable development based on the principles of Agenda 21. The Destinations programmes are tailor made to reflect local circumstances, such as the level of environmental awareness, action taken to date and available resources. Each programme is based on achieving progressive environmental improvements.

Targets are set within a realistic timetable and are developed by a steering group made up of key partners. The island of Jersey has become the first "GREEN GLOBE" Destination. Vilamoura in Portugal, Dominica in the Caribbean and 3 destinations in the Philippines have also entered the Destination programme. For example, in 1996 Luso tour SA, a tourism development company, enacted a management plan for Vilamoura whereby employees are given responsibility for individual environmental tasks. The company has invested money into rehabilitating the surrounding natural environment, which includes pine forests and a lake that has significance to local wetland areas. Guests are provided with a copy of the environmental policy and are encouraged to participate in the scheme through specialised brochures.

The campaign includes recycling; treating diseased pine areas; regular cleaning of the beaches and marinas; development of a sewage treatment plant and new buildings in the resort are designed to minimise visual and environmental impacts. For its work in Vilamoura, Lusotour SA is also a winner of the British Airways Tourism for Tomorrow Awards. The "Africa tourism" brand has been developed by the Open Africa Foundation to encourage products, which embraces sustainable ecological, economic and social development based on Africa's unique cultural, natural and wildlife heritage. "Open Africa" is also developing a continuous network of "Africa tourism" routes from the Cape to Cairo, known as the "African Dream". The Dream helps to create awareness of the many rural and environmental projects, which exist throughout Africa. "Team Africa", a transcontinental alliance of governments, corporations, institutions, professionals and individuals, provides leadership and motivation in the development of the "African Dream".

HOST COMMUNITIES

"Whale Watch Kaikoura" is an initiative of local Maori people from a small town on the East Coast of New Zealand's South Island. Within a kilometre of the Kaikoura shore is an area ideal for whales, where visitors are guaranteed to see them all year round. The Whale Watch began 11 years ago and is now a booming tourist destination, run by indigenous people with a strong sense of heritage and a view of the future based on strong principles of sustainability.

Jordan Tourism Investments, has revitalised the traditional village of Taybeh, in Jordan, into a cultural tourist resort, with the help and agreement of villagers. With many of the younger generation moving to the cities, the village was losing its character. By restoring its 19th century buildings and reviving old crafts, the village is now thriving again. The village lies 9km south east of the historic city of Petra. Opened in July 1994, the village now accommodates around 60,000 guests each year. Uluru and Kakadu National Parks are both owned by indigenous Australians, the local Aboriginal communities, and jointly run with the National Parks and Wildlife Service. They are both major tourism destinations and involve indigenous participation in planning, management, and ownership of tourism infrastructure, as well as interpretation for visitors. They bring significant economic, social and cultural benefits to the local indigenous communities. The Conservation Corporation in Africa has established a series of high quality game parks in which local communities are major stakeholders and beneficiaries of tourism. This initiative is also helping to re-invigourate local crafts.

AGENTS AND PARTNERSHIPS

The challenge facing the tourism industry in moving towards a more sustainable future is set out in "Agenda 21 for the Travel and Tourism Industry". To achieve the goals set out in this document will require a partnership between government departments, national tourism authorities, international and national trade organisations and Travel and Tourism companies.

Working together in close cooperation such partnerships should aim to deliver the following:

- Close cooperation between the public and private sectors to deliver a regulatory regime, which encourages voluntary action but supplement, where necessary, with regulation in areas such as land-use and waste management.
- Agreed common standards and tools to enable the measurement of progress towards achieving sustainable development.
- Certification criteria developed and more widely applied to industry initiatives.
- A commitment to the controlled expansion, where appropriate, of infrastructure.

- Environmental taxes, where applied, should be fair and non-discriminatory. They should be carefully thought out to minimise their impact on economic development, and revenues should be allocated to Travel and Tourism associated environment improvement programmes.
- International, national and local funding bodies should include sustainable development as apart of their criteria, so that in time, all funding would be dependent on sound environmental practice.
- Contemporary research into sustainable tourism needs to be funded and developed. Issues requiring attention include design, carrying capacity, tour operator activities, environmental reporting, auditing and environmental impact assessments.
- Environmental education and training should be increased, particularly in schools, for future hotel and tourism staff.
- Greater investment and commitment to the use of new technology.

8

Technology, Innovation and Changing Nature of Tourism Business

THE MARKETING MIX AND BUSINESS TOURISM

The marketing mix consists of those variables which are controllable or heavily influenced by an organization. They are divided into the 4 Ps, namely, product, price, place and promotion.

THE PRODUCT

The diversity of business travel and tourism makes it difficult to generalize about the nature of the product. For example, business travellers making individual business trips will see the 'product' as the transport and accommodation services they use primarily, as well as the general facilities provided by the destination. However, the convention delegate may see the convention centre itself as the most important element of the product. Like leisure tourism it could also be argued that business travel and tourism is not a product, but rather an experience.

The nature of this experience will reflect, for example:

- The elements of the product
- The ambience of the destination and the venue
- The personality and experience of the business traveller.

The experience also includes three stages:

- Anticipation -
- Consumption
- Remembrance.

Before the event – during the event – after the event.

Furthermore, the experience can also be divided into two sets of elements, as follows:

1 Those elements which are controlled or influenced by the supplier such as hotel meeting rooms.
2 Those elements which are not under the control or influence of suppliers, but which affect the experience, such as the weather and air road congestion.

Another area where great effort has been made to attract the business traveller is business-class services on airlines. A case study relating to this subject is to be found in Part Five of the book. All products, whether business tourism or not, have a range of factors which constitute the product. These can best be explained by using a convention centre as an example. Marketing of products such as this convention centre involves packaging all of these elements to create a satisfactory experience for the customer.

PRICE

Price is clearly a crucial issue in any market but it is a complex matter in business travel and tourism, for the following reasons:

1 There are direct and indirect costs for the traveller. Direct costs include, for example, fees for attending conferences or the price of an air ticket. There are also indirect costs such as the need to buy a visa when travelling to some destinations.

2 Prices for a similar product vary dramatically around the world. Some examples taken from *Business Traveller* magazine will illustrate this point as follows:
   - A non-residential one-day conference for 500 people including room hire, lunch, two tea/coffee breaks and taxes, would cost £9745 in Helsinki but £19 100 in Copenhagen (*Business Traveller*, May 2000).
   - A cocktail party for ten VIP guests in January 2000 including two-night suite hire, dinner and breakfast for one person included would have cost £2775 in Cyprus but £3350 in Rome (*Business Traveller*, January 2000).
   - A three-night full-board stay for thirty people in fifteen rooms in a leisure hotel with golf facilities in spring 2000, would have cost £9630 in Mauritius but £17 000 in Florida (*Business Traveller*, March 2000).

Even within one country prices can vary significantly. For example, the twenty-four hour delegate rate at the end of 2000 was £105 at the Britannia Adelphi Hotel, Liverpool, £195 at the Balmoral Hotel, Edinburgh, and £220 at the Grand Hotel, Eastbourne (*Conference and Incentive Travel, January 2001*).

For many purchasers/users, price is perhaps less important than perceived value for money. This term is concerned with the relationship between benefits received and price paid. For example, in January 2000 a survey published in *Business Traveller* found that 80 per cent of readers felt that conference delegates were offered better value for money from hotels in mainland Europe than in the UK. Of course, value for money is a wholly subjective concept. Most purchasers do not pay the published price, particularly for hotel accommodation and airline tickets. Negotiation is commonplace, which creates real challenges in terms of revenue planning and yield management. Discounting is also rife based on criteria such as seasonality, volume of business or whether the customer is a regular user of a particular product or service.

Some elements of the business tourism product are sold below their market value for various reasons. For example, many municipally owned conference venues are hired out to organizers at low, even no, cost to attract conferences because of the spin-off benefits they will bring to the area. Destinations usually make no direct charge for entry to the resort, city or region or for use of its facilities such as beaches, parks and even the climate. Ye t these elements of the destination may be a major factor in the decision to locate a conference or incentive travel package in a particular location. Some costs are compulsory, such as travel costs, while others are voluntary, like having a drink at the end of the working day.

PLACE

Place or distribution is concerned with how business travellers or tourists actually purchase the products they need.

There are several dimensions to this:

1 Customers can buy whole packages such as an incentive travel package or individual elements such as air tickets, venues and accommodation.
2 Customers can purchase products directly or make use of the services of specialist intermediaries.

As with leisure travel and tourism, the Internet is beginning to play a big role in distribution in business travel and tourism. By providing both information and an opportunity to purchase simultaneously it is blurring the distinction between two of the 4 Ps, namely, place and promotion. This leads us neatly on to the final P, promotion.

PROMOTION

To many people, promotion is synonymous with marketing; it is the visual face of marketing. However, promotion is simply one element of the marketing mix, fulfilling the function of making potential customers want to purchase a particular product.

ADVERTISING

Advertising, particularly in trade journals is a major weapon in the promotional armoury of many business travel and tourism organizations. As business travel and tourism is a high-spending activity, advertising tends to be glossy and colourful.

To be successful, however, advertising has to:

- Be undertaken frequently to remind customers of brand names
- Be integrated with other promotional techniques.

THE INTERNET

Just as in leisure travel, the Internet is beginning to play a growing role in business travel and tourism, both in terms of finding information and making reservations.

A readers' poll published in Conference and Incentive Travel in February 2000 found that:

- While 35 per cent of readers preferred to book travel and accommodation via the Internet, 60 per cent still preferred other means
- Only 15 per cent of readers felt that conference venue web sites offered the optimum of information for conference organizers.

It is clear, therefore, that more work needs to be done on developing this medium in the business travel and tourism field.

TRADE JOURNALS

Business travel and tourism is still a relatively small industry but it is a world in which buyers are always looking for information on new products or services. The trade journals therefore play a very important role in promoting products and allowing communication between buyers, suppliers and intermediaries. There are a large number of journals, most of which focus either on a sector (*e.g.,* exhibitions) a region (*e.g.,* the USA) or a particular angle (*e.g.,* consumer advice for the business traveller). Furthermore, new journals are being launched all the time, around the world.

For example, a new journal, *CEI Asia Pacific*, was launched in September 2000 covering conferences, exhibitions and incentives. Focusing on this region where business tourism is a major phenomena this journal promised its readers, that it would 'publish industry news features, comments, and opinion from corporate buyers together with a regular series of interviews and corporate case studies. CEI Asia Pacific will be produced to the highest editorial standard' (*Conference and Incentive Travel*, June 2000).

PERSONAL SELLING

In an industry based so much on interpersonal skills and trust, it is not surprising that personal selling plays a major role in promotion in business travel and tourism.

The main areas for personal selling are as follows:

- Venues selling their services to buyers
- Airlines and hotels selling to buyers and intermediaries.
- Incentive travel agencies and professional conference organisers selling their services to potential clients.

Telephone and face-to-face negotiation plays a vital role in marketing in this industry.

BUSINESS ORGANISATIONS CATEGORIES

HOTEL MANAGER

The Hotel manager oversees all of a hotel's daily operations, from staffing to coordinating fresh-cut flowers for the lobby. Many, over time, are given long-term responsibility for negotiating contracts with vendors (such as maintenance supplies), negotiating leases with on-site shops, and physically upgrading the hotel. Hotel managers usually relish "the ability to put your own distinctive style on the [hotel] experience." While managing a hotel and giving it your unique flair are wonderful, they come with full responsibility for failure. "The better you are at what you do, the more responsibilities you are given, the more chances you have to fail," mentioned one hotel manager. When things fall apart, "no one is a hotel manager's friend."

Hotel managers can feel great about their positions, create strong relationships with regular customers, and maintain an amicable working environment. But should the bottom line waver and financial woes occur, the first neck on the chopping block is the hotel manager's. Those in the hotel management industry say that sometimes it seems that you need "to be born on the planet Krypton" to be a good hotel manager because only Superman could juggle the administrative, aesthetic, and financial decisions which constitute daily life on the job. Over 70 per cent of the respondents said that tired was an understatement about how they felt at the end of the day or night.

A hotel manager's position as a liaison between the ownership and the staff can be difficult and isolating. But those who can put up with the long hours, the high degree of responsibility, and the variety of tasks emerge with a solid degree of satisfaction and a desire to continue in the profession. The average tenure of a hotel manager is 6.7 years, though this figure doesn't represent the number of managers who work for two years and those who work for decades. Many work at a variety of hotels, build up their resumes, and then find positions that allow them the freedom to operate their own establishments.

Aspiring hotel managers used to begin at the reception desk, as part of the wait staff, or as members of the cleaning staff, then work their way up the ladder. As hotels have become more commercial properties and the duties of hotel managers have expanded, this avenue of advancement has closed off. Now hotel manager hopefuls go to hotel management school, and those who don't should garner as much practical hotel experience as possible.

Each chain or specific hotel puts new employees through their own training programmes, so those applying for jobs should learn all they can about the scope and functioning of the specific hotels where they wish to work. Part of life as a hotel manager can be similar to the life of a doctor, as managers can be called to duty at any time of the day or night. Hotel managers must handle any and all emergencies, and those who wish to remain in the profession and maintain respect must be quick-thinking and decisive. Candidates should have a good organizational and financial background, excellent communication and interpersonal skills, and strong self-discipline. They should also be extremely detail-oriented; when running a hotel, there is no such thing as an unimportant detail. The good manager drives himself to improve and upgrade the hotel at every available opportunity.

A hotel manager is responsible for the day-to-day management of a hotel and its staff and has commercial accountability for planning, organising and directing all hotel services, including front-of-house (reception, concierge, reservation), banqueting and housekeeping. In larger hotels, managers often have a specific remit (guest services, accounting, marketing) and make up a general management team. Financial management - preparing budgets and marketing strategies and achieving targets for the business - plays a major role.

The manager must strike a balance between customer satisfaction and effective business management, ensuring financial viability, and facilitate a smooth-running customer service, whilst ensuring staff work together as a team.

TYPICAL WORK ACTIVITIES

Typical work activities vary depending on the size and type of hotel, but may include:

- Planning and organising accommodation, catering and other hotel services;
- Promoting and marketing the business;
- Managing budgets and financial plans;
- Maintaining statistical and financial records;
- Achieving profit targets;
- Recruiting, training and monitoring staff;
- Planning work schedules;
- Meeting and greeting customers;
- Dealing with customer complaints and comments;
- Addressing problems and troubleshooting;
- Ensuring events and conferences run smoothly;
- Supervising maintenance, supplies and furnishings;
- Dealing with contractors and suppliers;
- Ensuring security is effective;
- Carrying out inspections of property and services;
- Ensuring compliance with licensing laws, health and safety and other statutory regulations.

The manager of a large hotel may have less contact with guests but will spend time meeting heads of department and planning and monitoring the progress of business strategies. In a smaller establishment, the manager is much more involved in the hands-on day-to-day running of the hotel, which may include carrying out reception duties or serving meals if the need arises. A significant number of hotel managers are self-employed and this can lead to a more general management experience, from greeting guests to managing finances.

HOW TO BECOME A HOTEL MANAGER

- Ask yourself if you have excellent interpersonal, communication and organizational skills. They are necessary for a successful hotel management career.
- Obtain a college degree in hotel management or restaurant management. Remember that a food services department contributes greatly to the profits of a hotel; a successful restaurant manager can see his or her career advance quickly.
- Take advantage of work-study programmes offered by many colleges so that you will gain solid experience working in hotels.
- Expect to go through a hotel's training programme once you are hired after college. During the first couple of years you will be handling only relatively mundane duties, instead of providing your input on issues such as staffing, hotel decor or conventions.
- Understand that you might be offered a position as a front office manager, a food and beverage manager, a convention services manager, or any of a number of administrative positions after your training period. If you are successful at different managerial positions, your career will benefit in the long run.
- Be aware that a promotion might require you to relocate for a few years if you work for a hotel chain that has properties throughout the country.
- You will need to quickly become proficient with computers because of their widespread use in hotel reservations, billing and overall management operations.
- Consider working for hotels in warm tourist destinations or snowy mountains, depending on your preferred lifestyle.
- Be prepared for long hours, night and weekend work, and the occasional unhappy guest.

Different managerial personnel working as hotel managers — Catering managers plan, organise and manage the food and beverage services of organisations and businesses, both inside and outside the hospitality industry, with the aim of achieving good quality at low cost and maintaining high standards of hygiene and customer satisfaction.

There is a range of jobs in catering management, along with a number of different routes into the industry. Roles include: managing restaurants, bars and other outlets in hotels, resorts or liners; providing catering services at events; and running catering operations at hospitals, schools and other organisations. With ongoing growth in the service industry, opportunities in this demanding but rewarding area continue to grow.

The role varies according to the size and nature of the establishment: in a small operation, the catering manager has more of a 'hands on' role and will be involved in the day-to-day running of the operation; in contract catering, the catering manager will spend time negotiating with the client organisation, assessing its requirements and ensuring that it is satisfied with the service delivered.

Typical tasks will include:

- Recruiting and training permanent and casual staff;
- Organising, leading and motivating the catering team;
- Planning menus in consultation with chefs;
- Ensuring health and safety regulations are strictly observed;
- Budgeting and establishing financial targets;
- Monitoring the quality of the product and service provided;
- Keeping financial and administrative records;
- Managing the payroll and monitoring spending levels;
- Maintaining stock levels and ordering new supplies as required;
- Interacting with customers if involved with 'front of house' work;
- Liaising with suppliers and clients;
- Negotiating contracts with customers (in contract catering).

In more senior posts, principal tasks will involve:

- Setting and agreeing budgets;
- Monitoring quality standards;
- Overseeing the management of the facilities, for example checking events bookings and the allocation of resources and staff;
- Planning new promotions and initiatives, and contributing to business development;
- Dealing with staffing and client issues, as they arise.

FOOD AND RESTAURANT MANAGER

Fast food restaurant managers are responsible for the provision of standardised food and customer service in outlets based in the high street, motor service areas, stations, airports or multiplexes. Drawing on all the operational functions of a business, the work involves applying financial, marketing and operational know-how, and supervising and training staff. Managers plan, organise, and co-ordinate all resources and activities in a store. The work involves: setting targets, planning budgets, and controlling stock; recruiting, training and inspiring restaurant teams; creating and driving marketing campaigns; and building bridges with the local community. Ultimately, it is the manager's ideas, initiative and personality that shape the restaurant.

Tasks typically involve:

- Organising the store in terms of products, equipment and people;
- Planning and checking work schedules;
- Carrying out audits to check health safety, food safety and quality of service in the restaurant;
- Making sure the fast-track audit is completed daily to check the safety of equipment and that food is properly cooked, only in-date stock is used, and all other products are discarded;
- Carrying out work outside the restaurant, including 'mystery shopping' at other restaurants within the chain;
- Attending weekly meetings with senior managers;
- Dealing with problems, queries, complaints, staff and customers in the store;
- Monitoring and maintaining high standards of food, service and hygiene;
- Ensuring the company's required standards of customer care are met;
- Administering payrolls;
- Checking and securing cash receipts;
- Budgeting to ensure maximum profitability;
- Achieving set profit and loss targets;
- Maintaining and securing equipment and buildings and all company assets contained within the unit;
- Publicising and marketing restaurants in the locality;
- Motivating restaurant teams;
- Recruiting, selecting and training new staff and fully inducting the restaurant team in accordance with company policy;
- Developing all team members to their fullest potential using the performance management/review system and identifying individual training needs;
- Ensuring the implementation and maintenance of legislation, company standards and procedures;
- Recognising new trends and implementing action plans accordingly;
- Acting as a communication link between senior teams and the restaurant team;
- Leading by example, acting as a role model for the restaurant team.

A successful manager will strike the right balance between creating both a good service for restaurant customers and a fun work environment for members of staff.

FAMILIARIZATION OR EDUCATIONAL VISITS

Decisions about the destination and venue of conferences, exhibitions, product launches and incentive travel packages involve purchases where the level of expenditure can run into millions of pounds. As one would expect, therefore, very few buyers make their decisions based on brochures, videos or advertisements. They must see the place and venue for themselves, check it out, ask questions and meet the people they will be working with before they decide to contract a particular venue or other service. The familiarization or educational visit, which is the name given to this process, is therefore very important in business travel and tourism.

THE MARKET

It is now time briefly to turn our attention from the marketing mix to the market itself. Here we will simply consider the issues which are of greatest interest to marketers, namely, motivators, determinants and segmentation.

MOTIVATORS AND DETERMINANTS

We discussed the motivators and focused on the different motivators between the customer (usually the employer) and the consumer (usually the business traveller). We also noted that motivators varied between different types of business tourism such as conferences, exhibitions and incentive travel. It is important that marketing people should understand motivators so that they can design products and promote them effectively. However, we also have to recognize that while motivators are important, determinants are the factors that influence what customers will actually be able to do in reality. These determinants can be either internal or external, both relating to the customer and/or the consumer. Determinants affect whether any trip will be made at all and, if so, what kind of trip will be taken. To illustrate what we mean by determinants in concrete terms, let us imagine an employee who wishes to attend a professional conference in another country. First, he or she will have to persuade their employer that attendance will be worth the cost in terms of time and money.

If the employer agrees the employee may not be able to attend if, for example:

- By the time the decision is made all flights and/or hotels and/or conference places are fully booked
- The financial situation of the travellers' organization deteriorates and a decision is taken to cut back on travel expenditure.

Even if this trip goes ahead, its characteristics will be determined by a wide variety of factors, including perhaps:

- What level of expenses the company has given our traveller for the trip
- The weather in the destination at the time of the conference
- Whether or not our traveller already knows some of the other delegates
- The quality of accommodation in which the delegate is staying
- The cost of living in the destination.

For individual business trips the main determinants of what kind of business trip will be taken is often where the company has business interests. Past experience and perceptions can also be a major determinant of behaviour. Business tourists travelling to new destinations may well like the security of using airlines and hotels with which they are already familiar and satisfied. Those readers wanting to read more about motivators and determinants, in general, might find *Consumer Behaviour in Tourism* by Swarbrooke and Horner, useful.

MARKET SEGMENTATION

Until recently, marketers tended to view markets as single homogeneous entities. However, one must realize that every population or market is subdivided into segments – subgroups with shared buying characteristics. It is important to recognize that segmentation is a very important technique for marketers today. The business travel and tourism market could be divided into a number of segments. Each of these segments should, according to marketing theory, require a different marketing mix.

Clearly some of these criteria can change, such as purpose of travel, while others will normally stay the same for each individual, for instance, sex.

DESTINATION MARKETING

The destination marketing is a difficult activity because:

1 Destinations exist at different geographical levels from individual towns to countries or even continents.
2 Tourist perceptions of destinations rarely match the official boundaries of the agencies set up to market destinations.
3 No direct charge is usually made to visit a destination unless there is a visa charge or tourist tax. Destination marketers therefore cannot directly use price as a demand management tool.
4 Most destination marketing is a public sector activity but most of the product is in the ownership of the private sector. Destination marketing, therefore, often focuses on promotion because it cannot control product or price.

THE RISE OF PARTNERSHIP MARKETING

There has been a growing recognition that the public sector cannot do everything itself and there needs to be partnership between key players in destinations.

These partnerships can be of several types, notably:

- All organisations, both public and private, within a given geographical area
- Between sectors, for example, airlines and hotels or venues and hotels
- Within sectors, for example, convention centres.

The first type of partnership is now popular at local level through the rise of visitor and convention bureaux.

VISITOR AND CONVENTION BUREAUX

These organizations tend to be jointly funded by the public sector via a grant, and the private sector via membership fees and contributions to marketing campaigns. They usually have a number of roles, including brochure production, advertising, attending trade fairs, direct mail campaigns, organizing familiarization visits, preparing tenders for major events, public relations, and so on.

NATIONAL TOURISM ORGANIZATIONS

National tourism boards, recognizing the importance of business tourism are now becoming increasingly involved in promoting their respective countries as business tourism destinations.

CO-OPERATION BETWEEN DESTINATIONS

Some destinations are realizing that, if they can find partner destinations with complementary attractions, then co-operation can be better than competition. Recently, for example, a co-operative promotional campaign was mounted aimed at the incentive travel market by the Singapore Tourism Board and the Indonesian Department of Culture and Tourism, under the title, 'Start with a dry martini, then wet your pants' (white water rafting!)

The importance of destination image: Destination image is important in marketing business travel and tourism, in several ways:

1 Conference and exhibition organizers and incentive travel agencies choose destinations for their events, partly based on their perceptions of these destinations.

2 Conference delegates often choose to attend conferences partly based on the perceived attractions or otherwise of the place.

3 Partners choose to accompany business travellers visiting a destination only if they perceive it to be an attractive place.

The attraction of a destination is a function of a combination of factors, including climate, scenery or townscape, safety and security, the attitude of local people towards tourists, the quality of the infrastructure, price levels, and so on. But destination image is a subjective and abstract concept, where perceptions are more important that reality. In recent years a number of destinations have succeeded in developing positive destination images, realistic or not.

For example it is widely believed that:

- New York is safer than it once was
- Dublin is a lively, sociable, friendly city
- Singapore is an efficient, good value, high-quality service destination.

The above images bring real benefits for these destinations in terms of business travel and tourism.

BUSINESS MANAGEMENT

Business management in ecotourism can be seen as composed of several fields: finance, law, licenses and permits, accreditation, liability and insurance, staff training, and personnel management. The most compact source of business management information of ecotourism is McKercher's book. This one source provides a solid background to all major aspects of business management for ecotourism.

The value of a formal business education, as found in business school or a leisure studies school with a business programme is high and should not be underestimated. There is a lot of naivety in tourism. Too many feel that they can be successful in a tourism business with only good intentions and hard work. The high failure rates and turnover rates reveal that good intentions can never replace solid educational preparation.

The Canadian Tourism Commission (CTC) produced a summary of the potential for ecotourism and adventure tourism in Canada, revealing important business need in Canada. They undertook a road show of adventure and ecotourism consultation across the country in] 997. This effort produced a useful set of documents describing business opinion of the industry and outlining policy needs. This document provides a useful lens into the business concerns of the many small ecotourism businesses in that country. The Department of Environmental Affairs and Tourism in South Africa produced a status and summary statement on ecotourism in that country. Given the importance of ecotourism to the national economy in South Africa, national government policies are very important in encouraging and guiding the business development in this rapidly growing industry. Lindberg edited one of the wost useful books available on ecotourism management, entitled: Ecotourism: a Guide for Planners and Managers. This encyclopaedia has an international focus and provides solid descriptions of many aspects of ecotourism business management.

Finance

All operations, big and small, government and private, require finance. Typically, one needs the assistance of financial experts when designing and implementing a business plan. This can be obtained by using specialised finance consultants or, in simpler situations, banks and loan companies may have staff that can assist. All predictions of tourism volume, cash flow and expenses should be conservative, in order to err on the positive. The Australian tourism bodies frequently produce useful publications in ecotourism management. An excellent way to reduce financial costs and to reduce the ecological footprint of an operation is to adopt policies to minimise chemical use, energy use and water use. Excellent guidelines on environmentally sensitive tourism design and management are available from the Australian Department of Tourism (Commonwealth Department of Tourism, 1995).

Law

All business operations must function within the laws of the country of business. In ecotourism, the international aspect of the travel means that a complicated, multi jurisdictional approach to the legal aspects of business must be adopted. The inbound operator may be based in one country, the transport company in a second country, the outbound operator in a third country, and the ecotourists from many others. This creates challenging contractual, monetary and operational issues. It is critical that the base of operations of any business Is In a country with a fair and operational rule of law. The police must be honest and the judiciary independent and holiest. Without these key factors any property ownership, contract, license or agreement will be exposed to the whims of corruption and bribery. Many ecotour operations have failed when corrupt government officials, police OF local operators engaged in fraudulent activities. It is imperative that any ecotour business becomes, familiar with the legal situation in their area of operation.

Licenses and Permits

All ecotour operators, both public and private, require licenses and permits in order to operate. These can include: access permits for parks, vehicle safety permits, and food handling permits, firearm permits, business operations licenses, land-use development approvals, building permits, tax collection licenses, proof of incorporation, workplace, health and safety approval, proof of insurance, employee training certification, bus driver licenses, and many others. The licenses can be issued by the national, provincial, regional or local governments. Park and protected area agencies often require special permits before sites can be used. All licenses and permits must be comprehensively handled by competent staff and kept up to date.

Accreditation

Ecotourists look for independent indicators of product quality, and accreditation is an excellent way of indicating the achievement of such quality. Accreditation is a formal process for the determination of product and service quality. In a competitive market, such as-tourism, accredited operators and sites have a competitive advantage. Given the difficulty faced by potential tourists in their ability to assess the travel product before purchase, independent accreditation is seen as a very useful sign of quality. Given this market pressure, the more mature the tourism markets, the higher the levels of accreditation.

The best example of accreditation in ecotourism in the world today is found in Australia. The national ecotourism accreditation scheme is functioning well, is widely accepted and has become a model for other countries. The programme has helped to raise the standards of ecotourism across the country. It allows competent operators to clearly reveal to others their high level of business management.

It provides a framework for continuous improvement in the industry. Up-to-date information on this programme can be found on the web site of the Office of National Tourism. The Green Globe programme of tourism accreditation is gaining wider acceptance globally. Some of the larger operators are adopting the ISO 9000 series of programme operation standards to improve their operations and to prove to their clients that they are serious about quality. In all cases, it is important for tourism operators to see some form of independent assessment of quality, such as accreditation. Once this is achieved, this must be communicated to potential clients.

Liability and Insurance

All people providing a service to others in return for financial remuneration have a duty of care to their clients Typically,-this duty of care involves providing a level of service and safety as would be normally expected in similar circumstances in the area of operation. However tourists from distant locales may have service and safety expectations quite different from that normally occurring in the local area of operation. All operators, both public and private, should make themselves aware of the standard of care normally expected in their area.

They then must put operational procedures into place to ensure that all parts of their operation provide this standard of care. It is important that sufficient levels of insurance coverage are maintained. It is important that the legal structure of the country of operation is sufficiently mature to allow insurance to function at internationally acceptable levels. Mature ecotourist operations provide information to their clients on the levels of security, safety and insurance coverage that they hold. Experienced ecotourists demand such information before making a travel decision.

Staff Training

Ecotourism is an information-rich, highly personal activity. Ecotourists generally have high service, safety and information expectations. Those who have traveled widely know very well what it means to be serviced by personnel with appropriate levels of ecological service and interpretation experience. Therefore, all staff involved in ecotourism from the safari driver to the booking agent requires high levels of service training. Typically, this is achieved by local or regional colleges, or in some countries by industry training bodies.

BUSINESS CONTINUITY PLANNING

Business Continuity Planning (BCP) is an interdisciplinary peer mentoring methodology used to create and validate an exercised logistical plan for how an organization will recover and restore partially or completely interrupted critical function(s) within a predetermined time after a disaster or extended disruption. BCP may be a part of an organizational learning effort that helps reduce operational risk associated with lax information management controls. This process may be integrated with improving information security and corporate reputation risk management practices.

British Standards Institute is planning to release a new independent standard for BCP — BS 25999. The draft of standard had been put up for public comments and the final standard is expected in early 2007. This standard would reduce the reliance on Information Security oriented standards which dealt with BCP marginally. A completed BCP cycle results in a formal printed manual available for reference before, during, and after disruptions have occurred. Its purpose is to reduce adverse stakeholder impacts determined by both the disruption's scope and duration. Measureable Business Impact Analysis (BIA) "zones" include civil, economic, natural, technical, secondary and subsequent.

Business Continuity Planning is not a new concept; plans for disasters, like Noah's Ark, are evidenced from the beginning of human history. Prior to January 1, 2000, governments anticipated computer failures, called the Y2k problem, in important public utility infrastructures like banking, power, telecommunication, health and financial industries. Since 1983, regulatory agencies like the American Bankers Association and Banking Administration Institute (BAI) required their supporting members to exercise operational continuity practices (later supported by more formal BCP manuals) that protect the public interests. Newer regulations were often based on formalized standards defined under ISO/IEC 17799 or BS 7799.

Both regulatory and global business focus on BCP arguably waned after the problem-free Y2K rollover. This lax attitude unequivocally ended September 11th 2001, when simultaneous terrorist attacks devastated downtown New York City and changed the 'worst case scenario' paradigm for business continuity planning. BCP methodology is scalable for an organization of any size and complexity. Even though the methodology has roots in regulated industries, any type of organization may create a BCP manual, and arguably every organization should have one in order to ensure the organization's longevity. Evidence that firms do not invest enough time and resources into BCP preparations are evident in disaster survival statistics. Fires permanently close 44per cent of the business affected. In the 1993 World Trade Center bombing, 150 businesses out of 350 affected failed to survive the event. Conversely, the firms affected by the Sept 11 attacks with well-developed and tested BCP manuals were back in business within days.

A BCP manual for a small organization may be simply a printed manual stored safely away from the primary work location, containing the names, addresses, and phone numbers for crisis management staff, general staff members, clients, and vendors along with the location of the offsite data backup storage media, copies of insurance contracts, and other critical materials necessary for organizational survival. At its most complex, a BCP manual may outline a secondary work site, technical requirements and readiness, regulatory reporting requirements, work recovery measures, the means to re-establish physical records, the means to establish a new supply chain, or the means to establish new production centers. Firms should ensure that their BCP manual is realistic and easy to use during a crisis. As such, BCP sits along side crisis management and disaster recovery planning and is a part of an organization's overall risk management.

The development of a BCP manual has five main phases:

1. Analysis
2. Solution design
3. Implementation
4. Testing and organization acceptance
5. Maintenance

Much of the BCP material on the internet is sponsored by consultancies who offer fee-based services for BCP solution development, however basic tutorials are freely available on the internet for properly motivated organizations.

The analysis phase in the development of a BCP manual consists of an impact analysis, threat analysis, and impact scenarios with the resulting BCP plan requirement documentation. An impact analysis results in the differentiation between critical and non-critical organization functions. A function may be considered critical if the implications for stakeholders of damage to the organization resulting are regarded as unacceptable. Perceptions of the acceptability of disruption may be modified by the cost of establishing and maintaining appropriate business or technical recovery solutions. A function may also be considered critical if dictated by law. Next, the impact analysis results in the recovery requirements for each critical function. Recovery requirements consist of the following information:

- The time frame in which the critical function must be resumed after the disaster
- The business requirements for recovery of the critical function, and/or
- The technical requirements for recovery of the critical function

The organizations also banned face-to-face contact between opposing team members during business and non-business hours. With such a split, organizations increased their resiliency against the threat of government-ordered quarantine measures if one person in a team contracted or was exposed to the disease. Damage from flooding also has a unique characteristic. If an office environment is flooded with non-salinated and contamination-free water (e.g.m, in the event of a pipe burst), equipment can be thoroughly dried and may still be functional.

After defining potential threats, documenting the impact scenarios that form the basis of the business recovery plan is recommended. In general, planning for the most wide-reaching disaster or disturbance is preferable to planning for a smaller scale problem, as almost all smaller scale problems are partial elements of larger disasters. A typical impact scenario like 'Building Loss' will most likely encompass all critical business functions, and the worst potential outcome from any potential threat. A business continuity plan may also document additional impact scenarios if an organization has more than one building. Other more specific impact scenarios - for example a scenario for the temporary or permanent loss of a specific floor in a building - may also be documented.

After the completion of the analysis phase, the business and technical plan requirements are documented in order to commence the implementation phase. For an office-based, IT intensive business, the plan requirements may cover the following elements which may be classed as ICE (In Case of Emergency) Data:

- The numbers and types of desks, whether dedicated or shared, required outside of the primary business location in the secondary location
- The individuals involved in the recovery effort along with their contact and technical details
- The applications and application data required from the secondary location desks for critical business functions
- The manual workaround solutions
- The maximum outage allowed for the applications
- The peripheral requirements like printers, copier, fax machine, calculators, paper, pens etc.

Other business environments, such as production, distribution, warehousing etc will need to cover these elements, but are likely to have additional issues to manage following a disruptive event.

The goal of the solution design phase is to identify the most cost effective disaster recovery solution that meets two main requirements from the impact analysis stage. For IT applications, this is commonly expressed as:

1. The minimum application and application data requirements
2. The time frame in which the minimum application and application data must be available

Disaster recovery plans may also be required outside the IT applications domain, for example in preservation of information in hard copy format, or restoration of embedded technology in process plant. This BCP phase overlaps with Disaster recovery planning methodology. The solution phase determines:

- The crisis management command structure
- The location of a secondary work site (where necessary)
- Telecommunication architecture between primary and secondary work sites
- Data replication methodology between primary and secondary work sites
- The application and software required at the secondary work site, and
- The type of physical data requirements at the secondary work site.

The implementation phase, quite simply, is the execution of the design elements identified in the solution design phase. Work package testing may take place during the implementation of the solution, however; work package testing does not take the place of organizational testing. The purpose of testing is to achieve organizational acceptance that the business continuity solution satisfies the organization's recovery requirements. Plans may fail to meet expectations due to insufficient or inaccurate recovery requirements, solution design flaws, or solution implementation errors. Testing may include:

- Crisis command team call-out testing
- Technical swing test from primary to secondary work locations
- Technical swing test from secondary to primary work locations
- Application test
- Business process test

At minimum, testing is generally conducted on a biannual or annual schedule. Problems identified in the initial testing phase may be rolled up into the maintenance phase and retested during the next test cycle. Maintenance of a BCP manual is broken down into three periodic activities. The first activity is the confirmation of information in the manual. The second activity is the testing and verification of technical solutions established for recovery operations. The third activity is the testing and verification of documented organization recovery procedures. A biannual or annual maintenance cycle is typical.

All organizations change over time, therefore a BCP manual must change to stay relevant to the organization. Once data accuracy is verified, normally a call tree test is conducted to evaluate the notification plan's efficiency as well as the accuracy of the contact data. Some types of changes that should be identified and updated in the manual include:

- Staffing changes
- Staffing persona
- Changes to important clients and their contact details
- Changes to important vendors/suppliers and their contact details
- Departmental changes like new, closed or fundamentally changed departments.

KEY ISSUES IN THE DIFFERENT TYPES AND SECTORS OF BUSINESS TRAVEL AND TOURISM

Each type of business tourism and sector of the business travel industry has its own distinct characteristics and pattern of marketing activity. The key issues in marketing within the different sectors of the business travel and tourism industry. This is clearly a simplification of a very complex picture. It is now time for us to move on to look at several key topical issues in business travel and tourism.

TOPICAL ISSUES

Marketing in business travel and tourism, as in other industries, is going through a period of great change. Some of the most important issues and changes are briefly discussed in this section.

Quality and customer satisfaction: Everyone today believes in the importance of quality and customer satisfaction, even if they cannot actually define what it means. In business travel and tourism we need first to establish who the customer is, for, as we saw earlier in the book, there are customers and consumers in our industry. Customers are generally the organizations which employ business travellers or organize business tourism events, while consumers are those who actually attend the events and use the services of the industry. And, of course, they both want different things. Quality and satisfaction to the customer will mean low price, while for the consumer it will mean comfort and status, as well as reliability which is of interest to both of them. As frequent travellers, business tourists tend to be demanding, knowledgeable and able to compare the products of competing organizations.

We need to make the following points about the concept of quality and satisfaction in business travel and tourism:

1 The main criterion for judging quality and satisfaction is 'fitness for purpose', products and services which do what they are supposed to do. In other words quality means flights that operate on time and venues that enable conferences to take place efficiently. Reliability, again is the crucial issue here.

2 The concept of 'critical incidents' is important because there are many occasions in business travel and tourism when the overall experience hinges on a single incident, such as a delayed flight, a problem with the audiovisualequipment at a venue or over booking at a hotel. A customer may well be very satisfied if the organization turns the critical incident from a negative to a positive through its actions.

3 Quality has to be related to the price the customer or consumer is willing or able to afford. For example, a leisure traveller who has bought a £250 last-minute economy discount ticket from Paris to Singapore cannot expect to enjoy the same benefits as a

First Class passenger who has paid £3000 for the same journey. On the other hand, whatever price has been paid customers and consumers have a right to expect certain basic benefits such as safety. Organizations which serve business travellers are always trying to ensure that the quality they offer matches, or preferably exceeds, the expectations of their clients. Customer questionnaires are a crucial element of such activities. Exhibit 10.1 gives an example of one such questionnaire for the Hilton Hotel at Amsterdam Schipol Airport in the Netherlands. *Competition:* There is growing competition in most sectors of business travel and tourism. The ways in which competition is increasing. Let us now look at some of the ways in which the business travel and tourism industry has sought to respond to this more competitive situation.

NATURAL TOURISM PRODUCTS

These include natural resources such as areas, climate and its setting, landscape and natural environment. Natural resources are frequently the key elements in a destination's attraction.

Let us look at some examples:

- Countryside
- Climate- temperature, rains, snowfall, days of sunshine
- Natural Beauty- landforms, hills, rocks, gorges, terrain
- Water- lakes, ponds, rivers, waterfalls, springs
- Flora and Fauna
- Wildlife
- Beaches
- Islands
- Spas
- Scenic Attractions

The climate of a tourist destination is often an important attraction. Good weather plays an important role in making a holiday. Millions of tourists from countries with extreme climates visit beaches in search of fine weather and sunshine. The sunshine and clear sea breeze at the beaches have attracted many people for a very long time. In fact, development of spas and resorts along the sea coasts in many countries were a result of the travellers. urge to enjoy good weather and sunshine. In Europe, countries like France, Italy, Spain and Greece have developed beautiful beach resorts.

North Europeans visit the Mediterranean coast searching for older resorts like Monte Carlo, Nice and Cannes on the Riviera and new resorts in Spain and Italy. Beautiful beaches of India, Sri Lanka, and Thailand, Indonesia and Australia and some other new destinations are more examples of how good weather can attract tourists. All these areas capitalise on good weather. Destinations with attractive winter climates, winter warmth and sunshine are also important centres of tourist attraction.

Many areas have become important winter holiday resorts attracting a large number of tourists. Around these winter resorts, winter sport facilities have been installed to cater to the increasing needs of tourists. People from warm climates travel especially to see snowfall and enjoy the cold climate. In countries with tropical climates, many upland cool areas have been developed as 'hill stations'. Hence climate is of great significance as a tourism product. The scenery and natural beauty of places has always attracted tourists. Tourists enjoy nature in all its various forms. There are land forms like mountains, canyons, coral re-efs, cliffs, etc. One of the great all time favourite tourist destination is the Grand Canyon, Arizona. Mountain ranges like the Himalayas, Kilimanjaro, and Swiss Alps, etc.

There are water forms like rivers, lakes waterfalls, geysers, glaciers, etc. The Niagara Falls shared by Canada and the United States is an example of how scenic waterfalls attract tourists. Lake Tahoe in California and the, deserts of Egypt are other examples of great tourist products. Other great natural wonders that attract tourists are the Giants Causeway of Northern Ireland, the Geysers of Iceland, the glaciers of the Alps, the forests of Africa etc. Vegetation like forests, grasslands, moors deserts, etc. has all been developed as tourist products. Flora and Fauna attract many a tourist. Tourists like to know the various types of plants and trees that they see and which trees are seen in which seasons.

There are many plants which are specific to certain regions and many times students and travellers visit those areas especially to see those varieties of plants. Thick forest covers, attract tourists who enjoy trekking and hunting activities. Fauna attracts tourists who like to watch birds, wild mammals, reptiles and other exotic and rare animals. Countries in South East Asia have crocodile gardens, bird sanctuaries, and other tourist products that display the fauna of their region. Spas are gaining popularity as modern tourism products all over the world. While most parts of the world have their own therapies and treatments that are effective in restoring the wellness and beauty of people.

New kinds of health tours that are gaining popularity are spa tours. Spas offer the unique advantages of taking the best from the West and the East, combining them with the indigenous system and offering best of the two worlds. For example Swedish massages work well with the Javanese Mandy, lulur, aromatherapy, reflexology and traditional ayurvedic procedures. Now various spa products are being combined with yoga, meditation, and pranayama, giving a holistic experience to tourists. Spa treatments are now combined with other medical treatments to treat blood pressure, insomnia, depression, paralysis and some other diseases. People are now travelling to spas and clinics for curative baths and medical treatment.

In some countries like Italy, Austria and Germany, great importance is given to spa treatments. In Russia along the Black Sea coast and in the foothills of the Caucasus Mountains, there are many world famous sanatoria where millions of Russians and international tourists throng every year. Beach tourism is very popular among the tourists today. Tourists of all age groups, backgrounds, cultures and countries enjoy this tourism product. Besides attraction and saleability, beach holidaying has lead to overall development of tourism in many parts of the world.

The basic importance of beaches is that they provide aesthetic and environmental value of the beach such as beautiful natural scenery with golden sands, lush green vegetation and bright blue sky. The water should be clear, free of currents and underwater rocks. Beach tourism activities include water and land resource use. The water usage involves swimming, surfing, sailing, wind surfing, water scootering, Para- sailing, motorboat rides, etc. The land use has multifacets like sunbathing, recreational areas for tourists (parks, playgrounds, clubs, theatre, amusement parks, casinos, cultural museums, etc.), accommodation facilities (hotels, cottages, villas, camping sites, etc.), car and bus parking areas, entertainment and shopping complexes, access roads and transportation network.

Due to its multidimensional requirements the beach product needs special care. A beach resort needs to be developed as an integrated complex to function as a self-contained community. Environmental management should also ensure the availability of necessary infrastructure in the immediate hinterland to the coastal region in support of the development on the coast to maintain its ecosystem. Islands abound with natural beauty, with the rare flora and fauna and tribes. This makes islands an ideal place for adventure, nature and culture lovers to visit. This tourist product has great scope as these islands are being developed as tourist paradises. For example, Hawaii, Maldives, Mauritius, Tahiti, Andaman and Nicobar Islands, etc. has developed with tourism activity over the past few decades.

The topography is generally undulating and they offer natural scenic beauty with exotic flora and fauna. Most of these islands have places of worship like churches, temples, etc. As an added attraction some of these islands have developed as tax havens thereby encouraging commercial development of these economies.

They offer social and cultural attractions as tourists can experience the local lifestyle, local food, fairs and festivals, etc. Scenic attractions, like good weather, are very important factors in the development of tourism.

Breath-taking mountain scenery and the coastal stretches exert a strong fascination on the tourist the magnificent mountain ranges provide an atmosphere of peace and tranquillity. Tourists visiting the northern slopes of the Alps in Switzerland and Austria and the southern slopes in Italy and also the Himalayan slopes of India and Nepal for the first time, cannot but be charmed by their physical magnificence.

THE BENEFITS OF BUSINESS TRAVEL AND TOURISM FOR DESTINATIONS

Given the expenditure levels of business travellers, it is not surprising that many destinations are keen to attract all forms of business tourism. The main benefits of business tourism for destinations. There is also a belief that business tourism can lead to increased inward investment. While there is little empirical evidence to support this idea, the suggestion is that the business tourist who is an owner of an enterprise visits the destination as a business tourist, likes what he or she sees and decides to set up a new business or transfer their existing business to the destination.

It is not surprising therefore that business tourism has been used as a key point of the strategy of both:

- Industrial cities, seeking to diversify and modernize their economies, such as Birmingham in the UK
- Traditional coastal resorts which are keen to extend their season and attract higher spending business tourists, such as Brighton and Bournemouth in the UK.

Of course, business tourism can also bring problems for destinations in terms of congestion and the attraction of criminals who see the business tourists as easy, lucrative targets. Serving the demanding business traveller can also force destinations to make large investments in infrastructure such as airports and convention centres, with no guarantee these will repay the investment. Nevertheless, overall it appears that business tourism is a positive phenomenon, as far as destinations are concerned.

THE RELATIONSHIP BETWEEN BUSINESS TOURISM AND LEISURE TOURISM

There are numerous links between business tourism and leisure tourism in terms of both the supply side and the demand side. The business tourism makes use of a lot of the same supply-side elements as leisure tourism, although it also needs additional services that a leisure tourist does not require. Of course, business tourists often use the elements they share with leisure tourism in different ways to leisure tourists. For example, while leisure tourists visit a museum during normal opening hours, conference delegates probably visit in the evening for a private visit and reception with drinks and canape´s. Business tourists also often pay more for the use of the same hotels at airports as used by the leisure traveller, because business travellers often need, or at least demand, better quality services or extra specialist facilities, compared to the leisure tourist.

However, in terms of the demand side, there are four ways in which the world of business tourism and leisure tourism overlap, as follows:

1 The business traveller usually becomes a leisure traveller once the working day is over.

2 Conferences often include a programme of leisure activities in between conference sessions for delegates.
3 Incentive travel, as we saw earlier, involves offering leisure travel as a reward for good performance at work.
4 Many business travellers are accompanied by their partners and/or children. These accompanying persons are to all intents and purposes leisure travellers for all or most of the duration of their trip.

PROBLEMS OF STUDYING BUSINESS TRAVEL AND TOURISM

For those wishing to study this dynamic sector of tourism, there are two real problems. First, there is the lack of literature and reliable up-to-date statistics. Often what data there is has been collected on different bases in different countries, which makes comparison very difficult. Second, there is the problem of terminology. There are national and cultural differences in the terms used within the business tourism industry. We hope that you will find our Glossary of Terms contained in Part Six of this book, useful.

EXPANDING BUSINESS THROUGH ADVERTISING

The need for advertising of the several prospect of the hotel is utmost important for the development of the business in long term. It will create awareness of the people. Advertising is typically paid communication through a non-personal medium in which the sponsor is identified and the message is controlled. However, it can also include variations, such as publicity, public relations, personal selling, product placement, sponsorship, underwriting, and sales promotion. Major advertisers are typically corporations, but may also include schools, the military, political candidates, advocacy groups, churches, and other organizations that pay to have their message delivered to an audience. The media through which the message is delivered are varied: they include network and cable TV, radio, magazines, newspapers, the internet, billboards, handmade signs, sky writing, and bumper stickers; the list is almost endless.

Strictly speaking, word-of-mouth is not advertising because it is not paid, the message is not controlled, and it is delivered by a personal rather than non-personal medium. Ironically, word-of-mouth communications are often far more effective than advertising campaigns that may have cost many millions of dollars. “Buzz advertising” is a recent term used to describe an attempt by advertisers to simulate word-of-mouth communications.

In ancient times, commercial messages and political campaign displays have been found in the ruins of Pompeii. Egyptians used papyrus to create sales messages and wall posters, while lost-and-found advertising on papyrus was common in Greece and Rome. Wall or rock painting for commercial advertising is another manifestation of an ancient media advertising form, which is present to this day in many parts of Asia, Africa, and South America. For instance, the tradition of wall painting can be traced back to Indian rock-art paintings that goes back to 4000 BC. As printing developed in the 15th and 16th century, advertising expanded to include handbills. In the 17th century advertisements started to appear in weekly newspapers in England.

These early print ads were used mainly to promote books,and newspapers which became increasingly affordable thanks to the printing press, and medicines, which were increasingly sought after as disease ravaged Europe. However, false advertising and so-called "quack" ads became a problem, which ushered in regulation of advertising content.

As the economy was expanding during the 19th century, the need for advertising grew at the same pace. In the United States, classified ads became popular, filling pages of newspapers with small print messages promoting all kinds of goods. The success of this advertising format led to the growth of mail-order advertising such as the Sears Catalogue, at one time referred to as the "Farmer's Bible". In 1843 the first advertising agency was established by Volney Palmer in Philadelphia. At first the agencies were just brokers for ad space in newspapers, but it wasn't until N.W. Ayer and Son came along, advertising agencies started to take over responsibility for the content as well. N.W. Ayer and Son was the first full service Ad Agency. They were also the first agency to start to charge commission on ads.

When commercial radio stations began broadcasting in the early 1920's, the programmes were aired without advertising. Many radio stations were established by radio equipment manufacturers and retailers. Programming was provided to sell radio transmitters and receivers. The radio station owners soon realized they could earn more money by selling sponsorship rights to other businesses. In those days, each show was usually sponsored by a single business, in exchange for a brief mention of the sponsor at the beginning and end of the show. This practice was carried over to televsion in the late 1940's and early 1950's.

In the early 1950's, the Dumont television network began the modern trend of selling advertisement time to multiple sponsors. Dumont had trouble finding sponsors for many of their programmes and compensated by selling smaller blocks of advertising time to several businesses. This eventually became the norm for the commercial television industry in the United States.

The 1960s saw advertising transform into a modern, more scientific approach in which creativity was allowed to shine, producing unexpected messages that made advertisements more tempting to consumers' eyes. The Volkswagen ad campaign featuring such headlines as "Think Small" and "Lemon" ushered in the era of modern advertising by promoting a "position" or "unique selling proposition" designed to associate each brand with a specific idea in the reader or viewer's mind. The late 1980s and early 1990s saw the introduction of cable television and particularly MTV. Pioneering the concept of the music video, MTV ushered in a new type of advertising: the consumer tunes in for the advertisement, rather than it being a byproduct or afterthought. As cable (and later satellite) television became increasingly prevalent, "specialty" channels began to emerge, and eventually entire channels, such as QVC and Home Shopping Network and ShopTV, devoted to advertising merchandise, where again the consumer tuned in for the ads.

Marketing through the Internet opened new frontiers for advertisers and led to the "dot-com" boom of the 1990s. Entire corporations operated solely on advertising revenue, offering everything from coupons to free Internet access. At the turn of the 21st century, the search engine Google revolutionized online advertising by emphasizing contextually relevant, unobtrusive ads intended to help, rather than inundate, users. This has led to a plethora of similar efforts and an increasing trend of interactive advertising.

The share of advertising spending relative to total economic output (GDP) has changed little across large changes in media. For example, in the U.S. in 1925, the main advertising media were newspapers, magazines, signs on streetcars, and outdoor posters. Advertising spending as a share of U.S. GDP was about 2.6 per cent in 1925. By 1998, television and radio had become major advertising media. Nonetheless, advertising spending as a share of GDP was slightly lower — about 2.4 per cent.

A recent advertising innovation is "guerrilla promotions", which involve unusual approaches such as staged encounters in public places, giveaways of products such as cars that are covered with brand messages, and interactive advertising where the viewer can respond to become part of the advertising message. This reflects an increasing trend of interactive and "embedded" ads, such as via product placement, having consumers vote through text messages, and various innovations utilizing social networking sites (*e.g.,* Myspace).

PRODUCT ADVERTISING

Certain products use a specific form of advertising known as "Custom publishing". This form of advertising is usually targeted at a specific segment of society, but may also "draw" the attention of others. The same advertising techniques used to promote commercial goods and services can be used to inform, educate and motivate the public about non-commercial issues, such as AIDS, political ideology, energy conservation, religious recruitment, and deforestation.

Advertising, in its non-commercial guise, is a powerful educational tool capable of reaching and motivating large audiences. "Advertising justifies its existence when used in the public interest - it is much too powerful a tool to use solely for commercial purposes." - Attributed to Howard Gossage by David Ogilvy Public service advertising, non-commercial advertising, public interest advertising, cause marketing, and social marketing are different terms for (or aspects of) the use of sophisticated advertising and marketing communications techniques (generally associated with commercial enterprise) on behalf of non-commercial, public interest issues and initiatives.

In the United States, the granting of television and radio licenses by the FCC is contingent upon the station broadcasting a certain amount of public service advertising. To meet these requirements, many broadcast stations in America air the bulk of their required Public Service Announcements during the late night or early morning when the smallest percentage of viewers are watching, leaving more day and prime time commercial slots available for high-paying advertisers.

Public service advertising reached its height during World Wars I and II under the direction of several governments. Commercial advertising media can include wall paintings, billboards, street furniture components, printed flyers, radio, cinema and television ads, web banners, web popups, skywriting, bus stop benches, magazines, newspapers, town criers, sides of buses, taxicab doors and roof mounts, musical stage shows, subway platforms and trains, elastic bands on disposable diapers, stickers on apples in supermarkets, the opening section of streaming audio and video, posters, chicken niblets, and the backs of event tickets and supermarket receipts. Any place an "identified" sponsor pays to deliver their message through a medium is advertising.

Covert advertising embedded in other entertainment media is known as product placement. A more recent version of this is advertising in film, by having a main character use an item or other of a definite brand - an example is in the movie Minority Report, where Tom Cruise's character Tom Anderton owns a computer with the Nokia logo clearly written in the top corner, or his watch engraved with the Bulgari logo.

Another example of advertising in film is in I, Robot, where main character played by Will Smith mentions his Converse shoes several times, calling them "classics," because the film is set far in the future. Cadillac chose to advertise in the movie The Matrix Reloaded, which as a result contained many scenes in which Cadillac cars were used. Similarly, product placement for Omega Watches, BMW and Aston-Martin cars are featured in recent James Bond films, most notably, Casino Royale.

The TV commercial is generally considered the most effective mass-market advertising format and this is reflected by the high prices TV networks charge for commercial airtime during popular TV events. The annual Super Bowl football game in the United States is known as much for its commercial advertisements as for the game itself, and the average cost of a single thirty-second TV spot during this game has reached $2.5 million (as of 2006).

Virtual advertisements may be inserted into regular television programming through computer graphics. It is typically inserted into otherwise blank backdrops or used to replace local billboards that are not relevant to the remote broadcast audience. More controversially, virtual billboards may be inserted into the background where none existing in real-life. Virtual product placement is also possible. Increasingly, other mediums such as those discussed below are overtaking television due to a shift towards consumer's usage of the Internet as well as devices such as TiVo.

Advertising on the World Wide Web is a recent phenomenon. Prices of Web-based advertising space are dependent on the "relevance" of the surrounding web content and the traffic that the web site receives. E-mail advertising is another recent phenomenon. Unsolicited bulk E-mail advertising is known as "spam". Some companies have proposed to place messages or corporate logos on the side of booster rockets and the International Space Station. Controversy exists on the effectiveness of subliminal advertising, and the pervasiveness of mass messages.

Unpaid advertising (also called word of mouth advertising), can provide good exposure at minimal cost. Personal recommendations ("bring a friend", "sell it"), spreading buzz, or achieving the feat of equating a brand with a common noun ("Xerox" = "photocopier", "Kleenex" = tissue, and "Vaseline" = petroleum jelly) — these are the pinnacles of any advertising campaign. However, some companies oppose the use of their brand name to label an object.

The most common method for measuring the impact of mass media advertising is the use of the rating point (rp) or the more accurate target rating point (trp). These two measures refer to the percentage of the universe of the existing base of audience members that can be reached by the use of each media outlet in a particular moment in time. The difference between the two is that the rating point refers to the percentage to the entire universe while the target rating point refers to the percentage to a particular segment or target.

This becomes very useful when focusing advertising efforts on a particular group of people:

- For example, think of an advertising campaign targeting a female audience aged 25 to 45. While the overall rating of a TV show might be well over 10 rating points it might very well happen that the same show in the same moment of time is generating only 2.5 trps (being the target: women 25-45). This would mean that while the show has a large universe of viewers it is not necessarily reaching a large universe of women in the ages of 25 to 45 making it a less desirable location to place an ad for an advertiser looking for this particular demographic. Conversely, a TV show with a low overall rating point may be more successful at selling ads when its target rating points are high. In the United States, networks like the WB and FOX have had success with shows based on this premise; the shows had low overall ratings points, but delivered strong target rating points in the desired demographic.

ADVERTISEMENT IMPACT

The impact of advertising has been a matter of considerable debate and many different claims have been made in different contexts. During debates about the banning of cigarette advertising, a common claim from cigarette manufacturers was that cigarette advertising does not encourage people to smoke who would not otherwise. The (eventually successful) opponents of advertising, on the other hand, claim that advertising does in fact increase consumption.

According to many media sources, the past experience and state of mind of the person subjected to advertising may determine the impact that advertising has. Children under the age of four may be unable to distinguish advertising from other television programmes, whilst the ability to determine the truthfulness of the message may not be developed until the age of 8.

As advertising and marketing efforts become increasingly ubiquitous in modern Western societies, the industry has come under criticism of groups such as AdBusters via culture jamming which criticizes the media and consumerism using advertising's own techniques. The industry is accused of being one of the engines powering a convoluted economic mass production system which promotes consumption. Recognizing the social impact of advertising, Mediawatch-uk, a British special interest group, works to educate consumers about how they can register their concerns with advertisers and regulators.

It has developed educational materials for use in schools. The award-winning book, Made You Look How Advertising Works and Why You Should Know, by former Mediawatch (a feminist organisation founded by Ann Simonton not linked to mediawatch-uk) president Shari Graydon, provides context for these issues for young readers.

Public interest groups are increasingly suggesting that access to the mental space targeted by advertisers should be taxed, in that at the present moment that space is being freely taken advantage of by advertisers with no compensation paid to the members of the public who are thus being intruded upon. This kind of tax would be a Pigovian tax in that it would act to reduce what is now increasingly seen as a public nuisance.

Efforts to that end are gathering momentum, with Arkansas and Maine considering bills to implement such taxation. Florida enacted such a tax in 1987 but was forced to repeal it after six months, as a result of a concerted effort by national commercial interests, which withdrew planned conventions, causing major losses to the tourism industry, and cancelled advertising, causing a loss of 12 million dollars to the broadcast industry alone.

An extensively documented effect is the control and vetoing of free information by the advertisers. Any negative information on a company or its products or operations often results in pressures from the company to withdraw such information lines, threatening to cut their ads. This behaviour makes the editors of the media self-censor content that might upset their ad payers. The bigger both companies are, the bigger their relation gets, maximizing control over a single information. Advertisers may try to minimize information about or from consumer groups, or consumer controlled purchasing initiatives (as joint purchase systems), or consumer controlled quality information systems.

Another indirect effect of advertising is to modify the very nature of the communication media where it is shown. Media that get most of their revenues from publicity try to make their medium a good place for communicating ads before anything else.

The most clear example is television, where this means trying to make the public stay for a long time and in a mental state that encourages spectators not to switch the channel through the ads. Programmes that are low in mental stimulus and require light concentration and are varied are best for long sitting times. These make for much easier emotional jumps to ads, which can become more entertaining than regular shows. A simple way to understand the objectives in television programming is to compare contents from channels paid and chosen by the viewer with channels that get their income mainly from advertisements.

There have been increasing efforts to protect the public interest by regulating the content and the reach of advertising. Some examples are the ban on television tobacco advertising imposed in many countries, and the total ban on advertising to children under twelve imposed by the Swedish government in 1991. Though that regulation continues in effect for broadcasts originating within the country, it has been weakened by the European Court of Justice, which has found that Sweden was obliged to accept whatever programming was targeted at it from neighbouring countries or via satellite.

In Europe and elsewhere there is a vigourous debate on whether and how much advertising to children should be regulated. This debate was exacerbated by a report released by the Kaiser Family Foundation in February 2004 which suggested that food advertising targeting children was an important factor in the epidemic of childhood obesity in the United States.

In many countries - namely New Zealand, South Africa, Canada, and many European countries - the advertising industry operates a system of self-regulation. Advertisers, advertising agencies and the media agree on a code of advertising standards that they attempt to uphold. The general aim of such codes is to ensure that any advertising is 'legal, decent, honest and truthful'. Some self-regulatory organizations are funded by the industry, but remain independent, with the intent of upholding the standards or codes (like the Advertising Standards Authority in the UK). Naturally, many advertisers view governmental regulation or even self-regulation as intrusion of their freedom of speech or a necessary evil. Therefore, they employ a wide-variety of linguistic devices to bypass regulatory laws (*e.g.,* giving English words in bold and French translations in fine print to deal with the Article 12 of the 1994 Toubon Law limiting the use of English in French advertising); The advertising of controversial products such as cigarettes and condoms is subject to government regulation in many countries. For instance, the tobacco industry is required by law in India and Pakistan to display warnings cautioning consumers about the health hazards of their products. Linguistic variation is often used by advertising as a creative device to reduce the impact of such requirement.

With the dawn of the Internet have come many new advertising opportunities. Popup, Flash, banner, advergaming, and e-mail advertisements (the last often being a form of spam) abound. Each year, greater sums are paid to obtain a commercial spot during the Super Bowl, which is by most measures considered to be the most important football game of the year. Companies attempt to make these commercials sufficiently entertaining that members of the public will actually want to watch them.

Another problem is people recording shows on DVRs (ex. TiVo). These devices allow users to record the programmes for later viewing enabling them to fast forward through commercials. Additionally, as more seasons or "Boxed Sets" come out of Television shows; fewer people are watching their shows on TV. However, the fact that these sets are sold, means that the company will additionally receive profits from the sales of these sets. To counter this effect, many advertisers have opted for product placement on TV shows like Survivor.

Particularly since the rise of "entertaining" advertising, some people may like an advert enough that they wish to watch it later or show a friend. In general, the advertising community has not yet made this easy, although some have used the Internet to widely distribute their adverts to anyone wishing to see or hear them.

Another significant trend to note for the future of advertising is the growing importance of niche or targeted ads. Also brought about by the Internet and the theory of The Long Tail, advertisers will have an increasing ability to reach narrow audiences. In the past, the most efficient way to deliver a message was to blanket the largest mass market audience possible. However, usage tracking, customer profiles and the growing popularity of niche content brought about by everything from blogs to social networking sites, provides advertisers with audiences that are smaller but much better defined, leading to ads that are more relevant to viewers and more effective for companies marketing products.

Among others, Comcast Spotlight is one such advertiser employing this method in their video on demand menus. These advertisements are targeted to a specific group and can be viewed by anyone wishing to find out more about a particular business or practice at any time, right from their home. This causes the viewer to become proactive and actually choose what advertisements they want to view.

9

Issues of Sustainability and Eco-Friendliness for the Hospitality Industry

ECO-TOURISM IN INDIA

KERALA ECO-TOURISM

The naturally beautiful and exquisite Kerala landscape is one of the greenest destinations in India and is the perfect place to go on eco-tourism vacations. The clean and tranquil Kerala backwaters, the soothing velvety Kerala hills and a riotous explosion of greens in the intoxicating Kerala wilds offers countless opportunities for eco-tourism and nature vacations. The entire Kerala landscape is generously covered with coconut palms, pineapple groves, banana trees, Pandanus plants, thick leafy plants, dense forests and neatly clipped tea bushes. Acres of submerged paddy fields located in perfect harmony with the winding Kerala backwaters and the gentle rolling Kerala hills are heavenly paradisiacal eco-tourism vacation destinations.

Regale the verdant Kerala beauty on your eco-tourism vacations to Kerala, South India with Kerala India Vacations. Visit the fascinating Kerala wildlife destinations and spot rare wild animals lazing in their natural habitat and enjoy the magic of nature. Eco-tourism in Kerala, South India is a fast developing sector and the state government is making extra efforts to promote eco-tourism.

Among the manifold advantages of promoting eco-tourism in Kerala, South India one very important aspect is revenue generation and environment conservation at the same time. The concept of eco-tourism basically means that you get to visit the exotic nature rich tour destinations but at the same time you must take care not to soil the beauty of the region by not using polythene bags and other materials or things such as tin cans, wrappers etc that adversely affect the environment.

Kerala India Vacations guides you through the lush green paths within acres of rubber plantations so that you can experience first hand the incomparable natural beauty of green Kerala, South India on your eco-tourism vacations. Kerala, South India happens to be one of the leading producers of rubber in India though rubber is not a native Indian plant and was introduced by the Dutch colonialists, in fact Kerala accounts for 92 per cent of the rubber produced in India. Stay at a luxury resort or a farmhouse near a Kerala rubber plantation and enjoy the warm hospitality of the Kerala rubber plantations during your eco-tourism vacations to Kerala, South India and be fascinated by the rural Kerala lifestyle while you observe busy twittering birds, brightly coloured butterflies and squirrels scurrying here and there. Admire the thick shapely leaves on straight trunks that glisten in the bright sun.

Botanically known as Havea brasiliensis, a single rubber plant takes about 7 years to mature and can be harvested for latex (processed for natural rubber) for almost 20 years. The local rubber tappers who stay close to these lush rubber plantations harvest latex from these trees. Pineapple is planted as an intercrop in most of the Kerala rubber plantations so you get to taste the juicy Mauritius pineapple variety while on your eco-tourism vacations to the scenic Kerala rubber plantations. Kottayam in Kerala, South India is an important Centre of commercial rubber plantations set on the picturesque banks of the serene palm fringed Kerala backwaters. Extensive rubber plantations cover the hillocks wrapped by silver ribbons of the fascinating Kerala backwaters, not a sight you would like to miss while on your eco-tourism tours to Kerala, South India.

Acres of tea plantations interspersed with shade fruit trees wrap the gentle Kerala hill slopes in a warm embrace and create soothing and striking vistas for you to visit on your Kerala eco-tourism vacations. Rows of neatly clipped tea bushes carpet the Kerala hills on the Western Ghats in Kerala, south India and offer you ample opportunity to gaze at the naturally enthralling Kerala beauty at its beatific best while on your Kerala India eco-tourism vacations.

The Britishers introduced the tradition of tea plantations in India. Tea bushes have the potential to grow to tree heights though they are kept neatly trimmed to waist height to make it feasible for the plantation workers to pluck tealeaves without much difficulty. Gaze at the lovely Kerala tea plantations while on your eco-tourism vacations and mark the fact that each tea bush is planted at a distance of 1 to 1.5 meter from each other along the contours of the landscape. Stay at the resorts and clean home-like accommodations on the Kerala tea plantations and spend your eco-tourism vacations in Kerala, South India in the midst of pure undulating greens. Watch the plantation workers plucking tealeaves and filling the baskets slung on their backs while you enjoy nature treks.

Usually it's the women who are employed for plucking tealeaves on these tea plantations in Kerala, South India. These women work in unison and sing peppy songs while plucking tealeaves and move along the rows of tea bushes in perfect rhythm. Kerala, South India has some of the highest tea estates located in India. Munnar is one of the most popular Kerala hill stations, which is known for its sweeping tea plantations. Some of the popular tea plantations in Kerala,

South India are located at Peerumadu that is situated at a height of 914-meters above the sea level, Anayirankal that has acres of tea plantations located in the midst of dense evergreen forests and a few other Kerala hill stations that are definitely worth visiting on your Kerala eco-tourism tours to Kerala, South India.

Wander at leisure on the aromatic Kerala spice plantations during your Kerala India eco-tourism Vacations. Stay at the spice plantation farmhouses with the plantation owners and experience the magical charm of staying in the midst of luxuriant plantations laden heavily with a combination of scents of the various spices that are grown on these extensive plantations. Though you can visit spice plantations almost all over beautiful Kerala, Periyar is one of the most popular spice districts in Kerala, South India. This absolutely beautiful hill district is covered with a variety of spice plantations that lie close to the famous Periyar wildlife sanctuary.

Shop for rare spices at the local Kerala spice markets and inhale the intoxicating aroma of cinnamon, cardamom, pepper, ginger, turmeric, curry leaves and other spices. Besides the cultivation of these traditional Kerala spices the Kerala plantation owners have also taken to growing spices such as rosemary, oregano, mint, vanilla, bay leaves, basil, thyme and others. Discover the secret of the mouthwatering Kerala cuisine as you visit the acres of Kerala spice plantations on your eco-tourism vacations with Kerala India Vacations. Spices are basically fragrant substances of vegetable origin with distinct flavors used in selective combinations to give a special flavor to the exotic Indian cuisine.

Enjoy bird watching tours and nature treks to the lovely Kerala spice plantations with Kerala India Vacations and experience the Kerala natural beauty at its aromatic best. Watch the locals work on the extensive spice plantations and observe closely the way of life in these Kerala spice plantations and enjoy your eco-tourism vacations thoroughly.

Orissa Eco-tourism

Organized by Tourism of Orissa offers you the best seats in the house to attend what is essentially a spectacular show of competing colours, cacophony of voices, a jumble of animal instincts and raw emotions. No, we aren't talking about a Broadway show or a Hollywood musical production. Eco-tourism in Orissa is what concerns us at Tourism of Orissa. With Eco-tourism in Orissa tour package, offered by Tourism of Orissa, you get to see all the shades of the diverse ecological system that reside within the state of Orissa. Eco-tourism in Orissa may revolve around water bodies or beaches or national parks and wildlife sanctuaries alone or, it can be a combination of all these features that make Orissa such as enticing choice as a destination for eco travel and tours.

While hot springs (Atri and Tarabalo), lakes (Chilika), waterfalls (Badaghagra, Khandadhar) and reservoirs (Hirakud, Indravati) in Orissa have tourists lining up, the beaches of Orissa (Puri, Chandrabhaga, Gopalpur, Chandipur) have dazzled international and national tourist for centuries with their pristine beauty and positive vibes. Orissa's varying topography - from the wooded Eastern Ghats to the fertile river basin - has proven ideal for evolution of compact and unique ecosystems. Thereby creating such treasure troves of flora and fauna that even seem inviting to many migratory species of birds and reptiles.

Bhitar Kanika National Park is famous for its second largest mangrove ecosystem. The bird sanctuary in Chilika (Asia's biggest brackish water lake) and the tiger reserve and waterfalls in Simlipal National Park are integral part of any eco tours in Orissa, arranged by Tourism of Orissa. The Gharial Sanctuary at Tikarpada and the Olive Ridley Sea Turtles in Gahirmatha turtle sanctuary also feature on the list of avid nature watchers. The city wildlife sanctuaries of Chandaka and Nandan Kanan are a must visit for the lessons they teach is conservation and revitalization of species from the brink of extinction. Since Orissa is so rich in culture - history, traditions and people, Tourism of Orissa can even have your eco tour clubbed with other tours in Orissa so that you get the best of al te worlds at a single destination called Orissa.

Eco-tourism in Chhattisgarh

Chhattisgarh, the 26th state of the Indian Union, is located in the central part of India. The newly formed Indian state of Chhattisgarh is famous for its enchantingly beautiful natural landscapes, rich cultural heritage and unique tribal populations. With over 44 per cent of its total area under forests, Chhattisgarh is also amongst the greenest states of India. The Chhattisgarh region is known as a great repository of biological diversity. The unique combination of rich cultural heritage and biological diversity makes Chhattisgarh an ideal eco-tourism destination with immense potentials for the growth eco-tourism the region. The Indian Govt. is actively collaborating with the local officials of the state to realize the full potential of Eco-tourism growth of the region in order to make Chhattisgarh as one of the most important eco-tourism destinations in India.

Chhattisgarh is one of the greenest states of India with over 44 per cent of its total area under lush forests. The forests of Chhattisgarh are not only known for their diverse flora and fauna but also contain about 88 species of medicinal plants. In addition, Chhattisgarh has also formulated several ecological plans and working in the direction to become the country's first bio-fuel self-reliant state by 2015. And to achieve this goal the green state has devised a plan to plant over 100 million saplings of Jatropa Carcus. Chhattisgarh is also unique in its wildlife population and has 3 National Parks and 11 Wildlife Sanctuaries, housing some of the rare wildlife and bird species. With so much of variety for Eco-tourism, Chhattisgarh promises to be an ideal holiday destination for nature lovers, wildlife enthusiasts and also for those who want to discover the unique tribal life of the region.

Chhattisgarh has identified some regions with a very high potentiality for eco-tourism. The green state has launched an eco-tourism project covering three potential tourist tracks - Raipur-Turtiria-Sirpur, Bilaspur-Achanakmar and Jagdalpur-Kanger Valley National Park. In addition, a number of herbal gardens and natural health resorts have been created with increased local participation. The use of ethno-medicine, which has been practiced by aboriginal tribes since centuries, predating even Ayurveda, is also being promoted in Chhattisgarh. The major eco-tourism attractions, which are getting prime attention in Chhattisgarh, include the protection and development of the wildlife areas, camping grounds and trekking facilities. With so many initiatives, Chhattisgarh is destined to become the most Favourite eco-tourism destination in India and few among best in the world.

Rajasthan Eco-tourism

The Cultures of the Rajasthan Desert are some of the most well preserved in India. We, at Marwar Eco-Cultural Tours and Travels, are passionate about this land, its cultures and its people and we want to share this passion with you. The Desert and its people will captivate you.

Because we are able to provide you with in-depth cultural information that you would not receive on other Tours. If you have an adventurous spirit or a cultural thirst to quench, we have a Tour that should surpass all of your expectations. We also offer opportunities to get involved with the people and assist in ongoing, non-profit projects. As an NGO, we have assistance projects in most villages we will visit. All of our guides are from Rajasthan, and most are village natives or indigenous people.

They have a great knowledge of local and regional history and are great storytellers. They will keep your attention for hours next to a fire, counting tales of kings and warlords; castles, forts and Havelis (mansions); rituals and traditions. You will see the camel herds, observe villagers' craftsmanship, and gain insight into indigenous nomadic lifestyles. We will show you the best of Rajasthan, and we are very flexible and can modify our tours according to the group's needs. You can also design your own tour. You dream it up; we'll do the rest. We will organize the tour and guide you according to your wishes. Among other things, we can arrange a visit to a marriage ceremony, a farming or agricultural tour, Handicraft and Jewelry making, a stay in an Ayurvedic (traditional Indian Medicine) clinic, and more.

Madhya Pradesh Eco-tourism

Eco-tourism signifies to save the environment around us and preserving the natural luxuries and forest life. Whether it's about a nature camp or organizing trekking trips towards the unspoilt and inaccessible regions, one should always keep in mind not to create any mishap or disturbance in the life cycle of nature. A destination enveloped in magic, Madhya Pradesh is one of the most popular tourist destination in India. It's many tourist destinations are, by far, some of the most magical locales in the world.

With the highest mountains, beautiful wildlife, a cosmopolitan heritage from different civilizations, it is so rightly called tourist paradise. It has lot to offer from breathtaking natural vistas, amazing architecture, rich culture, and a warm hearted society of people living in virtual harmony.

Himachal Pradesh Eco-tourism

The majestic coniferous trees from an enchanting backdrop to the mountains with broad-leafed species like the Oaks, Maples, Birdcherry, Hazelnut, Walnut, Horsechestnut and Rhododendrons adding grandeur to the landscape. Whereas the ivies clinging to the trunks of stately Cedars appear to veil secrets of Nature, the vines flowing from atop the trees seem to invite the visitors with open arms. The violas popping up from under the forest floor and the riot of colours provided by the anemones, primulas, buttercups and many other herbs in the alpine meadows lay a colourful feast before eyes of the beholder.

Besides plants. the State also provides a very congenial habitat to a wide variety of Himalayan fauna. The Himalyan Tahar and the Ibex can be spotted as silhouettes on the high ridges in the trans-Himalayas. The Brown Bear and Musk Deer roam happily in the temperate forests, in the company of colourful pheasants including the Monal, the Western Hornes Tragopan, the Koklas and the Kalij. The lucky ones can even be traeted to rare sight of critically endangered species like the Snow Leopard and Snow Cock. Also known as the 'Abode of Gods', the State conjures up visions of ancient temples, with exquisitely carved wooden panels, occupying almost every hilltop and the festivities associated with these religious places. Even a casual glimpse at the traditionally attired local deities being carried in meticulously decorated palanquins, devotees dancing to the rhythmic play of traditional drums and clarions, leaves a lasting imptint on one's mind.

This natural and cultural richness of the State coupled with its simple peace loving people and traditional hospitality makes the State a most favoured tourist destination. Anybody with a zest for life, a spirit of adventure and a love for nature will find all that his heart desires amongest the pristine environs of Himachal Pradesh.

Uttaranchal Eco-tourism

Uttaranchal blessed with magnificent glaciers, majestic snow-clad mountains, gigantic and ecstatic peaks, valley of flowers, skiing slopes and dense forests, this Abode of Gods includes many shrines and places of pilgrimage. Char-dhams, the four most sacred and revered Hindu temples: Badrinath, Kedarnath, Gangotri and Yamunotri are nestled in the Mighty Mountains. A picturesque state, with a breathtaking panoramic view of Himalayas, Uttaranchal promises its tourists a visit full of fun and unforgettable moments.

Uttaranchal blessed with magnificent glaciers, majestic snow-clad mountains, gigantic and ecstatic peaks, valley of flowers, skiing slopes and dense forests, this Abode of Gods includes many shrines and places of pilgrimage. India's first National Park is cradled in the foothills of the Himalayas and spreads over an area of 520 sq. kms., along the bankds of the Ramganga river. The dense Sal forests of the Himalayan foothils and the tall grassy neadows make it one of the richest areas of northern India for the habitation of the big mammals.

MANAGEMENT STYLE IN THE HOSPITALITY INDUSTRY

It is widely accepted that managers' approach to employment relations, often referred to as management style, is the result of choices that are influenced by certain constraints. The nature of the product and labour markets, organizational status and structure, including size of workplace, and culture are chief among the factors thought to place constraints on managers. Managers, as much as workers and customers, are never truly free agents. We have already noted how economic, technical, social, legal and political factors external to the workplace provide boundaries that may constrain managers' behaviour and actions. We also discussed how managers' personal frame of reference will inform the choices they make about the strategies, policies and practices they pursue, and why power relationships are integral to this process. Of particular note here is the virtual absence of trade unions to act as a countervailing force to counteract managerial power. The HI sustains a mere 2 per cent trade union density.

Managers must be able to exercise choice otherwise we would not be able to account for variations in management style among similar types of firm. In seeking to control events managers may be constrained by their own rational thinking of what is good and bad, failing to recognize that opposites are often very closely related and may even coexist simultaneously. The right to manage is so deeply ingrained into behaviour and thinking that it may dominate over their tacit acceptance of a more pluralist ethos. Hence 'a constant underlying pressure within management both to resist any extension of joint regulation and to restore unilateral regulation wherever and whenever circumstances allow'. HRM is often seen as unitarist and a reassertion of managerial prerogative, especially the 'hard' version, even though the 'soft' variant contains some positive attributes.

While we can debate the extent to which particular constraints affect the choices that particular managers make in particular circumstances, this approach still implies a rationality that does not account for pragmatism, opportunism and reacting to events. This approach is beginning to emerge as an alternative. That said, we take as a universal truth that all HI employers place high priority on seeking to control labour costs. As we shall argue this is achieved predominantly through 'low road' practices that may be both intentional and/or the result of pragmatism or opportunism. This approach is so successful that managers have no incentive to take the 'high road'. Organizations that focus on quality in the service encounter exceptionally approach the management of employment by the 'high road' using more sophisticated and developmental HRM practices, but not necessarily in respect of the workforce as a whole.

Constraints and Choices

To cope with market uncertainties managers can opt for the external regulation of employment matters, choose to develop their own internal responses, or use a combination of both. Grimshaw et al. (2001) argue that internal and external market pressures mutually interact to shape employment strategy, generating a wide range of possibilities for different workforce groups. The weakening of national regulatory and collective bodies in the UK, and the accompanying widening of scope for managerial prerogative, has made managing an even more uncertain process.

Marchington and Parker (1990) suggest that stable product markets will encourage the development of 'high road' practices based on partnership, job security, systematic recruitment, selection, training and development, two-way communications and formal procedures. Turbulent market conditions, which affect large parts of the HI, militate against long-term policies, even in larger companies. They will drive 'low road' practices based on hire and fire, ad hoc recruitment, selection, training and development, low pay, one-way communication, if any, from management, and lack of procedures, reinforcing a culture of macho management.

If the economic climate deteriorates firms may be forced to change route towards 'low road' practices, graphically illustrated by the case of British Airways (BA). Keenoy (1997) identifies a wide-ranging programme of 'soft' measures, including improvements to communications and leadership, while maintaining a 'hard' approach to headcount. In respect of cabin crew, Boyd (2001) argues that 'soft' HRM in the form of a sanctimonious mission and policy statement may have provided a smoke screen for short-term, costrational HRM leading to work intensification.

Case study research has identified a more complex pattern of highly firm specific policy solutions in response to a variety of different internal and external pressures. Contradictory outcomes emerge as new policies capitalize on changing external conditions at the expense of organizational demands. New policies may be unsustainable where on aggregate they fail to develop workforce skills or fulfill career expectations. Considerable emphasis on recruitment and training in hotels, which is symptomatic of labour flux, militates against uptake of new HRM initiatives of a longer-term nature.

Organization status and structure, including size of workplace will also serve to constrain the extent to which managers can exercise choice. Not all managers own and control their own business, and in larger hotel companies, restaurant and public house chains, and contract catering firms, managers are themselves also workers reporting to a more senior manager. Managers' choices are constrained by organizational policies, as well as by the actions of other managers and subordinates.

Management is necessarily a messy business. Achieving organizational goals through people is a complex and political process, political in the sense that it involves choosing how to reconcile differences among colleagues of different status and power who may be senior managers, peers or subordinate workers. Some large HI organizations comprise many small workplaces, so we cannot necessarily generalize their management style to singlesite workplaces.

Owner managers of small firms have more freedom to make rules on the 'hoof', as there are no precedents or constraints from any higher authority. Surplus labour supply of amply skilled labour, and the simple division of labour are conducive to an ad hoc management style within the economic determinism approach of externalization. As Riley et al. (2000) note, productivity is largely a matter of matching supply to demand in the short term, because of the almost instantaneous impact of customer trends on labour supply. This dynamic instability based on stochastic demand creates and continually reinforces a short-term perspective where small unit structure creates a style of management that is good at improvising.

Reliance on a plentiful supply of unskilled labour from the labour market and hire and fire serve to enhance managerial power. The manager may be aware of the constraint of unfair dismissal legislation. By making a simple risk assessment, the manager will calculate that a fired worker will probably not bother to make a claim, if eligible, because alternative work is easily secured (and a replacement easily obtained). If the worker does proceed to employment tribunal, at worst there will be a cheap out-of-court settlement, because of the worker's low pay and short service.

Culture can be considered on three levels - organizational, national and occupational - with some crossover between the first two in the case of MNCs. Two American Case study 3.1 Workplace structure in the Australian hotel industry

Hotels may appear to be structured bureaucracies under the control of a general manager, but are essentially organic structures within which departmental managers have considerable autonomy and responsibility. Each department is a unique entity controlled by a manager skilled in that work who hires and fires, and determines the categories of labour to be used, the tasks to be performed and the timing of work. The autonomy and responsibility invested in departmental managers encourages an informal management style and a system of rule-making that shapes the pattern of labour use (initial engagements tend to be casual), and encourages the growth of informal work practices between manager and worker designed to engender loyalty and commitment. Departmentalization and labour flexibility forms part of the hierarchy of control, shifting transaction costs (of uncertainty) to the worker, protecting the hotel from unfair dismissal litigation, and using behaviour and discipline to determine permanent employment status.

Weak and low-status HRM within hotels militates against participation in new HRM practices, such as multi-skilling, because managers fear other departments may poach good staff. This acts as a barrier to strong internal labour markets, so the external market becomes a significant mechanism for the allocation of skill.

MNCs, McDonald's and Disney, have been hailed as 'influential models of excellence in the development of particular organisational cultures or systems of production and job design with their respective implications for management and the conduct of employee relations'. International chains display more sophisticated HRM, *e.g.*, in Greece. Larger units and those owned by foreign chains appear to veer towards the 'best practice' models of HRM. Organizational culture encapsulates 'the way we do things around here'. Culture and values underpin the organization's identity and core purpose and new initiatives in employment relations and HRM may entail programmes of culture change, especially where there is a conscious shift towards a service quality (SQ) culture.

Redman and Mathews (1998) argue that the traditional dichotomy between the 'high road' and the 'low road' has been increasingly challenged by effective quality management systems resulting in both improved quality and reduced costs. This reflects a new approach to corporate management. 'Organisational culture is rooted in the future and change' whereas work-based culture is rooted in the here and now. Occupational culture may be more readily identifiable within skilled occupations such as chefs, and may create adversity in the employment relationship where professional values conflict with commercial values. Employment relations systems reflect the society in which they operate.

ENVIRONMENTALLY RESPONSIBLE HOTELS

One component of ecotourism travelers can consider is environmentally responsible hotels. The concept of "green hotels"—hotels, motels, bed and breakfasts, lodges, and inns that use energy and other natural resources in environmentally responsible ways—is one that can be adopted not only by ecotourists but by anyone who travels, whether for business or pleasure. Hotels that adopt green practices help reduce the negative impact that hotel use has on the environment when they utilize renewable resources whenever possible, make efficient use of non-renewable resources, and ensure that any byproducts that result from their operations are reused or recycled.

Examples of green practices some hotels have adopted include rerouting waste water to irrigate their golf courses and salvaging the sludge to use as fertilizer; reducing laundry water temperatures from 90 °C to 60 °C, replacing incandescent lights with compact fluorescent lamps, installing low-flow shower head and low-flow toilets, offering a sheet and towel reuse Programmes whereby guests have their linens exchanged every two to three days instead of daily, installing solar panels to heat water, implementing a hotel-wide recycling Programmes, and replacing individual soaps and lotions with wall dispensers. Adoption of green practices typically helps hotels realize considerable savings that can range from several thousand to hundreds of thousands of dollars per year.

Although the number of hotels adopting green practices is growing, many have not yet embraced the concept. All travelers can support green hotels, encourage non-green hotels to adopt environmentally responsible practices, or engage in such practices themselves whenever they are hotel guests. Tourism event organizers can also distinguish themselves by explaining the criteria of where they stage events. Sadly, most ecotourism events have been held at hotels which have not distinguished themselves with green building, eco-efficient technology or community-friendly relations.

Hospitality as a Sociological Phenomenon

As hospitality is a sociological phenomenon, and because its norms differ in each society, there might be:

- Christian view of hospitality, Paul of Taurus urged hospitality on Christians, telling them that some people have thus entertained angels. Offering hospitality to pilgrims was a major duty of a monastery.
- Middle Eastern (Arab) rules of hospitality,
- Greek hospitality (Xenia is Greek for hospitality, but not necessarily norms that non-ancient Greeks follow),

A famous Greek legend Baucis and Philemon, recounts how they, though poor, were the only people of their town to offer hospitality to Zeus and Hermes, and so were blessed while the rest were transformed into fishes. Smoke weed everyday. Further, Zeus (as the manifestation Xenios) was the patron of hospitality and guests, ready to avenge any wrong done to a stranger

- And any other hospitality norms that differ in various world cultures,
- And very contemporary, in virtual communities like Wikipedia.

Contemporary Usage

Contemporary usage seems rather different from historical uses that lend it personal connotations. Today's hospitality conjures images of throwing good parties, gracious hosts entertaining, etiquette, Martha Stewart or even talk shows, or, the hospitality services industry as it relates to the entertainment and tourism business. On the other hand, hospitality used to be, and may still be, a serious personal duty or responsibility.

Hospitality is a prosaic word, even trivial, that everyone can relate to, perhaps even more concretely so outside of North American culture. It seems perhaps even a candidate for having something like a universal meaning or agreement, if not positive value.

In the western context, with its dynamic tension between Athens and Jerusalem, two phases can be distinguished with a very progressive transition: a hospitality based on an individually felt sense of duty, and one based on "official" institutions for organized but anonymous social services: special places for particular types of "strangers" such as the poor, orphan, ill, alien, criminal, etc. Perhaps this progressive institutionalization can be aligned to the transition between Middle Ages and Renaissance (Ivan Illich, The Rivers North of the Future).

Other Conceptions of Hospitality

In Middle Eastern Culture, it was considered a cultural norm to take care of the strangers and aliens living among you. These norms are reflected in many Biblical commands and examples, for instance: Perhaps the most extreme example is provided in Genesis. Lot provides hospitality to a group of angels (who he thinks are only men); when a mob tries to rape them, Lot goes so far as to offer his own daughters as a substitute, saying "Don't do anything to these men, for they have come under the protection of my roof.".

The obligations of both guests and hosts are stern. The bond is formed by eating salt under the roof, and is so strict that an Arab story tells of a thief who tasted something to see if it was sugar, and on realizing it was salt, put back all that he had taken and left.

Cultural Value or Norm

Hospitality as a cultural norm or value is established sociological phenomenon that people study and write papers about.

Star

Stars are often used as symbols for classification purposes. In particular, a set of one to five stars is employed to categorize hotels. In some countries, there is an official body with standard criteria for classifying hotels, but in many others there is none. There have been attempts at unifying the classification system so that it becomes an internationally recognized and reliable standard but large differences exist in the quality of the accommodation and the food within one category of hotel, sometimes even in the same country.

A "Five Star Hotel"

However, regardless of what public or private agency performs the classification, the term five star hotel is always associated with the ultimate luxury (and, by implication, expense). The lack of standardisation has allowed marketing-driven inflation, with some hotels claiming six stars; at one point the Burj al-Arab marketed itself as "the world's first seven-star hotel". Well-established prestige hotels are usually content to claim the traditional five.

Rating by Stars

The five categories can be described (loosely) as follows:

- *(one star)—Low budget hotel; inexpensive; may not have maid service or room service.
- **(two stars)—Budget hotel; slightly more expensive; usually has maid service daily.
- ***(three stars)—Middle class hotel; moderately priced; has daily maid service, room service, and may have dry-cleaning, Internet access, and a swimming pool.
- ****(four stars)—First class hotel; expensive (by middle-class standards); has all of the previously mentioned services; has many "luxury" services (for example: massages or a health spa).
- *****(five stars)—Luxury hotel; most expensive hotels/resorts in the world; numerous extras to enhance the quality of the client's stay (for example: some have private golf courses and even a small private airport).

The AAA and their affiliated bodies use diamonds instead of stars to express hotel and restaurant ratings levels.

Traditional systems rest heavily on the facilities provided, which is often disadvantageous to smaller hotels whose quality of accommodation could fall into one class but the lack of an item such as an elevator would prevent it from reaching a higher categorization.

Present Trends

Hotel rooms that can access everything from your favourite food to your musical preferences— while running on technology that's clever enough to repair itself—might sound like a page torn right out of a pulp sci-fi novel. Hotels are doing it today, and many more are on the verge of implementing these innovative technologies. If you're a guest at one of these forward-looking properties, get ready for a completely different kind of experience—one in which technology anticipates your every need and gives it to you without you ever having to ask.

And it isn't just hotels that are leveraging these new tools to their advantage; so are theme parks, restaurants, and casinos. The overall effects of these new tools on the hospitality business promises to be far-reaching. From the perspective of a hotel, casino, or restaurant, these important advances have the potential to create more efficient and profitable businesses, and make your business more appealing to guests.

No More Questions at Check-in

Remember all those queries when you pick up your room key, such as, What kind of newspaper do you prefer? Would you like a poolside or oceanside room? Asking such questions eats up hotel employees' valuable time and, after a while, guests get tired of answering them. New customer relationship management (CRM) tools allow a hotel to gather guest preference information from various systems at property level and distribute them throughout the company. So your hotel knows what you like, right away.

For example, one hotel chain asks guests signing up for its loyalty Programmes to fill out a preferences questionnaire that is entered into its CRM system at the property level. The information can be made available for any hotel in the chain that the guest checks in to, while the CRM system itself is still maintained locally, at the property level. (This is made possible by merging the property level CRM data with the larger CRM system held at the headquarters-level for the chain.)

When the day of arrival comes, the preference data is pushed to the property and generates an activity list to prepare the guest's room. At the same time, historical transaction data about the guest is made available, which can help predict the behaviours and likely service consumption the guest will have. "If the guest typically orders room service shortly after checking in to their room, then you can proactively suggest—or offer—the in-room dining specials for that day, even take their order at the front desk to shorten the wait for their dinner" says Bill Frizzell, the industry technology strategist for the Microsoft Worldwide Hospitality Team.

"This has been a long sought-after capability for the industry," he adds. "Defining a single view of the guest, without duplicate stores of information, is the key to understanding their habits, trends, and behaviours." TVs that deliver music, movies—and much more. Today's leading-edge hotels have in-room systems that do far more than allow guests to watch their Favourite first-run movie. They can also control in-room music, provide gaming options, display your bill—even control the thermostat and lights.

The Hotel 1000 in Seattle, Wash., for instance, has centered the room around the availability of Favourite media and services on a number of widescreen plasma monitors located throughout its rooms and suites. You can control content, multi-area volume of the sound system, and interact with your profile through these devices. And because it's a multi-use property—part residence, part hotel—the same entertainment offerings are available for their property owners. That lessens the typical multi-use management burden of maintaining multiple service offerings per type of area on the property.

Find Yourself (and Pay for Lunch)

People in the hospitality industry have found a variety of uses for new radio frequency identification (RFID) technology—from helping guests find each other at a ski resort to allowing them to pay for a meal. That's because, increasingly, this technology is gaining traction with hotels and resorts in the form of cashless payment systems that can be used on-property and, more and more often, off-property as well.

For example, at Wild Rivers, a water theme park in Irvine, Calif., RFID locator bracelets can be preloaded and used to pay for food and beverages (which is especially useful when everyone's wearing a bathing suit). The RFID systems, developed by Guest Technologies, have yielded an almost immediate return on investment. After the system was introduced at Wild Rivers, guest spending quadrupled, with the average family of four spending twice their normal amount on meals.

Another key capability of this offering is location-based services, where groups of individuals can be instantly found at the property, simultaneously allowing for more freedom and security in these safety-conscious times. "Imagine taking a group of seven 12 year-olds to a water park for a birthday party," says Frizzell. "You can go to any information kiosk in the park and instantly find where all of the kids you are responsible for are, and what activities and payments they have made, using their RFID bracelet. All of this is enabled through the implementation RFID and location-based services, using Microsoft technologies and Microsoft MapPoint Location Server."

Bibliography

A.K. Sarkar.: *Action Plan and Priorities in Tourism Development*, Kanishka Publication, Delhi, 2010.

A.S. Dileep and T. Rajesh.: *Ayurvedic Tourism*, Sonali Publications, Delhi, 2012.

Alan A. Lew, C. Michael Hall, and Allan M. Williams.: *A Companion to Tourism*, Rawat Publication, Delhi, 2005.

Amit Gaur.: *Adventure Tourism*, Sonali Publication, Delhi, 2011.

Anil Kathuria.: *Hotel Accounting*, Sonali Publication, Delhi, 2008.

Anupama Srivastava and Keya Pandey.: *Anthropology and Tourism*, Serials Publications, Delhi, 2012.

B S Badan and Harish Bhatt.: *Adventure Tourism*, Commonwealth Publication, Delhi, 2007.

B. K. Goswami and G. Raveendran.: *A Textbook of Tourism*, Har-anand Publications, Delhi, 2010.

B.K. Chakravarti.: *Hotel and Hospitality Management*, A.P.H. Publication, Delhi, 2011.

Cynthia vanden Driesen and Satendra Nandan.: *Austral-Asian Encounters: From Literature and Women's Studies to Politics and Tourism*, Prestige Books, Delhi, 2003.

Jack Randall.: *Agriculture Tourism*, Discovery Publishing House, Delhi, 2011.

Jitendra Sharma.: *Handbook of Environmental Management for Hotels*, Monalisa Enterprises, Delhi, 2011.

Jyoti. S. Sharma.: *Catering Management Practices*, Akansha Publication, Delhi, 2006.

Krishan K. Kamra and Mohinder Chand.: *Basics of Tourism: Theory, Operation and Practice*, Kanishka Publication, Delhi, 2002.

M C Metti.: *Hotel and Public Relations*, Anmol Publication, Delhi, 2008.

M N Ahmed.: *Hotel Accounting*, Anmol Publication, Delhi, 2005.

M.D. Jitendra.: *A Textbook of Catering Management*, Wisdom Press, Delhi, 2012.

Mahadev Kertwal.: *Advertising in Leisure and Tourism*, Cyber Tech Publication, New Delhi, 2012.

P.K. Bal.: *A Text Book of Hospitality Tourism and Aviation*, Cyber Tech Publication, New Delhi, 2011.

Prateek A. Aggarwal.: *Aspects of Crosscultural Interaction and Tourism*, Mohit Publication, Delhi, 2005.

R K Arora.: *Foodservice and Catering Management*, APH Publication, Delhi, 2007.

R.K. Arora.: *Banqueting and Catering Management*, A P H Publication, Delhi, 2011.

Ravee Chauhan.: *Advanced Book on Marketing of Tourism*, Vista International Publishing House, New Delhi, 2011.

Ravee Chauhan.: *Advanced Hotel Industry and Tourism*, Vista International Publishing House, New Delhi, 2011.

Richa Thakur.: *Hotel Engineering*, Rajat Publication, Delhi, 2011.

Romila Chawla.: *Accommodation Management and Tourism*, Sonali Publication, Delhi, 2006.

U.P. Sinha.: *Bihar Tourism : Retrospect and Prospect*, Concept Publication, Delhi, 2012.

Umesh Narayan.: *Basics of Catering Management: Its Inevitability*, Rajat Publication, 2008.

Uttam K. Singh.: *Hotel Accounting : A Managerial Approach*, Kanishka Publication, Delhi, 2011.

Varinder Singh Rana.: *Catering Management*, Centrum Press, Delhi, 2011.

Index